GLOBAL WARMING
DISASTER

The Real Global Warming Disaster

Is the obsession with 'climate change'
turning out to be the most costly scientific
blunder in history?

CHRISTOPHER BOOKER

'In the night, imagining some fear,
How easy is a bush supposed a bear.'
A MIDSUMMER NIGHT'S DREAM, ACT V, SCENE 1

continuum

Published by the Continuum International Publishing Group

The Tower Building
11 York Road
London
SE1 7NX

80 Maiden Lane
Suite 704
New York
NY 10038

www.continuumbooks.com

First published 2009.

Paperback edition 2010

British Library Cataloguing-in-Publication Data
A catalogue record for this book is available from the British Library.

ISBN: PB: 978-1-4411-1970-4

Typeset in Sabon by Tony Lansbury, Tonbridge, Kent.
Printed and bound by MPG Books Ltd, Bodmin, Cornwall.

Dedication

This book is dedicated to Richard Lindzen, Fred Singer, Steve McIntyre, Anthony Watts, Bob Carter, Henrik Svensmark, Nir Shaviv, Syun-ichi Akasofu and all those who have valiantly fought to uphold the principles and disciplines of true scientific inquiry through a time when so many lost sight of them.

Contents

Contents

List of Graphs

Introduction

> 'To capture the public imagination we have to offer up some scary scenarios, make simplified dramatic statements and little mention of any doubts one might have. Each of us has to strike the right balance between being effective and being honest.'
>
> Dr Stephen Schneider, *Discover*, October 1989

As the first decade of the twenty-first century nears its end, there is ever more evidence to suggest that, thanks to global warming, the world may be heading towards an unprecedented catastrophe. But it is not the one which has been so widely and noisily predicted by the likes of Nobel Peace Prize winner Al Gore.

The real disaster to be brought about by global warming, it now seems highly possible, is not the technicolor apocalypse promised by Gore and his many allies – melting ice sheets, rising sea levels, hurricanes, droughts, mass-extinctions. It will be the result of all those measures being proposed by the world's politicians in the hope that they can avert a nightmare scenario which, as many experts now believe, was never going to materialise anyway.

This book tells the story of what has been, scientifically and politically, one of the strangest episodes of our time. Indeed, as a case study in collective human psychology, it is turning out to have been one of the most extraordinary chapters in the history of our species. In the closing decades of the twentieth century a number of scientists became convinced that the earth's atmosphere had suddenly begun to heat up to an extent never known before, and that this was caused by the activities of man. The emission of carbon dioxide and other 'greenhouse gases' from the burning of fossil fuels was now trapping the sun's heat to such an extent that the balance of nature had become dangerously disturbed.

Having created elaborate computer models which seemed to confirm their dire predictions, in a remarkably short time these scientists – vociferously urged on by environmental activists and the media – convinced key political figures, most notably the then-Senator Al Gore, that this rise in temperature was easily the most urgent challenge confronting the human race. Only by taking the most drastic action might it be possible for disaster to be averted.

The chief driver in promoting this cause was an organisation set up by the United Nations in 1988, the Intergovernmental Panel on Climate Change. Contrary to general supposition, the IPCC was essentially not a scientific but a political body. Although its findings would commonly be described by politicians and the media as representing a 'consensus' of the views of 'the world's top climate scientists', the vast majority of its contributors were not climate experts and a great many were not scientists at all.

The IPCC's brief was not to weigh the evidence for whether or not man-made global warming was taking place. It was to take 'human-induced climate change' as a given, to assess its likely impact and to advise on what should be done about it. Working to an agenda tightly controlled from the top, the IPCC's role was thus not to question the new orthodoxy but to promote it, and to inspire the political response to a threat the nature of which was assumed from the outset. By 1997 this had led to the signing by 180 countries of the treaty known as the Kyoto Protocol, many of them to reduce CO_2 emissions way below their existing levels.

By the early years of the twenty-first century governments were adopting an ever more ambitious series of policies, intended not just to meet those Kyoto targets but to go far beyond them. The bill for these measures, if all were put into effect, would be astronomic, making them by far the most expensive set of proposals ever put forward by any group of politicians in history. This would eventually necessitate such a dramatic change in the way of life of billions of people that it was hard to imagine how modern industrial civilisation could survive in any recognisable form.

As the first decade of the new century neared its end, however, just when governments had begun to implement these measures, the scenario began dramatically to change. Although CO_2 levels in the atmosphere were still steadily rising, it became obvious that the earth's temperatures were no longer following suit, as the IPCC's 'consensus' dictated they should. Far from continuing to hurtle inexorably upwards, the temperature curve had flattened out and was even dropping, in a way none of those officially approved computer models had predicted.

At much the same time, it emerged that the supposed scientific 'consensus' was nothing like so unanimous as the politicians and the media had been led to believe. By no means all the world's scientists were agreed even that the temperature rise towards the end of the twentieth century was unprecedented. An increasing number doubted that it had been caused by the rise in carbon dioxide levels.

With growing force, ever more climatologists and other experts were now showing that the evidence for a human link to such warming as had occurred had been not just seriously exaggerated but even deliberately manipulated, to produce findings which the data simply did not justify. They were also coming up with alternative theories as to what was shaping the world's climate which fitted the observed data much more plausibly.

Then in the autumn of 2008 the global economy was suddenly plunged into its deepest recession for more than 70 years. With the time approaching for agreement on a successor to the Kyoto Protocol, political attitudes towards global warming began to polarise.

On one hand, the majority of Western politicians, led by the new US President Barack Obama, were still locked into their belief that the IPCC's orthodoxy was correct, and that all those astronomically costly measures were still urgently necessary. Others began to argue that the immense economic sacrifices these would involve made them no longer affordable. Developing countries such as China and India continued to insist that, if they were expected to cut back on their 'carbon emissions', the bill for this must be picked up by those developed countries which in their view had created the problem in the first place, and whose economies were now in crisis.

The 'political consensus' was beginning to crack apart just as the 'scientific consensus' had done. Had the story of the panic over global warming reached a critical turning point? If the momentum towards committing mankind to all those steps designed to 'fight climate change' now seemed unstoppable, might it turn out to have been the most reckless and costly political gamble in history?

THE PATTERN OF A SCARE

There have already been enough books about global warming to fill a small library. Most of them set out the reasons why, in the past 20 years, so many scientists have come to believe that the late twentieth century rise in temperatures was man-made and threatening the world with disaster. More recently an increasing number of books have appeared, not a few by eminent scientists, strongly questioning that belief and putting the other side of the story.

What all these books have in common, however, is that they present the case for one side of the debate or the other in a series of snapshots, looking in turn at different aspects of the picture, What this book sets out to do, by contrast, is to put all these complex arguments into chronological context. It tells a story, that of how the scientific and political debate has unfolded through the two decades since it began.

The decision that this book should be written was taken in August 2008. I was sitting with my colleague Dr Richard North outside a hotel in Washington DC, near the White House. Twice within a few months we had been invited to the US to talk about a book we had published the previous year entitled *Scared To Death: From BSE to Global Warming, How Scares Are Costing Us The Earth*.

For 15 years we had found ourselves investigating a long succession of those 'scares' which had become such a conspicuous feature of Western life in the closing decades of the twentieth century. Repeatedly we had seen supposed experts hitting the headlines with some supposedly terrifying new threat to human health or wellbeing: food scares such as those over eggs and 'mad cows', Asian bird 'flu, the 'Millennium Bug', dioxins, lead in petrol, passive smoking, white asbestos and many more. And again and again we had seen how these scares had followed a remarkably similar pattern.

Each had originated in what would eventually turn out to be a misreading of the scientific evidence. Usually this was because scientists had put two things together and guessed, as it turned out incorrectly, that one was the cause of the other.[1] The scare had then been magnified by the media and campaigning groups, to the point where eventually politicians and governments gave way, launching a legislative response out of all proportion to the reality of the threat. This had invariably resulted in huge financial and economic damage. But finally in each case new evidence had come to light to show how the supposed threat had been wildly exaggerated, and that the panic had been based on misunderstanding or even a deliberate distortion of the scientific data.

What struck us when we came to look in detail into the history of the alarm over global warming was how uncannily it seemed to have echoed the pattern of all those other scares with which we were so familiar. There was the initial assumption that the rise in global temperatures must have been caused by the observed rise in CO_2 levels in the atmosphere. There was the way in which this scare had been adopted and obsessively promoted by the media and environmental lobby groups. There was the remarkable speed with which this cause had been taken up by politicians and governments, as they rushed to propose their regulatory response. Then finally, just when the awesome scale of that response was becoming evident, came the growing challenge to all the scientific assumptions on which the scare had rested.

Nothing alerted us more to the curious nature of the global warming scare than the peculiar tactics used by the IPCC to promote its orthodoxy, brooking no dissent. More than once in its series of mammoth reports, the IPCC had been caught out in very serious attempts to rewrite the scientific evidence. The most notorious instance of this was the extraordinary prominence it gave in 2001 to the so-called 'hockey stick' graph, mysteriously produced by a relatively unknown young US scientist, which completely redrew the accepted historical record by purporting to show temperatures in the late twentieth century having shot upwards to a level far higher than had ever been known before. Although the 'hockey stick' was instantly made the central icon of the IPCC's cause, it was within a few years to become one of the most comprehensively discredited artefacts in the history of science.

Similarly called into serious doubt was the reliability of some of the other temperature figures on which the IPCC based its case. Most notably these included those provided by NASA's Goddard Institute for Space Studies (GISS), run by Dr James Hansen, Al Gore's closest scientific ally, which were one of the four official sources of temperature data on which the IPCC relied. These were shown to have been repeatedly 'adjusted', to suggest that temperatures had risen further and more steeply than was indicated by any of the other three main data-sources.

Again the IPCC became notorious for the consistency with which it contrived to overrule or ignore any expert contributors, however distinguished, who failed to agree with its approved line, several of whom refused to continue participating in its work.

If the case the IPCC was set up to make was sufficiently robust and genuinely rooted in science, the question inevitably arose, why was it necessary to resort to such questionable methods to defend it?

All this made the story of how global warming had come to be elevated to the top of the world's political agenda uncomfortably reminiscent of many of the other scares we had studied. It played a large part in why we chose to make it the subject of the longest chapter in our book on the 'scare phenomenon'. But then in 2008 the scientific and political drama over global warming developed so rapidly that it prompted the extension of the story into a whole new book.

THE FORTHCOMING ENERGY CRISIS

Back in Britain during the months after our book was published in 2007 there came to the fore an alarming new twist to the story. Within only a few years, it had become clear, Britain would be facing a major energy crisis. After more than 20 years of neglect, caused in great part by the growing influence of the environmentalists, many of the nuclear and coal-fired power stations which supplied the country with 40 per cent of its electricity were due to close down. Unless replacements were built as a matter of the highest national priority, there was every chance that Britain would face prolonged power cuts, shutting down large parts of her now almost wholly computer-dependent economy.

Even some senior government officials and ministers had belatedly come to recognise this threat. But for so long had Britain's energy policy been skewed, in the name of 'fighting global warming', by the obsession with 'renewable energy' such as wind power, and by the bitter opposition of the environmental lobby to the building of any more nuclear and coal-fired power stations, that the chances that enough new power plants could be built in time to plug that fast-looming energy gap seemed increasingly remote.

As we repeatedly reported in 2008, this would face Britain with an unprecedented disaster. What we had not been prepared for when, that August, we made our second trip across the Atlantic in four months was to discover that a remarkably similar crisis was fast approaching in the USA, threatening to inflict just as great a disaster on the largest economy in the world.

Just as in Britain, environmental campaigners had come to exercise a near-complete stranglehold on the thinking of the country's poiiticians, at every level. For 30 years, ever since a minor leak of radioactivity from a reactor at Three Mile Island, the US had not added to her ageing fleet of 104 nuclear power stations. She was dependent on equally ageing coal-fired power stations for 50 per cent of her electricity. Yet almost every attempt to replace them was being vetoed by state politicians or becoming mired in legal protests, on the grounds that the contribution to global warming made by their 'carbon emissions' would make them wholly unacceptable .

Meanwhile at federal level, everywhere from Congress to the Supreme Court, the environmentalists seemed to be gaining ground in moves to heap prohibitive new costs and regulations on US industry and energy producers, to force them to slash their CO_2 emissions by an amount so great that it would be economically crippling.

Nor did it seem to matter, with the 2008 presidential election campaign under way, which of the two candidates would win. One evening in Washington we saw two television commercials, one from each side. Senators Obama and McCain were each shown in front of the same giant, supposedly telegenic windfarm, making an almost identical claim: that the best contribution America could make in helping to save the planet from 'climate change' was to spend tens of billions of dollars on building thousands more wind turbines.

I knew something about wind turbines. Having reported on them in the *Sunday Telegraph* for several years, I was aware just how easily politicians and journalists could be misled into exaggerating the negligible amount of electricity they could generate, through the wind industry's favourite trick of talking about them only in terms of their 'capacity'. In fact, of course, thanks to the wind's intermittency, the actual amount of power turbines produce, unreliably and unpredictably, amounts on average to only around a quarter of their 'capacity'.

Next day I checked on the actual output of the 10,000 wind turbines the US had already built. In total it averaged out through a year at just 3.9 Gigawatts.[2] This was no more than the output of a single large coal-fired power station. Yet here were the two candidates for the office of President seemingly so detached from reality by the alarm over global warming that they could seriously be proposing to make the need to build more wind turbines the centrepiece of their energy policy – at a time when the US could, like Britain, be heading for a massive shortfall in the energy supplies it would need to keep its economy functioning.

Faced with the evidence of such unreality, it was at that moment, sitting in that Washington hotel courtyard, that it was decided that I should write this book. Inevitably, since it is telling the same story, it goes over ground already covered in *Scared To Death*. But that original version is here greatly expanded, with a mass of new material. And of course since our earlier book was completed in the summer of 2007, the story has moved on a long way. It is now much clearer even than it was then just how far the political obsession with global warming is threatening to put at stake the entire future of our civilisation.

Hence the story set out in the pages which follow.

Notes

1. Thus, for instance, eggs were not the cause of the rise in salmonella poisoning as had been claimed in the 1980s; eating beef was not the cause of the brain disease vCJD; the chances of Asian bird 'flu mutating into a disease contagious between humans were so remote as to be statistically implausible; the '2YK' disaster was never going to happen; DDT did not cause cancer; lead in petrol did not cause brain damage in children; the health risks from exposure to 'white asbestos' cement were non-existent; and so forth. For detailed analysis of the scientific confusion behind all these scares, see Booker and North, *Scared To Death: From BSE to Global Warming, How Scares Are Costing Us The Earth* (Continuum, 2007).

2. 'Official energy statistics from the US Government', Energy Information Administration. Summary statistics for the United States, EIA website, Table ES1, data up to 2007, published 21 January 2009.

Part One: Forging the 'Consensus': 1972–1997

'Only an insignificant fraction of scientists deny the global warming crisis. The time for debate is over. The science is settled.'

Al Gore,1992*

'The work of science has nothing whatever to do with consensus. Consensus is the business of politics. Science, on the contrary, requires only one investigator who happens to be right, which means that he or she has results that are verifiable by reference to the real world.'

Michael Crichton, speech in
Washington DC, 25 January 2005

---

* Quoted by Lawrence Solomon, *Financial Post*, 2 June 2007.

Prologue

'*The science is beyond dispute and the facts are clear.*'
President-elect Barack Obama, December 2008

In London on Tuesday, 29 October 2008, the House of Commons spent six hours discussing what was potentially the most expensive piece of legislation ever put before the British Parliament.

The debate, one of the longest allowed in recent times, was on the final or Third Reading of something called the 'Climate Change Bill'. One reason for its length was that the government had introduced a last-minute amendment, moved by Ed Miliband, just appointed to head a new ministry, the 'Department for Energy and Climate Change'.

This change to the Bill would legally commit Britain, at that time uniquely in the world, to reducing its emissions of carbon dioxide within four decades by well over four fifths, more than 80 per cent.

The new opening words of the Bill would make it

'*the duty of the Secretary of State to ensure that the net UK carbon account for the year 2050 is at least 80 per cent lower than the 1990 baseline*'.

By any measure this was an astonishing requirement to impose, not just on the minister putting it into law, but on his successors over the next 40 years. Short of an almost unimaginable technological revolution, there was no way such a target could be achieved without closing down much of the country's industrial economy, rendering most motorised transport impossible and turning Britain's lights out.

Yet in that six hours of debate, as politicians of every party lined up to support the Bill (they had already approved it in principle on Second Reading by 463 votes to 5), only two MPs questioned the need for it. Only one, Peter Lilley, raised the matter of its potential cost.

Only rarely in its history had the House of Commons been quite so unanimous on anything. As if from a single script, one MP after another had intoned on the urgent need to curb the planet-threatening menace of runaway global warming. Then, right at the end of the debate, Mr Lilley drew the Speaker's attention to the fact that, outside the Palace of Westminster, snow was falling. It was the first October snow recorded in London since 1934, more than 70 years earlier.

With immaculate timing, a similarly unseasonal swathe of snow was covering much of the country. Britain was just about to experience its coldest start to a winter for 30 years.

Yet within minutes of the debate ending, hundreds of MPs were filing through the lobbies to record their final approval of the Climate Change Bill. It was passed by 463 votes to just 3.

Across the Atlantic, where the US presidential election was entering its final days. something remarkably similar was happening. So much snow had fallen in October across the US and Canada that the US National Oceanic and Atmospheric Administration (NOAA) reported that 63 places in the United States had experienced record snowfalls for the month and 115 places had recorded their lowest-ever October temperatures.

It was to be the prelude to a winter in North America so cold that snow would at one point cover the whole of Canada and half the United States for the first time in a generation, falling on cities as far south as New Orleans and Houston.

Towards the end of that chilly November, however, the new President-elect Barack Obama made his second major post-election policy statement. His theme was the threat of global warming. The statement took the form of a video, intended first for a gathering of state governors, then for the delegates to a vast international conference in Poland, organised under the UN's Framework Convention on Climate Change.

Mr Obama wished everyone to know that, after years when the US had lagged behind, under his presidency it was now intending to 'lead the world' in the fight against global warming. 'The science', he said, 'is beyond dispute.' 'Sea levels are rising, coastlines are shrinking, we've seen record drought, spreading famine, and storms that are growing stronger with each hurricane season.'

Far from being 'beyond dispute', the 'science' on each of these points suggested that the man about to become President had been seriously misinformed. Sea levels might have been modestly rising, but no faster than they had been doing for centuries. Al Gore's celebrated Oscar-winning film *An Inconvenient Truth* might have predicted a possible rise during the twenty-first century of 20 feet, inundating many of the world's major cities. But even the IPCC had only predicted a rise of between four and 17 inches.

The main focus of alarm on this point had been the fate of low-lying coral islands such as the Maldives and Tuvalu. Around each of these tiny countries, according to various studies, sea levels in recent decades had either remained stable or actually fallen. The Indian Ocean was higher between 1900 and 1970 than it had been since. Satellite measurements showed that since 1993 the sea level around Tuvalu had gone down by four inches.

Coastlines were not 'shrinking', as Obama claimed, except where land was subsiding, as on the east coast of England, where it had been doing so for thousands of years.

Far from global warming having increased the number of droughts, the opposite was the case. A comprehensive recent study showed that, of the twentieth century's 30 major drought episodes, 22 were in the first six decades, with only five between 1961 and 1980. The most recent two decades had produced just three.[1]

Mr Obama had again been misled over the data on hurricanes. Despite a recent press release from NOAA claiming that 2008's North Atlantic hurricane season 'set records', even NOAA's own graphs showed hurricane activity as having been higher in the 1950s than recently, and the worldwide incidence of cyclone activity had in the previous four years been declining.

Alarming though it might have been that the man about to become US President should have been briefed in such a one-sided fashion, even more worrying was what he was proposing to do in consequence of this when he reached the White House.

For a start he was planning to introduce a 'federal cap and trade system', a tax on 'carbon', designed to follow Britain's example by cutting America's CO_2 emissions 'to their 1990 levels by 2020' and by 'an additional 80 per cent by 2050'. As was true in Britain, such a target could only be achieved by closing down most of the US economy.

Mr Obama then announced his intention to spend $15 billion a year to encourage 'clean energy' sources, such as building tens of thousands more wind turbines. He was clearly unaware that wind energy is so ineffectual that the amount of electricity generated by the 10,000 subsidised turbines America had already built was so negligible that it was less than the output of a single large coal-fired power station.

He talked of allowing only 'clean' coal-fired power plants, using 'carbon capture and storage': piping off the CO_2 to bury it in holes in the ground, Not only would this double the price of electricity; the technology to make it work had not even been developed yet.

He went on to promise that his emphasis on renewable energy would be responsible for 'generating five million new green jobs'. But to anyone who knew about the economics of renewable energy, the only way this could be achieved would be to hire millions of Americans to generate power by running up and down on tread-mills, to replace all those 'dirty' coal-fired power stations which currently supplied the US with half its electricity.

All this was being proposed just when America was entering one of its coldest winters for decades. Obama's message was then beamed over to Europe, to be shown in the Polish city of Posnan, where at the start of December 10,000 delegates from all over the world were gathering in near-freezing temperatures to attend the latest conference on global warming organised by the UN.

The aim of all these politicians, officials, environmentalists and government-approved scientists in Posnan was to prepare the way for an even bigger conference planned for Copenhagen in December 2009 to draw up a successor to the famous 'Kyoto Protocol', the international agreement in 1997 which had laid out targets for almost every developed country in the world to reduce its emissions of CO_2.

The plan was that in Copenhagen they would commit themselves to even more drastic cuts in 'carbon emissions' than had been agreed in Kyoto 12 years earlier. But one of the chief stumbling blocks of Kyoto had been the refusal of the world's fastest-growing economies, notably China and India, to accept limits on their own emissions until they had caught up with the already developed countries which until this time had been the world's heaviest emitters of CO_2.

In Posnan not only were China, India and others still adamant that the same principle must apply to the successor to Kyoto, and that any limitations they agreed to must be paid for by the richer countries. The world's economy had just plunged into such a severe depression that many of the smaller developed countries could see no reason for agreeing to measures which would only damage their own economies still further.

Ironically, one of the countries most vociferous in this respect was that in which the Posnan conference was taking place. Poland was dependent on 'dirty' coal for 95 per cent of its electricity. The central heating by which those 10,000 delegates were keeping warm came from the very substance the IPCC was seeking in effect to ban.

On all sides, as the first decade of the twenty-first century neared its end, it was clear that the drive to 'save the planet' from global warming was beginning to falter. For 20 years the alarm over 'man-made climate change' had seemed to be developing an unstoppable momentum. But now it appeared to be running into a maze of contradictions.

On one hand, the scientific evidence used to support that alarm was suddenly beginning to look nothing like so convincing. Far from continuing to rise along with CO_2 levels, as the computer models were programmed to predict they should, global temperatures in 2007 and 2008 had shown that sharp drop. For two winters running, from Jerusalem and Greece to the deserts of Arabia and Iran, from Buenos Aires to Johannesburg, from Canada to China, many countries in both the southern and northern hemispheres had experienced snowfalls so abnormal that in many cases no one could recall anything like it having happened for decades.

When the sea-ice of the Arctic had shrunk in September 2007 to its lowest level ever recorded, this prompted a rash of excitable predictions that possibly as soon as 2008 the summer ice might vanish altogether. Yet two winters running it returned so strongly that in the winter of 2008 it briefly reached an extent equal to that recorded 30 years before in 1979. Polar bear numbers, far from diminishing towards extinction as predicted, were at their highest level ever recorded.

Likewise, most of the Antarctic continent, containing 90 per cent of all the ice on the planet, was colder than it had been at any time since satellite records began in 1979. Its surrounding sea-ice cover was in 2008 30 per cent greater than its 30-year average.

So far did this seem to contradict the predictions of those official computer models that even scientists committed to the belief in man-made global warming began to look around for explanations. Some, for instance, accepted that the warming process might be in temporary suspension, but suggested that this was only because the drop in temperatures caused by shifts in ocean currents was 'masking the underlying warming trend' which would eventually reappear.

To all this evidence of what was happening in the outside world, however, the politicians, particularly in the West, such as those MPs in Westminster who had so enthusiastically approved the new Climate Change Act, remained strangely impervious. So unquestioningly were the leaders of the European Union and the USA now fixed in their belief that global warming was the greatest challenge facing mankind that they were still blindly driving forward with all those astronomically costly measures which could only inflict untold damage on their own peoples and on the world's economy.

Rarely if ever in history can such a yawning gulf have opened up between the dreams of politicians and the realities of a world they aspired to change. How could such a remarkable contradiction have come about?

To answer that question, we must trace the story back to where it all began.

Notes

1. G. T. Narisma *et al.* (2007), 'Abrupt changes in rainfall during the twentieth century', *Geophysical Research Letters*, **34**, 10.1029.

1
How it all began
Cooling and warming: 1972–1987

'*A global deterioration of climate, by order of magnitude larger than any hitherto experienced by civilised mankind, is a very real possibility and may be due very soon.*'

Scientists' letter to President
Nixon, December 1972

As good a place as any to begin this story might be the apocalyptic letter sent by two scientists to the President of the United States in December 1972. What was worrying them was the possibility that the Earth might soon be facing a disastrous shift in its weather patterns.

The two men were Dr George Kukla, a Columbia University astrophysicist and Dr Robert Matthews, head of the Geological Sciences Department at Brown University, Rhode Island. In January that year, along with Murray Mitchell, the chief climatologist of the US National Oceanic and Atmospheric Administration, they had convened an international conference of scientists from America and Europe at Brown. So alarmed were they by its conclusions that in October Kukla and Matthews summarised its findings in the leading US scientific journal, *Science*.

When, two months later, they wrote to President Nixon, they wanted to warn him that the world's climate might be about to go through a change for the worse, by an 'order of magnitude larger than any hitherto experienced by civilised mankind'.[1]

As other scientists were coming up with similar fears around this time, it was not long before the story was picked up by the media, In 1973 it was being reported by *Science Digest*. In 1974 the BBC made it the subject of a a major two-hour television documentary, *The Weather Machine*. In June that year the science section of *Time* magazine was recording how 'a growing number of scientists' were beginning to suspect that 'the bizarre and unpredictable weather pattern of the past several years' – droughts, flooding, abnormally mild winters – might be the harbingers of 'a global climactic upheaval'.[2]

'There are ominous signs', reported *Newsweek* the following year, 'that the earth's weather patterns have begun to change dramatically, and that these changes may portend a dramatic decline in food production – with serious implications for just about every nation on earth'.[3]

Newsweek quoted a report by the US National Academy of Sciences that 'a major climactic change would force economic and social adjustments on a worldwide scale'. The evidence cited for such a change ranged from a two-week shortening since 1950 of the English grain-growing season to 'the most devastating outbreak of tornadoes ever recorded' in the US, where in 1974 '148 twisters killed more than 300 people'.

The fear they were all expressing, of course, was not that the earth was warming but that it was dangerously cooling. It had been noted that, for more than three decades, average temperatures across the globe had been dropping.

As a *New York Times* headline put it 'Scientists ponder why world's climate is changing: a major cooling widely considered to be inevitable'.[4] *Time* reported how 'telltale signs are everywhere – from the unexpected thickness of pack ice in the waters around Iceland to the southward migration of a warmth-loving creature like the armadillo'. The 1975 *Newsweek* article, entitled 'The Cooling World', asserted that evidence to support predictions of global cooling had now 'begun to accumulate so massively that meteorologists are hard-pressed to keep up with it'.

The *Science Digest* article in 1973 had been headed 'Brace yourself for another ice age'. This described how, as the earth gradually cooled and the icecaps of Greenland and Antarctica grew, winter would eventually last the year round, cities would be 'buried in snow and an immense sheet of ice could cover North America as far south as Cincinnati'.[5] In 1975 Nigel Calder, a former editor of the *New Scientist*, wrote that 'the threat of a new ice age must now stand alongside nuclear war as a likely source of wholesale death and misery for mankind'.[6]

Although some of the scientists who feared that the Earth might be heading for a dramatic cooling believed that its causes were entirely natural, others, such as Paul Ehrlich in his apocalyptic bestseller *The Population Bomb* (1968), were already suggesting it might be due to the activities of man.*

---

* See below.

In 1971 a young Columbia University PhD, Stephen Schneider, was joint author of a paper in *Science* comparing the predicted effects on global temperatures of human emissions of carbon dioxide and 'aerosols', minute particles being added to the atmosphere in ever-increasing quantities by the burning of fossil fuels on which modern industrial civilisation was based.[7]

Potentially by far the more damaging of the two, the paper suggested, would be the effect of the aerosols, which could lower global temperatures 'by as much as 3.5°C'. Sustained over 'a few years', they believed, such a decrease would be 'sufficient to trigger an ice age'. Their conclusions were based on the calculations of another young PhD with a particular interest in computer models, Dr James Hansen.[8]

For several years the fear of global cooling continued to inspire a spate of articles and books, such as Schneider's *The Genesis Strategy* (1976) and *Climate Change and World Affairs* by a British diplomat Crispin Tickell. *The Cooling: Has The Next Ice Age Already Begun?* (1976) by the US science writer Lowell Ponte, warmly endorsed on the cover by Schneider, claimed that 'the cooling has already killed hundreds of thousands of people in poor nations'. 'It is a cold fact', he wrote, that 'the Global Cooling presents humankind with the most important social, political, and adaptive challenge we have had to deal with for ten thousand years'.

But then quite suddenly, in the late 1970s, global temperatures began to rise again. The panic over global cooling subsided faster than it had arisen.

WARMING AND COOLING DOWN THE AGES

There was a simple explanation for this temporary hysteria over cooling in the 1970s. In imagining the future, as we know from the history of science fiction, human beings like to project onto it an exaggerated version of some tendency already evident in their own time. And what scientists were noticing in the 1970s was that, for more than 30 years, the average temperature of the earth had been in decline.

After several decades of rising temperatures earlier in the twentieth century, particularly between 1920 and 1940, the earth had suddenly begun to cool again. In Britain for 30 years we became used to harsher winters, like those of 1946/7 and 1962/3, when snow remained on the ground for nearly three months between December and March. This phase would eventually become known to climate scientists as the 'Little Cooling', to distinguish it from the generally higher temperatures in the decades before and after it.

The one thing certain about climate is that it is always changing. And in our own time we now have so many ways of measuring the changes in climate and temperature of the past, from the width of tree rings and organic residues in marine sediments to ice cores dating back hundreds of thousands of years, that we can get a pretty accurate picture of how the earth's temperatures have fallen and risen, stretching back not just to the start of the Ice Age a million years ago but even much further back into distant geological eras.

We have become accustomed, for instance, to the idea that we are still living in the period known as the 'Ice Age'. At least four times in the last million years, since the start of the Pleistocene, the world has gone through long periods of freezing so intense that up to 30 per cent of its land surface has been covered in ice, drastically lowering sea levels and reducing much of the remaining land to cold, dry deserts.* But these have been punctuated by warmer, interglacial periods, lasting up to 20,000 years before the ice returns. It is in one of these 'interglacial warmings', that which began around 18,000 years ago, that we are living today.[9]

By 15,000 years ago the earth had warmed sufficiently for glaciers to be in retreat and for sea levels to begin rising. Since the end of the last glaciation, the average temperature of the earth has risen by around 8.8°C, and the sea by 300 feet (separating Asia from Alaska 8,000 years ago and Britain from the continent 6,000 years ago).

But this rise in temperature has been far from consistent. Within the general overall rise, there have been marked fluctuations between warmer and cooler times. During the warmest period of man's time on earth, known as the Holocene Maximum or Climate Optimum, roughly between 7000 and 3000 BC, the evidence shows that the world was on average significantly warmer than it is today.

Average temperatures then declined slowly, dropping even more sharply in the three centuries around 700–400 BC, to create what is known as the 'pre-Roman Cold' phase. But this was followed by another rapid rise. Between around 200 BC and the sixth century AD,

---

* Although it has long been recognised that there were four major stages of glaciation in the Pleistocene period, these between them contained up to 14 individual glaciations.

coinciding with the pre-eminence of Rome, the world enjoyed what is called 'the Roman Warming'. Vine-growing for the first time spread up through Italy into northern Europe, as far as Britain. By the fourth century AD the climate in many parts of the globe was warmer than it is now.[10]

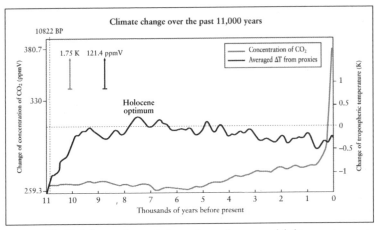

Figure 1: The black line on the graph shows changes in average global temperatures over the past 11,000 years, beginning with the Earth's emergence from the last ice age (data based on proxy studies by G. Bond, *et al.*). The grey line shows CO_2 levels (based on Parrenin, *et al.*).[11]

The Roman Warming came to an abrupt end in the sixth century, coinciding with dramatic meteorological events around 540 AD which were followed by a sharp cooling. This ushered in the cold period of the Dark Ages, lasting more than three centuries. But around 900 AD temperatures again began to rise, leading to the 400-year-long period known as the 'Mediaeval Warm Period'. The Vikings colonised Greenland. Vines returned to Britain. The European civilisation of the High Middle Ages flowered, as a new prosperity and spiritual and artistic confidence gave rise to the great Gothic cathedrals. Physical evidence from across the world again indicates that temperatures at the height of the Mediaeval Warming were generally higher than those of the present day.[12]

Around 1300, shortly before the Black Death reached Europe in 1347, temperatures again began to drop significantly, leading to the four centuries of what is called the 'Little Ice Age'. This became particularly severe after 1550, when average temperatures dropped to their lowest level since the end of the last glaciation.

As usual, there were temporary reversals of the trend. The 1730s in Central England, for instance, recorded seven of the eight hottest years since accurate records began to be kept in 1659.[13] But in general the Little Ice Age was to last until the early nineteenth century. In human terms we associate the chilling winters of those centuries with the snowscapes of Pieter Brueghel, images of ice fairs on the River Thames and records of the sea freezing for miles round the coasts of Europe and Iceland. Glaciers all over the world advanced dramatically. Greenland become uninhabitable. All this reflected an exceptional period of cooling which has again been confirmed by physical data from all over the world.

The last recorded freezing over of the Thames was in the winter of 1813/14, a year after much of Napoleon's *Grande Armée* froze to death in the snows of Russia. Slowly average temperatures again began to rise through the nineteenth century, giving rise to what is known as 'the Modern Warming'.

As always, however, there have been anomalies. A temporary advance of glaciers across the world at the end of the nineteenth century first prompted speculation about the approach of a new ice age, which was to continue on and off for several decades. In 1923, under the front-page headline 'Scientist says Arctic ice will wipe out Canada', the *Chicago Tribune* quoted Professor Gregory of Yale University warning that North America would disappear as far south as the Great Lakes and that huge parts of Asia and Europe would be 'wiped out'.[14]

Already in fact, as we have seen, temperatures in those decades between the two world wars were rising rapidly, faster than in any other phase of the Modern Warming. By the end of the 1920s this too was attracting attention. A US government meteorologist in 1933 noted that 18 of the previous 21 winters in Washington DC had been warmer than normal. In light of this 'widespread and persistent tendency towards warmer weather', he asked, 'is our climate changing?'[15]

Within a decade he had an answer: that sharp drop in temperatures which was to lead to nearly four decades of the Little Cooling. But no sooner had this given rise, by the 1970s, to those widespread predictions that the world was fast heading for a new ice age than 'climate-change' again went into reverse. By the 1980s it was obvious that surface temperatures were again quite rapidly rising. Increasingly we began to hear two hitherto generally unfamiliar phrases: 'global warming' and 'the greenhouse effect'.

THE 'GREENHOUSE EFFECT'

As early as 1824, the French mathematician and engineer Josephe Fourier had theorised that the earth's atmosphere plays a crucial part in determining surface temperatures by trapping heat radiated by the sun, thus preventing it from escaping back into space. This 'greenhouse effect' was crucial to the survival of life on earth because, without it, the global average temperature of around 15°C would drop to −18 degrees, creating an intense, world-wide ice age.[16]

In 1860 John Tyndall, an Irish physicist, established that only certain gases in the atmosphere had this invaluable property. As the earth is heated by the sun, the commonest gases, nitrogen and oxygen, do not prevent this heat, in the form of infra-red radiation, escaping back into space. But the 'greenhouse gases' do, thus retaining the sun's heat. By far the most important of these greenhouse gases is water vapour, contributing around 95 per cent of the 'greenhouse effect'. This is followed by carbon dioxide, CO_2 (3.62 per cent); nitrous oxide (0.95 per cent); methane (0.36 per cent) and others, including CFCs, or chlorofluorocarbons, (0.07 per cent).[17]

In 1896 the Swedish chemist Svante Arrhenius attempted to calculate what might be the consequences of mankind continuing to burn vast amounts of fossil fuels, thus adding to the natural quantity of CO_2 in the atmosphere. If CO_2 was to double, he suggested, this would increase the average temperature by 5°C, equivalent to more than half the warming which had carried the earth from the depths of the last ice age to its present state.

In 1938, inspired by the rapidly rising temperatures of the 1920s and 1930s, a British meteorologist Guy Callendar suggested that the cause of this rise might be the marked increase in the burning of coal and oil in the age of mass-industrialisation, electricity and the motor car. Far from seeing this as an unqualified disaster, however, he saw it as likely in several ways 'to prove beneficial to mankind'; not least in allowing for greater agricultural production. It might even hold off the return of a new ice age 'indefinitely'.[18]

What Callendar was recognising, of course, was that although CO_2 makes up only a minuscule proportion of all the gases in the earth's atmosphere − compared with nitrogen, oxygen and the rest it represents a mere 0.04 per cent of the total − it plays an absolutely vital role in the survival of life. Of the estimated 186 billion tons of CO_2 which enter our atmosphere each year from all sources, only

3.3 per cent comes from human activity. More than 100 billion tons (57 per cent) is given off by the oceans. 71 billion tons (38 per cent) is breathed out by animals, including ourselves. And on that supply of CO_2 depends the survival of the entire plant kingdom, without which the rest of life could not exist.

Trees and all other plants absorb CO_2 from the atmosphere, transforming it by photosynthesis into the oxygen essential to all animal life. And, as Callendar was aware, an increase in CO_2 serves to promote plant growth, which was why he foresaw a higher CO_2 level as likely to boost human food production.[19]

Scarcely had Callendar made his prediction, however, than the Little Cooling arrived. As temperatures began dropping again, there now seemed little immediate cause for concern over global warming. But the essence of what he and Arrhenius had been on about was not forgotten. And this was particularly true when the 1960s saw the rise of the modern environmentalist movement, rooted in a conviction that man's reckless greed in despoiling the planet was threatening to disturb the balance of nature to such an extent that the very survival of life was in doubt.

FINDING THE FOCUS

Even at the height of that 1970s panic over a new ice age, a number of scientists had already begun to speculate that the real danger which lay ahead for mankind might not be an ice age but disastrous global warming.*

The first populariser to pick up on this was Paul Ehrlich, an entomologist from Stanford University, whose book *The Population Bomb* in 1968 quickly became (after Rachel Carson's seminal 1962 bestseller *Silent Spring*), one of the key texts of the new 'environmentalism'.

Ehrlich caught the mood of the time by painting mankind as the ultimate villain in the story of Planet Earth, predicting doom in every direction. Not only was the world's exploding population fast outrunning humanity's ability to feed itself, leading Ehrlich to predict

---

* In recent years advocates of global warming have tried to argue that very few scientists in the 1970s were seriously concerned by global cooling and that this was just a 'scare' got up the media. This is not supported by the evidence, e.g. the 1972 international scientific conference at Brown University.

that 'in the 1970s and 1980s hundreds of millions of people will starve to death ... at this late date nothing can prevent a substantial increase in the world death rate'.[20] Within a few decades 'the sea would be virtually emptied' of harvestable fish. By 1980, thanks to toxic pesticides, the average age of death in the US would be only 42. And, 'even more important', mankind was now dumping so much 'junk into the atmosphere' that this had the potential, by altering global temperatures, to change 'the climate of the Earth'.

Here, however, Ehrlich was equivocal as to which way temperatures were likely to move. On one hand, the 'greenhouse effect' was now being enhanced 'by the greatly increased level of carbon dioxide in the atmosphere', caused by the burning of fossil fuels, meaning the world was likely to get hotter. On the other, the greenhouse effect was being 'countered by low-level clouds generated by contrails, dust and other contaminants that tend to keep the sun from warming the surface', causing the world to become colder.

Whether temperatures rose or fell, even 'very small changes' could have 'very serious' impact. 'With a few degrees of cooling, a new ice age might be upon us, with rapid and drastic effects' on agricultural productivity. But 'with a few degrees of heating, the Greenland and Arctic ice caps would melt, perhaps raising ocean levels 250 feet'.

Similarly hedging its bets was the article cited earlier from the *Science Digest* in 1973 predicting a new ice age. This ended by quoting two geologists that 'man's tampering with the environment' might lead to the opposite effect: a 'global heatwave' caused by an excess of carbon dioxide emissions. Through 'the so-called "greenhouse effect"', they said, this could lead to such a rise in temperatures that the 'nine million cubic miles of ice covering Greenland and the Antarctic' would melt. The world's sea levels would be raised to such an extent that every coastal city would be flooded.

Even the BBC's 1974 documentary on global cooling, *The Weather Machine*, had included a sequence featuring a Swedish meteorologist Professor Bert Bolin, who for more than a decade had been speculating that the real problem facing the world might be warming rather than cooling.

When, in the late 1970s, measurements showed surface temperatures reversing upwards again, all might have seemed set for a revival of the belief that the ever-increasing emissions of CO_2 resulting from human exploitation of the planet's resources were about to lead to a wholly unnatural and potentially catastrophic degree of global warming.

Certainly by the early 1980s this concern was being voiced ever more widely. Newspapers and scientific journals sporadically featured articles and papers discussing the rise in temperatures, in particular predicting how this might lead to a dramatic rise in sea levels, due not just to melting ice but to the expansion of the volume of sea water caused by heating of the oceans.* But at this stage there still seemed considerable uncertainty as to what might be the prime cause of the world's modest warming or what, if anything, could be done about it.

One notable concern at this time, for instance, was the speed at which the Amazon and other tropical forests round the world were being felled for agriculture. In 1983 *Science* published a paper, reported in the *New York Times*, suggesting that the most effective way to slow global warming would be to introduce much tighter controls on deforestation, thus reducing emissions of CO_2 to the atmosphere.[21]

Another problem causing increasing alarm in the early 1980s was the damage supposedly being done to the earth's ozone layer by fast rising emissions of chlorofluorocarbons or CFCs, the gases widely used as coolants, fire retardants and aerosol sprays.† In 1985, when the British Antarctic Survey discovered a startlingly large 'ozone hole' above the South Pole, this made headlines across the world. Moves had already been made to ban the use of CFCs on the grounds that thinning the protective ozone in the upper stratosphere, allowing more ultra-violet radiation to reach the earth, could cause skin cancer and other human ills. But it was also noted that CFCs were a powerful greenhouse gas, raising the possibility that they too might be playing a part in the rise in global temperatures.

Hence in January 1986 a paper in *Nature* by two scientists from the US National Center for Atmospheric Research suggested that increasing emissions of 'trace gases' including CFCs could cause global temperatures to rise over the next 65 years by as much as 5°C or

---

* A statement to this effect was put out in 1986 by the German Physical Society (*Deutsche Physikalische Gesellschaft*), warning of an impending 'climate catastrophe'. This inspired an oft-cited 16-page story by *Der Spiegel*, with the cover headlined 'Klima Katastrophe' showing Cologne Cathedral half-submerged in sea water.

† In the 1970s it had been established that when CFC molecules interact with ozone (O_3), this creates an ongoing chemical reaction whereby their chlorine atoms detach part of the oxygen, turning the ozone into carbon dioxide. Thus it loses its ability to absorb ultra-violet rays from the sun, removing the protection the ozone layer provides to life on the Earth's surface.

more. If this rise continued into the twenty-second century, they predicted, temperatures might reach 'higher values than have occurred in the past 10 million years'.[22]

The most remarkable feature of the alarm over CFCs, however, was the speed with which the international community agreed to take action to phase out their use. In 1987, only two years after the discovery of the Antarctic ozone hole, more than 100 countries signed an international treaty known as the 'Montreal Protocol on Substances that Deplete the Ozone Layer'.

Politically this was highly significant. The Montreal Protocol marked the first time the governments of the world had taken collective action on such a scale, to remedy what was seen as an environmental problem affecting the entire planet. But if CFCs were a problem it was quite specific, and the threat they were perceived to pose was immediate. The more general problem potentially posed by greenhouse gases such as CO_2 was much vaguer and more diffuse. And the possibility of any agreement on similar collective action to counter the threat of global warming seemed distinctly remote.

A good snapshot of the uncertainty still surrounding all these issues was given by a rambling *Time* cover-story in October 1987, entitled 'The Heat Is On'.[23] The piece began with an account of a $10 million US research project into the ozone layer, part-sponsored by NASA and NOAA. This involved repeated flights by a DC-8 airliner and a high-flying 'spy plane', from Chile over the Antarctic, in an effort to discover how much the ozone was thinning and why.

In fact these had been the scientists whose data led to the Montreal Protocol, looking for evidence to confirm that CFCs were the cause of the problem rather than natural fluctuations in sunspots, as others had argued. A British scientist on the project, Dr Robert Watson, working for NASA, told *Time* 'we can forget the solar theories'. He and his colleagues believed the evidence that chlorine from CFCs was destroying the ozone layer – and therefore that the problem was man-made – was now overwhelming.

This provided *Time* with a cue to ask whether the same might be true for the part played by man-made greenhouse gases in making the world hotter. 'It is too soon to tell whether unusual global warming has begun', the article cautiously pronounced. But some scientists were sure it had, and that mankind was responsible. One of these was Stephen Schneider, back in the 1970s a leading advocate for global cooling. Now convinced that the problem was warming, he said:

'humans are altering the earth's surface and changing the atmosphere at such a rate that we have become a competitor with natural forces that maintain our climate. What is new is the potential irreversibility of the changes that are now taking place.'

After reviewing the possible causes and effects of global warming caused by greenhouse gases, *Time* then quoted Schneider on the possibility that lesser 'trace gases', such as CFCs and methane, were so increasing the effect of rising CO_2 levels that, by the year 2030, the world could well be facing the 'equivalent of a doubling of CO_2'. These might be 'the little guys', said Schneider, 'but they nickel and dime you up to the point where they add up to 50 per cent of the problem'.

It was one thing to identify the problem – but what could be done about it? Despite the precedent of the recently-agreed Montreal Protocol, *Time* somewhat despairingly concluded that 'any similar attempt to ease the greenhouse effect by imposing limits on CO_2 and other emissions is unlikely':

'obviously the most far-reaching step would be to cut back on the use of fossil fuels, a measure that would be hard to accomplish in industrialised countries without a wholesale turn to energy conservation or alternative forms of power. In developing countries, such reductions ... would be all but impossible to carry out, politically and economically.'

Thus, as late as the autumn of 1987, it seemed that, despite the conviction of a number of individual scientists that man-made global warming posed an alarming challenge to the future of the planet, the prospects of any concerted international effort to meet it were remote.

Within a short time, however, the picture would look very different, and in bringing that transformation about, three men in particular were to play a crucial part.

THREE MEN WHO WOULD HELP TO CHANGE HISTORY

No one knew more at that time about rising CO_2 levels than a team of American scientists who, for nearly 30 years, had been systematically recording the amount of CO_2 in the Earth's atmosphere from a weather station near the summit of a 13,679-foot high Hawaiian volcano, Mauna Loa.

The oceanographer Dr Roger Revelle was an outstanding scientist in his field. Back in the 1950s, he and his colleagues at the University of California's Scripps Institution of Oceanography were well aware that, as part of the earth's climatic regulatory system, the oceans not only give out a huge amount of carbon dioxide but also absorb it from the air above them. At the time of the International Geophysical Year in 1957 they had surmised that so much carbon dioxide was now being pumped out by the burning of fossil fuels that there might be too much for the oceans to absorb it all. Might this excess be leading to a gradual build-up of the CO_2 in the atmosphere?

To test this theory, Revelle commissioned Dr Charles Keeling and a Scripps team to begin taking detailed readings at Mauna Loa. In 1959, the first year of their study, they measured the amount of CO_2 in the atmosphere at 316 parts per million (316ppm). By 1980 this had risen to nearly 340ppm, an increase of more than 7 per cent in just 20 years. Since even this represented less than one-3,000th of all the gases making up the atmosphere, it might still have seemed insignificant – had not readings based on ice cores taken by the Vostok research station in East Antarctica begun to show that CO_2 levels stretching 650,000 years back into the Pleistocene age had been as low as 180ppm during glaciations, only rising occasionally as high as 300ppm during interglacial warmings.

Furthermore, it was widely accepted that, until the late eighteenth century, CO_2 levels had for 10,000 years not been higher than around 280ppm. Only with the coming of the Industrial Revolution and the ever-increased burning of fossil fuels had this level begun to increase. Now, according to Keeling's researches, it was rising at such a rate that, within a few decades, it might be above 400ppm.[*]

Here, it might have seemed, was the 'smoking gun'. The obvious explanation for why CO_2 was rising to record levels was the reinforcing of the 'greenhouse effect' by man's unprecedented burning of coal, oil and other fossil fuels. This created too much CO_2 for oceans and plants to absorb the excess. The earth's natural regulatory system was breaking down. The result, as Arrhenius and others had long indicated, was the rise in global temperatures.

[*] For long periods of geological time, covering some 250 million of the last 600 million years, isotope readings and other evidence indicate that CO_2 levels in the atmosphere were far higher than in more recent times, rising as high as 3000ppm. The last such epoch was in the Jurassic, the 'age of the dinosaurs', between 150 million and 200 million years ago.

Unless urgent and drastic action was taken to curb CO_2 emissions, the temperature rise would soon be so great as to unleash catastrophic consequences. The ice caps would melt. Sea levels would rise. Deserts would expand. The world's climate systems would be thrown into chaos.

This was how some would choose to read the evidence from Dr Revelle's weather station on top of that Hawaiian volcano. But they did not include Dr Revelle himself.

When interviewed by *Time* in 1987 for the article cited above, Revelle was much too cautious to respond to any invitation to sound the alarm about global warming, 'Climate', he said, from his decades of experience, 'is a complicated thing, and the changes seen so far may be due to some other cause which we don't yet understand'. As we shall see, he was to remain similarly cautious to the end of his life.[24]

This was not the case, however, with one of his former pupils, who had first heard Revelle lecturing on rising CO_2 levels when he was a student of politics at Harvard in the late 1960s. That young aspiring politician had now succeeded his oil-millionaire father as a Senator for Tennessee. In the years that lay ahead, his interest in global warming, originally inspired by Revelle's lectures 20 years before, would help to make Al Gore one of the most famous politicians on the planet.

A second man who was to play a key part in the events of the next few years has remained almost unknown to the wider public. Maurice Strong was been born into a poor home in Canada in 1929, and as a boy knew the hardships of the Great Depression. He was brought up to believe passionately in socialism and that the collective power of the state could be used create a better world. But as a young teenager during World War Two he was also inspired by the plans of Roosevelt and Churchill when the war was ended to set up a United Nations organisation.

This vision of what he saw as the embryo of a future 'world government' so fired Strong's imagination that it was to become the guiding light of his life. At the age of 18 he applied for a humble role on the UN's security staff in New York. But he soon realised that to rise to any position of influence in the organisation he would need rather better qualifications. He therefore embarked on a successful career in the Canadian energy industry, which allowed him to develop contacts with senior politicians, In the 1960s he was asked by Canada's prime minister Lester Pearson to run the country's overseas development agency; and he became a fervent early recruit to the fast-emerging 'environmentalist' movement, seeing it as a cause which it would help to further the UN's progress towards 'world governance'.

In 1971 Strong's new passion and skills at high-level networking led to him being chosen by UN Secretary-General U Thant to organise and chair the first 'UN Conference on the Human Environment', staged in Stockholm in 1972. This led to the launching of the UN Environment Program (UNEP), of which Strong became the first director, establishing its headquarters in Nairobi, Kenya.

In a speech at Windsor, Ontario, in 1974, he laid out the essence of his philosophy. Many of the problems of mankind, he believed, lay with the selfish materialism of the rich Western countries, which laid such a heavy burden on the poorer nations of the under-developed world. This was posing an 'acute moral, economic and political dilemma to the whole global community'. And one notable expression of this, he had been advised by scientists, was that 'we may already be in the beginning stages of a major shift in the dynamics of the earth's climate system'.

In 1976 Strong retired from UNEP to build up a sizeable fortune back in Canada through various business enterprises. But he had also become a member of the Club of Rome. This was a shadowy body set up in 1968 to bring together 'world leaders' to discuss many of the concerns being voiced rather more luridly in the same year by Ehrlich's *The Population Bomb*.* These centred on the need for global action to meet the dangers of over-population and the over-exploitation of the world's resources, risking various potential disasters from the exhaustion of food and oil supplies to catastrophic environmental pollution. A book along these lines, *Limits To Growth*, published by the Club of Rome in 1972, sold 30 million copies, making it the top-selling 'environmentalist' title in history.

In 1983 Strong returned more publicly to the global stage when he was picked by the UN's Secretary-General Kofi Annan to serve as a key member of its 'World Commission on Environment and Development', chaired by the Norwegian prime minister, Gro Harlem

---

* According to its website (2009) the Club of Rome is composed of 'scientists, economists, businessmen, international high civil servants, heads of state and former heads of state from all five continents'. Its members have included Prince Philip and Prince Charles.

Brundtland. The Commission's aim was to consider how the world's natural resources could be shared out more equitably between developed and under-developed nations, and how the global environment could be better safeguarded for the benefit of all.

What more than anything convinced Strong that one of the chief preoccupations of the commission's report should be the threat posed by man-made global warming was a little-reported conference held in Villach, Austria, in 1985, under the sponsorship of two other UN bodies, his own creation, UNEP, and the World Meteorological Organisation (WMO).

As early as 1979 the WMO and UNEP had organised the first 'World Climate Conference' in Vienna, calling on the world 'to prevent potential man-made changes in climate that might be adverse to the well-being of humanity'. This had led in 1985 to the conference at Villach, chaired by Strong's successor as director of UNEP, Dr Mustafa Tolba, to discuss 'the Role of Carbon Dioxide and of Other Greenhouse Gases in Climate Variations and Assorted Impacts'.

The key figure at the Villach conference, who had drafted a 560-page report for consideration by its delegates, was the third man who was to play a crucial role in what lay ahead, the Swedish meteorologist Professor Bert Bolin.

Bolin had been concerned by the possibility of global warming for many years, having published his first paper on the subject in 1960.[25] In the wake of the 1973 world oil crisis, he was drawn into politics, when his old school friend and tennis partner Olof Palme, now Sweden's Social Democratic prime minister, wanted to free Sweden from over-dependence on imported oil by building 24 nuclear reactors. These were strongly opposed by Sweden's new, strongly anti-nuclear 'green' movement. Palme therefore used Bolin's warnings that rising CO_2 levels from fossil fuels were soon likely to cause a disastrous degree of global warming as a central argument in favour of using 'carbon free' nuclear power plants to generate electricity.[26]

When Palme lost office in 1976, Bolin switched his efforts to warn of the dangerous consequences of global warming to the two UN bodies, the WMO and UNEP. He played a central part in the 1979 World Climate Conference, which led in turn to the Villach conference of 1985, the keynote for which was set by Bolin's lengthy paper.

Bolin's report argued that climate change was a 'plausible and serious probability'. The conference endorsed his proposition that 'as a result of the increasing greenhouse gases, it is now believed that in the first half of the next century a rise of global mean temperature could occur which is greater than any in man's history'. 'Current modelling', delegates agreed, showed a likely rise in surface temperatures of up to 4.5°C, which in turn could lead to a sea level rise of up to '140 centimetres', or more than four feet.[27]

There was, therefore, the conference concluded, an urgent need for more research into climate change. There must be 'internationally agreed policies for the reduction of the causative gases', and strategies 'to minimise and cope with the climate changes and rising sea levels'. No nation had either 'the political mandate or the economic power to combat climate change alone'. Mankind's response would need to be co-ordinated at the highest international level, through the WMO and UNEP. And, if necessary, their efforts should be 'backed by a global convention'.*

Strong and Tolba were among those members of the Brundtland Commission ensuring that the Villach recommendations featured strongly in its report, completed on March 30 1987.† This 'global agenda for change', which was to put the term 'sustainable development' into the vocabulary of politicians and bureaucrats for decades to come, predicted that the 'greenhouse effect' caused by the burning of fossil fuels

> *'may by early next century have increased average global temperatures enough to to shift agricultural production areas, raise the sea level to flood coastal cities and disrupt national economies.'*

It added that urgent action should also be taken to limit the use of greenhouse gases other than CO_2, particularly CFCs. These, it was estimated, would by 2030 'cause about half the problem' (precisely the claim echoed by Schneider when he was interviewed by *Time*). But international action would above all be vital to curb the use of CO_2 emitting fossil fuels, as the greatest single contributor to rising temperatures.[28]

* Quoted in Brundtland report, 'Our Common Future', see below.
† Brundtland paid particular tribute in her foreword to the part played by UNEP's director Dr Tolba, who had warned so strongly of the dangers of 'human-induced climate change' at Villach.

Behind the scenes Strong then played a part in ensuring the sign-ing of the Montreal Protocol in his native Canada six months later, on 16 September 1987. This was based above all on evidence pro-vided by a UNEP team chaired by Dr Robert Watson from NASA.[29] The treaty to limit use of CFCs provided a crucial model for what could be done, But among those intimately involved, a powerful head of steam was gathering behind the idea that they could now be aiming for something very much more ambitious.

Firstly, by the end of 1987, the WMO and UNEP had agreed that 'an inter-governmental mechanism' should be created to provide 'sci-entific assessments of climate change', and to formulate 'realistic response strategies for national and global action'.[30] Beyond that, Strong and his allies looked to the setting up of that 'global con-vention' recommended by Bolin at Villach which could move 'cli-mate change' to the centre of the international political agenda.

The following year, 1988, was to see the most significant turning point of the whole story.

Notes

1. Robert W. Reeves, *et al.* (2004) 'Global Cooling and the Cold War', US National and Atmospheric Administration (NOAA), National Weather Service, *www.meteohistory.org/2004polling_preprints/docs*. The letter to Nixon was taken very seriously, leading to the National Climate Pro-gram Act of 1975 and eventually to the setting up of what is now known as NOAA's Climatic Prediction Center. See Lawrence Solomon's *The Deniers* (Richard Vigilante Books, 2008), pp. 167–170.
2. *Time*, 24 June 1974.
3. *Newsweek*, 28 April 1975.
4. *New York Times*, 21 May 1975.
5. *Science Digest*, February 1973.
6. *International Wildlife Magazine*, July/August 1975.
7. S. I. Rasool and S. Schneider, 'Atmospheric Carbon Dioxide and Aerosols: Effects of Large Increases on Global Climate' (*Science*, 173, 138–141).
8. See 'US scientist predicts new ice age', *Washington Post*, 9 July 1971, which describes Hansen as designing the computer model on which the paper's calculations were based.
9. Graphs on temperature: Gerard Bond, *et al.*, 'Persistent Solar Influence on North Atlantic Climate During the Holocene', *Science*, Vol. 294, No. 5549 (7 December 2001), pp. 2130–2136. Graph on CO_2: Parrenin, F., Loulergue, L., & Wolff, E. (2007), EPICA Dome C Ice Core Timescales EDC3. IGBP. PAGES/World Data Center for Paleoclimatology Data

Contribution Series #2007–083. NOAA/NCDC Paleoclimatology Program, Boulder CO, USA.

10. This was originally suggested in the 1960s by Hubert Lamb, founder of the Climate Research Centre at the University of East Anglia, a pioneer in documenting climate changes over the past 2000 years (Lamb, *Climate, History and the Future*, 1977) but has since been confirmed by a mass of physical data.

11. For a general account of temperature and climate changes over the past 10,000 years, based on a wide range of sources, see *Unstoppable Global Warming: Every 1500 Years* (2008) by Fred Singer and Dennis Avery. Chap. 3, citing some 50 sources, is based on human recorded evidence. Chap. 4, citing more than 120 sources, shows how this has been confirmed by a mass of recent physical studies, covering every continent and ocean, using data ranging from pollen and stalagmites to boreholes and tree lines.

12. Singer, *op. cit.*

13. Data from Meteorological Office, cited in evidence given to House of Lords Select Committee on Economic Affairs (2005), *The Economics of Climate Change, Vol. II: Evidence*, pp. 229–231.

14. *Chicago Tribune*, 9 August 1923. This is quoted in an entertaining and well-researched anthology of climate-change predictions reported in the American press between 1895 and the present day, by R. Warren Anderson and Dan Gaynor, published by the Business and Media Institute on *www.businessandmedia.org*.

15. J. B. Kincer, *Monthly Weather Review*, September 1933.

16. Sir David King, evidence to House of Lords committee, *op. cit.*, p. 96.

17. 'Global warming: a closer look at the numbers' (2003), *www.geocraft. com*. These figures do not represent quantities but allow for the different heat-retention properties of the various greenhouse gases.

18. Callendar, G. S. (1938). 'The Artificial Production of Carbon Dioxide and Its Influence on Climate', *Quarterly J. Royal Meteorological Society*, 64, pp. 223–240.

19. Arrhenius too had hypothesised that an increase in atmospheric CO_2 would, by stimulating plant-growth, be on balance beneficial. See 'Arrhenius's little known claim about the beneficial effects of increased CO_2', *Watts Up With That*, 13 April, 2009, citing NASA Earth Observatory website.

20. In 1971 Ehrlich was to publish a rather more sober statement of his case in a paper co-authored with a young physicist John Holdren (Paul R. Ehrlich and John P. Holdren, 'Impact of Population Growth', *Science*, 26 March 1971 (Vol. 171, No. 3977, pp. 1212–1217). Nearly 40 years later, in 2009, President Obama was to appoint Holdren, by now a leading advocate for man-made global warming, as his chief

scientific adviser and director of the White House Office of Science and Technology Policy.

21. *Science*, 9 December 1983; 'Study urges action to curb climate trend', *New York Times*, 12 December 1983. Also arousing concern at this time was whether anything could be done to prevent 'acid rain', caused by man-made emissions of sulphur dioxide and nitrous oxide, blamed for killing off forests and lakes. A first international agreement on measures to reduce these emissions had been reached in 1979.

22. Robert E. Dickinson and Ralph J. Cicerone, 'Future atmospheric warming from atmospheric trace gases', *Nature*, 319, pp. 109–115, 9 January 1986.

23. 'The heat is on', *Time*, 19 October 1987.

24. Revelle had in fact been sceptical about global warming for a long time. In one of *Omni* magazine's interviews with 'top scientists of the twentieth century' (March 1984), he was asked whether he thought the increasing levels of CO_2 in the atmosphere could cause the earth's climate to become warmer.

    Revelle: 'I estimate that the total increase over the past 100 years has been about 21 per cent. But whether the increase will lead to a significant increase in global temperature, we can't absolutely say.'

    Interviewer: 'What will the warming of the earth mean to us?'

    Revelle: 'There may be lots of effects. Increased CO_2 in the air acts like a fertiliser – you get more plant growth. Increasing CO_2 levels also affect water transpiration, causing plants to close their pores and sweat less. That means plants will be able to grow in drier climates.'

    Interviewer: 'Does the increase in CO_2 have anything to do with people saying the weather is getting worse?'

    Revelle: 'People are always saying the weather is getting worse. Actually the CO_2 increase is predicted to temper weather extremes ...'

25. 'On the exchange of carbon dioxide between the atmosphere and the sea', *Tellus*, 12, pp. 274–281. See also Bolin, obituary, 'Meteorologist and first chair of the IPCC who cajoled the world into action on climate change', *The Independent*, 5 January 2008.

26 As early as 1974 Palme was warning that, by the turn of the century, climate change would be the biggest political problem confronting mankind (*Svenska Dagbladet*, 27 November 1974). Bolin now had a quasi-official role as scientific adviser to Palme, and was being generously funded by the Swedish government for his computer-based climate modelling studies (information based on unpublished paper by Stefan Björklund, 2009).

27. In Bolin's own account of the Villach conference, he emphasised later that he had taken a fairly cautious view. 'The conference was opened by Dr Tolba, who gave a very powerful message about possible future disasters because of a human-induced climate change. In light of the

uncertainty that still prevailed about a number of issues I was not willing to paint such a scary picture of the future ... I stressed that the scientific community should be careful not to become engaged in the political process beyond providing information about available knowledge.' Bert Bolin, *A History of the Science and Politics of Climate Change* (Cambridge University Press, 2007).

28. *Our Common Future, Report of the World Commission on Environment and Development*, World Commission on Environment and Development, 1987. Published as an Annex to General Assembly document A/42/427, and by Oxford University Press.

29. 'A group of scientists that had been brought together by UNEP had played an invaluable role in evaluating available knowledge in the field, under the leadership of its dynamic chairman, Dr Robert Watson of NASA.' Bolin, *op. cit.*, p. 46.

30. See IPCC website, '16 Years of Scientific Assessment in Support of the Climate Convention', 10th anniversary brochure, p. 2. See also Bolin, *op. cit.*, p. 47, in which he records that the WMO made this recommendation at its congress in May 1987, endorsed by the UNEP council later in the year.

2

The road to Rio

Enter the IPCC and Dr Hansen:
1988–1992

'1988 will be the warmest year on the record.'
Dr James Hansen, testimony to
the US Senate, 23 June 1988

*'Humanity is conducting an unintended, uncontrolled, globally perva-
sive experiment whose ultimate consequences could be second only to
a global nuclear war.'*
Statement from 'World Conference on the
Changing Atmosphere', Toronto, June 1988

*'What do you mean the President's not going to go to the Earth Summit?
It's the most important gathering in the history of the world.'*
Eileen Claussen recalling discussions on
whether President George Bush Sr should
attend the Rio Convention in 1992[1]

Looking back on the year 1988 we can see how belief in the threat
of global warming was a classic example of an idea whose time had
come.

The key event of 1988, although not widely noticed at the time,
was to be the setting up of the UN's Intergovernmental Panel on
Climate Change, the IPCC, which was to be the central player in the
debate for years ahead.

But on all sides 'global warming' suddenly became the cause of the
moment. It was the time when politicians finally took to promoting
'climate change' as one of 'the greatest challenges facing mankind'.
It was the time when most journalists in the mass-media finally came
off the fence, to promote it as a truth which should not be questioned. It even became a fashionable cause to champion among the
stars of Hollywood and show business.

The immediate trigger for all this excitement was a curious
episode which took place in Washington in June 1988. The Senate
Committee on Energy and Natural Resources, chaired by Senator

Tim Wirth of Colorado, was conducting an ongoing investigation into 'the greenhouse effect and global climate change'.

Wirth had been one of the first US politicians to take the alarm over global warning seriously, and he was determined to raise it up the political agenda. As the first witness to appear before his Committee on 23 June, he had therefore invited the scientist who was reputed to be more outspoken on this issue than any other: Dr James Hansen, who since 1981 had been director of NASA's Goddard Institute for Space Studies (GISS).

The summer of that year was unusually hot in the USA and this June day was as hot as any, with Washington thermometers hitting 95 degrees. When Hansen took the stand, it seemed appropriate to the message he was about to deliver that he was visibly perspiring.

The brief statement he began with electrified his audience. The results of researches carried out with his colleagues at the Goddard Institute, he said, showed that 'the earth is warmer in 1988 than at any time in the history of instrumental measurements'. This degree of global warming was so great that, 'with a high degree of confidence', it could now be ascribed to 'the greenhouse effect'.[2]

'Computer climate simulations', Hansen went on, 'indicate that the greenhouse effect is already large enough to begin to effect the probability of extreme events such as summer heatwaves' (like the one which at the time was causing droughts and crop failures across the USA). He then asked an assistant to put up a graph showing the temperature record over the previous 100 years. This showed that the present temperature, as Hansen pointed out, was the highest of the entire period. The four hottest years ever recorded had all been in the 1980s, rising to a peak in 1987. And all the indications were that 1988 would be even hotter, 'the warmest year on the record'.

No one in the room was better pleased by these starkly dramatic statements than Wirth and his Senate colleague Al Gore. The hearing room was crowded with journalists and TV cameras, who had been promised a story worth reporting. Within hours, just as Wirth and Gore had hoped, Hansen's claims, far more extreme than anything said publicly by any US scientist before, were making headlines across the nation.[3]

Only years later did it emerge just how carefully Wirth and his team had worked for this effect. In 2007, on a US public service TV programme which supported the cause of man-made global warming, Wirth recalled how 'we knew there was this scientist at NASA who had really identified the human impact before anybody else had done so, and was very certain about it. So we called him up and asked if he would testify.'[4]

Wirth then described how his team had called the Weather Bureau to discover what was likely, historically, to be the hottest day of that summer. 'So we scheduled the hearing that day, and bingo, it was the hottest day on record in Washington, or close to it.'

The presenter then asked 'did you also alter the temperature in the hearing room that day?' Wirth replied:

> '*what we did is that we went in the night before and opened all the windows inside the room ... so that the air conditioning wasn't working ... so when the hearing occurred,* there *wasn't only bliss, which is television cameras in double figures, but it was really hot.*'

The interview then cut to a clip of Hansen in 1988 beginning to speak, sweating profusely, with Wirth commenting in voice-over 'the wonderful Jim Hansen was wiping his brow at the table at the hearing, at the witness table, and giving this remarkable testimony'.

A senior *New York Times* journalist of the time was cut in, claiming that if Hansen had not said what he did in 1988 'it would not have become the major issue and scientists would not have taken it up the way they did after that. It was a major breakthrough.'

Cut back to Wirth saying 'I mean this was a very, very brave statement. I mean he was on the edge of the science. He's working for the federal government, and certainly, this was not cleared, you know, far up the line, what he had to say....'

What only came to light even more recently was another extract from the Congressional Record, which shows that this was not in fact the first time that Wirth's committee had interviewed Hansen. He had already appeared before them seven months earlier, in November the previous year. But on that winter's day his remarks had been so much denser and more technical that they attracted no media attention.[5] Clearly, in the time intervening, careful deliberation had gone into how most effectively to stage a second appearance by Hansen, so as to achieve maximum impact.

Thanks to what the presenter gleefully called 'stagecraft', global warming had at last become a hot political issue, as was evidenced in the flood of coverage given to Hansen's comments. A major piece in *Time*, headed 'Is The Earth Waming Up?', observed that, until now, most scientists had 'cautiously avoided definitive statements' about when man's contribution to the greenhouse effect might become obvious. But Hansen's claim that he was '99 per cent certain' this was now the cause of rising temperatures, as measured by '2,000 meteorological stations round the world', was the most definitive statement by any scientist so far. As Hansen himself had put it, 'it is time to stop waffling and say that the evidence is pretty strong that the greenhouse effect is here'.[6]

Other scientists contacted by *Time* were not prepared to be so unequivocal. Stephen Schneider, while agreeing that the planet was heating up, said that the evidence for this being due to human activity was only circumstantial: 'it doesn't prove the greenhouse effect.' Another 'climate specialist' from the Climate Analysis Center observed 'it's still not clear whether this is the CO_2 signal. The hard evidence isn't there.'

But overnight, thanks to Wirth's *coup de theatre*, global warming had moved way up the US political and media agenda. It had also given James Hansen that central place in the drama he was to enjoy for years to come.

THE IPCC – 'BERT BOLIN'S BABY'

The scientists quoted by *Time* were far from alone in being uneasy at Hansen's testimony to the Senate. As Bert Bolin was to recall years later, 'an intense debate among scientists followed, and most of them disagreed strongly with Hansen's statement.' The data showing the increase in global temperature 'had not been scrutinised well enough'. There was also 'insufficient evidence that extreme events had become more common'.[7]

Bolin went on,

> 'this was to me a clear warning of how chaotic a debate between scientists and the public might become, if a much more stringent approach to the assessment of available knowledge was not instituted.'

No one was to play a more influential role in attempting to provide the politicians with such an 'assessment' than Bolin himself. By the end of the previous year, the two UN bodies, WMO and UNEP, had agreed to set up an 'intergovernmental panel' to carry out three tasks: (1) to provide a comprehensive assessment of the scientific evidence for 'human-induced climate change'; (2) to assess its likely impact on the environment and human activity; (3) to recommend ways in which climate change and its impact might be mitigated.

During 1988 this proposal was discussed with representatives of the WMO's member governments, notably that of the USA. At the same time discussions were going forward on how to implement the recommendations of the Brundtland Commission. On the initiative of Strong, this led in June 1988 to an international gathering in Toronto billed as a 'World Conference on the Changing Atmosphere'.[8]

The conference was addressed by Bolin, Brundtland herself and Canada's prime minister Brian Mulroney. It issued a statement including the words quoted at the head of this chapter:

> *'Humanity is conducting an unintended, uncontrolled, globally pervasive experiment whose ultimate consequences could be second only to a global nuclear war.'*

The delegates agreed that there must be a concerted international effort to cut back emissions of CO_2 and other trace gases to 80 per cent of their current levels by 2005 (which Bolin later said he had thought 'unrealistic'). They also supported the idea of an 'intergovernmental panel on climate change'.

When invitations went out to a meeting in Geneva in November to set up the IPCC, only 28 countries responded (as Bolin later observed, 'the climate issue was still not high on the political agenda'). By the time the relatively modest gathering took place, its organiser, Dr Tolba of UNEP, had already persuaded Bolin to act as the new body's chairman.[9]

Tolba also proposed that three 'working groups' should be formed, to take responsibility for each of the three main tasks the IPCC had set itself. The first chairman of Working Group I to assess 'scientific information on climate change' was Dr John Houghton, head of the UK Meteorological Office, already a keen advocate of the idea of man-made global warming. Chairman of Working Group II, to assess the 'environmental and socio-economic impacts of climate change', was Dr Yuri Israel of the Soviet Union. Head of Working Group III, to formulate 'response strategies', was Dr Frederick Bernthal, an assistant secretary of state at the US State Department.

On a Maltese initiative, it was agreed that each of these groups should produce a report, to be presented to the UN General Assembly at its autumn session in 1990. At the same time, Malta persuaded the Assembly to invite the IPCC to submit its first 'review on the issue of human-induced climate change' by the same date.

Thus did the IPCC come into being. Few present at that obscure meeting in Geneva in November 1988 could have had any idea just what an influential part it was to play in shaping world affairs in the decades which lay ahead.

A 'CONSENSUS' IS BORN

Hansen's comments to the Senate committee may have been greeted with scepticism by most scientists, even those committed to the idea of man-made global warming. But in the wider world they triggered an explosion of support for the cause, which was quickly taken up not just by politicians and the media but notably by the leading environmentalist pressure groups and even by some of the most famous names in show business.

One of the first politicians to express concern was Britain's prime minister, Margaret Thatcher, whose international standing was then at its height. Having worked earlier in her career as an industrial chemist, Mrs Thatcher had taken an interest in the issue for some time, not least thanks to the lobbying of one of her senior advisers. Sir Crispin Tickell. In the 1970s, after taking a year's sabbatical from his diplomatic career to study climate science at Harvard, he had written a book on global cooling, *Climate Change And World Affairs.* Now he had become an evangelist on the dangers of global warming. He was also Britain's Permanent Representative at the UN.

In September 1988 (on Tickell's suggestion, as she records in her memoirs), Mrs Thatcher gave a talk to the Royal Society, Britain's most venerable scientific body, at the Fishmongers' Hall in London. She emphasised that climate change caused by rising levels of CO_2 and CFCs was a potential threat to mankind which must be taken seriously:

'We are told that a warming effect of 1°C per decade would greatly exceed the capacity of our natural habitat to cope. Such warming could cause accelerated melting of glacier ice and a consequent increase of the sea level of several feet over the next century ... it is noteworthy that the five warmest years in a century of records have all been in the 1980s.'[10]

This last sentence showed that those helping to draft her speech were familiar with Hansen's Senate testimony, since no one else had made such a claim. Thatcher went on to say that she would approve new funding for climate research in Britain. This resulted in the UK Met Office setting up its Hadley Centre for Climate Prediction and

Research, which she was to open in 1990, and which was also to play a very key role in the drama which lay ahead.[11]

Another politician becoming increasingly vocal on the issue was Wirth's Senate ally Al Gore. Although he hadn't yet focused on global warming as the issue to override all others, he liked to recall what he had heard about rising CO_2 levels from Dr Revelle in the 1960s; and when in May 1989 he wrote an impassioned article for the Washington Post , he described how

> *'humankind has suddenly entered into a brand new relationship with the planet Earth. The world's forests are being destroyed; an enormous hole is opening in the ozone layer. Living species are dying at an unprecedented rate. Chemical wastes, in growing volumes, are seeping downward to poison groundwater while huge quantities of carbon dioxide, methane and chlorofluorocarbons are trapping heat in the atmosphere and raising global temperatures. How much information is needed by the human mind to recognize a pattern? How much more is needed by the body politic to justify action in response?* [12]

Already noticeable even at this stage was how impatient the advocates of global warming were becoming toward anyone who dared to question whether the evidence to support their case was as unambiguous as they liked to claim.

Another witness called before Wirth's committee in 1988 had been Lester Lave, a respected professor of economics at the Carnegie-Mellon University in Pittsburgh. Unlike Hansen, he told the senators that the issue of global warming was still 'controversial'. By no means all scientists were agreed on it, and the science was still very uncertain as to what the causes of climate change might be. Senator Gore expressed particular irritation at this, claiming that anyone who said such a thing couldn't know what he was talking about, and suggested there was no point in the senators hearing any more of Professor Lave's evidence.[13]

Lave was so surprised to be dismissed by Gore and the committee in such summary fashion that he wrote to one of America's most eminent climate scientists, Richard Lindzen, to ask whether he had got it wrong. As the Albert Sloan Professor of Meteorology at the Massachusetts Institute of Technology, Lindzen was arguably the most respected climatologist in the country. He confirmed to Lave that the case for global warming was not only 'controversial' but also, in his own view, implausible.[14]

In 1992 Lindzen was to write a long informal paper entitled 'Global warming: the origin and nature of the alleged scientific consensus'. He described the extraordinary pressure which had built up in the late 1980s to create the impression that global warming was supported by an overwhelming 'consensus' of scientists.

He described, for instance, how fervently the cause had been taken up at that time by the leading environmental lobby groups, such as Greenpeace, Friends of the Earth, WWF and the Environmental Defence Fund. These campaigning organisations, which had originally emerged out of the 'environmental awakening' of the 1960s, set in train by Rachel Carson's *Silent Spring*, had now attained considerable status and influence as 'non-governmental organisations'.

Lindzen noted how the chief target of these campaigning groups had previously been the need to save the world from nuclear weapons and nuclear power stations.* But with remarkable unanimity, as the Cold War approached its end, they all suddenly switched the focus of their attention to this new threat to the planet. As he put it

> 'these lobbying groups have budgets of several million dollars and employ about 50,000 people. Their support is highly valued by many political figures. As with any large groups, self-perpetuation becomes a crucial concern. "Global warming" has become one of the major battle cries in their fundraising efforts. At the same time, the media unquestioningly accept the pronouncements of these groups as objective truth.'

In March 1989 the main NGOs formed an umbrella organisation, the Climate Action Network, to co-ordinate their campaigning on the global warming issue. This shadowy body would eventually be structured into seven regional networks covering the world, supported by hundreds of individual organisations, large and small.

In the same year, another such group, the 'Union of Concerned Scientists', originally formed to campaign for nuclear disarmament and now campaigning against nuclear power, organised a petition urging for the recognition of global warming as potentially the greatest danger

---

* Friends of the Earth was originally founded in the US in 1969 to protest against nuclear power stations. When Greenpeace was launched by a group of US anti-war protestors in 1971, their first act had been to try to halt US nuclear weapons testing on an island off Alaska. Its most famous action had been a bid to halt French nuclear weapons tests in the Pacific in 1985, which ended in the sinking of its ship the *Rainbow Warrior* in Auckland Harbour by France's secret service.

faced by mankind. Of the eventual 700 signatories, including Nobel prizewinners and many members of the National Academy of Sciences, 'only about three or four', according to Lindzen, were climatologists. At the 1990 meeting of the NAS, its president, referring specifically to the petition, went out of his way to warn members against 'lending their credibilty to issues about which they had no special knowledge'.[15]

The cause became equally fashionable among leading figures in show business. In the summer of 1989 the Hollywood actor Robert Redford, then at the height of his fame, hosted a much-publicised seminar on global warming at his Sundance Ranch in Utah, proclaiming that it was time to 'stop researching and begin acting' (as Lindzen commented, this might have seemed a 'reasonable suggestion for an actor to make'). Barbra Streisand pledged financial support to the work of the Environmental Defence Fund. The actress Meryl Streep made a television appeal for global warming to be halted.

Although, with the explosion of interest in global warming among politicians and government agencies, there was suddenly a great deal of public money available for research into climate change, it soon became clear that projects which cast any doubt on global warming were not popular. Lindzen recalled how, In the winter of 1989, the National Science Foundation had withdrawn funding from one of his MIT colleagues, Professor Reginald Newell, when his data analyses failed to show that the previous century had seen a net warming ('reviewers suggested that his results were dangerous to humanity').*

Lindzen himself submitted a critique of the global warming thesis to *Science*, the journal of the American Association for the Advancement of Science. His article was rejected as being of 'no interest' to its readership but, to his astonishment, *Science* then proceeded to attack his unpublished paper in print. Although it was eventually published by the *Bulletin of the American Meteorological Society*, the editor made 'a determined effort to solicit rebuttals', including an attack on Lindzen by Stephen Schneider, now one of the leading advocates of warming.

---

* At the same time Lindzen was surprised, when invited to a seminar on global warming at another university, to find he was the only scientist on a panel of 'environmentalists'. 'There were strident calls for immediate action and ample expressions of impatience with science.' A Congresswoman from Rhode Island acknowledged that 'scientists may disagree, but we can hear Mother Earth, and she is crying'.

The letters the paper aroused from the *Bulletin's* readers, however, were predominantly sceptical of the case being made for 'anthropogenic' or man-made global warming. Indeed a subsequent Gallup poll of climate scientists belonging to the American Meteorological Society and the American Physical Union showed that no fewer than 49 per cent rejected anthropogenic warming. Only 18 per cent thought that some warming was caused by man, while 33 per cent didn't know.

Written in 1992, the main theme of Lindzen's article was the peculiar pressure which had developed to push this insistence that the man-made global warming thesis was now accepted by an overwhelming 'consensus' of scientific opinion, when there was so much evidence to the contrary. But, as one of the world's most distinguished climate experts, he was also deeply troubled by the scientific methods the upholders of the new orthodoxy were using to promote their thesis.

In his article he went on to spell out his central concern in some detail, because by this time the believers in global warming had won their most powerful support so far. This came when, in 1990, the Intergovernmental Panel on Climate Change presented the UN with its 'First Assessment Report'.

THE IPCC'S FIRST ASSESSMENT REPORT

From 1990 onwards the organisation chaired by Bert Bolin was to become, through its succession of scientific reports, the most important single player in the global warming story.

All those responsible for running the IPCC, from Bolin downwards, were already convinced that 'human-induced climate change' was taking place. The role of the IPCC, as they defined it, was not to test the hypothesis or to carry out new research but to review the existing scientific evidence for global warming from all over the world, to assess its likely impact and to make recommendations as to what might be done.

As exemplified by the First Assessment Report (FAR as it came to be known), this was to be carried out by an elaborate three-stage process. The first stage involved compiling a three-part technical report, under each of the three main headings of the IPCC's agenda. This was compiled by the three 'working groups', made up of scientists nominated by governments representing a variety of different disciplines, along with many contributors who were not strictly scientists at all, ranging from economists and sociologists to environmental activists. These 'authors' each contributed often not more than a page or two to a series of 'chapters', under the guidance of 'lead authors' answerable to a 'lead chapter author'.

By far the most important of the three sections of the technical report was that compiled by Working Group I, under the chairmanship of Dr John Houghton, head of the UK Met Office. This was because Houghton's group was the only one concerned with the scientific evidence for how much climate change was likely to take place, and Houghton's Hadley Centre played a key part in selecting which authors should be invited to contribute. The intention was that the other two working groups should take the findings of Working Group I as their starting point.[16]

Then came the second stage when the resulting drafts were circulated to hundreds of 'expert reviewers' throughout the world for comment. These were submitted back to the Working Group and 'chapter authors' to decide whether the original draft needed modification. Their comments would lead to a revised draft.

The final and crucially important stage came with the drafting of a 'Summary for Policymakers': in effect an 'executive summary' for the benefit of governments, the media and anyone wanting a brief statement of what the expert reports said. This process began with the submission of the technical reports and the draft Summary to governments, any of which could ask for changes before a plenary meting at which the Summary was finally agreed.

The result, as soon became apparent, was that the Summary would often become significantly different in key respects from the main technical report itself, although it was the Summary which would be most widely read, publicised and quoted.

The way this was to work in practice was illustrated by the IPCC's first report. The Summary for Policymakers of Working Group I's technical report, drafted by Houghton as its chairman, began by saying virtually everything the believers in global warming could have hoped for. The IPCC was not only 'certain' that there was a 'greenhouse effect' (hardly controversial) but that this was enhanced by 'emissions from human activities'. It was 'confident' that the increase in $CO2$ alone had been 'responsible for over half the enhanced greenhouse effect', and that this would 'require immediate reductions in emissions from human activities of over 60 per cent to stabilise their concentrations at today's levels'.

'Based on current models', the Summary predicted that, unless action was taken, global mean temperatures would increase through the twenty-first century by between 0.2 and 0.5°C. per decade. This was an increase greater than any 'seen in the past 10,000 years'. Over the previous 100 years, it found, surface temperatures had already increased by between 0.3 and 0.6 degrees, but the IPCC was now thus predicting the possibility of a roughly similar increase every 10 years. Hence, it argued, the need for such drastic action.

This was pretty dramatic stuff. But the Summary then went on to admit, rather curiously, that this twentieth-century increase could have been 'largely due to natural variability'. This appeared to contradict its earlier claim that increased CO_2 was responsible for half the increase in greenhouse warming. To make the picture still more confused, the Summary hastened to add that natural and 'other human factors could have offset a still larger human-induced greenhouse warming'. Finally, the Summary conceded that to reach an 'unequivocal' view of the 'enhanced greenhouse effect' would not be possible for 'a decade or more'.

These ambiguities were at least in part explained by comparing the Summary with the hundreds of pages of the main report. Here the findings of the technical experts turned out to be often very much more cautious and even flatly contradictory, supporting nothing like so straightforward a set of conclusions as Houghton's Summary tried to suggest.

One passage in the Working Group I report, for instance, allowed that although 'the evidence points consistently to a real but irregular warming over the past century',

> '*a global warming of larger size has almost certainly occurred at least once since the end of the last glaciation without any appreciable increase in greenhouse gases, Because we do not understand the reasons for these past warming events, it is not yet possible to attribute a specific proportion of the recent, smaller warming to an increase of greenhouse gases.*' *

None of this uncertainty was reflected in the Summary for Policy-makers.

---

* Because the IPCC's first report needed to be produced so quickly, Working Groups II and III could not wait for the findings of Working Group I but had to start work immediately from scratch.

When Prof Lindzen came to review the report in 1992, this was one of his central criticisms. Noting how startlingly it differed from the scientific report, he wrote that the Policymakers Summary

> *'largely ignores the uncertainty in the report and attempts to present the expectation of substantial warming as firmly based science.'* [17]

Another academic critic similarly observed how 'comments that were not welcomed by the main authors stood little chance of being considered seriously'.[18] He went on to quote Houghton himself confirming this, in admitting that:

> *'whilst every attempt was made by the lead authors to incorporate their comments, in some cases these formed a minority opinion which could not be reconciled with the larger consensus.'* [19]

Lindzen's chief objection to the report, however, was directed at the methods used to arrive at the evidence on which the IPCC rested its entire case. He did not, of course, deny that limited warming had taken place in the twentieth century, or that CO_2 in the atmosphere had risen. But the predictions of future temperatures and climate behaviour on which the IPCC relied were all based on computer models. And what particularly struck Lindzen was the technical inadequacy of these models. Their programming, in his view, was much too crude. By failing to allow for the subtle complexities and interactions of the earth's climatic system, their findings were demonstrably misleading.

In particular, by concentrating their attention on CO_2 and other man-made contributions to greenhouse gas, the models had tended to overlook or seriously to misjudge the part played by far the most important greenhouse gas of all, water vapour, comprising all but a tiny fraction of the total. They had also failed to allow for the 'negative feedback' effect of cloud-cover.[20] A warming of the sea would increase humidity, creating more water vapour and clouds which would feed back to lessen the impact of solar warming. In both these respects the models, Lindzen bluntly put it as a specialist in these areas, had 'neither the physics nor the numerical accuracy' to come up with findings which were not 'disturbingly arbitrary'.

Put these two factors properly into the equation, he argued, and it could be seen that the 'greenhouse effect' caused by rising CO_2 levels had been wildly overstated. What was more, this could be demonstrated by running those same computer models retrospectively, to 'predict' where temperatures should have been throughout the twentieth century.

It became glaringly obvious that these over-simplified programmes failed to explain the actual variations which had taken place in twentieth-century temperature levels. In the 1920s and 1930s, when CO_2 emissions were comparatively low, temperatures had sharply risen, But in the very years when emissions were rising most steeply, during the Little Cooling between the 1940s and the 1970s, temperatures had been in decline.

In fact the assumptions on which the models were based would have led them to predict a twentieth-century warming four times greater than the rise that had been actually recorded (with most of that rise taking place before atmospheric CO_2 had reached anything like its present level). On this basis, how could any trust now be placed in their attempts to estimate future rises?

This clearly showed, in Lindzen's view, how crucially important factors were being missed out by the 'modellers' as they made their extravagant predictions of future warming. Their models had an in-built bias, in that they were programmed to look for evidence of CO_2 warming while not making due allowance for those factors which would create 'negative feedback'. This was the very element in the equation on which Lindzen himself was an unrivalled expert.

As he summed it up, trying to be reasonably fair to the IPCC's findings, 'the report as such has both positive and negative features'. But

> 'methodologically, the report is deeply committed to reliance on large models, and within the report models are largely verified by comparison with other models. Given that models are known to agree more with each other than with nature (even after 'tuning'), that approach does not seem promising. In addition a number of the participants have testified to the pressure put on them to emphasise results supportive of the current scenario and to suppress other results. That pressure has frequently been effective, and a survey of participants reveals substantial disagreement with the final report.'[21]

Lindzen's criticisms, however, had little impact on the way the IPCC was to proceed (although minor 'tweaking' would be made in future to bring the findings of the models more into line with observed past temperature patterns). The upholders of the 'consensus' had by now become so impatient of anyone who dared question their new orthodoxy that Lindzen had already been singled out for attack in various articles and books. These included *Global Warming: the Greenpeace Report* by a geologist-turned-environmental activist, Jeremy Leggett (1990); and *World On Fire: Saving An Endangered Earth* written by George Mitchell, the Democrats' majority leader in the Senate (1991).

As Lindzen recalled, 'climate sceptics' such as himself were by now being regularly subjected to dismissive ridicule in the media, as in an article in the *New York Times* by Al Gore, comparing himself and his allies to Galileo, standing for the truth against the blinkered intolerance of his time.

'Why, one might wonder', Lindzen asked, was 'there such insistence on scientific unanimity on the warming issue'?

After all, unanimity in science is virtually non-existent on far less complex matters. Unanimity on an issue as uncertain as 'global warming' would be surprising and suspicious. Moreover, why are the opinions of scientists sought regardless of their field of expertise? Biologists and physicians are rarely asked to endorse some theory in high-energy physics. Apparently, when one comes to 'global warming', any scientist's agreement will do.

But however ill-founded these claims of 'consensus' and 'unanimity' might have been, the IPCC's 1990 report had given the global warming campaign tremendous momentum. Its most dramatic consequence came two years later in 1992, with a proposal that all the governments of the world should meet in Rio de Janeiro for an 'Earth Summit'.

'THE MOST IMPORTANT GATHERING IN THE HISTORY OF THE WORLD'

If the IPCC was 'Bolin's baby', the Rio de Janeiro 'Earth Summit' was very much the 'baby' of its chosen secretary-general and chief organiser, Maurice Strong. As a gifted top-level political networker and behind-the-scenes operator, it was the high point of his career. As a lifelong crusader for world government and the need to redress the balance between the world's richer and poorer nations, it perfectly expressed his long-held belief that the ideal cause to further those aims was 'environmentalism', above all 'climate change', which he argued would hit the poorer nations hardest.

The 'United Nations Conference on Environment and Development' (UNCED) was sponsored by the Brundtland Commission on which Strong had played such an influential part in the 1980s. Although it covered other environmental issues, such as 'bio-diversity', it was also that 'global convention' on climate change called for by the UNEP and WMO conference at Villach back in 1985.

The world had never seen anything like the gathering which assembled in Rio at the end of May 1992. Strong, who chaired the conference, had long believed in using the influence of the leading environmentalist campaign groups, such as Greenpeace, Friends of the Earth and the World Wildlife Fund, of which he was to become a board member. Many of them, as members of the Climate Action Network, had received official funding through UN bodies to rally support for his Rio conference. No fewer than 20,000 activists had been sponsored to come to Rio itself.

This seeming evidence of worldwide popular concern did much to ensure that politicians from 172 countries agreed to fly in to Rio for the great occasion. They included no fewer than 108 prime ministers and presidents, ranging from President George Bush of the USA to President Fidel Castro of Cuba. Also attended by 10,000 representatives of the media, it was easily the largest such political get-together in history.

Strong, with his passion for the idea of 'world governance', opened the two-week long conference by proclaiming that:

> *'The concept of national sovereignty has been an immutable, indeed sacred, principle of international relations. It is a principle which will yield only slowly and reluctantly to the new imperatives of global environmental cooperation. It is simply not feasible for sovereignty to be exercised unilaterally by individual nation states, however powerful. The global community must be assured of environmental security.'*

While most of the activists staged a giant non-stop rally nearby, known as the 'Non-governmental Organisation Forum', 2,400 of them had been invited as official delegates to the main conference itself. And here, on 12 June, they cheered as politicians from 154 countries queued up to sign a 'UN Framework Convention on Climate Change' (UNFCCC).

On ratification this would commit all the signatory governments to a voluntary reduction of greenhouse gas emissions, with the aim of 'preventing dangerous anthropogenic interference with Earth's climate system'. These actions were aimed primarily at industrialised countries, with the intention that, by the year 2000, their CO_2 and other greenhouse gas emissions would be no higher than they had been in 1990.

At this stage the commitment was only voluntary. But the Convention's aim was that, in close co-operation with the IPCC on the science, it should soon be replaced by a series of treaties or 'Protocols', setting targets for curbing emissions which would be mandatory. The first would be that to be agreed five years later in Kyoto.

For Strong it was 'a historic moment for humanity'. For the campaigners against global warming it was the headiest moment they had known so far. Barely four years after the campaign had begun in earnest, their issue was being raised towards the top of the world's political agenda.

Notes

1. *http://www.pbs.org/wgbh/pages/frontline/hotpolitics/interviews/ wirth.html*. Ms Claussen was being interviewed in 2007, having become President of the Pew Center on Global Climate Change.
2. Transcript from *Congressional Record* of 'Hearing before the Committee on Energy and Natural Resources', First Session on the Greenhouse Effect and Global Climate Change, 23 June 1988, Pt. 2, available in facsimile via Climate Audit website 'Thoughts on Hansen *et al.* 1988', 16 January 2008.
3. E.g., 'Global warming has begun, expert tells Senate', *New York Times*, 24 June 1988.
4. *Frontline, http://www.pbs.org/wgbh/pages/frontline/hotpolitics/interviews/ wirth.html*
5. For transcript from the *Congressional Record* see second link to 'Hansen' on Climate Audit website, 16 January 2008, cited above in n. 2.
6. 'Is The Earth Warming Up?', *Time*, 4 July 1988. This was followed on 11 July by a much more one-sided cover story in *Newsweek*, headed 'The Greenhouse Effect: Danger, More Hot Summers Ahead', which was to establish the magazine as one of the most consistent media cheerleaders for climate alarmism in the years to come.
7. Bolin, *op. cit.*, p. 49.
8. Bolin, *op. cit.*, p. 48.
9. Bolin, *op. cit.*, pp. 49–50.
10. Quoted by Bolin, *op. cit.*, p. 56.
11. Thatcher repeated her main points in further speeches to the UN General Assembly in November 1989 and to the Second World Climate

Conference staged by the WMO in 1990. By the time she came to write her memoirs in 1993, however, she had moderated her position dramatically. Omitting any reference to the scientific details, she now insisted that the relationship between CO_2 and climate change was 'a good deal less certain than the relationship between CFCs and ozone depletion'. The only quotation she included from her speech to the Royal Society blandly referred to the need for further research and that any political response to climate change must be based on 'good science to establish cause and effect' (*The Downing Street Years*, Harper Collins, 1993, pp. 640–641).

12. *Washington Post*, 13 May 1989.
13. Richard Lindzen, 'Global warming: the origin and nature of the alleged scientific consensus', proceedings of the OPEC seminar on the environment, Vienna, 13–15 April 1992 (available on Cato Institute website); also interview with Lindzen, *Die Weltwoche*, 3 March 2007.
14. Lindzen, *op. cit.*
15. Lindzen, *op. cit.* Lindzen's view of the petition was that it showed how global warming had become 'part of the dogma of the liberal conscience – a dogma to which scientists are not immune'.
16. Lindzen, *op. cit.*
17. Houghton J. T., *et al.* (1990), *Climate Change: The IPCC Scientific Assessment*, Cambridge University Press.
18. Lindzen, *op. cit.*
19. C. R. de Freitas, 'Are observed changes in the concentration of carbon dioxide in the atmosphere really dangerous', *Bulletin of Canadian Petroleum Geology*, 50, No. 2, June 2002 (available on *www.friendsof science.org*).
20. Houghton J. T., *et al.* (1990), *op. cit.*
21. Lindzen, *op. cit.*, p. 7.

3

The road to Kyoto

Enter Vice-President Gore and IPCC 2

'Today the evidence of an ecological Kristallnacht *is as clear as the sound of glass shattering in Berlin.'*
Al Gore, Earth in the Balance, 1992[1]

'Climate change is increasingly recognised as one of the most serious threats to humankind ... that the majority of world leaders are now convinced of this peril ... is due largely to the work of one organisation, the Intergovernmental Panel on Climate Change (IPCC).'
Sir John Houghton on Madrid meeting of IPCC in 1995[2]

'The balance of evidence suggests that there is a discernible human influence on global climate.'
Summary for Policymakers, Second
IPCC Assessment Report, 1996

'In my more than 60 years as a member of the American scientific community, including service as president of both the National Academy of Sciences and the American Physical Society, I have never witnessed a more disturbing corruption of the peer-review process than the events which led to this IPCC report ... if the IPCC is incapable of following its most basic procedures, it would be best to abandon the entire IPCC process.'
Professor Frederick Seitz, *Wall Street Journal*, 12 June 1996[3]

In no country up to this time had alarm over the threat of global warming been expressed more vociferously than the USA. But the concerns expressed by scientists, environmentalists and the media had conspicuously not been echoed by the US government.

President Bush had been profoundly uneasy about attending the 'Earth Summit. He was well aware that, as the world's leading emitter of CO_2, America would be cast in Rio as the chief villain of the story. He and his advisers were also aware that, thanks to the pronounced ideological slant given the conference by Strong and the Brundtland Commission, intense pressure would be put on rich countries such as the US to accept highly damaging curbs on their emissions, while developing countries such as China and India would be largely exempted.[4]

This impression was confirmed by the fact that, after Bush's arrival in Rio, his cavalcade driving through the streets was received in silence or with boos, while Communist Cuba's President Castro was feted by cheering crowds.

Bush did at least sign the 'Climate Convention', and in his speech afterwards wes anxious to talk up his country's record on environmental issues. But he referred only to measures such as those the US had taken to remove lead from petrol or to conserve forests. On global warming he pointedly remained silent.[5]

In the absence of any lead from America, the one 'government' keener than any to fill the gap was that of the European Community, based in Brussels. 1992 was the year when the 12 countries then making up the EC signed the Maastricht Treaty, transforming their bloc into the 'European Union'. Their leaders were now at the height of their enthusiasm for that political and economic integration which was always at the heart of the 'European' agenda. It was the Maastricht treaty which set up the single currency and laid the foundations of much closer integration in defence and foreign policy. But they had also already singled out the 'environment' as another ideal cause – high-minded and involving issues which ran across international borders – to justify extending yet further the powers of the 'supranational' government they were now so busily constructing.

In October 1991, in response to the IPCC report the previous year, the Brussels-based European Commission published a long document setting out 'a Community strategy to limit Carbon Dioxide emissions'.[6] The IPCC, the document began, had reflected for the first time 'a consensus amongst scientists on the possible impact and risks of the greenhouse effect'. 'Immediate action' was called for and 'a decision to stabilise CO_2 emissions is a first important step'.

'With the completion of the Internal Market', the paper went on, 'the European Community will be the biggest economic/trading partner in the world, with the potential to exercise an important level of moral, economic and political influence and authority'. To adopt a common policy on 'the greenhouse problem' would give the Community the chance to fill a 'vacuum in global foreign policy'.

To this end, the Commission proposed, the Community should adopt a wide range of measures. These were to set a template for how Brussels was to legislate on 'climate change' for years to come.

They included the active promotion of renewable energy sources, such as wind turbines (but excluding large scale hydro-electric power, seen to be competitive with more conventional power sources); stepping up the recycling of waste; regulations to limit CO_2 emissions from industry, vehicles and household appliances (including lighting); and steps to encourage a major switch from private to 'collective transport'.

In addition, to penalise CO_2 emissions and to encourage more efficient use of energy, the Commission proposed the imposition of a substantial new 'carbon tax', some of the proceeds of which should go towards subsidising renewable energy. This was taken further in 1992 by a formal 'Proposal for a Council Directive Introducing a Tax on Carbon Dioxide Emissions and Energy'.[7]

Thus did the government of what was soon to become the European Union set in train that aspiration to set a 'moral' example to the rest of the world on 'climate change' which was to shape its agenda through the years to come.

MR GORE AND DR REVELLE

If the US had not so far chosen to lead the world on global warming, there was one politician in America who was determined that it should do so. As a leading Democrat contender in the 1992 presidential race, Al Gore had now decided to make his stand on climate change the defining issue of his political career.

In bidding for the nomination, Gore published a book, *Earth In The Balance*. Although this also referred to other environmental issues, such as waste, deforestation and toxic chemicals, he made clear his view that global warming was 'the worst threat we have ever faced'.[8] A shaping experience of his life, he recalled in the book's introduction was how, at Harvard in the mid-1960s, he had been introduced to rising CO_2 levels as 'a global environmental threat' by Roger Revelle, the father of the research project which had given the world those epoch-making figures on the rise in carbon emissions.

> 'Professor Revelle explained that higher levels of CO_2 would create what he called the greenhouse effect, which would cause the earth to grow warmer. The implications of his words were startling ... if this trend continued, human civilisation would be forcing a profound and disruptive change in the entire global climate.'

When he wrote those words in 1992, Gore seemed unaware that Revelle had long been taking a very much more cautious line on global warming than fitted in with his own agenda. In July 1988, after Hansen had made headlines with his testimony to Wirth's Senate committee, Revelle had written to a member of Congress:

> 'Most scientists familiar with the subject are not yet willing to bet that the climate this year is the result of "greenhouse warming". As you very well know, climate is highly variable from year to year, and the causes of these variations are not at all well understood. My own personal belief is that we should wait another 10 or 20 years to really be convinced that the greenhouse effect is going to be important for human beings, in both positive and negative ways.'[9]

Four days later Revelle had written to Senator Wirth himself, cautioning that:

> 'we should be careful not to arouse too much alarm until the rate and amount of warming becomes clearer. It is not yet obvious that this summer's hot weather and drought are the result of a global climatic change or simply an example of the uncertainties of climate variability. My own feeling is that we had better wait another 10 years before making confident predictions.'[10]

In 1990, at a conference of the American Association for the Advancement of Science in New Orleans, Revelle presented a paper on the theory that seeding the world's oceans with nutrients such as iron filings would stimulate the growth of plankton, thus increasing marine absorption of CO_2. After the lecture he was approached by an old friend, Dr Fred Singer, professor of environmental science at the University of Virginia and the man who, as its first director in the 1960s, had worked in conjunction with NASA to design and set up the US National Satellite Weather Service. Next day the two men met to discuss writing an informal paper together on global warming, later inviting Dr Chauncey Starr, an energy expert, to join them.

Singer drafted the paper, which, after discussion, was submitted to a new, small-circulation journal, *Cosmos*. When he and Revelle met to discuss the proofs, Revelle expressed scepticism about computer climate models (Singer tried to assure him that within 10 years they would be greatly improved). After they had agreed several amendments, the article was published in April 1991, entitled 'What to Do About Greenhouse Warming: Look Before You Leap'.

Their main argument, echoing the views that Revelle had expressed earlier in his letters to the members of Congress, was that

> *'Drastic, precipitous, and especially unilateral steps to delay the putative greenhouse impacts can cost jobs and prosperity and increase the human costs of global poverty without being effective. Stringent economic controls now would be economically devastating particularly for developing countries....'*

They concluded that:

> *'the scientific base for a greenhouse warming is too uncertain to justify drastic action at this time. There is little risk in delaying policy responses.'*

The article attracted little attention. Three months later, professionally active to the end of his life, Revelle died aged 82. Later that year Singer was invited to contribute to a book on global warming and, being busy, suggested that the article be republished.

The following summer of 1992, when Gore was running hard for the vice-presidential nomination, the *New Republic* picked up on the contrast between the references to Revelle in his new book and the views Revelle had expressed in the article he had co-authored in *Cosmos*.[11] This was followed up by *Newsweek* and elsewhere in the media and, by the time Gore had won the nomination, was even raised in a televised election debate.

Gore's response was angrily to protest that Revelle's views in the article had been 'taken completely out of context'. In light of the somewhat embarrassing coverage which ensued, Singer was called by one of Gore's close associates, Dr Justin Lancaster of Harvard University, who asked that Revelle's name be removed from the article. Singer explained that this was not possible, since the piece had already been published. But Lancaster persisted in his request, claiming that Revelle had not really been a co-author of the article at all and that his name had only been included 'over his objections'. He even suggested that Singer must have been pressuring a sick old man whose mental capacities were failing.

Similar damaging accusations were then made by a member of Gore's personal staff to the publishers of the book in which the article was to be reprinted, again demanding that it be removed. When, after Gore had become US vice-president, Lancaster repeated his charges, Singer in April 1993 sued him for libel.

This led to a remarkable revelation, When the two sides exchanged documents under the process known as 'legal discovery', it emerged that Lancaster had been rung by Gore after the *Newsweek* article appeared, and that Gore had particularly pressed him about Revelle's mental state towards the end of his life. Hence Lancaster's earlier suggestions to Singer that Revelle had been losing his faculties.

Lancaster was now willing to agree that Revelle had in fact been 'mentally sharp to the end'. He also admitted that Revelle had shown him the *Cosmos* article before it was published, with the comment that there did not seem to be anything in it that 'was not true', and that 'it was honest to admit the uncertainties about green-house warming'.[12]

This was not the first occasion on which Gore had been associated with attempts to distort or suppress the views of those who disagreed with him. In one of the last hearings of a Senate sub-committee he had chaired, Professor Lindzen appeared as a witness. In the course of arcane exchanges about the role of water vapour in the upper troposphere, Lindzen admitted he had now had to revise a point he had argued two years earlier about the effect of water vapour from clouds. Subsequent research had shown that another process, probably ice crystals from the clouds, must also be involved (even though this did not alter the overall effect).

Gore picked up Lindzen's admission that he had changed his mind, asking whether he was now rejecting what he had said two years earlier. When Lindzen agreed, Gore called for the recording secretary to note that Professor Lindzen had 'retracted his objections to global warming'.[13]

Others present assured Gore that Lindzen had done nothing of the kind and that he was confusing matters. But soon afterwards, in the *New York Times*, Tom Wicker, a prominent journalistic ally of Gore's, repeated the charge that Lindzen had retracted his opposition to global warming. Lindzen tried to correct this with a letter, which was only eventually published more than a month later.[14]

In February 1994, an ABC News presenter, Ted Koppel, revealed on his *Nightline* programme that Vice-President Gore had rung him to suggest that he expose the political and economic forces behind the 'anti-environmental movement'. Gore had urged him to expose the fact that Singer and other US scientists who had voiced sceptical views about global warming were receiving money from the coal industry and other industrial interests.

Such charges were to become an only too familiar feature of the debate. Any prominent scientist who dared to challenge the global warming orthodoxy would be likely to face accusations that he was funded by energy firms, 'Big Oil' or even the tobacco industry.[15] Not only did Koppel call Gore's bluff by reporting their conversation on air, he observed that there was

> 'some irony in the fact that Vice President Gore – one of the most scientifically literate men to sit in the White House in this century – (is) resorting to political means to achieve what should ultimately be resolved on a purely scientific basis. The measure of good science is neither the politics of the scientists nor the people with whom the scientist associates. It is the immersion of hypotheses into the acid of truth. That's the hard way to do it, but it's the only way that works.'

Gore's attempt to use a leading news programme to denigrate his opponents in this way provoked such political embarrassment that, shortly afterwards, Lancaster settled his case with Singer by issuing a full retraction and apology.[16]

One bid to promote the illusion of 'consensus' had failed. But it was now to be followed by another, very much more public, and conceived on an altogether grander scale.

IPCC 2: 'A MAJOR DECEPTION'

By the mid-1990s, the Clinton-Gore administration had become closely involved in pushing America's energy interests across the world. In particular it was close to the new Texas-based energy giant, Enron, a significant contributor to Democratic Party funds. The federal government supported Enron with $4 billion of loans, and supported the company's bids for a series of huge contracts to open up new oil and gas fields and to build power stations and pipelines in India, Russia, China, the Philippines, South America and Africa.

Gore took a close interest in some of these projects. In particular, in December 1995 he visited South Africa to lobby the country's new president, Nelson Mandela, on behalf of Enron's bid to develop a large new gas field in Mozambique.[17]

The vice-president had not, however, lost his interest in the battle against global warming, and his visit to South Africa coincided with final political agreement being given to the next report of the Inter-governmental Panel on Climate Change, due to be launched the following summer.

The IPCC's 'second assessment report' (SAR) went considerably further than the first in endorsing an anthropogenic explanation for global warming. The biggest media headlines were reserved for its claim that 'the balance of evidence suggests that there is a discernible human influence on global climate'. These words were to be quoted far more often than any others in the report. But the story behind how they came to be included in the Summary for Policy Makers was curious.[18]

The source of this sentence was given as Chapter 8 of the scientific working group's report, the 'lead author' of which was Ben Santer, a scientist working for the US government's Lawrence Livermore National Laboratory. This included much the same wording: that 'the body of statistical evidence' now 'points to a discernible human influence on the global climate'.

When the report containing these sentences was published, however, some of the scientific contributors who had signed off the working group's chapters the previous year were seriously dismayed. These words had not appeared in the draft they had formally approved. It seemed they had been added subsequently, by the 'lead author' himself. Santer had also, it emerged, deleted a number of key statements from the agreed text, all of which reflected serious scientific doubt over the human contribution to global warming. They included these passages:

> '• *None of the studies cited above has shown clear evidence that we can attribute the observed changes to the specific cause of increases in greenhouse gases.*
>
> • *No study to date has positively attributed all or part (of the climate change observed) to (man-made) causes.*
>
> • *Any claims of positive detection and attribution of significant climate change are likely to remain controversial until uncertainties in the total natural variability of the climate system are reduced.*
>
> • *When will an anthropogenic effect on climate be identified? It is not surprising that the best answer to this question is "We do not know".'*

All these sentences had mysteriously vanished from the original agreed version. What was particularly odd about the new additions to the text was that the only source cited in support of them appeared to be two papers co-authored by Santer himself, which had not yet been published. That much-cited claim about 'discernible human influence on climate change' was based on what were known as 'fingerprinting studies'. These compared the patterns of climate change predicted by computer models with changes actually observed in the real world. Where these coincided (or displayed the same 'fingerprint'), this was taken as evidence that the computer model was correct.[19]

However, when Santer and several colleagues published their first, all-important paper, two other scientists, Dr Patrick Michaels and a colleague, examined their evidence. They were surprised to discover that its conclusions in favour of global warming had been based only on part of the data. The supposed 'fingerprinting' parallel between the computer models and observed data applied only to the years between 1943 and 1970, during the 'Little Cooling'. When the full set of data was used, showing earlier years going back to 1905 and years after 1970, the warming trend claimed by Santer and his colleagues disappeared.[20]

This was surprising enough, in view of the significance attached to Santer's revised wording of Chapter 8 by the Summary for Policymakers and all the publicity which followed. But the realisation that a single contributor could have been allowed to make such a crucial change after the scientific text had been formally approved, soon gave rise to a considerable uproar.

Even *Nature*, which published the Santer paper, was not happy about the rewriting of Chapter 8 to 'ensure that it conformed' with the Summary. A week after the report was published, the *Wall Street Journal* not only expressed outrage in an editorial ('Cover-up in the Greenhouse').[21] The following day it published an excoriatory article by Frederick Seitz, a much-respected former president of the US National Academy of Sciences.[22]

It was Seitz who, under the heading 'Major Deception on Global Warming', quoted some of those passages in the original draft of Chapter 8 which had been mysteriously removed. As he put it in his article, the IPCC report would 'surely be hailed as the latest and most authoritative statement on global warming', because the IPCC itself was generally regarded as 'the best source of scientific information' on the subject. Its latest report would be held in high regard:

'largely because it has been peer-reviewed. That is, it has been read, discussed, modified and approved by an international body of experts. These scientists have laid their reputation on the line. But this report is not what it appears to be – it is not the version that was approved by the contributing scientists listed on the title page. In my more than 60 years

as a member of the American scientific community, including service as president of both the National Academy of Sciences and the American Physical Society, I have never witnessed a more disturbing corruption of the peer-review process than the events which led up to this IPCC report.'

Seitz went on to illustrate his point that the crucial changes had been made 'after the scientists had met and approved what they thought was the final peer-reviewed version'. They had assumed that 'the IPCC would obey the IPCC rules', nothing in which permitted changes to be made after the wording of a report had gone through the prescribed approval process. And, initially, everything had been done according to the rules.

Twenty-eight scientists representing the authors of the technical report had approved the final draft at a meeting in Madrid in November 1995, also attended by 177 government delegates from 96 countries and 14 representatives of NGOs or non-governmental organisations.[23] It had then been given final political approval by a plenary meeting of the IPCC in Rome the following month. Yet now the document was published, it emerged that, subsequent to the Madrid meeting

'more than 15 sections in Chapter 8 of the report – the key chapter setting out the scientific evidence for and against a human influence over climate – were changed or deleted after the scientists charged with examining this question had accepted the supposedly final text.'

Furthermore, the effect of every one of these changes and deletions had been to suppress expressions of doubt about man-made warming, and to convey the false impression that the scientists had all accepted by 'consensus' that anthropogenic warming was taking place. Professor Seitz suggested that, for what had happened, the chapter's 'lead author, Benjamin D. Santer, must presumably take the major responsibility'.

'IPCC reports' he went on, are often 'called the "consensus" view. If they were to lead to 'carbon taxes and restraints on economic growth, they will have a major and almost certainly destructive effect on the economies of the world.' Whatever 'the intent was of those who made these significant changes, their effect is to deceive policy makers and the public into believing that scientific evidence shows human activities are causing global warming'.

In a final outraged paragraph, Seitz wrote:

'*If the IPCC is incapable of following its most basic procedures, it would be best to abandon the entire IPCC process, or at least that part that is concerned with the scientific evidence on climate change, and look for more reliable sources of advice on this important question.*'

The *Wall Street Journal's* assault provoked a storm, not least from the IPCC itself. A letter from Santer, claiming that his conduct had been entirely within the IPCC's rules of procedure, was also signed by his fellow 'lead author' Tom Wigley, one of Gore's chief scientific advisers.[24] This was published on 25 June, along with a considerably shortened version of a letter from Bolin and Houghton, making a similar claim.

This point was later developed at length in a paper co-authored by Stephen Schneider, who had been present at the Madrid meeting.[25] He described how, when various sections of the draft had aroused objections from national delegations, he and other scientific contributors, including Santer, Wigley and Kevin Trenberth, had gone into another room with the objectors to talk through the science behind them, apparently convincing them that it was sound. But Schneider also described how the changes to Chapter 8 which had caused all the fuss were made by Santer only 'in early December', subsequent to the Madrid meeting. As he reiterated in his paper:

'*Santer made the changes himself, and the final version of the chapter was not reviewed again by others. However, as he and his colleagues continually stressed, this procedure was the normal and agreed IPCC process.*'

Nor, in Schneider's lengthy account, did he refer to the 15 passages from the agreed text which Santer had altered or deleted and which were the real cause of the storm.[26]

Even murkier, however, seemed to be the sequence of events which had preceded these changes to the text, to which Schneider referred somewhat obliquely but which were only to come fully to light three years later in evidence to a Congressional committee.

Shortly before the scientists gave their final approval to the text in Madrid, the scientific working group's chairman Sir John Houghton* had received a communication from the State Department in Washington, dated November 15. This read:

---

* Houghton had been knighted in 1991, after the first IPPC report, and was therefore now 'Sir John'.

'*It is essential that the chapters not be finalised prior to the completion of the discussions at the IPCC Working Group I Plenary in Madrid, and that chapter authors be prevailed upon to modify their text in an appropriate manner following the discussion in Madrid.*'[27]

This instruction that 'chapter authors' should be 'prevailed upon to modify their text' came from the office of Timothy Wirth, chairman of those Senate committee hearings on climate change in 1988 and now the US Under-Secretary of State for Global Affairs. As an ardent advocate of global warming, Wirth was a close political ally of Vice-President Gore.[28]

In his account of the Madrid meeting some years later, as part of a series on 'Meetings that changed the world', Houghton described how the longest discussion had centred on a sentence drafted for the Summary for Policy Makers which originally read 'the balance of evidence suggests human influence on the climate'.[29] When this was objected to, after a debate lasting well over an hour, during which 'various alternatives were proposed', the UK delegate proposed the addition of the crucial word 'discernible' before 'human influence'. This was 'spontaneously applauded' as a version all could accept, and the new version went into the Summary.

What Houghton completely omitted from his article, however, was any mention of why the word 'discernible' agreed at political level should then have been inserted into Chapter 8 of the technical report, along with all the other changes, after the contributing scientists had agreed its text.

Without explicitly referring to this, Schneider's account does provide an explanation of why both Wirth and those in charge of the IPCC should have been so eager for the report to reinforce the case for man-made global warming in this way. As Schneider puts it, the forthcoming report 'was fraught with political significance'. Its chief purpose was to provide an underpinning for the major international treaty due to be agreed the following year in Kyoto. Based on the Rio Framework Convention on Climate Change, this would embody a 'Protocol' laying down the first practical foundations for the world's response to global warming.

A preliminary pre-Kyoto conference was due to be held in Geneva in June 1996, just after the IPCC's report was published. Nothing was viewed as more important to its success than that the US should throw all its weight behind Kyoto, which meant that there must be 'a sea change in American climate policy'.

Until now, as Schneider put it, the official US position had only allowed for 'voluntary, non-binding emissions targets and further scientific research. If the United States were to abandon its resistance to binding emissions targets, a strong international greenhouse policy would become much more likely. Since the more-research, no-binding targets position was officially based on assertions of high scientific uncertainty, the SAR's expressions of increased scientific confidence were viewed as critical.

Subsequent events, as Schneider confirmed, were to bear this out. When Wirth addressed the Geneva conference, he announced for the first time that the US was prepared to accept 'a realistic but binding target'. He conveyed that the 'proximate cause' of this dramatic change in US policy was the IPCC's increased certainty that 'the science is convincing, concern about global warming is real'.

Nothing had done more to assist the US administration in making its case for this policy change than the changes made to the IPCC's report the previous year, following the State Department intervention instigated by Wirth himself.

THE KYOTO PROTOCOL

The two years before the world's politicians were finally to gather in Kyoto to sign the historic treaty were taken up with long and complex negotiations. These were conducted through a process set up under the UN Framework Convention on Climate Change (UNFCC) known as the 'Conference of the Parties', or COP.

The first COP meeting held in Berlin between 28 March and 7 April 1995 had agreed the framework and goals of the negotiating process, supported by a preliminary budget of $18,664,200 and a permanent secretariat based in Bonn.[30] Among those endorsing the so-called 'Berlin Mandate' were Tim Wirth, representing the US, and the British environment minister John Selwyn Gummer, representing the EU.

The most fractious feature of these negotiations, which included the Geneva meeting in June 1996 referred to above, was a split between the industrialised nations, mainly in the northern hemisphere, held to have been responsible for most 'greenhouse forcing' up to this time, and the still-developing countries of the Third World, such as China, India and Brazil. These were adamant that they could not be made to accept restrictions on their economic growth which would prevent them catching up with the developed world.

In these fraught discussions, both Wirth and Gore played an active role. But on 21 July1997, with less than six months to go before the treaty was due to be signed, they had a serious setback. The US Senate voted by 95 to 0 for a resolution opposing the proposed treaty. As international treaties require the support of two-thirds of the Senate, this meant the US would be unable to ratify it.

This unanimous veto on US participation was precisely on the grounds that the proposed Protocol was to be so damagingly one-sided. It was now being formally proposed that the already developed countries, led by the US, would have to accept very severe restrictions on their greenhouse gas emissions, while the still-developing countries, led by China and India, would be exempted, even though their economies were now growing so fast that they would soon be among the world's major CO_2 contributors.

If such a treaty left out the developing world, the Senate noted, the reductions required of the industrialised world would be so great that this would 'result in serious harm to the US economy, including significant job loss, trade disadvantages, increased energy and consumer costs'.

Despite the likelihood that the world's leading economic power and CO_2 emitter would not take part, the planned treaty remained on course. But in November 1997, only two weeks before the Kyoto conference was due to begin, it was dealt another blow, when President Clinton himself endorsed the Senate's decision. When he confirmed that the US could not agree to the treaty unless the developing countries agreed to participate, a shocked Tim Wirth resigned his post at the State Department.[31]

Finally, in December 1997 10,000 participants gathered in Kyoto for what was officially known as 'COP III', or 'the Third Meeting of the Conference of the Parties' to the UNFCCC. Two thousand were official government delegates, politicians and officials representing 160 countries. Some 3,000 represented the world's media. Nearly half, some 5,000 more, were lobbyists and activists representing nearly 200 NGOs, most of them given official funding to take part, as Maurice Strong had arranged at Rio five years earlier.[32]

A key part was played behind the scenes by organisations such as Greenpeace, with 44 official lobbyists, Friends of the Earth, WWF and the Environmental Defence Fund. The Climate Action Network had 117. Activists swarmed around the Kyoto International Conference Hall, chanting slogans, waving placards and staging displays of 'street theatre', such as dressing up as dinosaurs to symbolise the fate of mankind if action were not taken to halt global warming. A youth orchestra funded by the UNFCCC launched a world concert tour in support of the need of 'protecting the earth by reversing global warming'. The front page of the city's main newspaper carried a picture of a member of Japanese Greenpeace, ceremonially drinking tea with water warmed by solar panels.[33]

At the last minute, amid a clatter of helicopters, the 'star' of the conference descended on the heliport of the main conference hotel, Vice-President Gore himself, who had been billed to give the opening keynote speech. Despite the refusal of his President and Congress to endorse the treaty, he soldiered bravely on, assuring his vast audience on Monday 1 December that

> *since we gathered at the Rio Conference in 1992, both scientific consensus and political will have come a long way. If we pause for a moment and look around us, we can see how extraordinary this gathering really is. We have reached a fundamentally new stage in the development of human civilization, in which it is necessary to take responsibility for a recent but profound alteration in the relationship between our species and our planet.'*

'The most vulnerable part of the Earth's environment', Gore went on:

> *'is the very thin layer of air clinging near to the surface of the planet, that we are now so carelessly filling with gaseous wastes that we are actually altering the relationship between the Earth and the Sun – by trapping more solar radiation under this growing blanket of pollution that envelops the entire world …*
>
> *Last week we learned from scientists that this year, 1997, with only three weeks remaining, will be the hottest year since records have been kept. Indeed, nine of the 10 hottest years since the measurements began have come in the last 10 years. The trend is clear. The human consequences – and the economic costs – of failing to act are unthinkable. More record floods and droughts. Diseases and pests spreading to new areas. Crop failures and famines. Melting glaciers, stronger storms, and rising seas.'*

Maurice Strong delivered a personal message from Kofi Annan, the UN Secretary General, appealing to national delegations to accept mandatory targets for curbing their CO_2 emissions, Thus began

11 days and nights of haggling, designed not least to find a compromise which the US might be able to accept. The Chinese delegation in particular remained adamant that the developing countries could not accept curbs to their emissions. Only on the morning of Thursday 11 December, after yet another marathon session lasting through the night, was a much-revised text of the Protocol finally agreed. Despite his President's insistence that the US would not sign unless China and India agreed to be participants, Gore signed a treaty which exempted them.

The Protocol's declared aim was to achieve 'stabilization of greenhouse gas concentrations in the atmosphere at a level that would prevent dangerous anthropogenic interference with the climate system'. It applied to all those industrialised countries listed in its Annex I (including Russia and its former satellites). These countries agreed by 2008–2012 to reduce their collective emissions of greenhouse gases to a level 5.2 per cent below where their emissions had been in 1990. Because most of their emissions levels had since increased, the true effect of these restrictions was estimated as equivalent to a cut by 2010 of 29 per cent.

The developing countries, including China and India, were not to be bound by these terms, however rapidly their own CO_2 emissions might be increasing. Some industrialised countries would be permitted to increase their emissions (Australia, for instance, by 8 per cent). The substantial emissions from international aviation and shipping were excluded. And the Protocol would come into force only when it had been ratified by enough developed countries to have accounted in 1990 for 55 per cent of the world's CO_2 emissions.

Just how these targets were to be achieved, no one as yet had any real idea. It would be up to each country to work out its own way to meet them. But the treaty also introduced the idea of 'emissions trading', whereby countries or firms which were failing to meet their reduction targets could buy 'carbon credits' from those which had already more than met them, thus offsetting 'failures' against 'successes'. The UNFCCC itself would administer a global trading scheme, to be called the 'Clean Development Mechanism'.

One of Kyoto's most obvious intentions was to discourage the use of fossil fuels, such as coal, oil and gas, and to promote a switch to those energy sources which did not emit greenhouse gases, such as 'renewables' (wind, wave, solar and hydro). Nuclear power also offered a much more effective source of large-scale 'carbon free' energy than any of them. But most of the proponents of Kyoto, including all the 'environmentalist' campaigning groups, were vehemently opposed to it, since they viewed it as potentially 'polluting the planet' in a different way, by threatening repetition of the 1986 Chernobyl disaster and creating dangerous radioactive wastes.

Revealingly, no official attempt was made to put a figure on just how much all this was going to cost the economies of the developed world. But in a study funded by the National Science Foundation and the US Department of Energy, William Nordhaus, an eminent Yale University economics professor, estimated that, if the US was eventually persuaded to ratify Kyoto, the cost of the first phase of emissions reductions required by the treaty would be $716 billion. Two thirds of this would fall on the United States, as the world's leading CO_2 'polluter'.[34]

In terms of 'saving the planet', however, what would all this expense and effort achieve? If all the Kyoto targets for emissions reduction were met, it was generally agreed, even by supporters of the Protocol, that the resulting reduction in global temperatures by 2050 would be equivalent only to 0.05°C, or one 20th of a degree.[35] By 2100, it was famously calculated by Tom Wigley, one of Gore's scientific advisers, Kyoto would delay the world's warming process only by six years.[36]

Recognising this, the 'environmentalists' expressed disappointment that the targets had not been tougher. But they rested their hopes on the prospect of much more drastic emissions reductions being agreed in a new 'Kyoto Two' treaty after 2012.

The important thing was that the nations of the world were now for the first time formally committed in principle to those curbs on the emission of CO_2 for which the IPCC and environmentalists had been calling for nearly a decade. For Gore's 'consensus', less than 10 years after those Senate hearings in 1988, it was quite an achievement.

TWO MOUNTAINS STILL TO CLIMB

Despite their apparent triumph at Kyoto, the supporters of the 'consensus' still had two sizeable obstacles to overcome. One was political, the other scientific.

The first was that the Protocol could not come into effect until it had been ratified. This required formal approval by enough countries to have between them been responsible for 55 per cent of the world's total man-made CO_2 emissions in 1990. In the heady atmosphere generated around the Kyoto agreement this hurdle did not seem insurmountable, although in fact it was to take rather longer than anyone in 1997 could have predicted (and would only finally be brought about by a very curious political deal).

The other problem bothering the scientists most committed to the 'consensus', however, was what had become the most awkward single anomaly in their argument. This was their claim that, thanks to the rise in greenhouse gas emissions, the world in the late twentieth century had suddenly become hotter than ever before in human history.

It was all very well to produce temperature charts showing that the hottest years ever recorded were in the last two decades of the twentieth century, temperatures having apparently risen during that time in harmony with rising levels of CO_2, but up to this time it had been generally accepted, not least by the IPCC itself, that during the so-called Mediaeval Warm Period temperatures had been even higher than they were now in the 1990s. Obviously this could not be blamed on those soaring levels of CO_2 emitted by the reliance of modern industrial civilisation on fossil fuels. So how was this to be explained?

As the 1990s wore on, the advocates of the 'consensus' within the IPCC had already become increasingly frustrated by the apparent anomaly posed by that Mediaeval Warm Period, In fact, miraculously, their problem was about to be resolved. But the way in which this was brought about would eventually make it one of the more bizarre episodes in the history of science.

Notes

1. Al Gore, *Earth In The Balance* (Houghton Mifflin/Earthscan Publications, 1992), p. 177.
2. John Houghton, 'Meetings That Changed The World', *Nature*, 9 October 2008.
3. Frederick Seitz, 'A Major Deception On Global Warming', *Wall Street Journal*, 12 June 1996.
4. Bush was also concerned that Senator Gore might be present in Rio. Although Gore was excluded from the official US delegation, Strong, now working closely with Gore on global warming, gave him a personal invitation to attend (interview with Strong, *Executive Intelligence Review*, 29 January 1999).

5. In fact Bush's White House advisers were more worried by the rising alarm of US environmentalists than was publicly admitted. As his chief of staff John Sunonu later recalled, in 1989 they called in some of the leading US scientists who were expressing alarm over global warming and subjected them to serious questioning on the science, notably on the failure of their computer models to take proper account of interactions between the atmosphere and the oceans. Sunonu, himself a qualified scientist, told them that they needed seriously to improve the quality of their research. For this purpose the federal government was prepared to increase its funding programme for climate research from around $200 million annually to $2 billion. Two decades later he wryly expressed regret that it was the Bush government which had thus given the biggest ever financial boost to research underpinning climate alarmism (speech by Sunonu to Heartland Institute Conference in New York, 11 March 2009, available on Heartland Institute website).

6. 'A Community Strategy to limit Carbon Dioxide emissions and to improve energy efficiency', Communication from the Commission to the Council, Commission of the European Communities, Brussels, 14 October 1991.

7. COM 92/266. Outside the EU the Swedish and Norwegian parliaments had already pioneered the way in voting for a tax on CO_2 emissions in 1988 and 1989 (Bjorklund, *op. cit.*).

8. Gore, *op. cit.*, p. 40.

9. Letter to Congressman Jim Bates, 14 July 1988. See website of Heartland Institute, article by Fred Singer under 'Environment and Climate News', 1 January 2000.

10. Letter to Senator Tim Wirth, 18 July 1988. Heartland Institute, *op. cit.* See also Fred Singer. 'The Revelle-Gore Story: attempted political suppression of science', 2003 (see Hoover website). The account in the following pages is based largely on Singer's version, although inevitably this has been attacked by global warming campaigners.

11. *New Republic*, 6 July 1992.

12. These last details emerged from a computer disk containing a draft letter sent by Lancaster to Gore (Singer, Hoover, *op. cit.*).

13. Lindzen, *op. cit.*

14. Lindzen, *op. cit.* This was not the first time Wicker had been involved in similarly rewriting history. A year earlier Robert White, former head of the US Weather Bureau, wrote an article for the *Scientific American* suggesting that the scientific basis for global warming predictions was totally inadequate to justify any costly actions. The only actions which should be taken were those which would be justified even if there was no warming threat. Wicker reported this in the *New York Times* as a call by White for immediate action on global warming (Lindzen, *op. cit.*).

15. Singer himself would be vilified in this way for having participated with Professor Frederick Seitz, a distinguished physicist and former President of the National Academy of Sciences, in a report criticising the EPA's efforts to demonise passive smoking. The report's authors were described as 'corrupt' for having 'received funding through ideological partners of the tobacco companies' (see the ecosyn website, which also accused the Bush family of having supported genocide and financing Hitler).

16. Twelve years later, in 2004, Lancaster issued a 'retraction' of his 'retraction' on a website ('The Cosmos Myth'). However, he omitted any reference to the evidence which had come to light during the discovery process of the legal action. This included his admission that Revelle had told him that he agreed with the main point the article sought to make: that the science on global warming was not yet sufficiently settled to justify drastic action.

17. 'Enrongate', *www.craigslist.org*. Gore's personal and family links with the oil industry went back a long way. His father, Senator Albert Gore Sr, had been a close friend and protégé of Armand Hammer, the head of Occidental Oil, who helped to set him up in the businesses which were the basis for the Gore family fortune. Hammer, who died in 1994, had been a friend of Lenin and throughout the Cold War was under official suspicion for his exceptionally close ties to the Soviet Union.

18. Reconstructed from de Freitas, *op. cit.*, and Singer and Avery, *op. cit.*

19. Santer, *et al.* (1996), 'A search for human influences on the thermal structure of the atmosphere', *Nature*, No, 382, pp. 39–46.

20. Michaels, P. J., and Knappenburger, P. C. (1996), 'Human effects on global climate', *Nature*, No. 384, pp. 522–523.

21. *Wall Street Journal*, 11 June 1996.

22. *Wall Street Journal*, 12 June 1996.

23. John Houghton, 'Meetings That Changed The World', *Nature*, 9 October 2008.

24. Santer, B., Wigley, T., *et al.*, 'Response to Wall Street Journal Editorial of June 12, 1996, by Frederick Seitz', WSJ, 25 June 1996.

25. Paul N. Edwards and Stephen H. Schneider, 'The 1995 IPCC Report: Broad Consensus or "Scientific Cleansing"?', *Ecofable/Ecoscience* 1.1 (1997), pp. 3–9.

26. Schneider also insisted that 'nowhere do IPCC rules explicitly address the question of when a report chapter becomes final (i.e. when all changes must cease)' and that Santer's conduct had been entirely within the 'spirit' of the IPCC process, He added that 'a careful reading of the IPCC's formal rules' revealed that they 'neither allow nor prohibit changes to a report after its formal acceptance' (Schneider, *op. cit.*, p. 6).

27. Quoted in Singer and Avery, *op. cit.*

28. Singer and Avery, *op. cit.* This political background to the IPCC's 1996 report emerged in evidence given to the US House Committee on Small Business, chaired by Congressman James Talent, in August 1998.

29. Houghton, *Nature, op. cit.*

30. UN Framework Convention on Climate Change, Report of the Conference of the Parties, First Session, 6 June 1995, *http://unfccc.int/resource/docs/cop1/07a01.pdf*

31. 'Kyoto Report', *http://sovereignty.net/p/clim/kyotorpt.htm*

32. In April 1996 the Global Environment Facility reported that three NGOs, the WWF, the World Resources Institute and the World Conservation Union had been listed as 'executing agencies' or 'collaborating organisations' to receive grants totalling $350 million from UN and other governmental bodies, to be passed on to the network of lobbying organisations. See 'A Two-Headed Monster', *http://sovereignty.net/p/clim/kyotorpt.htm*

33. *Ibid.*

34. W. D. Nordhaus and J. G. Bayer (1999), 'Requiem for Kyoto: An Economic Analysis of the Kyoto Protocol', *www.econ.yale.edu/~nordhaus/homepage/Kyoto.pdf*

35. M. Parry, *et al.* (1998), 'Adapting to the inevitable', *Nature,* 395, 741. See also Nordhaus, *op. cit.*

36. Tom M. L. Wigley, 'The Kyoto Protocol: CO_2, CH_4 and Climate Implications', *Geophysical Research Letters,* 25 (13), 1998 (cited in Bjorn Lomborg, *The Sceptical Environmentalist* (Cambridge University Press, 2001)).

Part Two
The 'consensus' carries all before it: 1998–2007

'The overwhelming majority of scientific experts, whilst recognizing that scientific uncertainties exist, nonetheless believe that human-induced climate change is already occurring and that future change is inevitable. It is not a question of whether the Earth's climate will change, but rather by how much, how fast and where.'

Dr Robert Watson, Chairman
of the IPCC, 2000[*]

'It has become common to deal with the science by referring to the IPCC "scientific consensus". Claiming the agreement of thousands of scientists is certainly easier than trying to understand the issue or to respond to scientific questions; it also effectively intimidates most citizens. However, the invocation of the IPCC is more a mantra than a proper reflection on that flawed document [the 2001 IPCC Report].'

Dr Richard Lindzen, IPCC
lead author, 2001[†]

---

[*] Dr Robert T. Watson, Chairman of the Intergovermental Panel on Climate Change, Report to the Sixth Conference of the Parties of the United Nations Framework Convention On Climate Change, 20 November, 2000.
[†] 'Testimony of Richard S. Lindzen before the Senate Commerce Committee, 1 May 2001': *http://www.lavoisier.com.au/articles/climate-policy/science-and-policy/Lindzen_McCain.pdf*

4

The 'hottest year ever'

Enter the 'Hockey Stick' and IPCC 3: 1998–2003

'We have to get rid of the Mediaeval Warm Period.'
Professor John Overpeck, IPCC Lead Author, 1995[1]

'He who controls the past, controls the future. He who controls the present, controls the past.'
George Orwell, *Nineteen Eighty-Four*

'The hockey stick debate is thus about two things. At a technical level it is about flaws in methodology and erroneous results in a scientific paper. But at a political level, the debate is about whether the IPCC betrayed the trust of governments around the world.'
Professor Ross McKitrick, 2005[2]

Although it had long seemed peculiarly important to the advocates of man-made global warming to insist that their beliefs were supported by a 'consensus' of the world's scientists, outside the bubble of commitment they had created it was not always easy to see the evidence for this.

In 1996, for instance, the *UN Climate Change Bulletin* had reported on a survey of 400 American, Canadian and German climate researchers. When asked whether it was 'certain that global warming is a process already underway', only 10 per cent were prepared to express 'strong' agreement. Nearly half those surveyed, 48 per cent, said they didn't have faith in the forecasts of the global climate models.[3]

In 1997, a survey of US State Climatologists found 90 per cent agreeing that 'scientific evidence indicates variations in global temperature are likely to be naturally occurring and cyclical over very long periods of time'.[4]

Even among those scientists most strongly committed to the orthodoxy, one problem which disturbed them as much as any was all the evidence that, at times in the historical past, temperatures had been higher than they were now at the end of the twentieth century.

The IPCC's first assessment report in 1990 had accepted this without question, showing a graph which reflected the received scientific view of how climate had changed over the past 1,000 years. This showed temperatures during the Mediaeval Warm Period markedly higher than those of the 1980s; falling steeply during the Little Ice Age; rising again in the nineteenth century with the Modern Warming. The graph showing this had been given the personal imprimatur of John Houghton himself, as chairman of the scientific working group, since his name headed the list of academics to whom it was credited.[5]

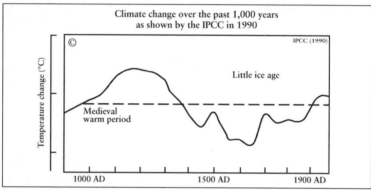

Figure 2: Climate change over the past 1,000 years: J. T. Houghton *et al.*, IPCC First Assessment Report, 1990.

In those early years, no one had seriously sought to challenge this picture of the rising and falling of temperatures through the centuries. In the chapter on 'Climate and Civilisation' in his book *The Earth In The Balance*, for instance, Al Gore had gone along with the received view just like everyone else. He described how the Roman Warming was ended by a marked cooling during the Dark Ages, followed by that 'shift in the global climate pattern' which gave rise to the Mediaeval Warm Period. Then a catastrophic drop in temperatures around 1350 had ushered in the centuries of the 'Little Ice Age', ending, according to Gore, around 1850.[6]

But because this picture contradicted the idea that late-twentieth century temperatures had suddenly shot up to a level never known before in history, it naturally gave upholders of the othodoxy serious concern. So, to a lesser degree, did the apparent anomaly of global temperatures having fallen during the Little Cooling between 1940 and 1975, just when post-World War Two economic expansion was causing CO_2 emissions to rise at an unprecedented rate.

Ever anxious to emphasise the influence of human activity on climate, they tried to explain this latter point by arguing that the warming effect of rising CO_2 emissions had been masked during the Little Cooling by the 'dimming' effect of tiny aerosol particles produced by sulphur dioxide emissions from power stations burning coal and oil. These, it was claimed, had shut out enough sunlight to counteract the effect of the increases in greenhouse gases.[7] But, as even the IPCC was to accept in its 2001 report, most of these aerosols were emitted in the northern hemisphere, which should have meant that, while its temperatures fell, the southern hemisphere continued to warm. Yet the Little Cooling had been experienced worldwide, showing no distinction between north and south.[8]

A very much larger problem to explain away were those fluctuations in temperature which had occurred in earlier times, notably in the early Middle Ages; and here the IPCC's growing concern was reflected in a curious episode in 1995 which was only eventually to be made public some years later.

Considerable interest was being shown at this time in the use of ground boreholes to assess past climatic conditions; and a pioneer in this field was Professor David Deming, a geoscientist at the University of Oklahoma. In 1995 he published a paper in *Science*, reporting on borehole data going back 150 years, entitled 'Climate warming in North America: analysis of borehole temperatures'.[9] Perhaps because of the reference to 'warming' in his title, Deming's article won him what he later described as 'significant credibility in the community of scientists working on climate change'.

Because 'they thought I was one of them', as he later explained, he was contacted by a 'major person working in the area of climate change and global warming'. The identity of this scientist was later to be revealed as Professor John Overpeck of the University of Arizona, an IPCC lead author. Overpeck 'let his guard down' in sending Deming an 'astonishing email that said "We have to get rid of the Mediaeval Warm Period"'.[10]

At much the same time, the IPCC's second assessment report (SAR, 1995), dropped the earlier Houghton graph and began to undermine the belief that temperatures in the historic past might have been higher than they were in the twentieth century, on the grounds that there was insufficient data to support such a claim.

Such evidence as was available, the IPCC now argued, suggested that the twentieth century was at least as warm as any time for 600 years:

> 'The limited available evidence from proxy climate indicators suggests
> that the twentieth century global mean temperature is at least as warm as
> any other century since at least 1400 AD.'

This was not in dispute, since by 1400 the Mediaeval Warm Period was giving way to the Little Ice Age. But going back before that
date, to the time of the supposed Mediaeval Warm Period, the IPCC
went on to argue, even less evidence was available:

> 'Data prior to 1400 are too sparse to allow the reliable estimation of
> global mean temperature.'

Two years after this first attempt to cast doubt on the Mediaeval
Warm Period, however, a further unprecedentedly comprehensive
record of temperatures derived from borehole data was published
by a team from the University of Michigan.[11] Their study, based on
more than 6,000 borehole records from every continent round the
world, went back 20,000 years. A graph covering the past 1,000
years clearly confirmed both the Mediaeval Warm Period and the
Little Ice Age. It showed global temperatures having risen up to 1°C
between 1000 and 1400, then having fallen by as much as 1.75 degrees to the end of the eighteenth century.

At this stage in 1997 it seemed the problem which was so trou-
bling Overpeck and his IPCC colleagues was still as intractable as
ever. But the following year the whole debate was suddenly transformed, in a way no one could possibly have foreseen.

ENTER DR MANN AND THE 'HOCKEY STICK'

Out of the blue in 1998 Britain's leading science journal *Nature*,
long supportive of the warming orthodoxy, published a new paper
on global temperature changes over the previous 600 years, back to
1400.[12] Its chief author was Michael Mann, a young physicist-
turned-climate scientist at the University of Massachusetts, who had
only completed his PHD two years before. In 1999 he and his colleagues published a further paper, based only on North America but
extending their original findings over 1000 years.[13]

Their computer model had enabled them to produce a new temperature graph quite unlike anything seen before. Instead of the previously familiar rises and falls, this showed the trend of average
temperatures having gently declined through nine centuries, but then

suddenly shooting up in the twentieth century to a level that was quite unprecedented.

In Mann's graph such familiar features as the Mediaeval Warm Period and the Little Ice Age had simply vanished. All those awkward anomalies were shown as having been illusory. The only real anomaly which emerged from their studies was that sudden exponential rise appearing in the twentieth century, culminating in the 'warmest year of the millennium', 1998.

As would eventually emerge, there were several very odd features about Mann's new graph, soon to be known as the 'hockey stick' because its shape, a long flattish line curving up sharply at the end, was reminiscent of the stick used in ice hockey.* But initially none might have seemed odder than the speed with which this obscure study by a comparatively unknown young scientist came to be taken up as the new 'orthodoxy'.

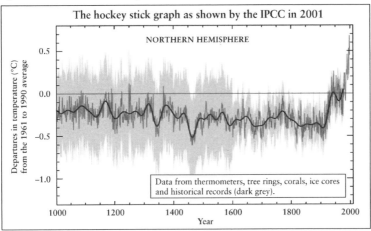

Figure 3: The 'hockey stick' graph: Mann M. E., *et al.* (1999), Northern hemisphere temperatures during the last millennium: inferences, uncertainties and limitations.

Within 12 months Mann's rewriting of climate science had become the major talking point of the global warming debate. In 2000, it was featured at the top of a major new report published by the US government, the *US National Assessment of the Potential Consequences of Climate Variability and Change*.

* The term 'hockey stick' was given to Mann's graph by Jerry Mahlman, head of a laboratory at the US government's National Oceanic and Atmospheric Administration.

In the following year, 2001, when the IPCC's Working Group I (still chaired by Houghton) published its 'Third Assessment Report' (TAR), Mann's 'hockey stick' was projected even more prominently. It was given pride of place at the top of the Summary for Policy-makers; elsewhere in the report, it was printed five more times, in one instance occupying more than half a page. At the press confer-ence to launch the Summary, Houghton appeared before the world's media in front of a large blown-up version of the 'hockey stick'.

Thanks not least to its new graph, the IPCC was emboldened to be markedly less equivocal than ever before on the degree to which recent warming had been caused by man-made greenhouse gases. 'There is new and stronger evidence', as the Summary for Policy-makers starkly put it, 'that most of the warming observed over the past 50 years is attributable to human activities'.

It wasn't just past history which the IPCC was now prepared to rewrite. Among its computer model projections of how high global temperatures were likely to rise between 1990 and 2100, the high-est estimate of 245 separate 'scenarios' (inevitably the one which made the headlines) showed temperatures soaring by 5.8°C. This was a startling 2.3 degrees higher than the IPCC's maximum guess of 3.5 degrees five years earlier.[14]

Mann was the hero of the moment. He had been made an IPCC 'lead author' on Chapter 2 of the scientific report in which his study was prominently featured (his two co-authors were named as 'au-thors'). He had been made an editor of the prestigious *Journal of Climatic Change*. He was besieged by the media. As one account put it,

> *'After the publication of the Third Assessment Report, the 'hockey stick' appeared everywhere, together with apocalytpic pronouncements of what would happen if we failed to cut greenhouse gas emissions. Graphic designers competed over who could design the most alarmist rendering of [the graph], with fire-engine red a favourite bordering colour.'*[15]

Versions of the graph were swiftly circulated all round the world, to be pinned up in the offices of countless academics, officials and 'environmentalists'. The 'hockey stick' had become the supreme iconic image for all those engaged in the battle to save the world from global warming.

It had been a remarkable coup. And what only served to reinforce the graph's terrifying message was a finding apparently confirmed by all the four official sources of global temperature data. In the 1990s, temperatures had risen even higher than in the previous decade, And, after a further spike upwards, 1998 was now generally accepted to have been the hottest year since records began.

AMERICA THE 'PARIAH'

Just as a key part of the political intention behind the IPCC's 1996 report had been to push the US into supporting Kyoto, so a key purpose in making the 2001 report as alarmist as possible was to push America into ratifying the treaty.

Four years after it had been signed, the Kyoto Protocol was in dire trouble. It could only come into effect if it was ratified by either America or Russia. But Russia seemed highly unlikely to agree, because its scientific establishment did not accept the case for man-made global warming. Thus the only real hope of getting Kyoto enforced, it seemed, lay with persuading the US to withdraw its opposition to the treaty. And with a strong possibility that Vice-President Gore might win the 2000 presidential election, that hope seemed very much alive.

No one was more aware of this than the small group of men running the IPCC. There had been changes at the top of the organisation. Houghton was still in charge of the scientific Working Group I. But in 1997 Bert Bolin had stepped down as overall chairman, to be replaced by Dr Robert Watson, the British-born chemist who had been running NASA's researches into the ozone layer back in the 1980s.

Watson had by now become well-versed in operating at the interface of science and politics at the highest level. In 1996 he joined the World Bank as the senior scientific adviser to its environmental division. In 1997, with the aid of his friend Al Gore, he had been appointed to a senior advisory post on environmental issues in the Office of the President in the White House. He had also been chosen in the same year to chair the IPCC, to take overall charge of drafting its next report.

In the autumn of 2000 the battle for the White House between Gore and the Republican candidate George W. Bush was so tight that it seemed either man could win. Shortly before polling day, a leak from inside the IPCC revealed that the draft Summary for Policymakers for its forthcoming report was predicting that global temperatures in the twenty-first century could rise by as much as '6°C', a much higher figure than anything previously claimed.[16]

Because of the dispute over votes in Florida, there was a delay of several weeks before it could be decided who had won the election. During that time Watson upped the political pressure further by making his strongest public speech so far on global warming, to a conference discussing the Kyoto ratification process under the UN Framework Convention on Climate Change. 'The overwhelming majority of scientific experts', he said, 'believe that human-induced climate change is already occurring':

> '*It is undisputed, that the two last decades have been the warmest this century, indeed the warmest for the last 1000 years, sea level is rising, precipitation patterns are changing, Arctic sea ice is thinning and the frequency and intensity of El-Nino events appear to be increasing. In addition, many parts of the world have recently suffered major heat-waves, floods, droughts and extreme weather events leading to significant loss of life and economic costs.*'[17]

By this time the Summary for Policymakers of the next IPCC report had already been drafted, since the scientific report had been all-but completed back in August. But in January 2001, after the draft Summary had been approved by a small number of the scientists responsible for the science report, the Summary was further amended at a meeting in Shanghai, in a way that was designed to ring the alarm bells even louder.

It was this Summary which gave such prominence to the 'hockey stick' and to its most quoted line; 'there is new and stronger evidence that most of the warming observed over the past 50 years is attributable to human activities'. As in 1996, this purported summary of the scientific report (not due to be published until April) dismayed not a few of the scientists who had worked on it, because it so blatantly disregarded some of the carefully qualified wording of the technical report they had agreed.

We know this because one of the 'lead authors' on the report, responsible for part of Chapter 7 on 'Physical Processes' was Dr Richard Lindzen of MIT, and in May 2001 he gave evidence on the report to a US Senate Committee.[18] Lindzen described how 'the vast majority of participants played no role in preparing the Summary', which involved only a small 'selected subset of the 14 co-ordinating lead authors'. But even then, the draft version of the Summary had been 'significantly modified at Shanghai'.

Lindzen showed, for instance, how one cautiously phrased passage in the original draft Summary had then at Shanghai been dramatically simplified. The original version had insisted that the accuracy of estimates of human contribution to warming 'continues to be limited by uncertainties in estimates of internal variability, natural and anthropogenic forcing and the climate response to external forcing'. The Shanghai version suppressed these doubts, merely insisting that, despite any 'remaining uncertainties, most of the observed warming over the last 50 years is likely to have been due to the increase in greenhouse gas concentrations'.

Lindzen had previously criticised the IPCC's methodology from the outside. Now he had been given an opportunity to observe its operations from the inside, he was able to described how not only the Summary but the preparation of the report itself was subject to constant pressure to push its findings in the desired direction:

> 'There were usually several people working on every few pages. Naturally there were disagreements, but these were usually hammered out in a civilised manner. However, throughout the drafting sessions, IPCC "co-ordinators" would go around insisting that criticism of models be toned down, and that "motherhood" statements be inserted to the effect that models might still be correct despite the cited faults. Refusals were occasionally met with ad hominem attacks. I personally witnessed co-authors forced to assert their "green" credentials in defense of their statements.'

He was surprised to find that, even when the report had been 'signed off' as supposedly complete by its authors, the text could still be modified.

As before, Lindzen was highly critical of the IPCC's over-reliance on computer models programmed to exaggerate any possible influence of 'CO_2 forcing' on temperatures, while failing to take proper account of many other factors affecting climate. His Chapter 7 had 'found numerous problems with model treatments, including those of clouds and water vapour'. But again the Summary suppressed these reservations in merely assuring its readers that 'understanding of climate processes and their incorporation in climate models have improved'.

Lindzen ended his Senate testimony with some general observations on how misleadingly the press and others liked to refer to the

IPCC as representing the views of 'hundreds and even thousands' of 'the world's leading climate scientists'. As he knew from personal experience, 'most of the top researchers (at least in the US) avoid the IPCC because it is extremely time-consuming and non-productive'. Not, he said, that this troubled the IPCC:

> *'as a UN activity it is far more important to have participants from a hundred countries – many of which have no almost no active effort in climate research. For most of these participants, involvement with the IPCC gains them prestige beyond what would be normally available, and these, not surprisingly, are likely to be particularly favourable to the IPCC. Finally, judging from the Citation Index, the leaders of the IPCC process like Sir John Houghton, Dr Robert Watson and Prof. Bert Bolin have never been major contributors to climate research. They are however enthusiasts for the negotiating process, without which there would be no IPCC, which is to say the IPCC represents an interest in its own right.'* [19]

Perhaps more surprisingly, another 'lead author' to criticise the just-published 2001 report was Stephen Schneider who, in an article in *Nature*, tore apart the way in which the IPCC's Summary had won such publicity for predicting that by 2100 temperatures could have risen by an unprecedented 5.8°C. [20]

As Schneider explained, the IPCC's computer models had run through no fewer than 245 different 'scenarios', according to how sensitive the climate might be to various levels of CO_2 emissions. These had produced a spread of predictions for the temperature rise by 2100 ranging between 1.4 degrees and 5.8 degrees. But the IPCC had refused to show how these computer predictions were distributed.

In fact, as Schneider showed, almost half the predictions had come in below 2.5 degrees. Only a quarter were above 3.6 degrees. Hardly any were above 5 degrees. But because the IPCC had refused to explain the weighting of probabilities (despite Schneider having asked them to do so), the one which forecast an apocalyptic 5.8 degrees was that which inevitably caught all the headlines.

However, all these revelations of how the IPCC had rigged the evidence emerged only months after that leak in the closing stages of the US presidential election campaign that the IPCC was about to announce a '6 degrees' temperature rise.

The leak had failed to have its desired effect. Despite receiving more popular votes than Bush, Gore narrowly failed to win the presidency. And when the new President began to reveal his hand on Kyoto, the IPCC's worst fears were realised.

Only weeks after entering the White House, Bush wrote on 13 March to Republican Senators to say

> '*I oppose the Kyoto Protocol because it exempts 80 per cent of the world, including such major population centers as China and India, from compliance, and would cause serious harm to the US economy.*'

The following week, Bush's National Security Adviser Condoleeza Rice privately told EU ambassadors in Washington that the new administration considered the Kyoto treaty 'dead'. A week later Bush's new head of the Environmental Protection Agency, Christine Todd Whitman, announced that the US had 'no interest' in implementing Kyoto, and would be taking steps to withdraw its signature from the treaty.[21]

Bush's decision provoked international uproar, notably from politicians in Europe. Italy's environment minister said 'the United States' rejection of the Kyoto Protocol should be denounced, and in a formal manner'. The EU's environment comissioner Margot Wallstrom said that it was to soon to discuss 'tactics to punish the United States', but that she would be leading an EU delegation to Washington the following week to 'seek clarification of the Bush administration's position'.[22]

France's environment minister Dominique Voynet called Bush's decision 'completely provocative and irresponsible'. Among many expressions of outrage in the European press, Bush was variously compared to the Taliban and to those US isolationists of the 1930s who stood by while Hitler led the world to war.[23] In Britain the Royal Society, now an active lobbyist for the global warming orthodoxy, announced that it was planning a 'response from the international scientific community'. Various wll-known scientists, including Stephen Hawking, Edward O. Wilson and Jane Goodall, signed an open letter of protest, published in *Time*. Twenty-seven senior environmental academics contacted by the *Times Higher Education Supplement* all-but unanimously condemned Bush's decision, one condemning it as making his government a 'pariah' which should be 'shamed' into reversing its policy.[24]

This furore highlighted the way in which the European Union now stood out as virtually the only real champion of Kyoto in the developed world. In June 2001, after a meeting in Sweden of the

European Council (equivalent to the Cabinet of the EU government), a communique announced that 'the European Union and its Member States are determined to meet their own commitments under the Kyoto Protocol'. The European Commission 'will prepare a proposal for ratification before the end of 2001', allowing the EU's 15 member governments 'to rapidly ratify' the treaty.[25]

This was greeted with acclamation from all the leading 'environmentalist' lobby groups such as the WWF, Friends of the Earth and Greenpeace, most of which were by now being handsomely funded by the EU and its member governments to maintain their campaigning pressure over global warming.

'We are pleased to see that the EU continues to lead the world on climate change' said a spokesman for the WWF (formerly the World Wildlife Fund). Friends of the Earth's 'International Climate Campaign Co-Ordinator' welcome the EU's decision 'at the highest political level to go unilaterally for the implementation and ratification of the Kyoto Protocol'. A 'spokesperson' for Greenpeace International said: 'We will harness the public outcry against Bush to show that Kyoto is the vital first step to save the climate.'[26]

If America had become a 'pariah' state and Vladimir Putin's Russia wouldn't play, it seemed as if the EU was the only major 'government' now left pushing for the planet to be saved.

THE EU RISES TO THE CHALLENGE

The EU had first signalled its wish to give a 'moral' lead to the world over global warming as long ago as 1991. One reason for the fervour with which it had taken up the cause of global warming was that this was a seemingly altruistic cause which played right into the hands of what had always been the 'European project's' core agenda: its desire through ever-increasing political integration to pose as 'the government of Europe'.

Those running the EU, including national politicians, were always looking out for new opportunities for it to take over more powers from national governments, and assuming the 'competence' to make laws on the 'environment' was a prime example. Problems such as pollution of the atmosphere were clearly not confined within national boundaries; and as early as 1986 (in the treaty known as the Single European Act), this had been used to justify ceding all power to decide policy on environmental issues to Brussels.

In this respect the EU was well aware that concern over 'green' issues such as global warming was a cause attracting wide popular
support. In several countries 'Green' parties enjoyed had been enjoying electoral success. In Germany Chancellor Schröder was only able
to take office in 1998 by forming a coalition with the Green Party,
which had piled up hefty majorities in former Communist East
Germany.

The political leaders now in power across much of the EU, such
as Tony Blair and many of his colleagues, belonged to a generation
which had grown up with the fashionable environmentalist ideal-
ism of the 1970s. They had absorbed the 'green' ideology of that
time more naturally than would have many of their predecessors.

Finally, as its 1991 strategy document had made clear, the EU welcomed the fight against global warming not least as a cause in which
it could hope to lead the world, filling the political 'vacuum' left by
the foot-dragging of the USA.

That 1991 document had laid out the template for ways in which
the EU could further the cause through new laws and policies: by
promoting renewable energy, greater 'energy efficiency' and recycling waste; by imposing ever tighter standards on vehicle emissions;
and, in due course, by imposing a 'carbon tax'.

As the years went by, ever more Brussels legislation had been justified
at least in part by the need to cut 'greenhouse gas' emissions. The far-
reaching Landfill Directive of 1999, for instance, designed to phase
out the landfilling of rubbish in favour of recycling or incineration,
referred in its preamble to the need to minimise the impact of waste
disposal 'on the global environment, including the greenhouse effect'.[27]

Another far-reaching directive in 2002 laid down a swathe of new
laws designed to improve 'the energy performance of buildings'.
Again this made clear in its preamble that buildings were among 'the
leading sources of carbon dioxide emissions'; and that 'increased
energy efficiency' constituted 'an important part of the package of
policies and measures needed to comply with the Kyoto Protocol'.
One requirement of the directive was that, when buildings were constructed, sold or rented out, owners should provide any prospective
buyer or tenant with an 'energy performance certificate'.[28]

On the international stage, the EU suffered something of a reverse
in April 2002 when it was outvoted in a bitter fight to retain Dr Robert
Watson as chairman of the IPCC. As chief architect of the most
alarmist IPCC report to date, Watson had hoped to be re-appointed

for a second five-year term. But he had aroused fierce opposition from the US administration.

President Bush and his advisers had long been aware of the highly political role Watson was playing as chairman, not least suspecting him (rightly or wrongly) of involvement in the leaks of extracts from the IPCC's forthcoming report during the 2000 presidential election campaign. As Watson's term of office approached its end, they were determined that he should go. At the IPCC's Geneva headquarters on 19 April 2002, the EU did all it could to keep Watson in office. But, in a secret ballot of 125 governments, he won only 49 votes against 76 for the US-backed candidate, Dr Rajendra Pachauri, an Indian academic economist, until now an IPCC vice-chairman.[29] The background of the IPCC's new chairman was in railway engineering. He had no expertise in climate science at all.

In no way did this hold back the EU from its determination to ratify Kyoto as soon as possible. Its leaders were already planning by 2005 to comply with one of Kyoto's main requirements by launching the world's first 'emissions trading scheme'. Under this hugely complex project every country had been assigned its 'Kyoto target' for reducing CO_2 emissions. Any large firm or organisation which 'polluted' the atmosphere with CO_2 would then be given its own target. If it continued to emit above its target level, it would then have to buy 'carbon credits' from those which had managed to lessen their emissions to a level below their given target.

Nevertheless, the EU was well aware that, globally, there were limits to what its members could hope to achieve on their own. One problem was that, because Kyoto only applied to the 37 developed countries listed in Annex 1, there were so many sources of CO_2 emissions in the world that the EU could do little about.

The second largest human cause of emissions, for instance, accounting for some 18 per cent or nearly a fifth of the world total, was deforestation. But this was mainly centred in countries not affected by Kyoto, such as Indonesia and Brazil, where the destruction and burning of their rainforests contributed 85 and 70 per cent of their total carbon output.

Just behind this, contributing around 14 per cent each, were agriculture, industry and transport. Again a significant part of agricultural emissions, as in those from rice growing which is particularly 'carbon-intensive', came from countries which would be unaffected by Kyoto. Some of the world's most polluting industries were in

China and India, which would also be unaffected. Steps were already being taken in the EU and other industrialised countries to reduce emissions from cars and lorries, but aviation (contributing around 3 per cent to the world total) and shipping (slightly more) were again not covered by Kyoto.

By far the biggest single contribution to greenhouse gas emissions, however, amounting to 40 per cent or two-fifths of the total, was the use of fossil fuels for generating electricity. Inevitably it was here that, in bidding to comply with its Kyoto targets, the EU would particularly have to focus its attention.

The most effective way to generate 'carbon-free' electricity on a large scale would have been to revive the use of nuclear power. But for two decades, after the scare over a relatively minor accident to the US Three Mile Island nuclear reactor in 1979, greatly reinforced by the much more serious disaster in 1986 at Chernobyl, using nuclear power to produce electricity had been distinctly unpopular.

The most nuclear-dependent country in the world was France, which, after the scare over future energy supplies following the 1973 Yom Kippur war, had built the 58 new nuclear power plants which now supplied 83 per cent of her electricity. But to the environmentalists, who since the 1980s had been so much in the ascendant, any talk of a return to nuclear power was anathema.

Several of the most influential environmentalist organisations had in fact owed their original inspiration to the nuclear issue. Friends of the Earth was founded in the US in 1969 explicitly to campaign against nuclear power stations. Greenpeace was launched in the US in 1971 to campaign against nuclear weapons. The US 'Union of Concerned Scientists' had first been launched to campaign against nuclear weapons, then extended its opposition to nuclear power stations. When the nuclear arms race identified with the Cold War came to an end in the late 1980s, all three organisations had immediately switched their main campaigning efforts to the new cause of global warming. But their opposition to nuclear power remained as uncompromising as ever, even though it offered by far the most practical solution to the problem they now claimed to care about more than any other: the rise in CO_2 emissions.

In terms of finding 'carbon-free' means to generate the electricity on which a computer-dependent civilisation now more than ever relied, this left those 'renewable' energy sources – solar, wave and tidal power, above all wind – which had now seized the imagination of the environmentalists as being the answer to all their dreams.

Everything about 'green' energy seemed appealing. It relied directly on the beneficence of nature itself, on such elemental forces as the sun, water and wind. It was pure, it was clean, it gave off no 'polluting' greenhouse gases, and, bar a little initial investment, it was free.

Thus it was that, from the early 1990s onwards, many EU countries (as was happening at the same time in the US) had embarked on a love affair with the idea of 'renewable' energy as something which governments must do all in their power to encourage. As early as 1989, in the last year of the Thatcher government, the British government introduced a 'non-fossil fuel obligation' (NFFO), whereby its newly-privatised electricity supply companies were obliged to buy a percentage of their power from 'renewable' sources.

Once the Kyoto Protocol was agreed, no one was more enthusiastic in its support than the EU, which was soon aiming to set its own 'Kyoto targets' whereby, by 2010, 10 per cent of all the EU's energy would be 'renewable'. In 2001 the member states committed themselves to an even more ambitious target, issuing a directive laying down that, by 2010, 'of the total electricity consumption of the Community', no less than 22.1%, more than a fifth, must be derived from renewable energy sources.[30]

This prompted the British government to introduce a 'Climate Change Levy' on all form of electricity not generated from renewable sources. And in 2002 the non-fossil fuel obligation was replaced by a 'Renewable Obligations Order' requiring electricity suppliers to buy an even greater and ever increasing percentage of their electricity from 'renewables'. For this and the Climate Change Levy the cost of electricity from wind and other renewable sources would soon thus be 100 per cent higher than the cost of the electricity itself. These additional costs would then be paid for by customers through higher electricity bills.

The most obvious source of additional renewable energy in Europe was wind.[31] By 2002 three EU countries had led the way, Denmark, Germany and Spain, each having already built thousands of subsidised wind turbines. Denmark in particular was now claiming to be generating almost 20 per cent of its electricity from the 6,000 windmills which towered over vast tracts of its flat countryside and coastline. With such cash incentives from governments, the wind industry offered its developers and manufacturers the prospect of ever growing profits.

But the country which supposedly boasted the 'largest potential wind resource in Europe' was Britain, with its windswept mountains, hills and long coastline. Until this time Britain had lagged far behind its continental counterparts in exploiting this 'resource', having built only 500 turbines, many relatively small, which between them generated less than half of 1 per cent of the country's electricity. But now her politicians had belatedly woken up to the idea that wind power might play a crucial part in enabling them to meet the country's EU and Kyoto targets, as was announced by Tony Blair in May 2002 and reflected in a White Paper on Britain's future energy strategy published by the government in March 2003.

Compared with how other European countries obtained their electricity, Britain was in a unique position. In the 1950s she had led the world in pioneering the use of nuclear power, opening the world's first commercial nuclear power station in 1956. In the 1960s and 1970s she built many of the nuclear power stations which, 40 years later, were still providing 23 per cent of her power. She also possessed the largest coal reserves in Europe, so that by 2002 she was still deriving 32 per cent of her electricity from coal-fired power stations.

In the 1970s Britain had begun increasingly to benefit from the discovery of rich oil and gas fields in the North Sea, so that by the 1980s she was enjoying a huge new income as a net oil and gas exporter. When Mrs Thatcher was faced in 1984 by the miners' strike, she welcomed this chance to break the power of a trade union which in the previous decade had caused such political havoc. In the early 1980s she had briefly favoured the idea of building a new generation of nuclear power stations, as another way to free Britain from overdependence on its coal industry. But when the first of the intended new reactors, Sizewell B in Suffolk, ran into interminable planning delays – not least thanks to the bitter opposition of environmentalists and the revulsion against nuclear power which followed Chernobyl – any further plans for nuclear power were abandoned (Sizewell only finally came on stream in 1996).

By 1988, following the closure of scores of inefficient loss-making pits after the strike, Britain had the most efficient coal industry in Europe. Despite having cut its workforce by two-thirds, production at around 100 million tons a year was much the same as it had been before the strike. But in 1992, as political concern began to grow over CO_2 and global warming, the Conservatives' environment minister Michael Heseltine decided to close down 32 modern pits, most of those which remained, and to opt instead for a 'dash for gas' (which as late as 1990 was being used to generate only 0.5 per cent of Britain's electricity). He was relying on the fact that, thanks to the North Sea, Britain was still self-sufficient in supplies of cheap gas, which as a source of electricity generated only half the 'carbon emissions' of coal.

This switch away from home-produced coal enabled Britain to claim a dramatic reduction in her CO_2 emissions. When her environment minister John Prescott went to Kyoto in 1997 he made much of this to his international colleagues and the media, even though three years earlier he had led parliamentary opposition to the pit-closures which alone had made his boast possible.

Only a few years later, however, the situation had suddenly begun to look very different. It was now clear that, thanks to the rate at which Britain had allowed her North Sea reserves to be exploited, they were running down so fast that by 2006 she would be a net importer of oil and gas, increasingly dependent on foreign imports, Similarly, she was now having to import two-thirds of the coal needed for the power stations which still provided a third of her electricity.

Worse still, eight of Britain's nine remaining nuclear power stations, built in the 1960s and 1970s, were ageing so fast that within 10 years or so they would have to close. Furthermore, it seemed likely that many of her larger coal and oil-fired power stations would also have to close by 2015 or earlier, under the EU's 'Large Combustion Plants directive', designed to curb the sulphur dioxide and nitrous oxide pollution which was blamed for causing acid rain.[32]

All this indicated that, within little more than a decade, Britain might well lose as much as 40 per cent of the generating capacity needed to meet her peak electricity demand. As energy experts were keenly aware, unless some way were found to make up this shortfall the country would run desperately short of power. So when in 2003 they learned that the government was to publish a White Paper on Britain's future energy supplies, they were eagerly expectant to see how it intended to fill the anticipated gap and to avert what threatened to be an unprecedented national crisis.

When the White Paper appeared, however, they were dismayed. A first clue to its contents was its title, 'Our energy future – creating a low carbon economy'. The opening page consisted of a signed personal message from the prime minister Tony Blair proclaiming that 'we need urgent global action to tackle climate change'. 'We are showing leadership', he went on, 'by putting the UK on a path to a 60 per cent reduction in its carbon emissions by 2050'. 'This White Paper', he claimed, 'is a milestone in energy policy', providing the strategy whereby Britain could be given 'a truly sustainable energy policy'.[33]

Chapter 1, headed 'Cleaner, smarter energy', then set the tone of the whole document by declaring that 'the first challenge we face is environmental. Climate change is real'. The first illustration in the text, apart from Mr Blair's photograph, was a highly exaggerated artist's impression of Mann's 'hockey stick', showing global temperatures soaring exponentially by what looked like 50°C or more (except that no temperature indices were given). This was nevertheless attributed to the IPCC's 2001 report, and was followed by a similarly exaggerated projection of soaring CO_2 levels, alongside 'shock horror' statements such as 'ice caps are retreating from many mountain peaks like Kilimanjaro'. The Thames Barrier, it claimed, has had to be raised 12 times more frequently in recent years than in the 1980s.

Much of the first 43 pages of a 126-page document supposedly devoted to mapping out Britain's energy future was devoted to further warning of the impending horrors of a warming which, the paper insisted, could only be man-made. 'Many millions more people' would be 'exposed to the risks of hunger, water stress, flooding and diseases like malaria'. 'Poor people in developing countries are likely to be most vulnerable.' Sea level rise would threaten small islands. 'Irreversible losses of diversity could be accelerated.' All this was decked out with references to the IPCC, Kyoto, the UN Framework Convention on Climate Change, the EU and the need for international action.

Only finally on page 44 did the White Paper turn to Britain's own electricity needs, with a chapter headed 'Low carbon generation' and the declaration that 'renewable energy' will play 'a vital part'. The government, it claimed, had already made a start by introducing its Renewables Obligation ('the cost is met through higher prices to consumers'), which by 2010, along with the 'Climate Change Levy', would be 'worth around £1 billion a year to the UK renewables industry'.

The government did admit that so far renewables ('excluding large hydro') only provided 1.3 per cent of Britain's electricity, not comparing well with her continental partners. But to meet its target to derive 10 per cent of power from renewables by 2010, it hoped within seven years to see the installation of '10,000MW of renewables capacity' (an increase of nearly 1000 per cent).

Only at the end of the chapter was there a dismissive throwaway reference to nuclear power, headed 'We do not propose new nuclear build'. 'The current economics of nuclear power make it an unattractive option for new generating capacity, and there are also important issues of nuclear waste to be resolved.'

Twenty-seven pages further on, after sections on reducing vehicle emissions, solar power and biofuels, there was a further brief section on coal, headed 'Handling the consequences of coal-fired generation'. This predicted that the EU's Large Combustion Plants directive and the rising costs brought about the EU's planned 'emissions trading scheme' would make coal 'less attractive as a source of power'. But it hoped that 'carbon capture and storage' – burying CO_2 back in holes in the ground using a technology which had not yet been developed – might offer 'a promising way forward'.

In terms of offering a solution to Britain's impending 40 per cent shortfall in electricity supplies, the White Paper thus said virtually nothing at all, except to speak briefly, vaguely and almost contemptuously about the future of the nuclear and coal-fired power plants which still provided 55 per cent of Britain's electricity (as opposed to the 0.5 per cent derived from wind turbines).

The only thing in the heads of the officials and ministers responsible for this document, it seemed, was the urge to spell out at great length the fearsome threat of global warming (represented by that grotesquely exaggerated version of the 'hockey stick') – combined with pages of mindless wishful thinking about how nice it would be if Britain could meet all those targets designed to give it a 'low carbon economy' (adding, the White Paper estimated, up to 15 per cent to household energy bills).

Unsurprisingly, many of the technical experts who read this summary of the government's energy policy were horrified.[34] But it was an eloquent tribute to just how far the alarm over 'climate change' had now gone in influencing the thinking and policies of governments.

ENTER MCINTYRE AND MCKITRICK

As Britain's new energy White Paper demonstrated. nothing had been more responsible for the unprecedented worldwide impact of the IPCC's 2001 TAR report than Dr Mann's 'hockey stick'. As one observer was later to put it:

> *'without it, the TAR would have been a very different document, it would not have been able to conclude what it did, nor could the IPCC have convinced world leaders to take the actions they subsequently took.'*[35]

So radically did the 'hockey stick' rewrite all the accepted versions of climate history that initially it carried all before it, leaving knowledgeable experts stunned. It was not yet clear quite how Mann had arrived at his remarkable conclusions, precisely what data he had used or what methods the IPCC had used to verify his findings. The sensational new graph which the IPCC made the centrepiece of its report had been sprung on the world out of left field.

Yet when, over the years that followed, a number of experts from different fields began to subject Mann's two papers to careful analysis, some rather serious questions came to be asked about the basis for his study.

For a start, although Mann and his colleagues had cited other evidence for their computer modelling of historical temperatures, it became apparent that they had leaned particularly heavily on 'proxy data' provided by a study five years earlier of tree-rings in ancient bristlecone pine trees growing on the slopes of California's Sierra Nevada mountains. 'Proxies' used to calculate temperature consist of data other than direct measurement, such as tree rings, stalactites, ice cores or lake sediments.

According to the 1993 paper used by Mann, these bristlecone pines had shown significantly accelerated growth in the years after 1900. But the purpose of this original study had not been to research into past temperatures. As was made clear by its title – 'Detecting the aerial fertilisation effect of atmospheric CO_2 enrichment in tree-ring chronologies' – it had been to measure the effect on the trees' growth rate of the twentieth-century increase in CO_2 levels.[36]

As the paper's authors had specifically pointed out, temperature changes could not account for the faster growth of these long-established trees. It must have been due to the fertilising effect of the increase in CO_2. The pine trees had been chosen for study because their position, high up on the mountains, made it likely that they would exhibit an unusually marked response to CO_2 enrichment.

Tree rings are a notoriously unreliable reflector of temperature changes, because they are chiefly formed during only one short period of the year, and cannot therefore give a full picture. This 1993 study of one group of trees in one untypical corner of the US seemed a remarkably flimsy basis on which to base an estimate of global temperatures going back 1000 years.[37]

Then it transpired that, in order to show the twentieth-century section of the graph, the terrifying upward flick of temperatures at the end of the 'hockey stick', spliced in with the tree-ring data had been a set of twentieth-century temperature readings, as recorded by more than 2,000 weather stations across the earth's surface. It was these which more than anything helped to confirm the most dramatic conclusion of the study, that temperatures in the closing decades of the twentieth century had been shooting up to levels unprecedented in the history of the last 1,000 years, culminating in the 'warmest year of the millennium', 1998.

Not only was it far from clear that, for this all-important part of the graph, two quite different sets of data had been used. Also accepted without qualification was the accuracy of these twentieth-century surface temperature readings. But the picture given by these was already being questioned by many expert scientists who pointed to evidence that readings from surface weather stations could become seriously distorted by what was known as the 'urban heat island effect'. The majority of the thermometers in such stations were in the proximity of large and increasingly built-up population centres. It was well-established that these heated up the atmosphere around them to a significantly higher level than in more isolated locations.

Nowhere was this better illustrated than by contrasting the temperature readings taken on the earth's surface with those which, since 1979, had been taken by NASA satellites and weather balloons, using a method developed by Dr Roy Spencer, responsible for climate studies at NASA's Marshall Space Centre, and Dr John Christie of the University of Alabama, Huntsville.

Surprisingly, these atmospheric measurements showed that, far from warming in the last two decades of the twentieth century, global temperatures had in fact slightly cooled.[38] As Spencer was at pains to point out, these avoided the distortions created in surface readings by the urban heat island effect. The reluctance of the IPCC to take proper account of this, he observed, confirmed the suspicion of 'many scientists involved in the process' that the IPCC's stance on global warming was 'guided more by policymakers and politicians than by scientists'.[39]

There was nothing the IPCC welcomed more in the 'hockey stick' than the way it showed the line hurtling upwards at the end, to portray 1998 as having been 'the warmest year of the millennium'. But, as many scientists had noted at the time, 1998 was likely to be exceptionally warm because of the unusually strong El Niño event of that year.

The long-observed El Niño phenomenon occurs when air currents in the Pacific fail to replace warm surface water off the western coast of America with colder water. This invariably results in warming over a considerable area of the earth's surface. The converse phenomenon, when the colder water becomes uppermost, is known as a La Niña, resulting in a tendency to cooling.

What was also remarkable about the 'hockey stick', as was again widely observed, was how it contradicted all that mass of evidence which supported the generally accepted picture of temperature fluctuations in past centuries. As was pointed out, tree-rings are not the most reliable guide to assessing past temperatures. Scores of more direct sources of proxy evidence had been studied over the years, from Africa, South America, Australia, Pakistan, Antarctica, every continent and ocean of the world.

Whether evidence was taken from lake sediments or ice cores, glaciers in the Andes or boreholes in every continent (Huang *et al.*, 1997), the results had been remarkably consistent in confirming that the familiar view was right. There had been a Little Ice Age, across the world. There had similarly been a Mediaeval Warm Period. Furthermore, a mass of data confirmed that the world had been even warmer in the Middle Ages than it was in 1998.

The first comprehensive study to review this point was published in January 2003 by Dr Willie Soon and his colleague Dr Sallie Baliunas of the Harvard-Smithsonian Center for Astrophysics. They had examined 140 expert studies of the climate history of the past 1,000 years, based on every kind of data. Some had given their findings only in a local or regional context, others had attempted to give a worldwide picture. But between them these studies had covered every continent.[40]

The question the two researchers had asked of every study was whether or not it showed a 'discernible climate anomaly' at the time of (1) the Little Ice Age and (2) the Mediaeval Warm Period; and (3) whether it had shown the twentieth century to be the warmest time in the Millennium.

Their conclusion was unequivocal. Only two of the studies they looked at had not found evidence for the Little Ice Age. Only seven of the 140 studies had denied the existence of a Mediaeval Warm Period, while 116 had confirmed it.

On the crucial question of whether or not the twentieth century had been the warmest of the past thousand years, only 15 studies, including that of Mann himself, had unambiguously agreed that it was. The vast majority accepted that earlier centuries had been warmer. The conclusion of Soon and Baliunas was that

> '*Across the world, many records reveal that the twentieth century is probably not the warmest nor a uniquely extreme climatic period of the last millennium.*'

But if Mann and his colleagues had got the picture as wrong as this survey of the literature suggested, nothing did more to expose just how this might have come about than a remarkable feat of analysis carried out later in the same year by two Canadians and published in October 2003.[41]

Stephen McIntyre, who began their study, was a financial consultant and statistical analyst specialising in the minerals industry, and was later joined by Ross McKitrick, a professor of economics at Guelph University. Neither made any pretensions to being a climate scientist, but where they did have considerable expertise was in knowing how computers could be used to play around with statistics. They were also wearily familiar with people using hockey stick-like curves, showing an exaggerated upward rise at the end, to sell a business prospect or to 'prove' some tendentious point.

Intrigued by the shape of the IPCC's now famous 'hockey stick' graph, in the spring of 2003 McIntyre approached Mann and his colleagues to ask for a look at their original data set. 'After some delay', Mann 'arranged provision of a file which was represented as the one used' for his paper. But it turned out not to include 'most of the computer code used to produce their results'. This suggested to McIntyre, who was joined later that summer by McKitrick, that no one else had previously asked to examine it, as should have been required both by peer-reviewers for the paper published in *Nature* and, above all, by the IPCC itself.[42]

When McIntyre fed the data into his own computer, he found that it did not produce the claimed results. At the heart of the problem was what is known as 'principal component analysis', a technique used by computer analysts to handle a large mass of data by averaging out its components, weighting them by their relative significance.

One of the first things McIntyre had discovered was that the 'principal component analysis' used by Mann could not be replicated. 'In the process of looking up all the data sources and rebuilding Mann's data set from scratch', he discovered 'quite a few errors concerning location labels, use of obsolete editions, unexplained truncations of various series etc.' (for instance, data reported to be from Boston, Mass., turned out to be from Paris, France, Central England temperature data had been truncated to leave out its coldest period, and so forth).

But the real problem lay with the 'principal component analysis' itself. It turned out that an algorithm had been programmed into Mann's computer model which 'mined' for hockey stick shapes whatever data was fed into it. As McKitrick was later to explain,

'had the IPCC actually done the kind of rigorous review that they boast of they would have discovered that there was an error in a routine calculation step (principal component analysis) that falsely identified a hockey stick shape as the dominant pattern in the data. The flawed computer program can even pull out spurious hockey stick shapes from lists of trendless random numbers.' [43]

Using Mann's algorithm, the two men fed a pile of random and meaningless data ('red noise') into the computer 10,000 times. More than 99 per cent of the time the graph which emerged bore a 'hockey stick' shape. They found that their replication of Mann's method failed 'all basic tests of statistical significance'.

When they ran the programme again properly, however, keeping the rest of Mann's data but removing the bristlecone pine figures on which he had so heavily relied, they found that the Mediaeval Warming once again unmistakably emerged. Indeed their 'major finding', according to McKitrick, was that Mann's own data confirmed that the warming in the fifteenth century exceeded anything in the twentieth century.[44]

One example of how this worked they later quoted was based on comparing two sets of data used by Mann for his second 1999 paper, confined to proxy data from North America. One was drawn from bristlecone pines in western North America, the other from a tree ring chronology in Arkansas. In their raw state, the Californian series showed a 'hockey stick' shape; the other, typical of most North American tree ring series, showed an irregular but basically flat line with no final upward spurt. When these were put together, however, the algorithm emphasised the twentieth-century rise by giving '390 times as much weight' to the bristlecone pines as to the trees from Arkansas.[45]

In other words, although Mann had used hundreds of tree ring proxies from all over North America, most showing a flattish line like that from Arkansas, the PCAs used to determine their relative significance had given enormously greater weight to those Californian bristlecones with their anomalous 'hockey stick' pattern.

Furthermore, McIntyre and McKitrick found that Mann had been well aware that by removing the bristlecone pine data the 'hockey stick' shape of his graph would vanish, because he had tried it himself. One of the files they obtained from him showed the results of his own attempt to do this. The file was marked 'Censored' and its findings were nowhere mentioned in the published study.[46]

What, however, concerned McIntyre and McKitrick as much as anything else about this extraordinary affair was what it revealed about the methods of the IPCC itself. Why had it not subjected Mann's study to the kind of basic professional checks which they themselves had been able to carry out, with such devastating results?

Furthermore, having failed to exercise any proper quality control, why had those at the top of the IPCC then gone out of their way to give such extraordinary prominence to

> '*the hockey stick data as the canonical representation of the earth's climate history. Due to a combination of mathematical error and a dysfunctional review process, they ended up promoting the exact wrong conclusion. How did they make such a blunder?*' [47]

Watson and Houghton themselves had never lost any opportunity to parade the 'hockey stick' as the 'evidence' which they hoped more than anything else would further their cause. They more than once appeared in front of blown-up versions of Mann's graph, as when Houghton was photographed launching the IPCC's 2001 Summary for Policymakers and again giving the prestigious 2001 Cambridge Lecture.[48]

Yet now, it seemed, the prize exhibit for their cause had been exposed as no more than a trick of smoke and mirrors.

When McIntyre and McKitrick first published their findings in October 2003, in a small circulation journal, these did not initially cause much of a stir. Mann and his colleagues posted a dismissive response on the internet, conceding nothing. When McIntyre and McKitrick then submitted a letter to *Nature*, pointing out some of the technical flaws in the study which *Nature* itself had published in 1998, the journal sat on their letter for eight months, before saying that it wouldn't appear. By a Catch 22 trick, *Nature* explained that they could only be allowed 500 words to make their point. But since in the editor's view, this would not be enough to explain their point properly, he did not propose to print anything.[49]

Despite this rejection, following a formal complaint by McIntyre and McKitrick in January 2004, Mann and his colleagues were invited by *Nature* to publish a face-saving 'Corrigendum', which appeared the following July. This conceded some of the non-technical mistakes in their paper but insisted that 'none of these errors affect our previously published results'.[50]

For the moment, the IPCC's rewriting of history still appeared to command the field. As George Orwell had written in *Nineteen Eighty-Four*:

> *'everything faded into mist. The past was erased, the erasure was forgotten, the lie became the truth.'*

In fact the most notable controversy in the history of the debate over 'human-induced climate change' had only just begun.

Notes

1. Ross McKitrick, 'What is the "hockey stick" debate about?', APEC Study Group, Australia, 4 April, 2005. See also Christopher Horner, *Red Hot Lies: How Global Warming Alarmists Use Threats, Fraud And Deception To Keep You Misinformed* (Regnery Publishing, 2008).
2. Ross McKitrick, *op. cit.*
3. Dennis Bray and Hans von Storch (1999), '1996 survey of climate scientists on attitudes towards global warming and related matters', *Bulletin of the American Meteorological Society*, 80, March 1999.
4. 'Survey of State experts casts doubt on link between human activity and global warming'. Press release, 1997, Citizens for a Sound Economy, Washington DC.
5. Although the graphic in the 1990 FAR report had been credited, *inter alia*, to Houghton, it appeared to be largely based on the work in the

1950s and 1960s of Professor Hubert Lamb, a distinguished British palaeoclimatologist. See Lamb's 'The Early Mediaeval Warm Epoch and its Sequel', *Palaeogeography, Palaeoclimatology, Palaeoecology* 1, 1965 (available through Climate Audit website), Lamb's later 1967 paper enlarging on the first and his book *Climate, History and the Future*, 1977. Although much of Lamb's study was based on data from Central England, he was clearly convinced that his 'Mediaeval Warm Epoch' was a much wider, probably worldwide phenomenon. Houghton, *et al.*, said nothing in 1990 to contradict this.

6. Gore, *op. cit.*, p. 66.
7. This was the point argued by Schneider and Rasool, *op. cit.*, as early as 1971.
8. The third IPCC report (TAR, 2001) accepted that between 1900 and 1940 the world had warmed by 0.4°C, that between 1940 and 1975 it had cooled by 0.2°C (the Little Cooling), and that from 1975 onwards it had warmed again by 0.4 degrees, thus giving an overall warming trend for the twentieth century of 0.6 degrees.
9. David Deming, 'Climate warming in North America: analysis of borehole temperatures', *Science*, 268, 1576–1577, See also McKitrick, *op. cit.*
10. Quoted in McKitrick, *op. cit.*
11. Shapoeng Huang, *et al.* (1997), 'Late Quaternary temperature changes seen in worldwide continental heat flow measurements', *Geophysical Research Letters*, 24, 1947-1950. See also McKitrick, *op. cit.*
12. Mann M. E., *et al.* (1998), 'Global-scale temperature patterns and climate forcing over the past six centuries', *Nature*, 392, 779–787.
13. Mann M. E., *et al.* (1999), 'Northern hemisphere temperatures during the last millennium: inferences, uncertainties and limitations', *Geophysical Research Letters*, 26.
14. SAR (1996) had predicted a rise of between 0.9°C and 3.5 degrees. TAR (2001) gave a range between 1.4 degrees and 5.8 degrees. FAR (1990) had predicted a rise between 1.5 degrees and 4.5 degrees, Thus, despite tens of billions of dollars spent on research funding, the range of uncertainty had progressively widened on each occasion.
15. Holland, *op. cit.*
16. Robert Foster, 'The Third IPCC Report: An Imagination Block', supplementary submission to the Joint Standing Committee on Treaties Inquiry Into The Kyoto Protocol, April 2001.
17. R. Watson, 'Report to the Sixth Conference of the Parties, United Nations Framework Convention on Climate Change, 20 November 2001'.
18. Testimony of Rochard S. Lindzen before the Senate Commerce Committee, 1 May 2001.
19. At a press conference in April, after the report had been published, Robert Watson denied at a press conference that there had been any

substantial disagreement among the scientists on the IPCC, or that there was any split within the scientific community as a whole over the human role in global warming. 'It's not even 80:20 or 90:10', he said, 'I personally believe it's something like 98:2 or 99:1.' Houghton on the same occasion claimed that there were 'not more than 10 scientists' in the world, versed in the arguments, who 'disagreed with the notion of human-induced climate change' ('UN expert: climate change skeptics a tiny minority', Reuters, 5 April 2001, quoted by McKitrick, *op. cit.*).

20. Schneider, S. H., 2001. 'What is "dangerous" climate change?', *Nature*, 411, 17–19. These 'scenarios' had originally been published in 2000 as a 'Special Report on Emissions Scenarios' (SRES).
21. 'Bush kills global warming treaty', *The Guardian*, 29 March 2001.
22. 'Bush firm over Kyoto stance', CNN, 29 March 2001.
23. 'Bush secedes from Kyoto, establishes roque state', *The Gully.com*
24. 'Bush's Kyoto stance angers UK scientists', *THE*, 6 April 2001.
25. 'Presidency Conclusions', Göteborg European Council, 15–16 June 2001.
26. Greenpeace press release, 16 June 2001.
27. Directive 2002/91/EC of the European Parliament and of the Council of 16 December 2002 on the energy performance of buildings. (*Official Journal* L 001 , 04/01/2003 P. 0065–0071)
28. Council Directive 1999/31/EC of 26 April 1999 on the landfill of waste (*Official Journal* L 182, 16/07/1999 P. 0001–0019)
29. 'Climate scientist ousted', BBC News, 12 April 2002. Friends of the Earth, Greenpeace and other environmental groups claimed that the Bush administration had only campaigned to get rid of Watson in response to pressure from ExxonMobil (see Greenpeace press release, 22 April, 2002).
30. Directive 2001/77/EC of the European Parliament and of the Council of 27 September 2001 'on the promotion of electricity from renewable energy sources in the internal electricity market' (*Official Journal* L 283 of 27.10.2001).
31. Apart from the handful of countries such as Switzerland and Norway which had mountains large enough to allow extensive use of hydro-electric power.
32. Large Combustion Plants Directive, 2001/80/EC, OJ. L 309/2, 27 November 2001.
33. 'Our Energy Future: Creating A Low Carbon Economy', presented to Parliament by the Secretary of State for Trade and Industry, February 2003. Cm 5761.
34. E.g. Professor Ian Fells of Newcastle University, who dismissed the White Paper as 'reckless' (BBC News website).
35. Ross McKitrick, *op. cit.*

36. D. A. Graybill and S. B. Idso (1993, 'Detecting the aerial fertilisation effect of atmospheric CO_2 enrichment in tree-ring chronologies', *Global Biochemical Cycles*, 7. See also Singer and Avery, *op. cit.*, Chap. 5.

37. Mann and his colleagues did seem to acknowledge this when, in their second paper, 'Global-scale temperature patterns' was changed to 'Northern hemisphere temperatures'.

38. National Research Council (2000), 'Reconciling observations of global temperature change' (National Academy Press).

39. Roy Spencer, 'When science meets politics on global warming', *Washington Times*, 3 September 1998. Spencer's scepticism over the IPCC's reluctance to refer to satellite temperature data was to be abundantly confirmed on pp. 28–29 of its 2001 Technical Summary, where a small graph based on his satellite data was dwarfed by yet another large colour reproduction of the 'hockey stick' covering more than half the page opposite. 'Like a magician misdirecting the audience's attention', as McKitrick was to comment, this 'sleight of hand' was obviously designed to draw attention towards Mann's graph and away from the graph of satellite temperatures which told such a different story (McKitrick, *op. cit.*, Fig. 1).

40. W. Soon and S. Baliunas, 'Proxy climatic and environmental changes of the past 1,000 years', *Climate Research*, 23, 89–110, 31 January 2003. The journal's decision to publish their paper so enraged the advocates of global warming lobby that this provoked a major internal row, resulting in half the 10 editors resigning. An account of this episode by one of them, Claire Goodess of the Climatic Research Unit, University of East Anglia, is published on the website of SGR (Scientists for Global Responsibility).

41. S. McIntyre and R. McKitrick, 2003, 'Corrections to the Mann *et al.* (1998) proxy databse and northern hemispheric average temperature series', *Energy and Environment*, 14, 752–771. In the analysis of McIntyre and McKitrick's work which follows, reference will also be made to their later paper, McIntyre and McKitrick, 2005b, 'The M & M critique of the MBH98 Northern Hemisphere climate index, Update and applications', *Energy and Environment*, 16, 69–99, and also to McKitrick (2005), 'What is the "Hockey Stick" debate about?', *op. cit.*

42. This account of the 'hockey stick' saga is based on several sources, in particular Ross McKitrick's paper already cited , 'What is the "hockey stick" debate about?' (2005), and his evidence to the House of Lords Committee on Economic Affairs, 'The Economics of Climate Change', Vol. II, Evidence, 2005. See also David Holland, 'Bias and concealment in the IPCC Process: the "Hockey Stick" affair and its implications' (2007), *op. cit.*

43. McKitrick, House of Lords evidence, *op. cit.*

44. *Ibid.*
45. McKitrick (2005), 'What is the "Hockey Stick" debate about?', *op. cit.*
46. *Ibid.*
47. McKitrick, House of Lords evidence, *op. cit.*
48. Holland, *op. cit.*, p. 957.
49. McKitrick, 'What is the "hockey stick" debate about?', *op. cit.*, p. 11.
50. *Nature*, Vol. 430, p. 105.

5

The political temperature rises
'A far greater threat than terrorism':
2004–2005

'A secret report, suppressed by US defence chiefs and obtained by The Observer, *warns that major European cities will be sunk beneath rising seas as Britain is plunged into a "Siberian" climate by 2020. Nuclear conflict, mega-droughts, famine and widespread rioting will spread across the world … deaths from war and famine run into the millions, until the planet's population is reduced by such an extent the Earth can cope. Access to water becomes a major battleground … Rich areas like the US and Europe would become "virtual fortresses", to prevent millions of migrants from entering, after being forced from land drowned by sea-level rise or no longer able to grow crops.'*

The Observer, 2004[1]

'Earlier this year a scientific conference at Exeter University, convened to provide the government with expert advice in preparation for this summer's G8 summit, became something like a contest between which horror stories – the Vanishing Gulf Stream, Millions Dead of Malaria in the Midlands, the Parboiled Polar Bear – would do the best job of making the public's flesh creep. As spin for the government's case that climate change is a threat greater than terrorism, this was no doubt effective. As guidance to policy-makers, it was a disgrace. Tall stories have no place at G8 summits.'

Rosemary Righter to House of
Lords committee, April 2005[2]

On both sides of the Atlantic by 2004 it might have seemed that there was no longer any real public debate over global warming.

The scientific establishments of the Western world had long been firmly lined up behind the 'consensus'. They were led by the US National Academy of Sciences, Britain's Royal Society and pretty well every other leading scientific body, such as the American Association for the Advancement of Science and the American Meteorological Society; not to mention all the more prestigious scientific journals such as *Science* and *Nature*.

Another of the most active promoters of the 'consensus' was the UK Met Office and its Hadley Centre. Set up by Houghton in 1990 and opened by Mrs Thatcher in the last days of her premiership as the Hadley Centre for Climate Prediction and Research, this organisation, thanks to Houghton, had been appointed by the IPCC to provide 'its primary data set to assess observed global warming'.[3] It had continued to play a key role in the IPCC's inner workings ever since, not least in selecting the authors for its crucial Working Group I reports.

The mass-media were now equally unanimous in pushing the threat posed by global warming. In the US they were led by the national TV networks, NBC, CBS and ABC, the *New York Times*, *Time* and *Newsweek*. To the fore in Britain was the BBC, tireless in promoting the alarmist agenda, flanked by the *Observer*, the *Guardian* and the *Independent*, with the rest of the media not far behind.

With the exception of the Bush White House and a few Republican Senators, America's politicians had increasingly been won over to support for the cause. In Britain and across the EU scarcely a single dissenting political voice could be heard to question it.

It was not least for this reason that by 2004 the temperature over global warming was visibly beginning to rise. It was not that the earth's temperature itself was continuing to rise. The El Niño year of 1998 was still generally regarded as having been the hottest on record. But so universally was the 'consensus' now accepted, without any obvious challenge, that there was now pressure to make claims of the supposed dangers of 'climate change' – hurricanes, floods, heat waves, droughts, melting ice caps, rising sea levels, diseases, species extinctions – more extreme than ever.

Nearly seven years after the Kyoto agreement, the most immediate political prize was still to get the treaty ratified, and here the British government tried to take the initiative. In January 2004, Sir David King, Chief Scientific Adviser to Tony Blair and the British government, published an article in *Science* warning that climate change was now 'the most severe problem we are facing today'. It was, he wrote in words which were widely quoted, 'a far greater threat to the world than international terrorism'.[4]

In Britain alone, warned King, the number of people at high risk of flooding was expected to more than double, to nearly 3.5 million by 2080. Damage to property could run to tens of billions of pounds every year. But, asserting that, as the world's largest 'polluter', the US was responsible for more than 20 per cent of the world's greenhouse gas emissions (compared with only 2 per cent from the UK), King then attacked the Bush administration for failing to play its proper role in tackling the crisis by refusing to ratify Kyoto. He did not mention that it was President Clinton and the US Senate which had first refused to accept the terms of Kyoto even before the treaty was agreed.

In March, King was warning MPs that the Antarctic had already lost 40 per cent of its ice and that the melting of the polar ice caps could cause a shift in the Gulf Stream which would lower temperatures in Britain and Europe by as much as 10°C. This 'could happen quite suddenly', said King, as could the 'switching off' of the Indian Monsoon. 'There could be a point, and it is quite likely', he went on, where temperatures rose too high for tropical forests to survive, so that they would 'got from being net absorbers of carbon dioxide to net emitters'. This could trigger a repeat of what had happened '55 million years ago', when CO_2 had risen to 1,000 parts per million of the atmosphere, causing mass-extinctions and making Antarctica virtually the only place on the planet which was habitable.[5]

In April 2004, Blair himself joined the assault, warning that the situation facing mankind was 'very, very critical indeed'. In May, launching 'a new alliance of governments, businesses and pressure groups' to tackle global warming, he said he could not think of 'any bigger long-term question facing the world community'.

Supporting Blair's initiative, with an interview headed 'Why Antarctica will soon be the only place to live', Professor King claimed that the earth's temperatures had risen to their highest level for '60 million years'. At that time, he said, repeating the point he had made earlier to the MPs, CO_2 levels had soared to 1,000 parts per million, causing a massive reduction of life.* 'No ice was left on Earth. Antarctica was the best place for mammals to live, and the rest of the world would not sustain human life', he went on, warning that, if humanity did not curb its burning of fossil fuels 'we will reach that level by 2100'. Thus, by the end of the twenty-first cen-

---

* King was referring to the extinction of the dinosaurs (and ammonites), which took place at the end of the Cretaceous 65 million years ago. Although various theories have been advanced as to the cause of this mass-extinction, leading to the rise of mammals and birds, an increase in CO_2 levels had not been generally suggested as one of them.

tury according to his own logic, Antarctica was likely to be the only continent on earth left habitable.[6]

It was not immediately obvious just why King should have set himself up as such an authority on climate change. His scientific specialism was 'surface chemistry'. He had first come to public prominence when, shortly after Blair appointed him as chief scientist, he found himself playing a central role in the unprecedentedly widespread epidemic of foot-and-mouth disease which hit Britain's countryside in 2001.

Ignoring the advice of the world's top veterinary experts on foot-and-mouth, it was King who advised that a computer modeller Professor Roy Anderson should be put in charge of the government's strategy for tackling the epidemic, even though Anderson and his modelling team had no experience of animal diseases. It was Anderson and his colleagues who used their computer model to design the highly controversial 'pre-emptive cull' policy, killing herds and flocks for miles around any outbreak of the disease, which, much to the dismay of the expert veterinarians, resulted in the mass-slaughter of an estimated nine million healthy animals.*

On climate change, another subject new to him, King was again to put his faith in computer models rather than on any detailed grasp of the science. In the summer of 2004 this led him into a curiously embarrassing episode, the repercussions of which would reverberate round the scientific community, if not the media, for quite a while to come.

KING GOES TO MOSCOW: 'A WAR AGAINST THE WHOLE WORLD'

Since Bush's confirmation of America's refusal to accept Kyoto, the only real hope of getting the treaty ratified lay with President Putin's Russia. But Putin seemed even more adamantly opposed to Kyoto

---

* Anderson and his team had specialised in modelling the epidemiology of human diseases, but had no previous experience in animal diseases whatever. Not only was their 'pre-emptive cull' strategy seriously questioned by some of the world's leading foot-and-mouth experts, such as Professor Fred Brown and Dr Simon Barteling, who strongly urged a mass-vaccination policy, but lawyers argued that it was illegal, since the law as it stood (the Animal Health Act 1981) only permitted the killing of animals which had been directly exposed to infection.

than the US. In December 2003 he reiterated that his country had no intention of ratifying, because the treaty was 'scientifically flawed' and 'even 100 per cent compliance with the Kyoto Protocol won't reverse climate change'.[7]

Unlike its Western counterparts, the Russian scientific establishment was profoundly sceptical towards the 'consensus' view that increased CO_2 levels were causing global warming. In the autumn of 2003 the Russian Academy of Sciences had put 10 key questions to the IPCC and been promised a response 'within a few days'. But nine months later still no answers had been received.[8]

Having also been put under continuous political pressure to ratify Kyoto by the EU, the Russians decided to stage a high-level international seminar in Moscow on 7 and 8 July 2004, chaired by Putin's chief economic adviser Alexander Illarionov. Leading scientists from all over the world would be invited to discuss some of the central issues at stake.

Among those who agreed to participate, with the full backing of the Blair government, was Professor King, who saw this as a fine opportunity to talk the Russians into changing their mind on Kyoto. When he arrived with a team of British scientists, however, he was shocked to see the names of some of the other scientists who had been invited.

He gave an ultimatum that two-thirds of the scientific contributors invited by the Academy were 'undesirable' and should not be allowed to speak. He appealed to Tony Blair's office and the British Foreign Secretary Jack Straw, who happened to be in Moscow, for pressure to be put on the Russian government and the conference organisers to insist that his demands were met.

When he failed to get his way and the conference commenced according to the planned agenda, many participants were astonished by the behaviour of King and his team.[9] Frequently they interrupted other speakers, or spoke themselves for much longer than their allotted time. On four occasions proceedings broke up in disorder, causing lengthy delays.

What seemed particularly to arouse King's anger were the contributions of speakers who, on a range of issues, dared to contradict the received IPCC line. Dr Nils-Axel Mörner, fo instance, had just stepped down after four years as President of the INQUA International Commission on Sea Level Changes, He was a professor of geology at the University of Stockholm with 30 years of experience

studying sea level changes all round the world and had been appointed as a lead reviewer on the IPCC's 2001 Assessment Report.
But he was also known to be deeply sceptical about the computer
modelling used by the IPCC to support its claim that sea levels were
rising (when appointed as an IPCC reviewer, he had been 'astonished' to discover that 'only one of the 22 authors of the section on
sea levels' was someone he recognised as 'a genuine sea level expert').

In Moscow Mörner strongly challenged the IPCC's position. He
asked why the graph produced by the computer model favoured by
the IPCC, based on Topex/Poseidon satellite data, had shown sea
levels to be roughly stable until 2003, but had then been republished
by the IPCC, using the same data, but now showing a pronounced
upward 'tilt'. One of King's team rather oddly explained that this
was 'because we needed a trend'.*

Dr Mörner further annoyed them by reporting that when he and
an expert team had carried out a series of studies of the Maldives,
where the IPCC's tide gauge data showed sea level to be rising, their
researches based on extensive field observations showed levels to
have fallen by between 20 and 30 centimetres in the 1970s, and since
to have remained stable.

Another speaker to arouse their ire was Professor Paul Reiter of
the Pasteur Institute in Paris, the world's leading authority on malaria
and other insect-borne diseases. As an expert adviser to the World
Health Organisation, Reiter had been a contributor to the IPCC's
2001 report, but disagreed strongly with its finding that global
warming would cause a spread of diseases. Malaria-carrying mosquitoes, he pointed out, could flourish at surprisingly low temperatures. There was simply no evidence to support the IPCC's alarmist
claims on this point.

When King himself then put forward the now familiar claim that
global warming was responsible for the melting of the ice on the

---

* Personal information from Dr Mörner. The IPPC's explanation for this
'correction' to its graph was that it was to take account of new data from
tide gauges. Mörner was very wary of tide gauges because their data
could be affected by rises or falls in the land on which they were sited. He
wryly noted that the new IPCC 'trend' line showed a general sea level rise
averaging 2.3mm, exactly in accord with the only one of six Hong Kong
tide gauges to show a 2.3mm rise. His own findings, showing no rise,
were derived from field studies carried out in many parts of the world,
based on measuring tide and shore lines, marine deposits and other direct
physical evidence.

summit of Kilimanjaro, Reiter challenged him by referring to various studies showing that the melting had been taking place since the 1880s. It was not due to global warming, these had concluded, but to deforestation causing a sharp drop in local precipitation. Apparently unable to answer Reiter's point, King broke off in mid-sentence and led his delegation out of the room.[10]

When the seminar ended, an angry Illarionov summoned a press conference. In a lengthy statement he described the background to the meeting and Russian frustration at the failure of the IPCC to reply to the 10 questions to which it had been promised an answer the previous year.

> *'Instead of getting replies to our questions, we kept on hearing that replies did not matter. What was important is that whether or not Russia trusts Britain, the European Union and the countries that have ratified the Kyoto Protocol and that have been exerting unprecedented pressure on Russia to ratify it. This is why it was so important for us to arrange a real meeting and a real discussion of real problems with the participation of foreign scientists who have different views.'*

Illarionov then turned to the Kyoto Protocol itself, which he described as 'one of the biggest, if not the biggest, international adventure of all times and nations. 'Frankly speaking, it's hard to recall something like this of the same scale and of the same consequences'. Yet, he said,

> *'none of the assertions made in the Kyoto Protocol and the "scientific" theory on which the Kyoto Protocol is based have been borne out by actual data.'*

We are not seeing, he went on, any of the consequences claimed for global warming – increased droughts, floods, hurricanes or other extreme weather events. There was no spread of contagious diseases.

> *'If there is an insignificant increase in the temperature, it is not due to anthropogenic factors but to the natural factors related to the planet itself and solar activity. There is no evidence confirming a positive linkage between the level of carbon dioxide and temperature changes. If there is such a linkage, it is a reverse nature. In other words, it is not that which influences the temperature on Earth, but it just the reverse: temperature fluctuations caused by solar activity influence the concentration of carbon dioxide.'*

Furthermore, said Illarionov,

'*The statistical data underpinning these documents and issued in millions of copies are often considerably distorted if not falsified.*'

In particular, he singled out the 'hockey stick'. 'A number of scientific works published lately', he said,

'*show that in order to produce this "hockey stick", intentional or unintentional, I don't really know, mistakes were made that led to distortions in initial data and final results. Using the words of famous poet Vladimir Vysotsky, everything is not the way it should be.*'

Illarionov then turned his attention in remarkably outspoken fashion to the part played in the seminar by King and his team. In the past two years, he said, he had taken part

'*in many international meetings, seminars, conferences and congresses on these issues both in Russia and in many of the countries, including the seminar that we had today and yesterday. Honestly, these papers [presented by King and his team] differed dramatically from what is usually offered at international congresses and conferences.*'

Simultaneously, they revealed an absolute – and I stress, absolute – inability to answer questions concerning the alleged professional activities of the authors of these papers. Not only the ten questions that were published nine months ago, but not a single question asked during this two-day seminar by participants in the seminar, both Russian and foreign, were answered.

When it became clear that [the King team] could not provide a substantive answer to a question, three devices were used. And I have to say it now, although it has not direct bearing on the Kyoto Protocol and the content of the extremely interesting presentations made during the past two days.

The British participants insisted on introducing censorship during the holding of this seminar. The chief science adviser to the British government, Mr King, demanded in the form of an ultimatum at the beginning of yesterday that the program of the seminar be changed and he presented an ultimatum demanding that about two-thirds of the participants not be given the floor ... Mr King spoke about "undesirable" scientists and undesirable participants in the seminar. He declared that if the old program was preserved, he would not take part in the seminar and walk out taking along with him all the other British participants. He has prepared his own program which he proposed, it is available here and my colleagues can simply distribute Mr King's hand-written program to change the program prepared by the Russian Academy of Sciences ...'

Illarionov then described the attempts made to apply political pressure to get the agenda changed through Straw and Blair's office. When this 'attempt to introduce censorship' failed,

> '*other attempts were made to disrupt the seminar. At least four times during the course of the seminar ugly scenes were staged that prevented the seminar from proceeding normally. As a result we lost at least four hours of working time in order to try to solve these problems. During these events Mr King cited his conversations with the office of the British Prime Minister and had got clearance for such actions.*
>
> *And thirdly, when the more or less normal work of the seminar was restored and when the opportunity for discussion presented itself, when questions on professional topics were asked, and being unable to answer these questions, Mr King and other members of the delegation, turned to flight, as happened this morning, when Mr King, in an unprecedented incident, cut short his answer to a question in mid-sentence realizing that he was unable to answer it and left the seminar room.*
>
> *It is not for us to give an assessment to what happened, but in our opinion the reputation of British science, the reputation of the British government and the reputation of the title "Sir" has sustained heavy damage.*'[11]

Finally Illarionov turned back to the Kyoto Protocol

> '*or more specifically, to the ideological and philosophical basis on which it is built. That ideological base can be juxtaposed and compared, as Professor Reiter has done just now, with man-hating totalitarian ideology with which we had the bad fortune to deal during the twentieth century, such as National Socialism, Marxism, Eugenics, Lysenkovism and so on. All methods of distorting information existing in the world have been committed to prove the alleged validity of these theories. Misinformation, falsification, fabrication, mythology, propaganda. Because what is offered cannot be qualified in any other way than myth, nonsense and absurdity.*'

In a resounding peroration, he concluded

> '*When we see one of the biggest, if not the biggest international adventures based on man-hating totalitarian ideology which, incidentally, manifests itself in totalitarian actions and concrete events, particularly academic discussions, and which tries to defend itself using disinformation and falsified facts. It's hard to think of any other word but "war" to describe this.*
>
> *To our great regret, this is a war, and this is a war against the whole world. But in this particular case the first to happen to be on this path is our country. It's unpleasant to say but I am afraid it's undeclared war against Russia ... a total war against our country, a war that uses all kinds of means.*

The main prize in this war for those who have started it and who are waging is the ratification by Russian authorities of the Kyoto Protocol. There is only one conclusion to be made from what we have seen, heard and researched: Russia has no material reasons to ratify this document. Moreover, such a ratification would mean only one thing: complete capitulation to the dangerous and harmful ideology and practice that are being imposed upon us with the help of international diplomacy.'

What was to happen only four months later no one could have predicted. Despite the vehemence of his own chief economic adviser and despite the strongly held views of Russia's leading scientists, President Putin made a startling U-turn.

It emerged that, on an initiative from Tony Blair, he had struck a political bargain with the EU which had no connection with climate change. Russia wished to enter the World Trade Organisation on favourable terms, by being classified as a 'developing country'. In return for the EU agreeing to support him, Putin agreed to ratify Kyoto.[12]

Putin had also been made aware that, because Russia had closed down large parts of its most polluting industries since the collapse of the Soviet Union, its carbon emissions had already dropped very drastically since the cut-off year of 1990. This meant that Russia would start off way below its Kyoto allowance and would thus be able to make billions of dollars a year under the UN's Clean Development Mechanism from selling those 'carbon credits' which were a key part of the Kyoto system.

By this curious deal, when Russia ratified Kyoto on 18 November 2004, the 55 per cent threshold had finally been reached. The Protocol could at last come into force, which it did on 16 February 2005.

'Consensus' had won the day. The Kyoto bandwagon could now start rolling in earnest.

THE GREAT WINDPOWER DELUSION

At least in one part of the world, as we have seen, the politicians had already been attempting to meet their Kyoto commitments for some time. In the European Union preparations were already well advanced for the launch of the world's first 'emissions trading scheme' in 2005. Ever more legislation was being designed to meet the EU's Kyoto targets in other ways.

Right at the top of the EU's agenda, however, were its plans to replace fossil fuels with 'renewable' sources for the energy needed to power Europe's transport and, above all, to generate its electricity. At the top of this list was the EU's ambition to produce an ever greater percentage of its electricity from 'wind farms'.

Where Denmark, Germany and Spain had led the way, the Briitish government, as was clear from its 2003 Energy White Paper, was keen to follow. But it was around this time that the penny began seriously to drop that this dream of deriving unlimited 'free' electricity from the wind was very far from being all it had been cracked up to be.

The first and most serious failing of wind power was the simple fact that wind does not blow at a consistent speed, and often not at all. The wind companies invariably liked to talk of their turbines in terms of their 'capacity'; in other words, their potential output if the wind was blowing at optimum speed all the time. Politicians and the media almost invariably fell for this trick, fondly imagining that a '2 megawatt turbine' could consistently be relied on to produce two megawatts (2MW) of electricity.

Because wind speeds are so inconsistent, however, this in fact meant that the average output of a turbine in the UK was only around 25 per cent or a quarter of its capacity (known as the 'load factor').* Indeed all too often, notably on cold days in winter when electricity demand was at its highest, high pressure meant that there was not enough wind to keep the turbines turning at all.

In short, wind turbines were extraordinarily unreliable. Furthermore, thanks to the vagaries of the wind, they were also unpredictable. This meant that, in order to guarantee a continuous supply of electricity to the customers, alternative sources of power had to be kept permanently on standby or 'spinning reserve', ready to step in at a moment's notice to make up for the lack of supply from the wind farms. Even when the wind was blowing, this back-up capacity, usually gas-fired, would have to be kept running, using fuel, generating steam, emitting CO_2, ready to ramp up its turbines the moment sufficient supply from the wind machines stopped coming.*

---

* The figure for 2003 was 24.1 per cent rising to 26.1 per cent in 2004 (UK Energy Statistics, DUKES Table 7.4 on BERR website). As can be seen from the Renewable Energy Foundation website, the load factor of turbines (which only generate with optimum efficiency at windspeeds between 34 and 56 mph) varies wildly according to location, from 57 per cent on Shetland to 7 per cent on the edge of London.

This remained one of the best-kept secrets of the wind industry, because what it meant was that the wind turbines were not saving anything like the amount of CO_2 they liked to claim. Even with conventional power stations, some 'spinning reserve' was needed, to provide cover for when they might go off-stream, But the greater the number of wind farms that were built, the more necessary it would become to build new conventional power stations just to provide them with back-up. When seeking planning permission to build a new wind farm, developers would invariably boast that it was going to help combating global warming by saving 'X thousand tonnes of CO_2' from being emitted to the atmosphere. In fact it was going to save very much less.[†]

In reality the contribution made by windpower, both in terms of the electricity it generated and its 'carbon savings', was derisory. By 2005 Britain was priding itself on having built 1,200 turbines, dominating hundreds of square miles of countryside. But the total amount of electricity they produced was much less than half that generated by a single 1,200MW coal-fired or nuclear power station; and barely a sixth of that supplied by the huge 3,900MW coal-fired plant at Drax in Yorkshire.

When it was proposed that the largest windfarm in England should be built at Whinash in Cumbria, 27 huge turbines each two-thirds the height of Blackpool Tower, the developers boasted that this would save '178,000 tons of carbon emissions a year'. Yet even the *Guardian's* George Monbiot, the most prominent global warming crusader in Britain's media, had to admit that 'a single jumbo jet, flying from London to Miami and back every day, releases the climate-change equivalent of 520,000 tonnes of carbon dioxide a year'. One Boeing 747 thus cancelled out three giant wind farms.[13]

---

* Gas-fired power stations provided the most efficient form of back-up for wind power because they could be switched on and off comparatively quickly. Nuclear power stations had to run continuously, which meant that their output was described as 'base-load'. Coal-fired plants took much longer than gas to bring onstream.

† In 2007 the British wind industry was rapped over the knuckles for these exaggerated claims by the Avertising Standards Authority, To justify its claims for CO_2 savings it had been making a comparison with coal-fired stations, but the ASA ruled that the proper comparison should be with the emissions from gas-fired stations, which were only half those from coal. Thus the British Wind Energy Association had been inflating its claimed savings by 100 per cent.

Another illusion about windpower was that it was cheap. In fact generating electricity by wind turbines was significantly more expensive than conventional power sources. A study carried out for the Royal Academy of Engineering in 2004 showed that the cost of a kilowatt hour of electricity produced by an onshore wind turbine, including the cost of standby generation, was 5.4p; more than double that of power from gas (2.2p), nuclear (2.3p) or the more efficient coal-fired plants (2.5p). From an offshore windfarm, the 7.2p cost made it well over three times more expensive.[14]

One reason why this was not more widely recognised was because of the ingenious way the government had managed to conceal the massive subsidy given to the owners of wind turbines. Under the Renewables Obligation, the electricity supply companies were required to buy an ever higher percentage of their electricity from turbine owners, due to rise from 3 per cent in 2002 to 15 per cent and more in future years. In addition they had to pay a Climate Change Levy on every MW-hour of electricity produced from conventional sources, from which renewables were exempted.

The net effect of all this was that the electricity supply companies were forced to pay twice as much for wind-generated electricity as they did for conventional power. In 2005 this amounted to around £90 per MW-hour compared with the normal price of £45. But this was hidden from the public because the additional cost was merely added, without explanation, to their electricity bills.[15]

For the turbine developers themselves this created an extraordinary bonanza. Each 2MW turbine, although on average producing only around 500 kilowatts of electricity, earned its owners around £400,000 a year, of which £200,000 was the value of the electricity and £200,000 the hidden subsidy. A big windfarm might have dozens of such turbines, like the 140 2.3MW giants being erected in 2006 at Whitelee south of Glasgow, the largest on-shore windfarm in Europe. Covering 30 square miles of moorland, with an installed capacity of 322MW, this was due to earn its developers £32 million a year in subsidies alone. Yet its total, intermittently produced output would be only 7 per cent of that of a nuclear power plant occupying less than a 30th of the same area.*

* In 2005 Sir Donald Miller, the former head of Scottish Power, announced that to meet the EU's target of 20 per cent of the UK's power from renewable sources would by 2020 have cost a total of £30 billion in subsidies through higher electricity bills.

In many people's eyes, of course, wind turbines had another serious failing. It seemed incongruous that, in the name of some supposed 'environmental benefit', these vast industrial structures were all too often being erected in particularly beautiful stretches of countryside, such as the Scottish Highlands or the mountains of mid-Wales, severely intruding on their natural environment. Rising as much as 400 feet into the air, the height of a tall city office block or the spire of Salisbury Cathedral, these incongruous towers of steel, with their blades giving off a dull, low-frequency 'whump' each time they revolved, dominated the once-unspoiled landscape for miles around.

To others these towers seemed beautiful, not least because they symbolised man's belated attempt to 'save the planet' from his own folly. But even the greatest enthusiasts for wind power might have had pause for thought had they bothered to discover just how little in practice it was solving the problem which so concerned them. And a further huge practical drawback to turbines only became really apparent as ever more thousands of them came to be built.

The European countries which had led the way in building wind turbines were Denmark and Germany. But in 2002 Denmark announced that its dash for wind was so unbalancing its electricity supply, for so little benefit, that it was not going to build any more. In 2004, although turbines nominally represented 20 per cent of Denmark's electricity production, the wind blew so inconsistently that it in fact provided only 6 per cent of the power the country consumed.

Because at almost any given time it either had too little wind or too much, Denmark either had to import power at considerable cost from other countries, or, worse, it had to export its surplus wind-generated electricity at a loss to Norway (because there was no means of storing it). In 2004 this represented a staggering 84 per cent of all the power Danish turbines produced.[16] Yet the cost of the turbines had made Denmark's electricity easily the most expensive in Europe.

The more dependent a country became on wind power, the more likely it was that this would create serious instabilities in its electricity grid, as conventional power stations had to be switched on and off to compensate for the vagaries of the wind. This was why Ireland in 2003 decided to follow Denmark by putting a moratorium on any more turbines.

In practical terms, it was becoming all too obvious that the prospect of wind turbines being able to make any contribution to the 'fight against climate change' was virtually non-existent. But to the politicians and the officials in charge of the EU's and Britain's energy policy such facts were quite immaterial.

Indeed, no politician was more obviously carried away by these dreams than Tony Blair, who had personally endorsed his government's plans to generate 10 per cent of Britain's electricity from renewables by 2010, mainly from wind power. In July 2005 he made tackling 'climate change' the keynote policy of his six months in the chair of the G8 nations (alongside 'making poverty history' in Africa). In announcing this he said 'the science is well established and the dangers clear. For example, the number of people worldwide at risk of flooding has increased twenty-fold since the 1960s'.[17]

When, on 6 December that year, the opposition Conservative Party elected David Cameron as its new leader, eager to give his Party a new 'modernising' and 'compassionate' image, he at once announced that the fight against 'climate change' would be at the top of his party's agenda, To highlight his environmental credentials, he was photographed bicycling to work at the House of Commons (his chauffeur driving discreetly behind with a clean shirt and shoes). He flew off to Spitzbergen, to be filmed watching glaciers melting and driving a team of huskies across the disappearing Arctic ice. He applied for permission to erect a mini-wind turbine on the chimney of his Notting Hill home. It seemed as if the need to tackle global warming was virtually his only policy.

'SCIENTIFICALLY UNSOUND': DR LANDSEA WALKS OUT OF THE IPCC

Nothing had done more to put climate change at the top of the world's political agenda (at least in theory) than the extraordinary prestige of the IPCC. So far this had scarcely been dented by the questioning of the 'hockey stick', the central inspiration of its 2001 Report (TAR). But the list of those prepared to criticise the workings of the IPCC, even from within its own ranks, was growing, as was shown by a disturbing episode in the autumn of 2004 involving one of the world's leading authorities on hurricanes, Dr Chris Landsea.

As a research meteorologist with the National Oceanic and Atmospheric Administration and chair of the American Meteorological Society's Committee on Tropical Meteorology and Tropical Cyclones, Landsea was an unrivalled expert on Atlantic hurricanes, He had been a contributing author to the IPCC's SAR in 1996, again to the TAR in 2001; and he had been invited to contribute, specifically on Atlantic hurricanes, to the Fourth Assesment Report (4AR), due to appear in 2007.

In October 2004 he was therefore astonished to receive an advance press release from Dr Kevin Trenberth, the IPCC Lead Author who had invited him to contribute only days earlier. The heading to the release, which invited the media to attend a press conference to be given by Trenberth and others at the Harvard Medical School's Center for Health and the Global Environment', read 'Experts To Warn Global Warming Likely To Continue Spurring More Outbreaks Of Intense Hurricane Activity'.[18]

Landsea was shocked. Not only did his own work fail to support any view that global warming was causing an increase in hurricane activity; nor did any scientific study he was aware of. Moreover, neither of the IPCC's previous two reports had made any such claim.

He therefore emailed Trenberth to express his concern. 'I am wondering', he said, 'what has led you to all this big conclusion. Are you all announcing a new published paper in the field?' Asking again what work they proposed to quote as justification for such a claim, he reiterated that 'there are no known scientific studies that show a conclusive link between global warming and observed hurricane frequency'.[19]

Trenberth's press conference nevertheless went ahead as advertised. 'With four hurricanes and tropical storms hitting the United States in a recent five-week period', the press summary began, '2004 already is being called "The year of the hurricane" ... this year's unusually intense period of destructive weather activity could be a harbinger of what is to come as the effects of global warming become even more pronounced in future years, according to leading experts who participated today in a ... Harvard Medical School briefing.'

The results were everything Trenberth could have wanted, The conference made headlines all round the world, Typical was a much-quoted Reuters report headed 'Global Warming Effects Faster Than Feared', which began

> *'Recent storms, droughts and heatwaves are probably being caused by global warming, which means the effects of global warming are coming faster than anyone had feared, climate experts said on Thursday. The four hurricanes which bashed Florida and the Caribbean within a five-week period over the summer, intense storms over the Western Pacific,*

heatwaves that killed tens of thousands of Europeans last year and a continued drought across the US southwest are only the beginning, the experts said ...' [20]

It was not only hurricanes which Trenberth had thrown in to win his headlines. In particular he cited the record heatwave experienced in Europe in August 2003. This had already been widely ascribed to global warming and blamed for causing 35,000 deaths. [21]

After his earlier email to Trenberth, Landsea was amazed to see the comments on hurricanes. He now emailed the IPCC's chairman Dr Pachauri and other senior IPCC figures, insisting that there were no studies on hurricane activity to support Trenberth's sensational claims:

> *'There are many legitimate reasons to be concerned with global warming, but the evidence just is not there with hurricanes no matter how much it is trumped up for the media and the public, Proceeding with such announcements outside the proper IPCC process taints the credibility of climate-change science and will in the longer run diminish our influence over public policy.'* [22]

Landea asked the IPCC leadership for an assurance that the 2007 report would be true to science and would 'reflect the best available information'.

The IPCC's response was that, since the Harvard press conference was not an official IPCC event, Trenberth had the right to say whatever he wished, Pachauri went even further, arguing that Trenberth 'did not in any way misrepresent the IPCC and apparently his statements accurately reflected the IPCC's [Third Assessment Report]'. [23]

Landsea tartly replied that Trenberth's statements had certainly not reflected the 2001 report, which he himself had helped to write. So shocked was he by the IPCC's unqualified defence of Trenberth that he then wrote a letter of resignation:

> *'Because of Dr Trenberth's pronouncements, the IPCC process on our assessment of these crucial extreme events has been subverted and compromised, its neutrality lost ...*
>
> *It is of more than passing interest to note that Dr Trenberth, while eager to share his views on global warming and hurricabes with the media, declined to do so at the Climate Variability and Change Conference in January where he made several presentations. Perhaps he was concerned that such speculation ... would not stand up to the scrutiny of fellow climate scientists.*

I cannot in good faith continue to contribute to a process that I view as both being motivated by preconceived agendas and being scientifically unsound. As the IPCC leadership has seen no wrong in Dr Trenberth's actions and have retained him as a Lead Author for the [Fourth Assessment Report]. I have decided to no longer participate in the IPCC AR4.' [24]

Landsea's resignation went virtually unreported. Its authority undiminished, the IPCC carried on as if nothing had happened.

THE IPCC AND THE HOUSE OF LORDS

The IPCC now came under fire from another and unexpected direction. In London in 2005 the House of Lords Select Committee on Economic Affairs decided to hold an inquiry into 'The Economics of Climate Change'. Most of its members held generally to the 'consensus' view. But one or two, including Lord Lawson of Blaby, better known as Nigel Lawson from the days when he was Mrs Thatcher's Chancellor of the Exchequer in the 1980s, were disposed to 'scepticism'. The committee's 'Specialist Adviser' Professor David Pearce, an emeritus professor of economics at University College, London, who had taken part in the workings of the IPCC, was also not convinced by its 'consensus'.

What therefore marked out this committee's work as highly unusual was its choice of the expert witnesses called to give evidence. These fell into two distinctly opposing groups (with some in the middle). On one hand, they included an array of leading figures representing the IPCC 'consensus', such as its chairman Dr Pachauri, Sir John Houghton and Sir David King. On the other, the committee invited some of the IPCC's more trenchant critics, such as Richard Lindzen, Nils-Axel Mörner, Fred Singer, Paul Reiter and Ross McKitrick, one of the duo who had exposed the 'hockey stick'. Never before had so many leading spokesmen for both sides of the argument been lined up together in the same forum.

The spokesmen for the 'consensus' all gave their versions of the orthodox IPCC view, often making dismissive references to its critics. Houghton told the committee that there were '20 or 25' climate computer models of 'top rank' in the world, but that the one run by his UK Met Office's Hadley Centre was believed to be 'the best in the world'. He spoke at length about Dr Lindzen, claiming that he was the 'only credible scientist in the world' who believed that water vapour as a greenhouse gas could give negative feedback (i.e. could lower rather than raise temperatures). He said that Lindzen's 'hand-waving arguments' on this point had been 'very thoroughly gone through by lots of other people' and that they had found no substance to them (to get a properly accurate picture 'you have to do very careful modelling').

Professor King laid repeated emphasis on the value of the IPCC's computer models to predict anything from the increased frequency of heatwaves such as that experienced in Europe in 2003 (which by 2030, he claimed, would be the norm) to droughts causing fires in the Amazon rainforest which 'would increase global warming quite substantially'.

He also attacked Lindzen as one of the 'very few' serious scientists to hold sceptical views. But the models had proved him wrong on water vapour. Otherwise, he said, the small group of sceptical scientists were 'not seriously regarded'. 'Without proper evidence' they claimed, for instance, that sea levels were not rising or that global warming was due to 'increased solar activity'. But the most vocal sceptics of all were merely well-funded 'professional lobbyists' who fell into the same category as those 'lobbyists for the tobacco companies who claim that links between smoking and ill-health are still not proven'.

These and other upholders of the IPCC 'consensus', supported by a lengthy memorandum from the Royal Society, were of course aware that Lindzen had also been invited to appear before the committee, and he duly obliged by being equally disparaging in his response.

In a written statement Lindzen agreed there was a basic 'consensus' that the world had seen a 'modest' 0.6 degree warming in the twentieth century, that human activity had contributed to a rise in CO_2 levels and that this would have a 'forcing' effect on temperatures. But from then on, as he amplified in his oral testimony, he set out some of the reasons why he differed so profoundly from the 'consensus'.

As on earlier occasions, he directed particular fire at both the inadequacies of the computer models and at the way the IPCC's Summaries for Policymakers were politically rigged to give such a distorted picture of the findings of the technical reports. He pointed out that if the assumptions programmed into the models about the effect of increased CO_2 were correct then temperatures should have risen in the twentieth century by a full 3 degrees rather than just 0.6. He gave chapter and verse, as he had earlier done to the Senate committee, on how the 2001 Summary for Policymakers had blurred over the clear admission of the scientific report that there were still major uncertainties about the effects of water vapour and cloud cover. His response to Houghton's views on water vapour was 'astonishment'.

In general, Lindzen concluded that, while enormous resources and tens of billions of dollars had gone into promoting an alarmist view of what was happening to the earth's climate, there was very little scientific basis for such alarm. 'The global warming issue', as he put it, 'parts company with normative science at a pretty early stage'. Such warming as might occur would not present society with any great challenge: 'nor would such (or even greater) warming be associated with more storminess, greater extremes, etc'. He ended by quoting Orwell that 'the slovenliness of our language makes it easier for us to have foolish thoughts', observing that

> 'there can be very little doubt that the language used to convey alarm has been sloppy at best. Unfortunately much of the sloppiness appears to be intentional. The difficulties of discourse in the absence of a shared vocabulary are, I fear, rather evident.'

Since this inquiry was being held by the Lords Economics Affairs committee, it was natural that many of its witnesses were economists.[25] One of these was Professor David Henderson of the Westminster Business School, formerly chief economist to the OECD (Organisation of Economic Co-Operation and Development). In 2002 he and a colleague, Ian Castles, formerly the chief statistician to the Australian government, had caused quite a stir by pointing out what they saw as a fundamental flaw in the methods used by the IPCC in its 2000 Special Report on Emissions Scenarios (SRES) to predict the future economic growth rates of developing countries, and therefore their likely emissions of CO_2.

Contrary to best academic practice, the IPCC had based its evaluations of future economic performance on 'market exchange rates' rather than on 'purchasing power parity', which gives a more accurate picture of a country's Gross Domestic Product in terms of the volume of goods and services it actually produces. This meant that, in real terms, the current size of economies in the developing world had been greatly underestimated (in the case of China, for instance, its actual output, according to Henderson, was around four times larger than the way it was generally presented in terms of exchange rate values).[26]

The significance of this was that the IPCC rested its forecasts on the assumption that by 2100 the economies of the developing world, such as China, would have converged with those of the existing developed world. It was on this projection that their predicted CO_2 emissions were based. But since, in real terms, their economies were already much larger than was indicated by 'market exchange rates', this meant that the IPCC was greatly exaggerating the degree of economic growth needed for them to catch up with the developed world.

Thus its forecasts of their likely CO_2 emissions, Henderson and Castles argued, had also become wildly exaggerated. The IPCC, for instance, forecast that real incomes across the whole of Asia would by 2100 be 70 times higher than they were in 2000. Current *per capita* GDP in the US would have been surpassed by, among others, North Korea, Libya, Algeria, Tunisia and Latvia. It was on this kind of projection that the IPCC rested its estimates of the rise in CO_2 levels.

In 2002 Castles had attempted to put this argument in two letters to Dr Pachauri, as the IPCC's chairman, but received no reply. Subsequently, however, their critique of the IPCC's methodology had attracted considerable attention, particularly when in 2003 it was prominently reported in two articles in the *Economist*. One of these began:

> *'you might think that a policy issue which puts at stake hundreds of billions of dollars of global output would arouse at least the casual interest of the world's economics and finance ministries. You would be wrong.'* [27]

A good many economists took the point made by the two men seriously, including another of the Lords committee's witnesses, an eminent Dutch economist, Professor Richard Tol of the University of Hamburg. Despite being an active participant in the IPCC, a supporter of the 'consensus' on global warming and differing from Henderson and Castles on other points, Tol agreed with them that to 'assume convergence based on market exchange rates' was 'ludicrous'.

So irked was the IPCC by the publicity given to Henderson and Castles that in December 2003 it put out an angry press release, originally in Dr Pachauri's own name, one of only two it issued that year. Running detailed computer models, it said, had shown that the claim that there was 'an upward bias in the SRES scenarios is totally unfounded'. The release poured scorn on the two economists for having 'completely ignored' the fact that, with greater prosperity, the developing countries would take steps to reduce their emissions. It ended 'there is absolutely no reason to believe that, in the longer term, lower economic development would, all things being equal, result in lower emissions'.[28]

Another witness highly critical of the IPCC was Professor Ross McKitrick, the Canadian economist, whose devastating comments on the analysis he and McIntyre had carried out on the 'hockey stick' graph have already been quoted, On this issue he was particularly anxious to emphasise the IPCC's failure to carry out even the most 'basic due diligence' in checking the methods used to produce the 'hockey stick'. 'Due to a combination of mathematical error and a dysfunctional review process they ended up promoting the exact wrong conclusion'.

But prior to this McKitrick also criticised the calibre of the team responsible for producing the SRES forecasts. A striking difference between the IPCC's second and third reports, he noted, was how so many 'mainstream economists' had dropped out. Since Castles and Henderson had focused expert attention on SRES, there had been 'a growing body of criticism of the IPCC's handling of economic issues'. SRES did not use 'conventional economic modelling' to produce 'what would normally be called "forecasts" or "predictions". They call their outputs "storylines" or "scenarios" and emphasise that they are speculative.'

The list of contributors to the SRES and the 2001 report had included only a

> *'small and non-representative sample of economists, among a long list of government bureaucrats and academics from other disciplines. Moreover I know that some of the contributing economists are quite critical of the final Reports, One of them is John Reilly of the Massachusetts Institute of Technology. In an article in Canada's* National Post *(27 November 2002) he said that the SRES exercise was "in my view a kind of insult to science" and the method was "lunacy". He said his lab refused a request from the IPCC to let their models be "tweaked" to support the IPCC scenarios.'*

McKitrick went on to say that he belonged to an international research group of some 100 academic economists drawn from universities across Canada and the US, many with international reputations. Not one of them was involved in the IPCC or had been asked to participate in the SRES exercise.

He and a colleague had recently carried out a study of the SRES emissions scenarios, using standard econometric methods, and found that the IPCC forecasts were absurdly high. Whereas it was highly implausible that peak emissions by 2050 could be higher than 10 billion tonnes, most of the IPCC scenarios showed between 15 and 30 billion tonnes. Only seven of the SRES scenarios were 'within five standard deviations of the current mean through to the year 2050'. Many departed 'more than 10 standard deviations above the observed mean; eight lie more than *fifty* standard deviations above the observed mean'.

Yet 'of even more concern', as McKitrick argued, was that,

> *'even after serious flaws in the SRES have come to light, the IPCC has chosen to use the same scenarios for the Fourth Assessment Report (AR4), even though it is not due out until 2007. In making this decision, the IPCC has effectively communicated to the scholarly community that external criticism will have little impact on its work.'*

When the Lords Committee came to draft its report, its members wished to produce a document which, despite their widely differing views, was nevertheless unanimous. Their findings therefore accepted that global warming was a real threat, calling for drastic action. But this was matched by a series of recommendations highly critical of the IPCC itself, somewhat forlornly calling on the British government to press for wholesale improvement in its procedures and the techniques used to reach its findings.

The real value of this Parliamentary inquiry lay in the evidence put forward by its array of witnesses. For the first time in any public report the leading spokesmen for the 'consensus' had been pitted against some of their most expert critics. One of these provided such a uniquely revealing picture of how the IPCC worked from the inside that his evidence merits a section to itself.

AN INSIDER'S VIEW OF THE IPCC AT WORK

Professor Paul Reiter was the man whose question about the melting snows of Kilimanjaro had prompted a flummoxed David King to storm off the platform in Moscow. A British-born professor at the Institut Pasteur in Paris and a senior adviser to the World Health Organisation, Reiter was the world's leading authority on mosquito-borne diseases. And in his evidence to the Lords committee, he explained how, before the IPCC's 1996 report, he had been invited to join its Working Group II, to act as a 'contributory author' to Chapter 18 assessing the impact of global warming on human health.[29]

Among his fellow 'contributing authors' he had been surprised to find one whose 'principal interest was the effectiveness of motor cycle helmets (plus a paper on the health effect of cell phones)'. Not one of the chapter's 'lead authors' had ever written a research paper on mosquito-borne diseases. Two were full-time 'environmental activists', one of whom had written articles on topics ranging from mercury poisoning to land mines.

It soon became clear that the preoccupation of the lead authors was to demonstrate that global warming would increase the range and intensity of 'vector-borne' diseases (those spread by insects and other carriers), as 'predicted' by a 'highly simplistic' computer model.

Reiter tried to explain that malaria was not a disease confined to hot countries, as was familiar to anyone versed in the history of the disease. One of the worst recorded epidemics of malaria had been in the frozen wastes of Siberia. The Palace of Westminster itself, as he pointed out to the members of the House of Lords, stood on the site of what had once been a notorious malarial swamp.

When he saw the chapter which had resulted from their deliberations, he was shocked at how 'the amateurish text' reflected the 'limited knowledge' of the 21 authors. Almost the only texts cited were 'relatively obscure' articles, almost all suggesting that disease became more prevalent in a warm climate. The text was riddled with 'glaring indicators of the ignorance of the authors', such as a claim that 'mosquito species that transmit malaria do not usually survive where the mean winter temperature drops below 16–18°C' (some species, Reiter pointed out, can survive temperatures of 25 degrees below zero).

In their determination to prove that greater warming was already causing malaria to move to higher altitudes, the authors quoted claims that 'had repeatedly been made by environmental activists', but which had been 'roundly denounced in the scientific literature'.

'In summary', Reiter went on, 'the treatment of this issue by the IPCC was ill-informed, biased and scientifically unacceptable'. Yet the Summary for Policymakers, drafted at political level, was able to use this chapter to support a claim that 'climate change is likely to have wide-ranging and mostly adverse impacts on human health, with significant loss of life'. It went on to predict that climate change at the upper end of the IPCC's predicted range would increase the proportion of the world's population vulnerable to malaria to 60 per cent, leading to 50–80 million additional cases every year.

Following the publication of the report, Reiter was shocked to see how

> *'these confident pronouncements, untrammelled by details of the complexity of their subject and the limitations of these models, were widely quoted as "the consensus of 1,500 of the world's top scientists" (occasionally the number quoted was 2,500). This clearly did not apply to the chapter on human health, yet, at the time, eight out of nine major web sites that I checked placed these diseases at the top of the list of adverse impacts of climate change, quoting the IPCC.'*

Reiter went on to describe how, when he was invited back to take part in preparing the third, 2001 report, he and a colleague, who were the only authors with any knowledge of vector-borne diseases, repeatedly found themselves 'at loggerheads with persons who insisted on making authoritative pronouncements, although they had little or no knowledge of our speciality'. Reiter eventually resigned, although when he saw a first draft of the report he was shocked to see his name still listed as a contributor. Only with great difficulty did he eventually succeed in having it removed.

For the IPCC's fourth report (AR4) due to be published in 2007, Reiter was nominated by the US government as a 'lead author'. He was rejected by the 'IPPC Working Group II Bureau' in favour of two 'lead authors', a hygienist and a specialist in fossil faeces. Neither had any knowledge of tropical diseases but they had both co-written articles with 'environmental activists'. When Professor Reiter questioned this with a relevant IPCC official (who worked for the UK Met Office's Hadley Centre in Exeter), she thanked him for his 'continued interest in the IPCC' and told him that selection was decided by governments: 'it is the governments of the world who make up the IPCC, define its remit and direction' according to 'the IPCC Principles and Procedures which have been agreed by governments'. To his question as to why the 'lead authors' chosen appeared to have no expertise in the chapter's subject matter, he got no answer.

Faced with such evidence, Reiter went on to muse how:

'the issue of consensus is key to understanding the limitations of IPCC pronouncements. Consensus is the stuff of politics, not of science ... in the age of information, popular knowledge of scientific issues – particularly issues of health and the environment – is awash in the tide of misinformation, much of it presented in the "big talk" of professional scientists.

Alarmist activists operating in well-funded advocacy groups have a lead role in creating this misinformation. In many cases they manipulate public perceptions with emotive and fiercely judgmental "scientific" pronouncements, adding a tone of danger and urgency to attract media coverage ... these notions are often reinforced by drawing attention to peer-reviewed scientific articles that appear to support their pronouncements, regardless of whether these articles are widely endorsed by the scientific community. Scientists who challenge these alarmists are rarely given priority by the media, and are often presented as "sceptics".

The democratic process requires elected representatives to respond to the concerns and fears generated in this process. Denial is rarely an effective strategy, even in the face of preposterous claims. The pragmatic option is to express concern, create new regulations and increase funding for research ...

In reality a genuine concern for mankind and the environment demands the inquiry, accuracy and scepticism that are intrinsic to authentic science. A public that is not aware of this is vulnerable to abuse.'

As we observed in our previous book, *Scared To Death*, Reiter's comments provided an admirably acute analysis not just of how the panic over global warming had been orchestrated but of how so many other lesser 'scares' had been propelled into the headlines in recent years. It caught the essence of the modern 'scare phenomenon'. And this time it had come from an 'authentic' scientist, puzzled by how mad the world had grown.

So far as the wider world was concerned, however, whatever was said within the confines of the British House of Lords mattered not a jot. The committee's report was scarcely noticed by the media, to much of which the IPCC still consisted of '2,500 of the world's top climate scientists' all agreed that global warming posed an unprecedented threat to the future of the planet.

What mattered to the wider world in 2005 was that Tony Blair, in chairing the G8, had put 'climate change' at the top of the world's political agenda. And whatever unusual events the world's weather now came up with instantly made headlines as being caused by global warming.

This had already happened with the European heatwave of 2003. Inevitably it now happened again with a vengeance when, at the end of August 2005, the sixth worst recorded hurricane in history brought catastrophe to the city of New Orleans.

'ITS REAL NAME IS GLOBAL WARMING'

Even before Hurricane Katrina hit the Louisiana coast on 29 August 2005, a clamant *Time* headline was asking 'Is global warming fuelling Katrina?'.[30] The verdict of ABC News was unequivocal: 'the finger of blame points quite clearly at global warming'.[31] And the day after the city began to disappear under the water pouring from Lake Pontchartrain over those collapsing earth banks known as levees, the *Boston Globe* widened out the story to pronounce, in terms that echoed much of the rest of the media:

> *'The hurricane that struck Louisiana yesterday was nicknamed Katrina by the National Weather Service. Its real name is global warming.*
>
> *When the year began with a two-foot snowfall in Los Angeles, the cause was global warming.*
>
> *When 124-mile-an-hour winds shut down nuclear plants in Scandinavia and cut power to hundreds of thousands of people in Ireland and the United Kingdom, the driver was global warming.*
>
> *When a severe drought in the Midwest dropped water levels in the Missouri River to their lowest on record earlier this summer, the reason was global warming.*
>
> *In July, when the worst drought on record triggered wildfires in Spain and Portugal and left water levels in France at their lowest in 30 years, the explanation was global warming.*
>
> *When a lethal heat wave in Arizona kept temperatures above 110 degrees and killed more than 20 people in one week, the culprit was global warming.*
>
> *And when the Indian city of Bombay (Mumbai) received 37 inches of rain in one day – killing 1,000 people and disrupting the lives of 20 million others – the villain was global warming.*
>
> *As the atmosphere warms, it generates longer droughts, more-intense downpours, more-frequent heat waves, and more-severe storms.*
>
> *Although Katrina began as a relatively small hurricane that glanced off south Florida, it was supercharged with extraordinary intensity by the relatively blistering sea surface temperatures in the Gulf of Mexico.*

The consequences are as heartbreaking as they are terrifying.
Unfortunately, very few people in America know the real name of
Hurricane Katrina because the coal and oil industries have spent millions
of dollars to keep the public in doubt about the issue.' [32]

Meanwhile, across the country in Hollywood, preparations were
afoot for the biggest popular wake-up call on the disaster facing the
planet yet to have been devised. Al Gore and his advisers, led by Jim
Hansen of NASA's Goddard Institute for Space Studies, were putting
together a documentary film that was destined to appear on cinema
and TV screens across the world.

In political and media terms, hysteria over global warming was
about to reach its height.

Notes

1. 'Now the Pentagon tells Bush: Climate change will destroy us',
   Observer, 11 November 2004.
2. Rosemary Righter, written evidence to House of Lords Select Committee on Economic Affairs, The Economics of Climate Change, Vol. II:
   Evidence, HL Paper 12-II, published 6 July 2005. Righter was the Chief
   Leader Writer on the *Times*.
3. Hadley Centre website.
4. *Science*, 9 January 2004.
5. Evidence given by King to Commons Select Committee on the Environment, Hansard, 30 March, 2004 *http://www.publications.*
   parliament.uk/pa/cm200304/cmselect/cmenvaud/490/4033003.htm
6. 'Why Antarctica will soon be the only place to live', interview with
   Geoffrey Lean, *The Independent*, 2 May 2004.
7. *New York Times*, 2 December 2003.
8. See transcript of press conference given by Alexander Illarionov on 8
   July 2004, available on *http://www.rightsidenews.com/200807241524/*
   energy-and-environment/results-of-the-climate-change-and-kyoto-
   protocol-seminar-in-moscow.html and other internet sources.
9. 'Bad manners at the Moscow Kyoto Protocol Seminar', *Financial Post*,
   13 July 2004.
10. Illarionov, *op. cit.*
11. *http://www.nationalreview.com/comment/murray200407230903.asp*
12. This is endorsed by David King in his book *The Hot Topic* (published
    with Gabrielle Walker, Bloomsbury, 2008). 'Following David King's re-
    port back from Russia', the book states (pp. 219–220), 'Tony Blair went
    to EU leaders to propose a horse-trade. If Russia ratified Kyoto, the EU

would support its entry into the WTO. This proved a powerful trump card.'

13. George Monbiot, 'An ugly face of ecology', *Guardian*, 26 April 2006. After a much-publicised public enquiry, the Whinash wind farm was turned down.

14. 'The Cost of Generating Electricity' (Royal Academy of Engineering, 2004).

15. According to Dr Paul Golby, chief executive of E-ON UK (formerly Powergen) 'without the renewable obligation certificates nobody would be building wind farms', *Daily Telegraph*, 26 March 2005.

16. ABS Energy Research 2006 Wind Power Report, quoting chief executive of Eltra.

17. *G8 2005* website.

18. This account is based on L. Solomon, *The Deniers, op. cit.*, pp. 29–36.

19. C. Landsea email to Kevin Trenberth and Linda Mears, 21 October 2004, *http://www.nuclear.com/archive/2005/01/20/20050120-001.html*

20. Maggie Fox, Reuters report, 21 October 2004.

21. Shaoni Battarchariya, 'European heatwave caused 35,000 deaths', *New Scientist*, 10 October 2003. The article cited the Earth Policy Institute (EPI) and the IPCC as warning that 'such deaths are likely to increase, as "even more extreme weather events lie ahead"'. Less excitable meteorologists pointed out that the cause of the 2003 heat wave was not global warming but a stationary high-pressure cell bringing hot air from North Africa to western Europe. It was an unusual but entirely natural phenomenon. A 2001 study in the *British Medical Journal* had reported that extreme cold caused 50,000 additional deaths a year in Britain alone, dwarfing the Europe-wide deaths attributed to 2003's extreme heat. This would not stop Gore and many others ascribing the 2003 heat wave to global warming for years to come.

22. Landsea, email message to Dr R. Pachauri, *et al.*, 'Hurricanes and global warming for the IPCC', 5 November 2004, website as above.

23. R. K. Pachauri's response, 20 November 2004, *ibid.*

24. Landsea, 'Open letter to the Community', 17 January 2005, *http://science policy.colorado.edu/prometheus/archives/science_policy_general/000318chris_landsea_leaves.html*

25. Other than Lindzen, one of the few witnesses concerned directly with the science of climate change was Dr Nils-Axel Mörner, until 2003 the chairman of the INQUA Commission on Sea Level Change. As in Moscow the previous year, he contrasted the picture given by the IPCC's computer models with the results of field observations all over the world which showed sea levels rising much more slowly, if at all.

26. Castles, I., and Henderson, D., 'The IPCC emission scenarios: an economic-statistical critique', *Energy and Environment*, 14 (2-3), 159–185.

27. *The Economist*, 8 November, 2003.
28. IPCC Press Release, 'IPCC Press Information on AR4 and emissions scenarios', Milan, 8 December 2003.
29. Written evidence given by Professor Paul Reiter to the House of Lords Select Committee on Economic Affairs, The Economics of Climate Change: Vol. II, Evidence, pp. 284–288.
30. *Time*, 29 August 2005.
31. ABC News, 14 September 2006.
32. 'Katrina's real name', *Boston Globe*, 30 August 2005.

6

Hysteria reaches its height
Gore and the EU unite to save the planet:
2006–2007

'The maps of the world will have to be redrawn.'

Sir David King, quoted in Al Gore's
An Inconvenient Truth, 2006

'This disaster is not set to happen in some science fiction future many years ahead, but in our lifetime. Unless we act now ... these consequences, disastrous as they are, will be irreversible.'

Prime Minister Tony Blair, October 29, 2006 [1]

'It is irresponsible, reckless and deeply amoral to question the seriousness of the situation, The time for diagnosis is over. The time to act is now.'

Gro Harlem Bruntland, May 9, 2007 [2]

'Almost everywhere, climate change denial now looks as stupid and as unacceptable as Holocaust denial.'

George Monbiot, *The Guardian*, 21 September 2006

Of all the world's politicians trying to identify themselves with the fight to 'save the planet' none was more prominent than the man who had been at the centre of this battle for nearly 20 years; who now liked to introduce himself to audiences all over the world with the words 'I used to be the next President of America'.

In the summer of 2006, with the full backing of the Hollywood publicity machine, Al Gore launched an unprecedented bid to project the threat of global warming to a worldwide mass-audience. His screen version of *An Inconvenient Truth* raced up the charts to become the highest-earning documentary film in history. The book version immediately became a runaway best-seller. [3]

The publicity-release for *An Inconvenient Truth* began:

'humanity is sitting on a ticking time bomb. If the vast majority of the world's scientists are right, we have just ten years to avert a major

catastrophe that could send our entire planet into a tail-spin of epic destruction involving extreme weather, floods, droughts, epidemics and killer heat waves beyond anything we have ever experienced.'

Much of the screen version was centred on Gore presenting a slide show to large, rapt audiences of mainly young people, interspersed with film clips. As with everything Gore did, his presentation was heavily larded with personal autobiography.

The movie opened with shots of his family's ranch in Tennessee, to convey his love of unspoiled but now threatened nature. A traffic accident which left his young son hovering on the edge of death was recalled to symbolise how he learned to appreciate the priceless value of something one is in danger of losing. His sister had died of smoking-related cancer because she believed the lies told by tobacco companies. This, Gore conveyed, was reminiscent of the similar lies now being told by those trying to deny the menace of global warming. Their father, Senator Albert Gore, had responded by ordering that the family farm must no longer grow tobacco.

Gore recounted how he had first come to see climate change as by far the greatest threat ever to face mankind when he attended those classes given by his hero Roger Revelle in the 1960s; the man who had first alerted the world to the soaring levels of CO_2. It was this which opened for Gore the 'window' on what was to become the overriding cause of his life.

With the aid of powerful imagery and dramatic graphs, Gore pulled out all the emotional stops. Beginning with shots of fragile Planet Earth from space, vanishing glaciers and those fast-disappearing snows of Kilimanjaro, he moved on to a redrawn version of the 'hockey stick', apparently based on his 'friend' Dr Lonnie Thompson's researches into ice cores from Himalayan and Andean glaciers. This allowed for the reappearance of the 'Mediaeval Warm Period', although this was now shown as only a tiny 'blip'. But then in the twentieth century the graph hurtled dramatically upwards to levels never before known (with Gore having to be hoisted up on a lift beside the graph to demonstrate how terrifyingly high they were now rising).

He took a side-swipe at the 'global warming sceptics', a group 'diminishing almost as fast as those mountain glaciers', who had 'launched a fierce attack on the "hockey stick"'. But, fortunately, he was able to explain how other scientists, above all Dr Thompson, had since confirmed Michael Mann's 'basic conclusions in multiple ways'.* And shown alongside it was the graph of CO_2 levels in the atmosphere, also hurtling upwards. It was obvious how the two matched almost exactly.

Nothing was missing from Gore's recital: poignant images of polar bears struggling to survive, even drowning as the Arctic ice melted; penguin populations plummeting by 70 per cent as their Antarctic ice shelves crumbled; chilling shots of the tragedy which had engulfed New Orleans only a few months earlier when it was devastated by Hurricane Katrina.

The horrors he used to illustrate his points fell into three main categories. The first was that the melting of all that ice, at the Poles, in Greenland, on the world's glaciers, would produce too much water. Sea levels would rise by 20 feet, inundating many of the most populous places on the planet. Computer-enhanced satellite images showed how part or all of many of its most famous cities would be engulfed, from Shanghai and Beijing to New York and San Francisco. 60 million people would be displaced in Calcutta and Bangladesh alone; another 20 million in China. As the world's climate systems were thrown into chaos, there was already evidence of cyclones, tornadoes and floods arriving with an intensity never recorded before (cue for shots of New Orleans under water).

Elsewhere the problem would be too little water. The melting of the Himalayan ice sheet, on which seven major river systems depended, would eventually rob 40 per cent of the world's population of their water supplies. Lake Chad in Africa, once the world's sixth largest lake, had already, thanks to global warming, all-but dried up: a significant factor in the tragedy wracking that whole region of Africa, from famine to the genocide in Darfur.

The third problem would be the massive disruption of nature wrought by the changing climate. This would lead to a mass-extinction of species, already 1,000 times higher than the normal rate; and to an explosion in 'vector-borne' diseases, as mosquitoes and other carriers rapidly extended their range into once-cooler parts of the world where people and forests were already dying as a result.

This apocalyptic vision, claimed Gore, was now endorsed by every climate scientist in the world (apart from that tiny handful of 'sceptics', who were vanishing as fast as the glaciers). Citing a recent study by Naomi Oreskes, he presented a graphic showing that the

---

* Mann was only named in the book version.

'number of peer-reviewed articles dealing with "climate change" published in scientific journals in the previous 10 years' was '928'. 'Percentage of articles in doubt as to the cause of global warming', he triumphantly revealed, 'zero'.

But all was not lost. What was called for was an unprecedented human effort to avert this catastrophe. Greenhouse gas emissions must be cut back by 60 per cent. And on all sides there was evidence of how this could be done: from the tens of thousands of wind turbines appearing in America and Europe to carbon emission trading schemes ('the European Union has adopted this US innovation' as he said in the book, 'and is making it work effectively').

Everyone, Gore exhorted, could make a contribution to this cosmic battle, by such means (he listed them) as using energy-efficient light bulbs; insulating homes; walking or using a bicycle instead of a car; eating less meat; composting food waste; unplugging the TV and computers instead of leaving them on standby.

The impact of Gore's skilfully made movie was enormous. Greeted with rapturous reviews, it was soon breaking box-office records. Urged on by such a call to arms, it was not surprising that, for those who shared Gore's view, their impatience with anyone still daring to question it reached new heights. For a long time, like Gore himself, they had liked to claim that the only scientists who 'denied' global warming were those who were in some way funded by energy companies or 'Big Oil'. But in April 2006, they had been given a new term of abuse for all these 'contrarians', when a long-time media crusader in the cause, Scott Pelley of CBS, was asked why his two latest reports on global warming on *60 Minutes* had not featured a single contribution from a scientist who was sceptical about global warming.[4]

'If I do an interview with Elie Wiesel', replied Pelley (referring to the concentration camp survivor who won the Nobel Peace prize in 1986), 'am I required as a journalist to find a holocaust denier?' This attempt to draw a parallel between global warming sceptics and those who denied the historical facts of Hitler's murder of six million Jews quickly caught on. By September, the *Guardian's* George Monbiot (as quoted at the head of this chapter) was writing that 'climate change denial now looks as stupid and as unacceptable as Holocaust denial'. He may well have been inspired by the contributor two days earlier to an American 'green' blog, praising Monbiot's latest book, who had carried this even further, exclaiming (in words which were themselves to win wide currency):

'When we've finally gotten serious about global warming, when the impacts are really hitting us and we're in a full worldwide scramble to minimize the damage, we should have war crimes trials for these bastards – some sort of climate Nuremberg.' [5]

'Holocaust deniers' or not, the chorus of media acclaim given to Gore's film had already begun to arouse some very different responses, from scientists such as Professor Bob Carter, an outspoken Australian palaeoclimatologist. So shocked was Carter by Gore's cavalier approach to the facts that, shortly after the film's launch, he exploded to a journalist that Gore's 'propaganda crusade is mostly based on junk science'. 'His arguments are so weak that they are pathetic. It is incredible that they and his film are commanding public attention'.[6]

MANY INCONVENIENT UNTRUTHS

Over the following months, others began to subject the claims in Gore's film to rather more measured analysis. In general they agreed that he had produced nothing but a caricature of the familiar case for global warming. He had picked over the literature for almost every extreme projection he could find, then exaggerated them still further. But it was when each of his claims came to be tested in detail against the latest scientific knowledge that the real flaws in his argument began to be exposed.

For a start there was his opening eulogy to his 'hero' Roger Revelle, without any reference to the fact that Revelle had in his later years consistently urged caution on taking any precipitate action to combat global warming.

Then there was Gore's unabashed reliance on his version of the famous 'hockey stick'. As a nod to the fact that Mann's original graph had been so trenchantly questioned, the graphic Gore made so much of did include three tiny warming 'blips' between 1100 and 1400. But even of these, he labelled only one, between 1360 and 1370, as the 'Mediaeval Warm Period', by the trick of showing the Middle Ages as having begun in 1200, rather than two centuries earlier as is common usage.

Still more puzzling was the question of how Gore had come by his version of the 'hockey stick'. He claimed it was based on the ice-core studies which his 'friend' Dr Thompson had used to measure temperatures in past centuries (film showed Thompson pulling out ice cores from glaciers). These 'independent' measurements, according to Gore (he called them 'Dr Thompson's thermometer'), had confirmed that Mann's original 'hockey stick' graph was right.

Assiduous researchers, however, could find no trace of the graph in Thompson's published work. It eventually appeared that Gore's graph had been cobbled together solely for the purposes of the film. It was not based on Thompson's data at all (which related only to precipitation levels at high altitudes). Gore's version had been created by splicing together elements of Mann's own graph with late twentieth-century temperature data from the UK's Hadley Centre. In other words, by strangely circular logic, Gore was using an adapted version of Mann's 'hockey stick' to 'prove' that Mann's graph was right.[7]

The other powerfully persuasive graph central to Gore's case, also based on ice core readings, was that showing the rises and falls in CO_2 over the past 500,000 years exactly matching the rises and falls in temperature. The two were shown as happening almost simultaneously, as if any rise in CO_2 had caused an almost immediate rise in temperature. Yet, as had been shown by the very studies on which Gore relied for his data, the fluctuations in temperature did not follow those in CO_2. The relationship was the other way round. First temperatures rose, then CO_2 levels followed, after a delay which could be long as 800 years.[8]

Then there were those iconic 'snows of Kilimanjaro', cited in the US Senate by Hilary Clinton and John McCain as evidence for global warming which could 'not be refuted by any scientist'.[9] In fact observers first noted the receding of the ice cap on the summit of Africa's highest mountain shortly after it was first climbed in 1889. Most of the retreat had taken place before 1950. Detailed recent studies concluded that this was due not to global warming but to a sharp drop in precipitation recorded in the area from 1880 on, primarily due to extensive local deforestation.[10]

Few images in Gore's film were made to seem more shocking than those of retreating glaciers in the Andes, the Alps and the USA, implying that glaciers were sharply receding all over the world. But the film ignored a number of recent studies reflecting a much more complex picture.[11]

Glaciers have been perpetually retreating and advancing for millennia, not in response to changes in CO_2 but synchronous with changing patterns of solar radiation.[12] They were thus generally in retreat during the Mediaeval Warm Period but advanced dramatically during the Little Ice Age, between the fifteenth and nineteenth centuries. The current retreat began with the start of the Modern Warming, long before any marked rise in CO_2. But there were significant exceptions to this pattern, not least in Greenland and the Antarctic, which between them contain 99.4 per cent of all the ice on the planet. In each case, although there was melting on the periphery of the land mass, the overall ice mass in the interior was increasing, and many of their glaciers were advancing.[13]

The Polar regions inevitably played a central part in Gore's thesis: partly because they provided emotive imagery in themselves (polar bears drowning, vast ice shelves collapsing into the sea); and partly because all that melting ice would provide the mass of water needed to raise the world's seas to unprecedented levels. But, again, almost every detail of his scenario was contradicted by expert evidence.

A series of studies, for instance, had shown that the Arctic was in general warmer at the end of the 1920–1940 warming phase than it was 60 years later.[14] After a drop in temperatures during the decades of the Little Cooling, they had risen again from the 1980s onwards, without yet reaching their levels of the 1930s.

Far from heading rapidly for extinction, polar bears across most of the region were in fact flourishing. Of 13 main polar bear groups in eastern Canada, 11 were growing in numbers or stable, only two were declining (it was on one of these, in west Hudson Bay, that environmentalists liked to focus attention).[15] An extensive study published in 2007 by the US National Biological Service similarly found that polar bear populations in western Canada and Alaska were so thriving that some had reached optimum sustainable levels.[16]

Gore's shocking reference to those 'drowning polar bears', it emerged, was equally unfounded. In his book he cited 'a new scientific study' showing that 'for the first time polar bears have been drowning in significant numbers' because the melting of the Arctic ice meant 'they have to swim much longer distances from floe to floe'. In fact the study paper of 2005 he based this on referred only to a single incident in which four bears had been found drowned following a violent Alaskan storm.[17] Their deaths had no connection with ice melting or global warming.

Similarly in Greenland, home to 9.9 per cent of the world's ice, the evidence again indicated that temperatures had been higher in the 1930s than in the 1990s.[18] Gore's computerised graphics showed a dramatic melting of the ice round the periphery of the world's largest island, particularly in the south, where there had been significant warming. This was based on a much-publicised paper which had claimed that in 2005 alone the ice had been melting at more than 200 cubic kilometres a year.[19]

Although this sounded immense, it in fact amounted to only eight-thousandths of one per cent of the total mass of the Greenland ice sheet (and very much more than this would have melted before Greenland could first be extensively inhabited during the Mediaeval Warming). But what both this paper and Gore's film ignored was a study published the previous year in the same journal, *Science*, showing that the peripheral ice loss was also being accompanied by a sizeable increase in the size of the ice-cap in Greenland's interior.[20]

Even more remarkable was the skewing of the evidence for what was happening at the other end of the world. The audiences for Gore's film were treated to more of those already familiar images of colossal chunks of ice calving off into the sea from the edge of the Antarctic, holding 89.5 per cent of all the world's ice. But these images and almost all the studies of the effects of global warming on the world's fifth largest continent, larger than Europe, had been focused on just one small corner of that immense frozen land mass, the Antarctic Peninsula, stretching up towards South America, and the coast of Western Antarctica adjacent to it.

Here there had indeed been dramatic evidence of warming, caused by a 0.3 degree temperature rise in the surrounding Southern Ocean. But a table of recorded temperatures across the rest of Antarctica, confirmed by satellite data, showed that, almost everywhere else, the preceding decades had seen a distinct cooling. This, combined with increased precipitation as the surrounding ocean warmed, had led, as in Greenland, to a thickening of the continent's vast ice-sheet and a lengthening of many of its glaciers.[21] According to one recent expert study based on satellite data covering 72 per cent of Antarctica, the ice was growing at a rate of 5mm a year. This was enough to suggest that, far from contributing to global sea levels rising, the water taken from the oceans in precipitation would actually lower them by 0.08mm per year.[22]

Gore's misrepresentation of the amount of water being released by melting of ice at the Poles thus led him on to absurdly exaggerating the projected rise in sea levels. His computer graphics showing the melting of the Greenland and Antarctic ice caps conveyed the impression that this was already happening with dramatic speed. Thus his enhanced satellite-images purporting to show the drowning of many of the world's major cities suggested (although he gave no time-line) that by the end of the twenty-first century sea levels would rise by as much as 20 feet. A similar figure was now being projected by his chief scientific adviser, Dr Hansen.[23] But even the IPCC, scarcely known for its understatement, forecast a rise only between 4 and 17 inches, and suggested that any serious melting of the polar ice caps could only take place over 'millennia'.[24]

Inevitably Gore referred to the widely-publicised belief that 'many residents of low-lying Pacific nations have had to evacuate their homes because of rising seas'. This was accompanied by a picture of homes apparently being swamped by waves in tiny Tuvalu, the fourth smallest nation in the world (formerly the British Ellice Islands).

In fact not a single resident of Pacific islands had been evacuated, despite the efforts of Tuvalu's prime minister since the early 1990s to describe his country as 'the world's first victim of climate change', in the hope of winning international help. Field studies by Dr Mörner's Commission on Sea Level Change had shown that since 1978 sea levels around Tuvalu had remained stable. These findings were confirmed by a separate French-US study reported in *Science* in 2001, based on Topex/Poseidon satellite and other data. This showed that in a large area of the central Pacific around Tuvalu, sea levels had between 1955 and 1996 gone down by a total of 105mm (4.1 inches), at an average rate of 2mm a year.[25]

When Gore blamed global warming for the fact that London's Thames Flood Barrier had already had to be raised far more frequently in recent years than ever before, he omitted to explain that the decision to build the barrier had been taken in the 1970s, when the fear was of global cooling. The reason for this was that London had long been sinking by inches every year, thanks to abstraction of water from subterranean aquifers and the general slow subsidence of Britain's east coast.

To reinforce his point, Gore took his graph back to 1930, to show that there had been virtually no flood alerts in those earlier decades. His cut-off point was significant. Had he taken it back just two more years, to 1928, he would have had to include the most damaging Thames flood on record. In fact, as the relevant authorities had reported, the reason why closures of the Barrier had become more frequent in dry years since 2000 was to keep river water in, not to keep sea water out.[26]

Gore again milked for all it was worth the recent flooding of New Orleans in the wake of Hurricane Katrina, to support his claim that global warming had produced a huge increase in the frequency of hurricanes and other 'extreme weather events'. This flatly contradicted the historical evidence, which showed that Atlantic 'Category 3–5' hurricane activity after 2000 was actually lower than it had been in the 1950s, a decade into the Little Cooling. It had fallen off between the 1960s and the 1990s, before rising again.[27] Whatever caused these oscillations, it was not global warming. The disaster which struck New Orleans in 2005 was predominantly caused by the tragic failure of the relevant authorities, despite warnings, to keep in proper repair the levees designed to protect a city built partly below sea and river level.

Virtually every point in Gore's case was based on similarly misrepresenting, distorting or even inverting the scientific evidence. According to researchers using data from NASA, for instance, the chief reason for the shrinking of Lake Chad (only a very shallow lake at the best of times, which had dried up completely more than once in the past) was over-abstraction for human and animal use, following a succession of local droughts unconnected to global warming.[28]

Gore naturally picked up on the increased frequency of droughts across the world as another consequence of global warming: in March 2007 he was to testify to Congress that 'droughts are becoming longer and more intense'. In October 2006, to coincide with a G8 meeting in Mexico to discuss the successor to the Kyoto Protocol, a team from the UK Met Office's Hadley Centre revealed the findings of a new study which showed that in the last decade of the twentieth century droughts had been 25 per cent more widespread than in the previous 40 years. Nearly a third of the world's land surface might be at risk of extreme droughts by the end of the twenty-first century, wreaking havoc on food production and water resources and leading to mass-migrations of 'environmental refugees'.[29]

Yet, only a few months later, a comprehensive study of the twentieth century's 30 most intensive droughts showed that seven of these had occurred in the first two decades of the century, seven between 1921 and 1940, eight between 1941 and 1960 and five between 1961 and 1980. Thus 27 of the world's 30 major drought episodes had been before 1980, while the figure for the century's last two decades was only three.[30]

Another popular myth which Gore had then vastly exaggerated was the predicted 'mass-extinction' of species caused by global warming. This had been largely inspired by local studies in the US and central America shown to have been based on seriously misinterpreting the data (if anything, warming encouraged many species to extend their geographical range).[31] As for Gore's excitable claim that warming was already leading to a spread of 30 diseases, including malaria, this was based not least on further exaggerating those basic errors by the IPCC which had already been magisterially dismissed by Professor Reiter.[32]

Finally there was Gore's triumphant citing of a 2004 study by Dr Naomi Oreskes, based on analysing the 'abstracts' of 928 peer-reviewed papers thrown up by a search for 'global climate change' on a scientific database. She claimed that 75 per cent of the 928 either explicitly or implicitly endorsed the 'consensus' in favour of man-made climate change, while none dissented from it. When a British academic, Dr Benny Peiser, checked her figures, he found that only 905 of the documents had abstracts and only 13 of these, 2 per cent, explicitly endorsed anthropogenic climate change. The vast majority did not mention it at all.[33]

Just as worrying as Gore's wholesale abuse of the science, however, were his recommended prescriptions as to how humanity should respond to this unprecedented threat. Having conjured up the prospect of a fast-approaching apocalypse, drowning cities, raging hurricanes, billions of people deprived of water and threatened with diseases running out of control, he ended in thudding anticlimax, with those suggestions that the human race might somehow avert catastrophe by using low-energy light bulbs and not leaving television sets and computers on standby.

But he also suggested two further ways in which global warming might be tackled on a more collective scale. One was that the power for all these devices could be provided from renewable sources, such as wind turbines. The other was that the world should cut back its output of CO_2 by adopting 'carbon emissions trading schemes', of the kind in which he claimed the EU had so 'effectively' led the way.

It was here as much as anywhere, as we shall shortly see, that Gore and his allies showed how completely their vision had parted company with reality. But first we must describe a remarkable episode taking place just as Gore's film was being launched on the world in the summer of 2006. This shed further dramatic light on the most important single piece of evidence he had used to promote his case: his version of the IPCC's 'hockey stick'.

ENTER THE US CONGRESS: THE 'HOCKEY STICK' IS DEMOLISHED

It was now nearly three years since McIntyre and McKitrick had published their first analysis of the methodology used to create the 'hockey stick'. For a while this had attracted little general attention, despite the grudging little 'Corrigendum' published by Mann and his colleagues in *Nature* in 2004. But such was the prominence which had been given to the 'hockey stick', and seemingly so damaging were the flaws the two Canadians had identified in it, that the controversy became increasingly public.

In view of the pride of place the IPCC had given to the 'hockey stick' in its 2001 report, there was inevitably some concern as to how the IPCC should handle the controversy in its next report, preparation of which was already well under way for publication in 2007. Mann and his allies decided that it might be helpful to the IPCC's deliberations if another authoritative new study could appear upholding his findings and confirming that his methodology was correct.

In May 2005 UCAR (the University Corporation for Atmospheric Research), a body strongly committed to the 'consensus' on man-made climate change, issued a press release announcing that two new research papers had been submitted to leading journals, *Geopysical Research Letters* and *Climatic Change*. These concluded that 'the highly publicised criticisms of the MBH graph are unfounded'.[34] Their authors were Caspar Ammann and Eugene Wahl, both associates of Mann. Ammann was one of his former students, who now worked for UCAR and was also a contributing author to the forthcoming IPCC report (AR4).

To put out a press release announcing merely that two scientific papers had been submitted for publication even before they had been accepted was so unusual that it was probably unprecedented. Still odder was the fact that two months later, on 4 July, in a statement to the House of Representatives Committee on Energy and Commerce, the European Geosciences Union cited these unpublished papers as having shown that McIntyre and McKitrick were wrong. On 21 July, in front of another congressional committee, Sir John

Houghton again cited the unpublished papers as evidence that the two men's criticisms of the 'hockey stick' could be discounted.[35]

The House Energy and Commerce committee had also interviewed Mann himself. When members asked to see the computer codes he had used to create the 'hockey stick', he refused, saying that he was not going to be 'intimidated'. The committee therefore decided that it would hold hearings specifically to look into the 'hockey stick', and would then make a formal request for the codes.

This so outraged members of another congressional committee, the House Committee on Science, that they invited the President of the US National Academy of Sciences to arrange for an investigation of their own. They invited him, through the National Research Council (NRC), to empanel a balanced group of scientists to provide Congress with expert guidance on the 'current scientific consensus' on the palaeoclimate record in general and the 'hockey stick' in particular.

Thus not one but two congressional committees had set in train their own rival inquiries. The Energy and Commerce Committee commissioned an investigation chaired by one of the most respected statisticians in the US, Dr Edward Wegman. For the Science Committee, the NRC set up a panel chaired by an expert in atmospheric sciences, Dr Gerald North.

Although in advance no one had any idea which way either investigation might go, the appointment of Dr Wegman seemed highly appropriate, since the criticism directed at Mann's methodology centred on his use of statistics and the processing of data by his computer model. Wegman's credentials to carry out such an investigation, with two other expert statisticians, were impeccable. As a professional statistician for 38 years, with a distinguished record. he was currently chairman of the National Academy of Sciences Committee on Applied and Theoretical Statistics, described by the NAS itself as occupying 'a pivotal position in the statistical community, providing expertise in methodology and policy formation'.[36]

The NRC panel, on the other hand, included several members well-acquainted with Mann who might have been anticipated to be supportive of the 'hockey stick'. One, a contributing author to the forthcoming IPCC report, had co-authored papers with Ammann and was his UCAR supervisor. Another, who also worked for UCAR, was presently collaborating not only with Ammann but with Mann himself. The panel's chairman, Dr North, had worked at

Hansen's Goddard Institute, and had been reported by *Science* as saying of the 'hockey stick' when he first saw it five years earlier that he found it 'more convincing' than the 'detection studies' which had preceded it.[37]

The North report was presented to the Science Committee in June 2006,[38] a month after the Los Angeles premiere of Gore's film. Wegman's report was published in July, a month later,[39] and each was then subject to committee hearings.

Although the NRC panel's findings were more cautiously worded, the verdicts of the two reports were in essence unequivocal. Each found that the methodology used by Mann and his colleagues (MBH) had in several crucial respects been deeply flawed. They had made incorrect use of principal component analysis. Their 'decentred methodology' was 'simply incorrect mathematics' (Wegman). Their use of tree rings from the bristlecone pines was so suspect that such proxy data 'should be avoided for temperature reconstructions' (North).

By contrast, Wegman found the analysis of McIntyre and McKitrick 'valid and compelling', and his report thus concluded that

> *'Mann's assessments that the decade of the1990s was the hottest decade of the millennium and that 1998 was the hottest year of the millennium cannot be supported by his analysis.'*

Wegman, whose report had been reviewed by nine eminent statisticians including several professors and a former president of the American Statistical Association, went rather further than North in the range and force of his criticisms. He found Mann's papers to be 'obscure and incomplete', 'written in a confusing manner, making it difficult for the reader to discern the actual methodology'. When Wegman's team had downloaded Mann's data from his website, 'unfortunately we did not find adequate material to replicate' his 1998 findings, whereas they were able to reproduce McIntyre and McKitrick's results without any difficulty.

If North's report was less trenchantly phrased, when he was asked by Joe Barton, chairman of the Energy and Commerce committee, whether he disagreed with 'the conclusions or methodology of Dr Wegman's report', he replied 'no we don't. We don't disagree with their criticism. In fact, pretty much the same thing is said in our report.'[40]

Wegman was keenly aware of the wider implications of his findings that such a crucial piece of evidence for the global warming cause was so deeply flawed. The fact that the graph produced by Mann and his colleagues fitted

> *'some policy agendas has greatly enhanced their paper's visibility … The "hockey stick" reconstruction of temperature graphic dramatically illustrated the global warming issue and was adopted by the IPCC and many governments as the poster graphic. The graphic's prominence together with the fact that it is based on incorrect use of [principal components analysis] puts Dr Mann and his co-authors in a difficult face-saving position.'*

Wegman was particularly scathing about claims that those other members of the 'palaeoclimatology community' who had attempted to defend Mann's work, notably Ammann and Wahl, had produced papers which validated it, while dismissing McIntyre and McKitrick's criticisms as the work of 'biased amateurs'.

McIntyre and McKitrick had, for instance, shown that, if the controversial bristlecone pines were removed from Mann's proxy data, leaving only the other proxies, the 'hockey stick' shape disappeared. But Wahl and Amman had argued, as if in answer to McIntyre and McKitrick, that 'if one adds enough principal components back into the proxy one obtains the hockey stick shape again'. 'This', as Wegman somewhat testily urged, was 'precisely the point of contention':

> *'A cardinal rule of statistical inference is that the method of analysis must be decided before looking at the data. The rules and strategy of analysis cannot be changed in order to obtain the desire result. Such a strategy carries no statistical integrity and cannot be used as a basis for drawing sound inferential conclusions.'*

Wegman was keenly aware that Ammann and Wahl had both worked with Mann. Therefore, as part of his investigation, he commissioned a 'social network analysis' of Mann's academic defenders, to ascertain how genuinely independent they were. How often had they co-authored papers with each other? How intimately linked were they professionally?

> *'Our findings from this analysis suggest that authors in the area of paleoclimate studies are closely connected and thus 'independent studies' may not be as independent as they might appear on the surface.'*

Mann's academic supporters were

> *'a tightly knit group of individuals who passionately believe in their thesis. However, our perception is that this group has a self-reinforcing*

feedback mechanism and, moreover, the work has been sufficiently politicized that they can hardly reassess their public positions without losing credibility.'

It was not surprising, Wegman observed, that these supposedly 'independent' scientists had come up with results similar to Mann's, because they had used much of the same controversial data. But what was also noticeable was the lack of statistical expertise of 'the paleoclimate community'. 'Even though they rely heavily on statistical methods', they did not seem ready to draw on the expertise of 'the statistical community'.

Wegman's report further regretted that the flaws in the 'hockey stick' had not been identified before it was so actively promoted by the IPCC. It was wrong that the authors of its reports, supposedly based on reviewing all the latest science in an objective fashion, should then be allowed to base their reports on their own work:

'Especially when massive amounts of public monies and human lives are at stake, academic work should have a more intense level of scrutiny and review. It is especially the case that authors of policy-related documents like the IPCC report, Climate Change 2001: The Scientific Basis, *should not be the same people as those that constructed the academic papers.'*

While it was noted that the North report was generally more guarded in its criticisms of the 'hockey stick' than Wegman, one prominent climate scientist. Eduardo Zorita, commented:

'in my opinion the Panel adopted the most critical position to MBH nowadays possible. I agree ... that [the North report] is in many parts ambivalent and some parts are inconsistent with others. It would have been unrealistic to expect a report with a summary stating that MBH98 and MBH99 were wrong (and therefore the IPCC TAR had serious problems) when the Fourth Report is in the making. I was indeed surprised by the extensive and deep criticism of the MBH methodology in Chapters 9 and 11.[41]

What this reflected, of course, was an awareness of the huge political embarrassment which might follow from confirmation that the most prominent piece of evidence in the IPCC's 2001 report, cited by governments across the world, could no longer be considered scientifically credible.

It was scarcely likely to be an embarrassment to Al Gore, whose film had now become one of the most fashionable talking points of the year. More thoughtful supporters of the 'consensus' on global warming, however, might have found it disturbing that the central icon of their cause had now become one of the more comprehensively discredited artefacts in the history of science.

As it turned out, the demolition of the 'hockey stick' left all the politicians committed to the cause quite unmoved, They had passed the point where they needed to worry about the evidence. The science, as they liked to say, was 'settled'. The time had come for action.

PAYING THE PRICE

Until now, all the increasingly frenzied talk about the threat of global warming had been little more than that: just talk. But, as with any scare, the tipping point had come, when politicians and governments felt the need to respond.

In October 2006, only months after Gore's film hit the cinema screens, Tony Blair launched a huge 712-page report, *The Economics of Climate Change: the Stern Review*,[42] by a Treasury official and former chief economist to the World Bank, Sir Nicholas Stern. Blair rather curiously called it 'the most important report on the future ever published by this government'.[43] It showed how the scientific evidence of global warming was now 'overwhelming' and that the consequences of failing to take action would be 'literally disastrous'.

Stern went even further than Gore's film. An *Observer* trailer for his report, headed 'Ten years to save the planet', said it would reveal that 'if governments do nothing, climate change will cost more than both world wars and make swathes of the planet uninhabitable'.[44] Stern predicted that up to 200 million people could become refugees as their homes were hit by drought. Floods from rising sea levels could displace up to 100 million more. Melting glaciers could cause water shortages for one in six of the world's population. Wildlife would be so devastated that up to 40 per cent of the world's species might become extinct. Climate change would be so damaging to the world's economies that it could reduce global GDP by as much as 20 per cent, certainly by at least 5 per cent, 'each year, now and forever'.

But all was not lost. Stern's purpose was to provide politicians with advice as to how they should act. He assured them that if measures were put in train immediately – needing to cost no more than 1 per cent of GDP – the worst of this apocalypse could be averted.

One of the chief sources of Stern's data was that leading promoter of alarm over global warming, the UK Met Office's Hadley Centre. Another inspiration cited for some of his report's more apocalyptic predictions was the work of Dr Richard Tol, one of the world's leading environmental economists, who had been involved in all three IPCC working groups and was the author of the UN's *Handbook on Methods for Climate Change Impact Assessment and Adaptation Strategies*.[45]

Tol, however, was far from enthused by his supposed disciple's work. Within weeks he had published an angry commentary, dismissing Stern's more lurid projections as 'preposterous'.[46]

Tol charged Stern with distorting his own findings and exaggerating them to reach absurd conclusions. One of Tol's studies, for instance, had given a range of estimates for the cost to the global economy of additional CO_2 emissions. Out of this wide range, Stern had picked the figure of $29 a tonne, without revealing that in the same study Tol had said that the most plausible figure was 'likely to be substantially smaller' than $14 a tonne. Stern had thus more than doubled Tol's most likely prediction.

Stern's report, Tol noted, had based all its estimates of the economic impacts of climate change on a single computer model, PAGE2002 by Hope (2006), which assumed that vulnerability to climate change would be the same whether a country was developed or undeveloped. This did not therefore allow for the ability of, say, the USA to adapt rather more easily to global warming than, say, Bangladesh).

Tol argued that Stern seemed to be counting in risks three times (including a 10 per cent risk that humanity would be extinct by 2100). 'In sum', he said, 'the *Stern Review* is very selective in the studies it quotes', invariably seeking to emphasise only 'the most pessimistic' of them. Along with all its other flaws, such as failing to have carried out a promised cost-assessment, the report could only be 'dismissed as alarmist and incompetent'.

An array of other leading economists joined in the assault, from Professor William Nordhaus of Yale to Professor Henderson, former chief economist to the OECD. But from the moment it appeared, the *Stern Review* was treated by politicians and policy-makers across the world with the reverence due to holy writ. At last they had a guide, more up-to-date and detailed than the IPCC's reports, as to what might be practically (and comparatively cheaply) done to save mankind from the catastrophe of climate change.

One of the most obvious means of doing this, Stern advised, would be to give a huge boost to renewable energy, particularly wind turbines. Shortly after his review appeared, however, came an episode which illustrated one of the more serious flaws in this strategy.

No country in the world had gone more overboard for wind turbines than Germany. Despite the Danish lesson, it had continued to build wind machines so fast that by 2006 it had no less 31 per cent of the world's entire wind capacity.[47] But power experts were keenly aware that, although this represented more than 20,000MW of installed capacity, in reality Germany's 18,000 turbines were generating on average only 3,480MW of usable electricity, comparable to that produced by a single large coal-fired power station.[48]

To produce this derisory amount of power, the Germans were already becoming worried about the amount of their country they were needing to cover not just with the turbines themselves but with costly high-voltage transmission lines to move the power to where it was needed. They were now having to plan another 2,700 kilometres just to cope with new wind farms.[49]

In addition to this, thanks to the wind's unpredictability, there was the threat of growing instability to the grid. On the evening of Saturday, 4 November 2006 a huge area of western Europe suddenly blacked out. Because of high winds and a surge of power into the 'pan-European grid' from German wind turbines, power from conventional generators had hurriedly to be closed off, causing repeated failures when they had to be reconnected. From France to Italy, it was reported that 'a real catastrophe' had been only narrowly averted. Heinz Kaupa, director of Austria's Power Grid, bluntly explained that his own country's system was becoming so unbalanced by the 'excessive' building of wind turbines that within two years the whole of Europe would be 'confronted with massive connector problems'.[50]

Despite these dire practical warnings, the blind faith of Europe's politicians in wind power seemed unshakeable. In the 2007 election campaign for the Scottish Parliament, the governing Labour Party promised that by 2020 Scotland would be producing no less than 40 per cent of its energy from renewable sources. At the time, Scotland was producing only 12 per cent from 'renewables', almost all of it from hydro-electric schemes built 50 years earlier. Only a fraction was coming from the country's 640 wind turbines. To achieve this new target would require building at least 8,000 more turbines, covering 7 per cent of Scotland's entire land area. But even these would generate on average only 3.3GW of electricity, equal to the output of just a single conventional power station such as the one at Didcot in Oxfordshire.[51]

The infatuation with wind power had become as much of a self-deluding fantasy as those windmills which Don Quixote took for giants,

THE EU DECIDES TO CONTROL
THE WORLD'S CLIMATE

On 9 March 2007, amid a fanfare of publicity, the European Council, the EU government's 'cabinet', including the leaders of all its 27 member states, met in Brussels to agree a new package of measures to fight 'climate change'.

For a start they wished to signal to the world 'the vital importance of achieving the strategic objective of limiting the global average temperature increase to not more than 2°C above pre-industrial levels'.[52] By way of reaching this target, Europe's leaders pledged that, by 2020, they would reduce the EU's carbon dioxide emissions to 20 per cent below their levels in 1990.

To achieve this they agreed that, by 2020, no less than 20 per cent of the EU's energy must be derived from renewable sources, such as wind turbines, solar power and 'biomass' (plants burned to generate electricity or heat). In addition, by 2020, 10 per cent of all transport fuel in the EU must be 'biofuels', derived from crops such as wheat, rape, maize (corn) or sugar beet which were supposedly 'carbon neutral'. All these targets were to be made mandatory.

In addition they proposed that by 2010 the EU should follow the example set by Fidel Catros's Cuba two years earlier by banning the sale and manufacture of conventional incandescent light bulbs. The EU's citizens would only be permitted to use 'low energy', mercury-vapour filled 'compact fluoresecent lamps' or CFLs (even though five years earlier, in its Restriction on Hazardous Substances directive, 2002/95, the EU had banned the use of mercury as a deadly substance).[53]

Although it was clear from the woolliness of their communiqué that the EU's leaders had not the faintest practical idea how such targets could be achieved (the details were all to be worked out later), they were beside themselves with excitement at the daring of what they had agreed to. This was meant to show, in the words of

Jose Manuel Barroso, the President of the European Commission, that 'Europe is now able to lead the way on climate change'.

The BBC reported that there was 'an air of real achievement in Brussels'. As Britain's Tony Blair put it, these 'groundbreaking, bold, ambitious targets' would give Europe a 'clear leadership position on this crucial issue facing the world'. Looking ahead to the next G8 meeting in June, he said that Europe's initiative would give 'a good chance' of getting the US, China and India on board as well.

Germany's Angela Merkel, who chaired the two-day meeting, said she was peronally 'very satisfied and happy that it has been possible to open the door to a whole new dimension of European co-operation in the years to come in the areas of energy and combating climate change'. But she did later admit that personally she had trouble at home with low-energy bulbs because they took so long to light up that she sometimes tripped up in the dark when she turned them on.

All these measures apart, however, as Gore had acknowledged in his film, the EU was already leading the world in pioneering the other main strategy devised to cut back on carbon emissions. On 1 January 2005, as enjoined by the Kyoto Protocol, it had launched the world's largest 'Emissions Trading Scheme' (or, as the Americans called it, 'cap and trade').

Each EU country had agreed to cap its CO_2 emissions at a certain figure, and individual enterprises within that country had then been allocated their own 'carbon allowances'. If they exceeded their allowance, they could continue to 'pollute', but only so long as they bought 'carbon credits' from those firms or countries which were emitting less than they were allowed.

A major flaw in the EU's version of this scheme was that each country was allowed to nominate its own national allowance, fixed for the first three years the scheme was in operation. Some, notably Britain, honouring the spirit of Kyoto, nominated figures substantially lower than their existing emissions level. Others, notably Germany, chose figures higher than their existing level. The total allowable emissions in the EU of 1,829 million tonnes a year were thus larger than its existing emissions of 1,785 million tons.[54]

A year later, in 2006, the first results of this lop-sided scheme became apparent. Several countries including Poland had chosen not to participate at all. Only four countries had been forced to buy carbon credits to remain within the allowances they had set themselves. By far the worst hit country was Britain, which had paid out

£470 million. Germany, on the other hand, had been able to make a profit of £300 million selling carbon credits to the losers. Over the first three years of the scheme, it appeared that British firms would be transferring nearly £1.5 billion to their competitors.

An even greater anomaly was revealed by comparing those organisations in Britain which were forced to pay out for credits with those which made a profit from selling them. NHS hospitals, for instance, had been obliged to spend £1.3 million on buying credits, while giant oil and energy firms had enjoyed a bonanza from selling them. BP had sold '1.4 million tons' of emissions credits across the EU, thus earning £17.9 million for doing nothing. Shell's first-year profit was £20.7 million. Even these sums were dwarfed by comparison with the profits enjoyed by the electricity generating companies, which, according to UK government figures, had enjoyed a windfall of up to £1.3 billion.[55]

The business pages were soon full of articles reporting on how the new 'carbon trading market' had become, according to viewpoint, either the best new investment going or a scandalous racket. Unwittingly, the biggest contributors were electricity consumers who had seen their bills rise by between 7 and 12 per cent to pay for the scheme, without their being told why.

But the most telling comment on the ETS, which had been praised by Gore as working so 'effectively', was the revelation that, in its first two years of operation, the EU's total carbon emissions, far from falling, had risen by up to 1.5 per cent.[56] At the same time it was announced that emissions in the US, universally reviled for its continuing refusal to sign up to Kyoto, had in 2006 fallen by 1.6 per cent.[57]

In face of figures like these, it was salutary to recall that the EU's leaders, led by Germany's Angela Merkel, were calling for a worldwide reduction in carbon emissions of 60 per cent by 2050.[58] A McKinsey study in March 2007 estimated that for the EU alone to reach its target of a 20 per cent cut by 2020 would cost up to €1.1 trillion (£747 billion).[59] Yet in 2004 EU countries had spent €5.6 billion subsidising the production of coal, and in 2006 Germany opened a giant new mine in the Ruhr producing brown coal, the most polluting fossil-fuel of them all, with plans to open 25 more new mines across the country.

It was equally salutary to recall just what a huge percentage of all the worldwide sources of CO_2 emissions was not covered by the

Kyoto Protocol. These included aviation, shipping and deforestation, the second largest contributor, and, of course, the two fastest-growing and potentially most polluting economies on the planet, China and India.

In face of such myriad contradictions, it seemed only appropriate that in the week of February 2007 when Hollywood was awarding Gore's film two Oscars, it should be revealed that his own 20-room home in Nashville, Tennessee, used 221,000 kilowatt-hours of electricity a year, 20 times the US national average.[60]

Having exhorted each of his fellow-American citizens to reduce their personal 'carbon footprint', Gore's only defence was that, as a multi-millionaire, he had bought 'renewable energy credits' to 'offset' his own carbon use. But it then emerged that he bought them from a London-based company called Generation Investment Management, run by one of his former staffers and of which he himself was chairman, a firm set up specifically to cash in on the multi-billion dollar boom in 'carbon offsets'.[61]

It was hard to recall any historical precedent for the outpouring of hypocrisy which had come to shroud the issue of global warming. So overwhelming now was the collective pressure to subscribe to the prevailing orthodoxy that scarcely a single politician in the western world dared challenge it.

Particularly in the EU, it was being used to justify almost any action governments might wish to take. In Britain this meant raising new taxes on anything from vehicle licences to airline tickets. The owners of buildings, under the EU's directive on energy efficiency, were being required to pay for expensive 'energy efficiency certificates'. In Britain these became a central part of the government's highly controversial plan to require property vendors to supply buyers with 'Home Information Packs'. The UK government, desperate to see the building of more wind farms, had also issued new rules allowing established planning laws to be overridden to force through wind schemes against the democratic wishes of local communities.[62]

Yet despite all this deluge of new measures, the EU's CO_2 emissions were still rising. And somehow this craze to impose new laws and costs in all directions did not seem to affect plans to increase the capacity of Europe's airports to handle millions more passenger-flights per year.

Governments were now annually pouring billions of dollars, pounds and euros into every kind of research related to global warming. But almost all these funds were conditional on that research coming up with results that the governments wanted to hear. Since few grants were available to those scientists who might challenge the official 'consensus', the only surprise was how many were still prepared to express a sceptical view.[63]

So rare had it become for the mainstream media, led by organisations such as the BBC, CBS and NBC, to voice anything but that orthodoxy that when one broadcaster dared put forward a dissenting view, as did Britain's Channel Four in March 2007, with a 90-minute documentary *The Great Global Warming Swindle*, featuring many of the leading academic dissidents on both sides of the Atlantic, this made headline news for days.[64]

Yet at the heart of this supposedly overwhelming political, scientific and media 'consensus' remained a glaring contradiction. On one hand, upholders of the orthodoxy were only too happy to proclaim that, unless the most drastic steps were taken to combat the threat of global warming caused by fast-rising greenhouse gas emissions, Planet Earth faced unprecedented catastrophe.

On the other, surveying the range of measures which were actually being taken to avert this apocalypse, it was quite clear that, even on their own terms, they were still at this stage astonishingly trivial in their effect. Not all of them combined would have the slightest influence on the world's climate. Even if the aspirations of Kyoto were met in their entirety, this would only supposedly delay the global temperature rise predicted for 2100 by six years. On the evidence of what had actually been achieved so far, it was obvious that even this was only wishful thinking.

The politicians of the developed world might well exhort the less developed nations to join them in a crusade which would deprive the vast majority of mankind of any hope of ever catching up with the rich minority; asking the peoples of rural Africa, for instance, to remain in the kind of poverty which would continue to kill them in tens of millions a year. But there was not the slightest chance that fast-developing nations such as China and India would agree to halt their drive to greater material prosperity, necessitating an explosion in carbon emissions which might before long put them even ahead of America as the world's leading 'polluters'.

Nothing more vividly brought home the unreality of all this than the fact that in 2006 alone China increased its electrical generating capacity by 25 per cent. The 102GW of capacity it added to its existing 400GW in 12 months was almost equivalent to the entire 112GW generating capacity of France. Furthermore 88.5 per cent of this came from new, heavily CO_2 emitting coal-fired power plants. By mid-2007 China was building a new coal-fired generating station every four days. It was on course to exceed the 978GW capacity of the USA within four years, and to become the world's leading CO_2-emitting nation even sooner.[65]

The rich Western nations themselves might be prepared to cover their countryside with wind turbines, impose new taxes on airline passengers, introduce regulations to curb emissions from the vehicles on their roads and play around with their 'carbon trading' schemes. But just as those wind turbines did little or nothing to reduce carbon emissions, so in reality did their airline traffic continue growing and their numbers of vehicles continue to increase. Measured against the scale of the forthcoming disaster about which they so liked to fantasise, none of these amounted to anything more than empty sentimental gestures.

So what chance was left that Planet Earth could be saved? There was perhaps just one ground for hope: that in conjuring up their vision of that future apocalypse and blaming it all on *homo sapiens* for allowing CO_2 to soar to 383 parts per million of the atmosphere, those scientists who set the whole fear of global warming in motion might in fact have been looking in completely the wrong direction.

Notes

1. *The Independent*, 30 October 2006.
2. Associated Press, 9 May 2007.
3. *An Inconvenient Truth* (2006), Bloomsbury, London. The summary which follows is based on both the film and book versions.
4. CBS 60 Minutes, March 19 2006. See also 'Public Eye', CBS News website, 23 March 2006.
5. '*Gristmill, the environmental news blog*', 19 September 2006.
6. *Canadian Free Press*, 12 June 2006. Carter was a senior research professor working for the Marine Geophysical Laboratory at James Cook University, Queensland, and Adelaide University.
7. See discussion on Climate Audit website, in particular 'Al Gore and Dr Thompson's Thermometer'. 9 and 10 November 2007, and 'Irreproducible results in PNAS', 24 April 2009.
8. See, for instance, H. Fischer, *et al.* (1999), 'Ice core record of atmospheric CO_2 around the last three glacial terminations', *Science*, 283,

1712– 1714; and N. Caillon, *et al.* (2003), 'Timing of atmospheric CO_2 and Antarctic temperature changes across Termination III', *Science*, 299, 1728–1731.We shall return to this point later.

9. Center for the Study of Carbon Dioxide and Glabal Change, *www.co2 science.org*, 10 March 2004.

10. Molg, T., Hardy, D. R., and Kaser, G. (2003), 'Solar-radiation-maintained glacier recession on Kilimanjaro drawn from combined ice-radiation geometry modeling', *Journal of Geophysical Research*, 108: Kaser, G., *et al.* (2004) 'Modern glacier retreat on Kilimanjaro as evidence of climate change: Observations and facts', *International Journal of Climatology* 24: These studies indicated that nearly two-thirds of the shrinkage had taken place before 1950, and that since the 1970s, as global temperatures rose, the rate of decline had actually slowed.

11. For sources see, for instance, Singer and Avery, *op. cit.*, Chap. 9.

12. See, for instance, P. J. Polissar, *et al.* (2006), 'Solar modulation of Little Ice Age climate in the tropical Andes', *Proceedings of National Academy of Sciences*, 13 June 2006, 103, 24.

13. Patrick J. Michaels (2006), 'Is the sky really falling? A review of recent global warming scare stories', Cato Institute, *Policy Analysis No. 576*, 23 August 2006. Michaels was formerly president of the American Association of State Climatologists.

14. E.g. Igor V. Polyakov, *et al.* (2003), 'Variability and trends of air temperature and pressure in the maritime Arctic, 1875–2000', *Journal of Climate* 16; Hansen, J. E., and Lebedeff, S., 1987: 'Global trends of measured surface air temperature', *J. Geophys. Res.*, 92, 13345–13372.

15. Dr Mitchell Taylor, research director for Nunavut Wildllife Service, in report to US Fish and Wildlife Service, dated April 6, 2006, arguing against a petition by Greenpeace and other environtemantal lobbyists to have polar bears put on the 'endangered species' list.

16. Steven Amstrup, *et al.* (2007), 'Polar bears in Alaska', Alaska Science Centre.

17. Monnett, C., Gleason, J. S., and Rotterman, L. M., 2005. Potential effects of diminished sea ice on open-water swimming, mortality, and distribution of polar bears during fall in the Alaskan Beaufort Sea. 16th Biennial Conference on the Biology of Marine Mammals, 12-16 December 2005, San Diego, CA (reported in *Sunday Times*, 18 December 2005).

18. W. Krabill, *et al.* (2000), 'Greenland ice-sheet: high elevation balance and peripheral thinning', *Science*, 289.

19. E. Rignor and P. Kanagratnam (2006), 'Changes in the velocity structure of the Greenland ice-sheet', *Science,* 311.

20. Ola M. Johannessen, *et al.* (2005), 'Recent ice-sheet growth in the interior of Greenland', *Science,* 310. This study was based on direct measurement of the interior ice-sheet, whereas the later paper used a computer

model to estimate this, by extrapolating from data of what was happening on the coast.

21. For table of temperatures and an analysis of the various competing and contradictory versions, with sources, see Michaels, *op. cit.*

22. Duncan Wingham, *et al.* (2006), 'Mass Balance of the Antarctic Ice Sheet', *Philosophical Transactions of the Royal Society*, 364, 1627–1635, 1844. As head of the Earth Sciences department at University College, London, and principal scientist of the European Space Agency's CryoSat satellite mission, Professor Wingham was one of the world's leading authorities on the climate physics of Antarctica.

23. James Hansen, 'The threat to the planet', *New York Review of Books*, 13 July 2006.

24. The third IPCC report (2001) found that the average sea-level rise in the twentieth century had been around 1.5mm a year (B4, 'Observed changes in sea-level'), and that 'no significant acceleration in the rate of sea level rise during the twentieth century has been detected'. This gave a total rise of 6 inches. The IPCC's projected rise in the twenty-first century was between '11 and 43 centimetres' (4.3–16.9 inches).

25. Cabanes, C., *et al.* (2001), 'Sea level rise during the past 40 years determined from satellite and in situ observations', *Science*, 294, 840–842. Figs 2 and 3 show falling sea levels in area around Tuvalu. See also Patrick Michaels, *Meltdown*, Cato Institute, 2004, pp. 202–206.

26. House of Commons *Hansard*, written questions, 18 January 2007, Col. 1251W. See also *www.ecn.ac.uk/iccuk//indicators/10.htm*

27. Graph showing hurricane activity 1900–2005 from the National Oceanic and Atmospheric Administration (NOAA) and National Hurricane Center (NHC). Oceanographers and climate scientists had long pointed out that the effect of climate change which warmed the Polar regions more than the Equator would be to level out disparities in sea-temperature, thus reducing rather than increasing the likelihood of hurricanes and cyclones. Gore's film similarly exaggerated the recent US incidence of tornadoes. For a discussion of how data on extreme weather events had been distorted to promote the global warming thesis, see Michaels, *op. cit.*

28. J. A. Foley and M. T. Coe (2001), 'Decline of Lake Chad', *Journal of Geophysical Research (Atmospheres)*, 106.

29. 'Extreme droughts will spread, say forecasters', *Guardian*, 3 October 2008.

30. G. T. Narisma, *et al.* (2007), 'Abrupt changes in raifall during the twentieth century', *Geophysical Research Letters*, 34, 10.1029.

31. For detailed discussion of these erroneous studies, see Michaels, *op. cit.*

32. For an interesting analysis of this passage by a lay critic, see 'Good news, Mr Gore, the apocalypse has been postponed', by Mary Ellen Tiffany Gilder, *www.sitewave.net*.

33. See Benny Peiser's website, *http://www.staff.livjm.ac.uk/spsbpeis/Oreskes-abstracts.htm*

34. *http://www.ucar.edu/news/releases/2005/ammann.html*

35. David Holland, *op. cit.*

36. *http://sites.nationalacademies.org/deps/BMSA/DEPS_047575*

37. Holland, *op. cit.*

38. *Surface Temperature Reconstructions for the Last 2,000 Years* (National Academies Press, 2006).

39. 'Ad hoc Committee Report on the "Hockey Stick" Global Climate Reconstruction', go*http://www.climateaudit.org/pdf/others/07142006_Wegman_Report.pdf*

40. *http://frwebgate.access.gpo.gov/cgi-bin/getdoc.cgi?dbname=109_house_hearings&docid=f:31362.wais*

41. *http://www.climateaudit.org/?p=715*

42. Stern (2007), *The Economics of Climate Change: the Stern Review* (Cambridge University Press). Page count based on paperback edition.

43. 'Running the rule over Stern's numbers', *BBC News* website, 26 January 2007.

44. 'Ten years to save the planet from mankind', *Observer*, 29 October 2006.

45. Solomon, *The Deniers, op. cit.*, to which I was indebted for much of this passage.

46. Tol, Richard S. J.,'The Stern Review of the Economics of Climate Change: A Comment', Economic and Social Research Institute, Hamburg, Vrije and Carnegie Mellon Universities, 2 November 2006, available on the internet.

47. European Wind Energy Association press release, 1 February 2007.

48. Website of Federal Ministry of Economics and Technology, 'Renewable Energy – Made in Germany – Wind Power', *http://www.german-renewable-energy.com/Renewables/Navigation/Englisch/wind-power.html*. This showed that the output of Germany's wind turbines in 2006 was 30.5 billion kilowatt hours, which translates into an average output of 3.48GW. The output of Drax, Britain's largest coal-fired power station is 3.9GW.

49. ABS Energy Research, *op. cit.*

50. News report from *www.financial.de/newsroom*, 5 November 2006.

51. *Sunday Telegraph*, 8 April 2007.

52. European Council, Presidency Conclusions, 2 May 2007.

53. 'Europe agrees renewable energy target', *BBC News* website, 9 March 2007. It was clear that the EU's leaders had not been properly briefed on this proposal to ban incandescent bulbs. The practical drawbacks would be immense. Since, to maximise their life, CFLs need to operate continuously, the energy savings would be minimal. For many purposes

they could not be used (e.g. in microwaves, ovens, freezers or other enclosed spaces). A study carried out for Defra in 2005 ('Energy scenarios in the lighting sector') had found that 'less than 50 per cent of the fittings installed in UK homes can currently take CFLs'. Replacing hundreds of millions of fittings in UK homes alone would thus cost upwards of £3 billion. Many people disliked the harsher light given off by CFLs, which were larger and heavier than normal lightbulbs, and when used for reading their rapid flicker could produce eye-strain. The fact that CFLs also contained mercury, now a banned substance in the EU, meant that disposing of CFLs at the end of their life would cause huge problems. As it turned out, the EU would in due course be forced to acknowledge some of these difficulties (see below). Even Philips, a giant EU lighting firm which had been lobbying for the change because it had invested heavily in CFLs, had not suggested that the transition could be made in less than 10 years.

54. Figures in this passage are taken from 'The high price of hot air: why the EU Emissions Trading Scheme is an environmental and economic failure', *Open Europe* report, 2006.

55. 'Carbon trade scheme is failing', *BBC News* website, 5 June 2007. Most of the 'carbon permits' on which the generating companies made these immense profits were given to them free. Across the EU as a whole the windfall profits enjoyed by the electricity supply industry under the Emissions Trading Scheme' were estimated at £13.6 billion a year (*Financial Times*, 18 June 2007).

56. *BBC News* website, *op. cit.*

57. US Energy Department figures, released May 2007.

58. 'Germany wants 60 per cent cut in CO_2 by 2050', *EU Observer*, 5 March 2007.

59. *The Guardian*, 28 March 2007.

60. *Daily Telegraph*, 28 February 2007.

61. 'Gore's carbon offsets paid to firm he owns', *WorldNetDaily*, 2 March 2007.

62. For smaller wind turbine projects, the Department of the Deputy Prime Minister (John Prescott MP), had issued new planning guidance (PPS 22), allowing local authorities to ignore normal planning rules in order to meet regional targets for 'renewable' energy. For larger schemes, above 50MW of 'capacity', the government could call these in for ministerial decision. In October 2005, for instance, the energy minister Malcolm Wicks gave the go-ahead to a giant wind farm on Romney Marsh in Kent, covering 1,000 acres with 26 370-foot high 2.5MW turbines, despite the fact that this had been opposed by every elected authority in the area, including two county councils, two district councils and 12 parish councils.

63. For one account of the pressure on scientists to follow the orthodox line, see Richard Lindzen's 'Climate of fear: global warming alarmists intimidate dissenting scientists into silence', *Wall Street Journal*, 12 April 2006.
64. See Chapter 7.
65. *Energy Tribune*, 'IEA revises China's 2Q demand', April 2007, 26. Reuters, 'China to become top CO_2 emitter in 2007 or '08 – IEA', 19 April 2007.

Part Three: The 'consensus' begins to crumble: 2007–2009

'That we are now entering a new period of climate change, there can be no reasonable doubt. However, this is not – as many of the climate sceptics tell us – simply just another one of the many periods of global warming that the Earth has experienced in its four-and-a-half billion year existence. All serious scientists agree that this time, it is being caused by Man, and it poses unprecedented risks to both human life and even to human civilisation itself.'

Jose-Manuel Barroso, President of the
European Commission, May 26, 2009 *

'Contrary to many self-assured and self-serving proclamations, there is no scientific consensus about the causes of recent climate changes. An impartial observer must accept the fact that both sides of the dispute – the believers in man's dominant role in recent climate changes, as well as the supporters of the hypothesis about their mostly natural origin – offer arguments strong enough to be listened to carefully by the non-scientific community. To prematurely proclaim the victory of one group over another would be a tragic mistake that I'm afraid we are making.'

President Vaclav Klaus to UN Climate Change
Conference, September 24, 2007 †

---

* Jose-Manuel Barroso, 'The business solution to the problem of climate change', eGov Monitor website, 26 May 2009.
† Vaclav Klaus (who was to become acting President of the EU at the same time as the European Commission President made the statement quoted above). *Blue Planet in Green Shackles* (CEI, 2008).

7

The temperature drops

IPCC 4, The modellers lose the plot:
2007

'It is another nail in the coffin of the climate change deniers and represents the most authoritative picture to date, showing that the debate over the science of climate change is well and truly over, as demonstrated by the publication of today's report by the IPCC.'

David Miliband, UK Environment Secretary, at launch of the
IPCC's Fourth Assessment Report, Paris, 1 February 2007[1]

'Faced with this emergency, now is not the time for half-measures. It is the time for a revolution, in the true sense of the term ... we are in truth on the doorstep of the irreversible.'

President Jacques Chirac, on the same occasion[2]

'Eleven of the last twelve years (1995–2006) rank among the twelve warmest years in the instrumental record of global surface temperatures.'

IPCC Fourth Assessment Report 2007[3]

'2007 is likely to be the warmest year on record globally, beating the current record set in 1998.'

UK Met Office, press release, 4 January 2007

'According to the new data published by NASA, 1998 is no longer the hottest year ever. 1934 is.'

Watts Up With That, August 2007

At the end of January 2007 it was reported that £120 million had been put into launching 'a new worldwide movement', Global Cool. It was backed not only by politicians and business leaders but by film actors such as Leonardo di Caprio, Orlando Bloom and Josh Hartnett, and pop groups such as Pink, Razorlight and The Killers. They were calling on 'one billion people to reduce their carbon emissions by just one tonne a year for the next 10 years'.

On 31 January some of the celebrities behind Global Cool met prime minister Tony Blair and 50 'business leaders' at 10 Downing

Street to plead for drastic cuts in carbon emissions and for greater use of renewable energy sources, such as 'solar, wind, water and hydrogen'.[4]

The timing of this publicity stunt was not accidental. It was one of the events planned to attract publicity to the unveiling in Paris two days later of the IPCC's long-awaited Fourth Assessment Report (4AR). Or, to be more precise, what was being released that day to the world's media was the politically-agreed Summary for Policymakers. As in 2001, it was not yet possible to compare the claims made in the Summary with the science it purported to summarise because the full technical report would not be available for several months.[5]

It was the most lavish launch of an IPCC report to date, attended by an array of political figures led by France's President Chirac. Unprecedented care had been taken to feed the media with what they needed to win headlines. The Summary began by starkly stating that

> *'Warming of the climate system is unequivocal, as is now evident from observations of increases in global air and ocean temperatures, widespread melting of snow and ice and rising average sea level.'*

Eleven of the previous 12 years, it went on, were among the 12 warmest years ever recorded. It was likely that Northern Hemisphere temperatures had become 'the highest in at least the past 1300 years'. Glaciers and snow cover were declining in both hemispheres. Droughts and heat waves had become more frequent. 'The incidence of extreme high seal level has increased worldwide'. There had been increases in 'intense tropical cyclone activity in the North Atlantic', the spread of vector-borne disease and much else.

Furthermore, the IPCC claimed that it now had new evidence to confirm that many of these problems were being caused by human activity. 'Advances since the TAR show that discernible human influences extend beyond average temperature to other aspects of climate', such as the rise in sea levels, changes in 'extra-tropical storm tracks', the greater risk of heat-waves, droughts and 'extreme precipitation'.

All this was projected with an eyecatching display of graphs, carefully drawn to show either a dramatic increase (temperatures, sea levels) or a dramatic decline (snow cover) according to the point the IPCC wished to convey.

The politicians stood by to provide the soundbites the media were looking for. The French President called, in the words quoted above, for a 'revolution in the true sense of the term', to meet this 'emergency' which had placed mankind 'on the doorstep of the irreversible'.

Britain's Environment Secretary David Miliband acclaimed the report as 'the final nail in the coffin of the climate change deniers'. On his return home he won more headlines by jointly announcing with the Education Secretary, Alan Johnson, that DVDs of Gore's film *A* *n* *Inconvenient Truth* would be sent to every one of the 3,385 secondary schools in Britain. 'I was struck', said Miliband, 'by the visual evidence the film provides, making clear that the changing climate is already having an impact on our world today, from Mount Kilimanjaro to the Himalayan mountains'.[6]

Although three months were to elapse before it would be possible to check what evidence the scientific report could cite to support the alarming claims made in the Summary, the launch was given the media coverage they were all after.

But at this point in the story, something unexpected happened. Although the scale of it would not be apparent for a year or more, at the very time the IPCC was launching its report global temperatures were beginning to register a sharp fall.

Over the next year, following another sharp spike in 2006 second only to that in 1998 (and similarly attributed to a rather smaller El Niño event), all the main sources of temperature data were to show a decline averaging 0.7°C. This was larger than the net rise of 0.6 degrees accepted by the IPCC for the whole of the twentieth century.

What did this mean? Was it just another temporary downward blip, of the kind which had been seen before, as in 1999 and 2000 when temperatures fell just as sharply back from their record high in the El Niño year of 1998? Or was it the first indication that something more fundamental might be going on?

All that could really be said at this stage was that the trend in global temperatures observed in the early years of the twenty-first century was no longer in accord with those predictions of the computer models on which so much of the concern over global warming rested. And this began to raise some rather important questions.

For a start it focused rather closer attention on the chief data sources to which the IPCC and everyone else looked for their picture of how temperatures were changing. There were four of these, two relying on measurements made since 1979 by NASA satellites and two on thermometer readings taken at the earth's surface.

One of the two satellite sources was based at the University of Alabama, Huntsville (UAH), run by Dr Roy Spencer, formerly a senior scientist with NASA, and Dr John Christy, a professor of atmospheric science who had been a lead author on the IPCC's 2001 report. Spencer and Christy had developed and refined the means whereby remarkably accurate temperature records covering almost the entire globe could be obtained indirectly by measuring the variations in microwaves given off by oxygen molecules in the atmosphere. The other satellite-based record was produced by a research team working for a California-based company, Remote Sensing Systems (RSS), under contract to NASA.

The remaining two sources were based on direct thermometer readings from a semi-worldwide network of surface weather stations on land and sea. One of these, HadCrut, was the Climate Research Unit at the University of East Anglia in Britain, working in association with the UK Met Office's Hadley Centre based in Exeter.* The other was NASA's Goddard Institute for Space Studies (GISS), run from New York since 1981 by Al Gore's old ally James Hansen (it might have seemed odd that a research institute under the aegis of NASA should rely not on satellite data but on surface thermometer measurements).

No single thing had done more to promote worldwide concern over global warming since 1988 than the fact that all these four temperature records had been broadly in agreement with each other, showing through most of that time that, despite fluctuations up and down, the earth's atmosphere had shown a consistent warming trend.

The 1980s had been warmer than the 1970s. The 1990s were warmer still, culminating in the peak year of 1998. All four data sources had shown a sharp post-El Niño fall, from which temperatures then recovered to show the years from 2001 generally higher than those of the 1990s.

What had also become noticeable, however, was that their overall trend was no longer continuing upwards. The trend line, all four sources showed, was flattening out (although the figures from GISS, it was noted, were now consistently higher than from the other three sources). And what was particularly interesting was that this trend was no longer in agreement with the predictions of the IPCC's com-

---

* It was ironic that the 30-strong CRU team worked in a building named after the late Hubert Lamb, the university's climate historian who had first identified what he called the 'Mediaeval Warm Epoch'.

puter models. For the first time the two lines were beginning clearly to diverge.

The significance of this was that those models had been programmed to assume that the main driver causing global temperatures to increase was the level of CO_2 in the atmosphere. So long as CO_2 continued to increase, according to the models, so temperatures must follow. But this was no longer happening.

There was no doubt that CO_2 levels were continuing to increase, having by 2007 reached 383 parts per million, up 20 per cent from their level when Keeling began his measurements on Mauna Loa back in 1958. But the fact that temperatures were no longer rising on the same curve, as the models predicted they should, inevitably began to raise a rather large question mark not just over the reliability of the models but also, even more significantly, over the theory on which they were based. If the trend line were actually to fall, those question marks would become even more insistent.

So confident still were the modellers in their theory that, in January 2007, the UK Met Office, aided by the predictions of its Hadley Centre super-computer, forecast that 2007 would probably overtake 1998 as 'the warmest year on record'.

It was at just this time, however, that, coinciding with a mild La Niña event, global temperatures were beginning a fall which, over the next 12 months, would at least temporarily take them down by a jump greater than their entire twentieth-century net rise. Did those computer modellers really know what they were doing? Or was it possible that the supporters of the 'consensus' had actually been looking in the wrong place to explain why temperatures over the previous 30 years had been rising?

THE MISSING PIECE OF THE JIGSAW?

One of the more worrying features of the 'consensus' theory that rising temperatures were caused almost entirely by rising levels of CO_2 was how much of the story of the earth's climate its advocates seemed to need to distort or suppress in order to make their case.

The most glaring instance of this was the lengths to which they had gone to strike out of the record all the evidence for temperature fluctuations in the past, notably the Mediaeval Warm Period, the Little Ice Age and the twentieth-century Little Cooling. This was because these events appeared to contradict the simplicity of their theory: not least in that the Mediaeval Warm Period had long pre-ceded any rise in CO_2 levels, while the Little Cooling coincided with a time when CO_2 levels were sharply rising.

Was there any other explanation which might more plausibly fit the facts? One of the most interesting features of the scientific debate as it had developed in the early years of the twenty-first century – outside the confines of the IPCC – was the growing number of sci-entists in many countries coming to the view that one hugely impor-tant factor had been overlooked. This was the link between what were far and away the two most conspicuous determinants of the earth's climate.

Whenever we talk of climate, even just of today's weather, two considerations dominate everything else. One is the sun. The other is how much cloud there is in the sky. It is this which determines the extent to which the earth is exposed directly to the sun's heat.

All attention in the public debate over global warming had been focused on the contribution man might be making to shaping the climate by producing gases which make it harder for heat from the earth to escape back into space. But nothing like enough attention had been paid to the source of all that heat in the first place: the great radiant ball of fire in the heavens without which no life could exist, and which is far and away the most powerful determinant of all the variations in climate on earth.

One of the first scientists to note an apparent connection between the state of the weather and that of the sun itself was the astronomer William Herschel, who in 1801 suggested that there seemed to be a correlation between the price of wheat and the number of sunspots. These are the seemingly dark patches which appear on the sun's disk, associated with intense magnetic activity. The regularity of their appearance is generally governed by various overlapping cycles, of which the shortest is every 11 years.* Fewer sunspots, Herschel observed, seemed to bring colder weather and lower crop yields. There-fore the price of wheat rose.

Later in the nineteenth century, two scientists – a German astronomer Gustav Spörer followed by Edward Maunder, keeper of sunspot records at the Greenwich Royal Observatory – noted the remarkable decline in sunspot activity between 1645 and 1715. In

---

* The economist William Stanley Jevons (1835–1882), who had some scientific background, also suggested that there appeared to be a link between the rises and falls of sunspot activity and business cycles.

one 30-year period barely 50 sunspots had been recorded, instead of the usual 40–50,000. The particular significance of what is now known as the 'Maunder Minimum' is that it coincided with the coldest period of the Little Ice Age.

For long no one was aware of quite what mechanism might allow sunspot activity to influence the earth's climate, although scientists from several different disciplines contributed what would eventually be seen as vital pieces of the jigsaw. One was Victor Hess, an Austrian physicist, who was to win a Nobel prize in 1936 for having discovered the constant bombardment of the earth by what he called 'cosmic rays'. These are fast-moving, highly-charged atomic particles originating from astronomical events in many parts of the universe, such as exploding stars. Some of these particles manage to penetrate the earth's lower atmosphere (indeed the earth itself), taking the form of secondary particles known as muons, or 'heavy electrons'.

Two pieces of the jigsaw were particularly important. One was the discovery that sunspot activity, creating what is known as the solar wind, stretching out throughout the solar system, determines how many of these cosmic particles reach the earth. When the magnetic force from the sunspots is high, cosmic rays are deflected from the earth. When sunspot activity is low, the quantity reaching the earth increases.[7]

The other more recent discovery has been how these cosmic particles are related to the cloud-cover in the lower atmosphere which plays such a crucial part in shaping the earth's climate. Many scientists have played a part in this story, one of the most remarkable in modern science.[8]

In 1991 two Danish scientists, Knud Lassen and Eigil Friis-Christensen of the Danish Meteorological Institute, published a paper noting a striking correlation between quickening of sunspot activity and the rise in temperatures in the Northern Hemisphere in the twentieth century.[9] At the end of 1995 their colleague Henrik Svensmark, a physicist, began studying data compiled by NASA's Goddard Institute for the International Cloud Climatology Satellite Project. Drawn from satellites all over the world, this charted changes in cloud-cover between 1983 and 1990. They showed a remarkable correlation between the extent of cloud and the relative intensity of cosmic rays.

In 1996 Svensmark and Friis-Christensen decided that their findings were so striking that they should be published.[10] It was some time before these could find a publisher because they diverged so far from the 'consensus' view, which wanted to see CO_2 as the only driver of climate change. In 1992, when a Danish delegation had suggested to the IPCC that the influence of the sun on climate should be added to the list of topics worthy of further research, the proposal was rejected out of hand. In 1996, when the IPCC's chairman Bert Bolin was asked to comment on the two men's findings, after they had been previewed at a conference of the Royal Astronomical Society in Birmingham, he angrily dismissed them as 'scientifically extremely naïve and irresponsible'.[11]

Threatened with loss of funding, the two men continued to receive derisive comments from fellow-scientists, not least at a conference of Nordic scientists addressed by Svensmark later that same year. But when Markku Kumala, the Finnish chairman of the International Commission on Clouds and Precipitation, was invited to join in the general scorn he surprised everyone present by observing that Svensmark's idea 'could be right'.

At the end of 1997 Friis-Christensen became director of what was to become the Danish National Space Center. In 1998 he asked Svensmark and an English colleague Nigel Marsh to join him, giving them the opportunity for a much more systematic review of the data linking solar radiation with cloud cover round the globe. By 2000, they had reached their conclusions. The link between 'solar variability' and 'low clouds' was inescapable.

By this time other studies were beginning to lend credibility to the theory that variations in global temperature had been influenced by fluctuations in cosmic rays, not just in recent times but far back into prehistory.

In 2001 a team led by a Columbia University geologist, Gerard Bond, came up with remarkable confirmation of this point, correlating evidence of past cosmic ray levels from beryllium-10 isotopes in sediment cores with the pattern of climate shifts shown by fragments dropped by 'armadas' of icebergs in the North Atlantic during different Ice Age glaciations.[12] Although Bond and his Swiss colleague Jurg Beer could not accept Svensmark's view that the final explanation lay in cloud-cover (they were not cloud experts), their overall findings significantly reinforced the thesis that climate change over the past 10,000 years had been much more plausibly driven by solar radiation and cosmic rays rather than by CO_2. Their rises and falls simply coincided much better with the evidence, including that for all the major climate shifts up to the present day.

Other studies were following thick and fast. When Charles Perry of the US Geological Service and Kenneth Hsu looked at the correlation between solar radiation and carbon-14 in tree rings over 90,000 years, they found the matches so exact that any idea of modern global warming being 'caused solely by an increase in CO_2 concentrations' must be regarded as 'questionable'.[13]

A cross-disciplinary study published in 2003 by Nir Shaviv, an astrophsyicist at the University of Jerusalem, and Jan Veizer, a University of Ottawa geologist, analysed data showing world temperature levels going back 500 million years. They found little correlation between the earth's climate and CO_2 levels (at times CO_2 levels had been as much as 18 times higher than today's and were 10 times higher even during the intense Ordovician glaciation).[14]

The more evidence that became available, the more the correlation with solar activity and cosmic rays seemed to explain all those past fluctuations in temperature which had previously been such a puzzle, from the Mediaeval Warm Period and the Little Ice Age (coinciding with the Maunder Minimum) to the Little Cooling (when solar magnetic activity again fell) and the resumed warming of recent decades.[15]

Such coincidences were all very well, but the one thing missing was a proper explanation of how the 'stardust' particles of cosmic rays could in themselves have a part in forming those clouds which are such an important factor in shaping the world's climate. Building on all that was known about the processes behind cloud formation, going back to researches carried out in the nineteenth century by a British engineer John Aitken, a final clue was provided by a series of experiments begun by Svensmark in Copenhagen in 2004.

It had long been established that the molecules of water vapour which form clouds require an initial 'seed' to begin forming up together. Most often this consists of minute droplets of sulphuric acid in the atmosphere. But a question which had never been answered was how such 'seeds' themselves are formed. Do they in turn require some even smaller speck of matter to begin the process?

Svensmark and his colleagues built a large box, full of artificially pure air, together with traces of sulphur dioxide and ozone as are found in unpolluted air in the atmosphere. For months they subjected it to rigorous experiments, designed to replicate conditions in which sulphuric acid droplets form in the air to set off the process of cloud-forming. By the summer of 2005, after checking and cross-checking every detail, they had their cloud formation. The results were even more conclusive than they had anticipated.

The SKY project had shown that the seeding which initiated the process leading to cloud vapour could only have originated from the electrons liberated by cosmic-ray muons passing through the box. It looked as though those muon particles did indeed play a key part in cloud formation. The more cosmic rays enter the earth's atmosphere, the more clouds are likely to form and thus the more the climate is likely to cool. The more solar radiation deflects the cosmic rays, the fewer the clouds that can form and the more the temperature will rise.[16]

So far did the findings of Svensmark's experiment differ from the prevailing orthodoxy that one scientific journal after another refused to publish them. Eventually they were accepted by the Royal Society of London for publication in 2007, under the title 'Experimental evidence for the role of ions in particle nucleation under atmospheric conditions'. In October 2006, the society released an advance draft of the paper online. A press notice went out from the Danish National Space Center, accompanied by a comment from its director Professor Friis-Christensen:

> *Many climate scientists have considered the linkages from cosmic rays to clouds to climate as unproven. Some said there was no conceivable way in which cosmic rays could influence cloud cover. The SKY experiment now shows how they do so, and should help put the cosmic ray connection firmly onto the agenda of internation climate research.'* [17]

On 8 March 2007 Svensmark's thesis was for the first time introduced to a mass-audience by a televison documentary made by Martin Durkin for Channel Four, *The Great Global Warming Swindle*. This was to become the most controversial television programme on global warming ever made, because it featured many of the scientists who had long been attempting to argue an alternative view to the orthodoxy represented by the IPCC.

For years the leading television networks, such as the BBC in Britain, had presented viewers with nothing but the 'consensus' view, reflected not just in numerous documentaries but routinely in supposedly impartial news programmes. Now for the first time, a TV audience was to be allowed to hear another side of the story.[18]

THE GREAT GLOBAL WARMING SWINDLE

Durkin's 90-minute documentary was as unashamedly one-sided in making its case as all those BBC documentaries had been in presenting the 'consensus' view. Among the scientists it interviewed, most of them currently or formerly holders of professorial chairs, were Dr Lindzen, Dr Singer, Dr Spencer and Dr Christy of UAH, Dr Pat Michaels, Dr Nir Shaviv, Dr Syun-ichi Akasofu, former director of the International Arctic Research Center in Alaska, Dr Tim Ball of Winnipeg University's Department of Climatology, Dr Paul Reiter, Dr Eigel Friis-Christensen and Patrick Moore, a co-founder of Greenpeace. He, like other contributors to the programme, had over the years completely changed his view on global warming.

A first main point made by several contributors, including Lindzen, Singer and Christy, was that the nature of the warming seen in recent years did not fit with what the orthodox theory predicted. The classic 'fingerprint' of CO_2-induced warming, said the theory, was that warming is most pronounced in the middle and upper troposphere, to where man-made CO_2 rises to amplify the greenhouse effect. Yet satellite and weather balloon measurements consistently showed recent warming to have been greater at the earth's surface.

The next section of the programme was directed at the belief that rises in CO_2 lead directly to rises in temperature. This was illustrated by the graphs based on ice-core studies which played such a key part in Gore's film, appearing to show a direct causative correlation between CO_2 levels and temperature . But the reality was not as Gore had shown it. 'What Al Gore doesn't say', explained Professor Ian Clark, an expert on ice-cores from Ottawa University, 'is that the link is the wrong way round'. Although Gore had carefully fitted his CO_2 and temperature graphs together, to show them rising and falling more or less simultaneously, a series of ice-core studies had shown that rises in CO_2 levels don't precede rises in temperature, they follow them. It is the rising temperature which eventually causes a rise in CO_2: but only very slowly, as much as 800 years later.[19]

The chief reason for this, as was explained by Dr Carl Wunsch, professor of physical oceanography at MIT, is that the oceans are by far the largest reservoir of CO_2 on the planet, infinitely larger than all other sources of CO_2 put together. When temperatures are cool the oceans absorb CO_2, when the sea warms up it releases it. But the oceans are so huge that this takes a long time. As Wunsch put it, the ocean thus 'has a memory of past events'.

So if CO_2 wasn't driving the climate, asked the programme, what does? Here Dr Friis-Christensen and Nigel Calder, who had just written a book with Svensmark,[20] explained the theory that by far the most plausible driver of climate change is the magnetic activity of the sun, and its interaction with the earth's cloud cover. In the twentieth century, the intensity of the sun's magnetic field had more than doubled: hence the prime reason for the earth's recent warming.

The programme made other familiar points. Professor Philip Stott, a retired University of London geographer, who for years had been almost a lone voice arguing a sceptical view of global warming in the British press, pointed out that the IPCC was not, as it was generally perceived, a scientific body but was 'politically driven'. Several contributors including Lindzen referred to the way research funding had become so skewed in favour of projects designed to support the 'consensus' that grants to promote its orthodoxy had risen to some $20 billion a year.

The programme ended by arguing that the most obvious victims of the global warming scare would be hundreds of millions of people living in poverty in the undeveloped world, many dying early because their only means of cooking was to burn animal dung or firewood in smoke-filled huts. Paul Driesser, the US author of *Eco-Imperialism: Green Power, Black Death*, and an African economist, James Shikwati, explained how they were already being held down in poverty because environmentalists from rich countries were determined to deny them the right to improve their lives through use of fossil fuels.

A doctor in charge of a clinic in rural Kenya showed how his surgery was only permitted by his government to derive its electricity from solar panels. So small and unreliable was the amount of power these produced that he had to choose between running a light to examine his patients or running the refrigerator in which he kept his drugs. He could not do both. Yet at the same time, not far away in Nairobi, the film showed 6,000 politicians, officials and environmentalists from across the world, driving up in SUVs to an air-conditioned conference centre for a gathering sponsored by the UN Environment Program under the UNFCCC process. Their purpose was to discuss the need to halt global warming, and for the Third World to learn to depend on renewable energy.[21]

Because its arguments had been so rarely heard amid the relentless promotion of the 'consensus' version, *The Great Global Warming Swindle* attracted considerable coverage in the British press. Some of it was extremely hostile. The *Guardian's* environmental crusader

George Monbiot savaged its contributors as 'cranks' talking 'bunkum', whose views had long since been 'discredited' by proper scientists.[22]

But even this paled beside the outrage the programme provoked from the more official pro-warming establishment. An avalanche of complaints began descending on Ofcom, the regulatory body charged with ensuring that British broadcasters obeyed certain rules relating to fairness and impartiality. Altogether there were 265 of these, including a pile of objections from a Mr Bob Ward, former head of media for the Royal Society, and '37 professors'. Another, 175 pages long, came from a Mr Dave Rado, supported by various scientists including Bert Bolin. Finally, most impressive of all, was one from the IPCC itself.

Scarcely a detail of Durkin's programme had not aroused their ire, from every kind of alleged scientific 'error' and charges that it had shown misleading graphs (this from the champions of the 'hockey stick') to complaints that the IPCC had not been given enough time to comment on the programme before it was shown.

Such a mountain of complaints would take Ofcom more than a year to consider. But one complainant whose protests were immediately reported in the press was Dr Wunsch, the oceanographer, whose filmed comments, he claimed, had been shown 'out of context'. Had he been told the nature and purpose of the programme, he said, as someone who accepted that man-made global warming was a serious threat he would never have agreed to take part. As it was, he told the *Observer*, *The Great Global Warming Swindle* was 'as close to pure propaganda as anything since World War Two' (by which he presumably meant the efforts of Josef Goebbels).[23]

Since everything he was shown as saying was on film, Wunsch could scarcely complain he had not said it, But his views, he said, had been 'distorted by the context in which they placed them'.

What enraged the upholders of the 'consensus' more than anything else, however, was the publicity Durkin's programme gave to those scientists who believed that the real cause of global warming (and cooling) lay in the activity of the sun, particularly the theories of Friis-Christensen and Svensmark. Friis-Christensen's work, it was pointed out on various blogs, had been wholly discredited. One graph shown in the film, it was claimed, had deliberately omitted the last few years of solar activity, because to have included these would have shown that it had been declining just when global temperatures were rising, thus exposing the theory as false (Durkin amended this for the DVD version of his film by adding the missing years).

So concerned were the advocates of the 'consensus' by the interest now being shown in the view that global warming might be related to the activity of the sun that some more formal riposte was inevitable. On 11 July 2007 it came. Bearing all the signs of a carefully planned operation, the media, led by the BBC and *Nature*, suddenly came out with a rash of news items trailing a new study which, it was claimed, had completely demolished the 'solar warming' thesis.[24]

The paper, published online by the Royal Society, was by Professor Mike Lockwood, a physicist at the Rutherford Appleton laboratory, and Claus Frölich of the World Radiation Center in Davos, Switzerland.[25] They claimed that a fresh look at the data for the previous 100 years showed that Svensmark's solar data were seriously wrong. They conceded that the sun's magnetic activity had been higher in the twentieth century than in previous centuries, and also, perhaps surprisingly, admitted that in earlier years this had significantly influenced global temperatures. But in 1985 it had peaked and started to decline, and it was at just this time that global surface temperatures had continued to rise, higher than ever. This was the proof, they claimed, that solar activity could not be the cause of recent warming.

Supporters of the 'consensus' were exultant at their coup. 'This paper is the final nail in the coffin for people who would like to make the Sun responsible for present global warming', one German climate scientist told *Nature*.[26] 'This should settle the debate', said Lockwood himself, expressing particular anger at the Channel Four programme, which he described as 'so bad it was almost fraudulent'.[27]

Yet the Royal Society's paper had a number of odd features. One was that its seven pages of text were written so opaquely, citing so many sources, that it looked as though the authors' chief purpose was just to put across their central headline message.

They were at pains, for instance, not to argue with the mass of research showing that, up to recent times, solar effects had played a significant part in influencing global temperatures ('it is becoming feasible', they conceded, 'to detect genuine solar forcing in climate records'). The focus of their concern was the period since 1985, in assessing whether 'solar variations could have played any role in observed present-day global warming'. Here, having established that solar activity had weakened, they could put across their central message: that, because surface temperatures had continued to rise, there could be no connection between current warming and the Sun.

But herein lay several disconcerting features of their argument. One was that a graph allegedly showing the cosmic ray count (gleefully reproduced by the BBC) in fact showed something quite unrelated to cosmic rays.[28] A graph of the actual cosmic ray count (from the Climax neutron monitor) showed, for instance, that in the early 1990s it was very low, indicating the likely onset of a strong warming phase over the following years. Why had this evidence been misrepresented and omitted?

Then why had they only included a graph of recent surface temperatures and not one showing satellite data? The latest satellite record of lower air temperatures since 1979 showed that, following the El Niño year 1998, levels had fallen markedly, even, in 2000, by as much as a full degree. Although it had risen again, with a spike in 2006, a further sharp fall in 2007 had already taken it down to a level 0.6 of a degree lower than it was in 1998. Indeed it was slightly lower than a level it had reached in 1983.[29]

Not to include this was suspect enough. But even more so was the way in which the record of surface temperatures on which Lockwood and Frölich hung their case, instead of giving year-by-year figures, was smoothed out to show a continuous warming. Looked at on a year-by-year basis, the latest data from the Hadley Centre gave a very different picture. These showed that, in the six years between 2000 and 2006, even the trend line of surface temperatures had not continued to rise, flattening out around an average level more than 0.2 degrees lower than in 1998. Now in 2007, as was already apparent, it was falling further still.

Why did the authors prefer such long-term averages to the simpler message of year-by-year data? The latter would have exposed a crucial flaw in their argument. If rising CO_2 levels were the main driver of global warming, then temperatures should also have continued to rise. If temperatures were flattening out at a time when CO_2 levels were still increasing, this questioned the entire case for CO_2-driven global warming.

Despite such determined efforts being made to discredit the findings of Svensmark's SKY experiment, not all the world's more established scientists were so easily satisfied. It had already been announced that in 2010 an international team at CERN, the world's largest subatomic particle laboratory based in Geneva, would be carrying out a very much larger-scale test of Svensmark's theory, in a project named CLOUD.

Thus there were now two quite different theories as to why global temperatures had risen in the twentieth century. Each, according to its supporters, could account for all the observed net temperature rise of 0.6 degrees. The explanation could not lie in both equally. Which one more closely fitted the evidence? It already seemed clear that the next few years would provide powerful clues as to which was nearer the truth.

Meanwhile, yet another puzzle had been coming to light which might complicate the debate even further.

In recent years, the world's astronomers had been observing something very odd going on in different parts of the solar system. This had first been noticed in 1998, when researchers at MIT reported that, according to observations by the Hubble telescope, Triton, the largest moon of the planet Neptune, seemed to have heated up significantly since it was visited by the Explorer space probe in 1989. The moon's surface frozen nitrogen appeared to be melting into gas.[30]

In 2002 there had been reports that the atmospheric pressure on Pluto had tripled in 14 years, indicating a 2°C rise in temperature.[31] In 2006 this had been confirmed by astronomers in Tasmania, who said that if anything Pluto's atmosphere had got even denser.[32]

In 2003 the project manager for NASA's Odyssey mission, orbiting Mars, reported that there was also evidence of global warming on Mars.[33] In 2005 NASA confirmed that the CO_2 'ice caps' near Mars's South Pole had been diminishing three summers in a row.[34]

In Russia, many of whose leading scientists had long been convinced that the solar activity played a much larger part than man-made CO_2 in driving the earth's climate, the country's most eminent astronomer, Habibullo Abdussamatov, head of the Pulkovo Observatory in St Petersburg, described this as evidence confirming that current global warming was being caused by changes in the Sun. 'Man-made greenhouse warming', he said, 'has made a small contribution to the warming seen on Earth in recent years, but it cannot compete with the increase in solar irradiance'.

In 2006, scientists from Berkeley reported that Hubble was now providing evidence from the emergence of a new red 'storm spot' on Jupiter that temperatures on that planet too seemed to be rising, in places by as much as 10 degrees.[35]

In other words, there seemed surprising evidence that warming was taking place throughout the solar system. Even though the mechanism for this might not yet be clear, it implied that some common cause might be at work which was not limited just to events on Planet Earth. And on how many other bodies orbiting round the sun were the inhabitants driving around in SUVs or failing to unplug their TV sets before going to bed at night?

HOW THE 'HOCKEY TEAM' SAVED THE 'HOCKEY STICK'

When, at the end of April 2007, the IPCC finally released online the full version of its scientific report 'The basis of physical change' – nearly three months after the publication of its Summary for Policymakers – one question was bound to attract particular interest. How would the IPCC respond to the comprehensive discrediting of the 'hockey stick', which in 2001 it had made the star of the show?

The message of the 'hockey stick' after all remained absolutely crucial to the global warming 'consensus' because it was the only real evidence to suggest that the warming of recent decades was without precedent in human history. If temperatures had been as high or even higher in pre-industrial times, the theory that the current warming could not have been caused by natural means would lose its central underpinning. At all costs this dramatic image of temperatures having suddenly hurtled upwards at the end of the twentieth century to levels never known before must somehow be kept alive.

McIntyre and McKitrick's first questioning of Mann's 'hockey stick' in 2003 had set off widespread discussion of the issue on the internet. This helped to give a whole new dimension to the climate change debate as, away from the main public arena, an increasingly important part came to be played in the debate by specialist blogs. These used the internet to carry on technical discussions with an intensity of interchange which the mainstream media and even scientific journals could not emulate.

In 2004, Mann and a group of scientific allies set up a blog called RealClimate to defend their case and generally to promote their particular view of global warming, Calling themselves the 'Hockey Team', they liked to insist that they were 'genuine climate scientists', in contrast to the unqualified 'amateurs' who dared to criticise them.

Mann's RealClimate colleagues, whose work was centred on computer models, included Gavin Schmidt, a British-born senior colleague of Hansen's at GISS; Ray Bradley, one of Mann's co-authors on the original 'hockey stick' studies; and Caspar Ammann, a Swiss palaeoclimatologist employed by the National Center for Atmospheric Research in Colorado and one of Mann's most active defenders.

Other key allies of the 'Hockey Team' included two senior staff members of the Climate Research Unit at the University of East Anglia in Britain. Dendrochronologist Dr Keith Briffa specialised in tree ring studies. The CRU's director, Professor Phil Jones, ran the world-ranking temperature series operated by the CRU with the Hadley Centre. Almost all of them, Mann, Bradley, Briffa, Jones and Ammann, were not only key contributors to IPCC reports but, as Wegman observed in 2006, had extensively collaborated with each other on a succession of papers defending the 'hockey stick' and the methods used to reach its conclusions.[36]

On the other side of the debate, in 2005 Steve McIntyre launched his own blog, Climate Audit, specialising in the analysis of data related to climate change. Having by now established something of a reputation in this field, he was to play a central part in the drama which followed, as the IPCC and the 'Hockey Team' attempted to salvage the 'hockey stick's' reputation.

This mini-saga was to become so murky and so complex that here it will only be summarised, reserving some of the details for an appendix.[37] But it was a story which had begun back in May 2005 when UCAR (the University Corporation of Atmospheric Research) issued a press release announcing that new papers submitted by a pair of Mann's close allies, Ammann and Wahl, to two scientific journals would show that 'the highly publicised criticisms' directed at Mann's graph were 'unfounded'.

These papers were intended to be the 'secret weapon' which would finally demolish McIntyre and McKitrick. The fact that they were promptly cited by Sir John Houghton and others in front of two congressional committees, indicated that the IPCC establishment was looking to the Ammann and Wahl papers to banish any further doubts about the 'hockey stick'. It could then be brought back again in the IPCC's 2007 report without any further embarrassment.

The story which followed divided into two stages. The first was the extraordinarily chequered career of the Amman and Wahl papers, after their submission in 2005 to the two journals, *Geophysical*

Research Letters and *Climatic Change*. Under the IPCC's rules, in order for the papers to to be cited in its 2007 report, they would have to be published (or at least 'accepted for publication') by the prescribed deadline of 16 December 2005.

However, the plan then ran into a succession of unexpected glitches. The paper sent to *Geophysical Research Letters* was rejected as unfit for publication. Then the editor of *Climatic Change*, Stephen Schneider, mischievously sent the other paper for peer-review to McIntyre himself. He soon spotted that the study had repeated exactly the same basic errors as Mann's original. Furthermore, missing from it were the crucial 'validation statistics' which any such computer study requires to establish whether or not its methodology can be relied on. When Ammann and Wahl refused to provide them, this led to the paper being held in abeyance.

As the clock was now ticking down to the December deadline, heavy pressure was put on both journals to bring the papers back into play. Mann was able triumphantly to announce on RealClimate that both papers were to be published after all. Just four days before the deadline, *Climatic Change* announced that, with McIntyre now removed from his role as peer-reviewer, its flawed paper had been 'accepted for publication'.

Thus in the nick of time, albeit in very odd circumstances, the IPCC had got clearance for at least one of the papers it needed to cite in its report (even though, after further hold-ups, the paper would not actually be published until months after the 2007 report had already appeared).

Then began the second part of the drama, The lead author chosen for the relevant section of the 2007 report, Chapter 6 on 'Palaeoclimate', was Dr Briffa, a key member of the 'Hockey Team', with Ammann himself named as a 'contributing author'. They would thus be in an ideal position to ensure that Ammann and Wahl's paper was used to full effect. But among the experts chosen to review this chapter were McIntyre and McKitrick.

This meant that the two men were able to get an early sight of how the IPCC proposed to deal with the 'hockey stick' controversy. Battle-hardened though they were, what they found in the first draft astonished them, prompting them as reviewers to a stream of highly critical comments.

For a start, they could see that their own work had been absurdly misrepresented. The initial draft made out that they had tried to produce their own reconstruction of northern hemisphere temperatures, claiming to have used the same proxies as Mann. But the draft then accused them of having 'omitted several important proxy series used in the original reconstruction' and thus having reached false conclusions. This was, of course, the very reverse of what McIntyre and McKitrick had done. Their sole purpose in running Mann's model without the atypical bristlecone proxies had been to demonstrate how completely the inclusion of the bristlecones had skewed Mann's results.

The draft went on to claim that Mann's 1999 findings had been 'successfully reproduced by Wahl and Ammann'. This, as McKitrick commented, was simply untrue. Despite several attempts to replicate them, he pointed out, 'Mann's results have never been reproduced', by Ammann and Wahl or anyone else. As for the charge that McIntyre had left out the bristlecones in order to skew his own results, this was such an inversion of the truth that McKitrick suggested the IPCC's author must have got his 'material off the RealClimate website rather than from following the debate in the literature'.

Although each of McIntyre and McKitrick's comments were officially marked 'noted', as if they were being taken account of, when the second draft arrived it was clear they had been ignored. If anything, the new version was even more one-sided than the first. Not only did it persist in claiming that Wahl and Ammann had shown that the sole reason why McIntyre and McKitrick were 'unable to replicate Mann's results was due to their omission of 'several proxy series used by Mann, *et al.*'; it went on to claim that Mann's findings had subsequently been confirmed by several other studies 'using different methods to those of Mann, *et al.*'.

McIntyre reiterated his criticisms, pointing out that all these studies had merely repeated the errors identified in Mann's original version. His points were again ignored and the text remained unchanged. He wrote to Susan Solomon, a co-chair of the WG I report, asking that reviewers should be allowed to see the data and methodology of papers they were asked to review. She replied forbidding him to make any further attempts to ask for the data. She warned him that if there was further evidence that he was using his position to challenge the rules governing access to 'unpublished and therefore confidential material', then 'we will no longer be able to continue to treat you as an expert reviewer for the IPCC'.

The mystery which remained was why, since all their comments had been rejected, the IPCC should have asked McIntyre and Mc-

Kitrick to act as reviewers in the first place. One possible explanation was that, knowing the report was going to condemn their work
in no uncertain terms, the IPCC wanted to be able to say that it had
given them every chance to defend their position but that they had
failed to make their case.

Thus did the IPCC manage to salvage its dependence on the 'hockey
stick'. In light of all the controversy which had surrounded it, not
least its demolition by Wegman and North a year earlier, the IPCC
at least knew better than to reproduce yet again the same graph
which in 2001 it had published five times. But it did manage to
smuggle in a version of Mann's original version (Fig. 6.10), heavily
disguised as part of a multiple graphic of northern hemisphere 'temperature reconstructions' (which became known, from its tangled
web of lines, as the 'spaghetti diagram'). Below it, another graphic
showed an 'overlap of reconstructed temperatures' displaying an
unmistakable 'hockey stick' shape which looked remarkably similar
to Mann's original.

Even these graphics had drawn criticism from several reviewers,
including McIntyre, who pointed out that the 'spaghetti' version, in
a way which was 'statistically invalid', spliced together graphs based
on proxies up to 1980 with lines based on temperature records for
the past two decades.

Why, he asked, had up-to-date proxies not been used as the basis
for showing temperatures for the last section of the graph? Was it
because the latest proxy records failed to show the dramatic rise in
late twentieth-century temperatures the IPCC wanted? But if proxies had not proved reliable indicators for recent temperature records,
did this not cast doubt on their value as a measure of temperature
in previous centuries?

Another reviewer, Per Holmund, commented that 'very few pale-
oclimatologists agreed with the shape of the "hockey stick" curve'
and 'nowadays we have much better data to use'. It might be natural 'to describe the Mann curve in a history of science perspective but
not as a valid data set'. The IPCC's comment was that 'the Mann *et
al.* curve is included for consistency and to maintain a historical context for the current state of the art'.

All those three years of plotting and agonising had finally borne
fruit. Maybe the bruised and battered 'hockey stick' could only be
smuggled back in with a blanket over its head. But it was still there,
on page 467 of the full report. The IPCC's face had been saved –

and along with it the crucial idea that the temperature rise of the late twentieth century was without historical precedent.

'A SIZZLING SUMMER'

In June 2007 the leaders of eight of the world's richest countries assembled for a G8 meeting at Heiligendam in Germany. Their host, the German Chancellor Angela Merkel (who had previously been her country's environment minister) invited her fellow politicians to discuss ways in which they could limiting the world's future temperature rise to just 2°C.

How heady it must have felt to imagine that they had the power to determine the future climate of the planet with such fine-tuned precision. England's King Canute might have smiled to know of it, as he sat enthroned on his beach to demonstrate to his courtiers that even a great ruler like himself could not order a halt to the advance of the incoming tide. As it happened, however, although Merkel's proposal won support from several prime ministers, including Blair, it did not find general approval.

In fact the summer of 2007 was not a good one for the 'warmists', as some were now beginning to call them. After its January forecast that 2007 would be the hottest year ever, the UK Met Office was reported as predicting, during an unusually warm April, that Britain was 'set to enjoy another sizzling summer', with temperatures 'above average'. If CO_2 emissions continued to rise at current rates, predicted Derrick Ryall, the Met Office's head of government meteorological research, 'the heatwaves of 2003 could become common'.[38]

As it turned out, the UK's summer was cooler and very much wetter than average, with much of the country affected by disastrous floods. Not that this stood in the way of journalists rushing to blame the torrential rains on 'climate change'.

So unquestioningly had most of the media now accepted the 'global warming' mindset that whenever there was any kind of unusual weather event, heatwaves, storms, floods, droughts, journalists could be relied on to describe it as 'further confirmation of climate change'. This became particularly anomalous when, unthinkingly, they described an event as the 'hottest/coldest/wettest' since some specific date in the past, unaware of how this implied that weather might have been just as extreme in the days before 'global warming' began. In 2007, for instance, they had no hesitation in ascribing to 'climate change' Britain's 'warmest April since 1865', followed by Britain's 'wettest summer since 1912'.

On 8 July, just after freak snow had blanketed Johannesburg[39] and two days before Buenos Aires was to see its first snow in 89 years,[40] the ever-loyal BBC devoted no less than 15 hours of coverage to LiveEarth, a series of rock concerts organised across the world by Al Gore to publicise his views on 'climate change'.[41] At London's Wembley Stadium, day-long music from an array of rock bands was interspersed with propaganda videos for the Gore thesis. This extravaganza failed to attract anything like the 'two billion viewers' predicted by its advance publicity. In Britain the average audience was well under two million, and the bad language freely used by many of the performers led to the event being dismissed by the tabloid press as 'a foul-mouthed flop'.

A UK-wide poll taken at the same time by Ipsos Mori showed that, despite the best efforts of the BBC, 56 per cent of the population still did not think there was any 'consensus' on global warming. Fifty-nine per cent said they were doing nothing about it, and most of those who said they were doing something thought that it was enough just to recycle their rubbish.

In August there was bad news for the government when the *Guardian* published a highly embarrassing internal paper leaked from inside the Department for Business, Efficiency and Regulatory Reform (BERR), the ministry responsible for Britain's energy policy (formerly the Department for Trade and Industry, or DTI). Their officials had been looking at the prospects of Britain meeting its target under the policy agreed by the EU's leaders in March, whereby the member states would collectively by 2020 have to generate 20 per cent of their energy from 'renewable' sources.

That autumn Britain's energy minister was scheduled to go to Brussels to explain to the EU's energy commissioner, Andries Piebalgs, how it intended to comply with this target. What still had to be agreed with Brussels was how much each country would be expected to contribute to the overall figure. The purpose of the leaked document from the DTI was to brief the minister in advance of his Brussels meeting on the practical implications of the obligation signed up to by Blair in March.

The news they brought was not good. They began by pointing out that attempting to reach the renewables target would 'be difficult to reconcile with other measures to tackle climate change'. Already in place, for instance, was the EU's Emissions Trading Scheme. If Britain was to cut back by 20 per cent on the CO_2 emissions involved in its energy mix, this would make the ETS 'redundant' and cause carbon 'prices to collapse'.

Rather more seriously, the officials advised that there was not the slightest chance that Britain could raise its current 2 per cent of energy derived from renewables (excluding hydro) to the agreed target of 20 per cent. Even if this were practically possible, it would cost the country £22 billion a year, nearly two-thirds of the £36 billion a year Britain was already spending on electricity from all sources. The best that could conceivably be hoped for was to raise the figure to 9 per cent, less than half what the European Commission was looking for. And even this would be extremely difficult.

So much for Britain's ambition to 'lead the world' in renewable energy. The chief means available to trying to improve its figure would inevitably have to be a massive expansion in wind power. But, as the government was keenly aware, schemes for new onshore wind farms were already becoming highly unpopular almost wherever they were proposed.

The method it had devised to override the wishes of local communities was to give every region and county council a target for the amount of 'renewable' electricity they were required to contribute, and then to instruct planning authorities and the government inspectors who presided over planning inquiries that meeting those targets must now override all other considerations.

In an unspoiled stretch of Devon countryside, for instance, the residents of North Tawton and Den Brook had been fighting for two years against a proposal to build nine 394-foot turbines, each almost the height of Salisbury Cathedral spire. These huge installations would dominate their views of distant Dartmoor across the open fields. In February, after the scheme had been rejected by the local council, a government inspector, David Lavender, dutifully observed that under Britain's 'international commitment' (i.e. to the EU) Devon had been ordered to contribute 151MW of electricity to the national target. For this reason alone he must give the Den Brook turbines the go-ahead. Any impact this might have on the local environment was immaterial.[42]

Yet now, it seemed, ministers were having to face up to the fact that not only were these inefficient turbines unpopular; the likely cost of this switch to 'renewables' they were required to make was so prohibitive that they would have to plead with the European Commission in Brussels for Britain's target to be reduced.

Another potential embarrassment touched on by the DTI's confidential briefing paper was that, as part of the same package of 'climate change' measures to which Blair had agreed in March, Britain was committed by 2020 to produce 10 per cent of all the fuel needed to power her transport from 'biofuels'.

The fact that this was to be made a legal obligation on oil companies meant that a highly lucrative and guaranteed new market was opening up for those firms capable of making the huge capital investment needed to create a major 'biofuel' industry in Britain virtually from scratch. One such firm was BP, the country's largest oil producer. Since one of the largest potential sources of biofuels in Britain would be wheat, in June 2007 BP announced plans to build a £200 million plant in Hull to process a million tons of wheat a year into fuel.

In fact, to meet the EU's target from homegrown crops, Britain would need to grow 14 million tons of wheat or its equivalent every year. But its total wheat harvest grown for food in 2006 had been only 11 million tons. Thus by 2020, to meet her need for food and biofuels, she would need to import 13 million tons of wheat annually, 2 million more than she currently grew. But this EU target had been laid down just when a world wheat shortage had already led by 2007 to a doubling of wheat prices on the international market in less than two years. Even if other crops, such as sugar beet, were used to meet the 10 per cent biofuel target, this would still take a similar area of farmland out of food production, necessitating a colossal increase in imports from the outside world.[43]

After all the years when politicians had blithely talked about the need to 'fight climate change', proposing measure after measure that they imagined would one day in the future enable them to meet their imaginary targets, an increasingly unpalatable reality was at last beginning to close in on them.*

---

* Another embarrassment brought on the government at this time by its need to comply with EU directives on 'climate change' was the ongoing debacle of its attempt to force home owners selling property to pay for a 'Home Improvement Pack'. So great were the problems which had arisen over the introduction of this ill-conceived and unpopular scheme that in May 2007 the government was forced to delay its introduction, initially limiting it only to homes with four or more bedrooms. There was a

'1998 NOT THE HOTTEST YEAR'

In the summer of 2007, Britain's ministers were not alone in experiencing some embarrassment. As McIntyre, through his blog Climate Audit, became ever more centrally involved in the debate on climate change. He had formed an informal alliance with Anthony Watts, a California-based meteorologist who ran another recently launched blog, Watts Up With That? With the aid of his readers, Watts was engaged in systematically checking the reliability of the 1,221 weather stations recording surface temperatures across the US.

This had become particularly relevant to the data underlying the global warming debate because two of the four main sources of temperature records were based on surface temperature readings. But a significantly high percentage of the worldwide network of surface weather stations were sited in the US. Even with compensating adjustments, US temperature readings thus made a disproportionate contribution to the global figure.

It had also become apparent in the previous few years that the temperature graph shown by one of these two sources, GISS, run by Hansen and Schmidt (Mann's RealClimate colleague), was now consistently showing temperatures markedly higher than the others, including the other source based on surface readings, HadCrut.[44] This was also important because the satellite records went back only to 1979, so that for earlier decades surface records provided the only source of directly measured temperature data.

From Watts's survey, as he reported on his *www.surfacestations. org* website, it was emerging that well over half the US weather stations were affected by a localised version of the 'urban heat island' effect. They were sited in places where their temperature readings had become distorted by nearby artificial heat sources, such as where thermometers had been surrounded with new buildings, or placed on asphalt parking lots or next to air conditioning vents.

At the end of July 2007 Watts was particularly intrigued by a report from one of his readers on a weather station in Michigan. Around

---

general clamour for the government to recognise that HIPs were an expensive fiasco and to scrap them altogether. But the government could not do this because a key element in HIPs were the 'energy performance certificates' which it had been compelled to introduce by the EU's directive 2002/01, issued as part of its fight against 'climate change'.

2000 it seemed that its temperature record had suddenly leaped upwards. Initially suspicion focused on the fact that two air conditioning units had been placed nearby in May 1999. But when this didn't seem to provide a plausible explanation for the temperature jump seven months later in 2000, this prompted Watts's ally McIntyre to carry out an exhaustive study of all the data obtained from the US Historical Climate Network (USHCN) on which GISS based its US temperature figures.

Since GISS refused fully to reveal the computer source codes and formulae used to calculate its graphs, it was far from easy to work out how these had been constructed. But when McIntyre, by what is called 'reverse engineering', managed to reconstruct what had been done with the USHCN data, he was astonished by what he discovered. It emerged that in January 2000 GISS had carried out wholesale 'corrections' to its figures, which resulted in recent winter temperatures being adjusted upwards by a whole degree C, and annual temperatures by 0.8 degrees. By any measure these were very substantial increases.

McIntyre discovered other 'adjustments' which affected the GISS figures not just for the period after 2000 but also for earlier years. Invariably scrupulous and courteous in all he did, he alerted GISS by email to what he had uncovered. Almost immediately, on 7 August, the GISS website posted a revised version of its top ten hottest years in the past century.[45]

The new list was indeed startling. Hitherto Hansen and Schmidt's website had been showing 1998 as the hottest year on record, with five of the warmest years ever recorded having been since 1990. Now 1998 gave way to 1934 as the hottest year since the record began in 1880. Four of the warmest years were now shown as having been in the 1930s, remembered in America as the time when drought and intense heat had reduced millions of acres of the Middle West to a dustbowl. The only year since 2000 to feature in the new 'top ten' was 2006, which now came fourth behind 1921.[46]

Considering the importance which had been attached to the belief that 1998 was easily the hottest year ever recorded, not least by the IPCC, this represented something of an earthquake in perception. Although the GISS website acknowledged McIntyre's part in drawing attention to the need for correcting the error, Hansen wrote to various journalistic allies such as Andy Revkin of the *New York Times* dismissing the episode as no more than 'a tempest inside someone's teapot dome'. He posted an online note which made no reference to McIntyre, suggesting that the adjustments were so minor as to be virtually irrelevant, since 'the 1934 and 1998 temperatures are virtually the same'.[47]

McIntyre responded by pointing out that in 1999 Hansen had put out a press release claiming something rather different. This had not only stated that 'in the US the warmest decade was the 1930s and the warmest year was 1934', but had been illustrated by a graph of US temperature history since 1880 showing 1934 as almost 0.6 degrees warmer than 1998. Only subsequent to this had Hansen 'adjusted' history by making the claim for 1998 he had now been forced to retract.[48]

Supporters of the 'consensus' were of course quick to point out that the new figures only referred to US surface temperatures, not to the rest of the world. But because much of the world's surface record was based on US figures, they exercised a highly disproportionate influence on the way the global figures were calculated and therefore on the figures on which GISS based its overall temperature record. Yet the very fact that the GISS figures were higher than any others helped to give them prominence and to boost the combined temperature graph on which the IPCC and so many others relied.

In fact, having looked again at the GISS data, McIntyre was at the same time able to report that Hansen had not only been changing his US figures. He had also done so in his figures for the Arctic.[49] In a paper published in 1987 he had included a graph showing Arctic temperatures in the 1930s as significantly higher than they had been at any time since.[50] But now GISS was showing a totally different graph. The 1930s temperatures had been substantially reduced by 0.4°C, while the figures given for the present day had risen well above them.

This was particularly pertinent because of the increasingly central part now being played in discussion of global warming by fears that summer sea-ice in the Arctic seemed to be rapidly disappearing. Satellite images from the US National Snow and Ice Data Center showed the area of ice getting smaller year by year.[51] Al Gore at his lectures now liked to stand before a huge blown-up photograph of two polar bears standing forlornly on what looked like the remains of a fast-melting iceberg.

The yearly ice-melt in that summer of 2007 had by September taken the area of ice down from 14 million sq. km. to barely 3 million sq. km., easily its lowest point since the satellite record began.

Eagerly reported by the media, Gore and others predicted that within a few years the ice might have vanished from the Arctic altogether.

It was convenient for their thesis that the satellite record should only have begun in 1979, just when the Little Cooling was giving way to the renewed warming of the late twentieth century. Otherwise, like Hansen in his 1987 paper, they might have recalled all the evidence indicating that Arctic temperatures were higher in the 1930s than they were in the early twenty-first century. But Gore's ally Hansen had now helped to rewrite the story. Fortunately, 70 years earlier, there had been no satellites to contradict them.

THE 'NINE INCONVENIENT UNTRUTHS' OF NOBEL PRIZE-WINNER GORE

In that autumn of 2007 the 20-year long crusade to alert the world to the threat of global warming was symbolically accorded its highest international recognition yet. In Oslo on 12 October it was announced that the joint winners of that year's Nobel Peace Prize were the IPCC and Al Gore, 'for their efforts to build up and disseminate greater knowledge about man-made climate change'.

Gore issued a statement to say that he was 'humbled', and that the award was 'even more meaningful because of sharing it with the IPCC – the world's pre-eminent scientific body devoted to improving our understanding of the climate crisis'. Back in India, acknowledging receipt of the prize on behalf of all those who had contributed to the IPCC's work, Dr Pachauri said that he looked forward to future collaboration with Gore. More than once, the former railway engineer with his PhD in economics was described by the media as 'one of the world's leading climate experts' or even 'the world's leading climate scientist'. In all the circumstances, it seemed an appropriate tribute.

For Gore in particular, his global reputation at this moment had never stood higher. It was the crowning point of his career. It must have seemed that all he had worked for was at last being vindicated and that all who doubted him had been routed. Earlier in the year he had compared any scientists who still remained sceptical towards the 'consensus' view on global warming to members of 'the Flat Earth Society'.[52] On another occasion he likened them to 'the people who believe the moon landing was actually staged in a movie lot in Arizona'.[53]

In fact not quite everything was going Gore's way at this time. A magisterial new book had just been published by Professor William Nordhaus of Yale, generally recognised to be one of the world's leading experts on the economics of climate change. In no way did Nordhaus wish to challenge the 'consensus' case on global warming; but he had used his own computer model to estimate the cost of various proposals put forward to mitigate its effects.

The two most 'ambitious' scenarios he analysed in *The Challenge of Global Warming: economic models and environmental policy*, were those suggested by Stern and Gore. In each case, he estimated, their proposals might result in reducing the increase in global temperatures by between 1.3 and 1.6°C. But by requiring cuts in greenhouse gas emissions that were 'too sharp and too early in time', they would end up costing very much more than they were likely to save, by as much as $25 trillion.[54]

The emissions cuts proposed by Gore, for instance, might theoretically save $12 trillion. But this would only be at a global cost of $34 trillion. In other words, the costs would be nearly three times greater than the benefits. It hardly looked like the bargain of the century.

Then, in the same month that Gore was awarded the Nobel Prize, he might not have been best pleased by a highly unusual judgment in the London High Court. Back in February, after the launching of the IPCC's Summary for Policymakers, Britain's Environment Secretary David Miliband had announced that the education ministry would be sending DVDs of Gore's Oscar-winning film to every secondary school in Britain.

This proposal so angered Stewart Dimmock, a school governor in Kent, that he sought a High Court ruling that to show *An Inconvenient Truth* to pupils in this way would be in breach of the law, namely two sections of the 1996 Education Act. He asked for screening of the film in schools to be banned.

Section 406 of the Act, headed 'Political indoctrination', laid down that schools must not allow 'the promotion of partisan political views in the teaching of any subject'. Section 407, headed 'Duty to secure balanced treatment of political issues', ruled that 'where political issues are brought to the attention of pupils in schools they should be offered a balanced presentation of opposing views'.

Dimmock had been guided to bring his action by Lord Monckton, formerly a senior policy adviser to Mrs Thatcher when she was prime minister and now a vocal sceptic on the science of global warming. He was particularly aware of these provisions of Britain's educational legislation since, in his time as a government political adviser, he had been responsible for drafting them.

Having heard the arguments put for Dimmock that the film constituted 'political propaganda' and contained serious scientific inaccuracies, Mr Justice Burton refused to ban its showing. But he did accept that, in Gore's desire to promote alarm over global warming, he had been guilty of nine exaggerations and scientific errors so serious that, unless pupils were told that these were controversial and given a balancing view, they were in breach of the Act.

The points on which Burton ruled that Gore's film had overstepped the mark included his claims that sea-levels could rise 'in the near future' by 20 feet; that Pacific atolls were having to be evacuated; that global warming might divert the Gulf Stream from Europe; that historic rises in CO_2 and temperatures had taken place simultaneously; and that global warming was the cause of the ice receding on Kilimanjaro, the drying up of Lake Chad and the devastation of New Orleans by Hurricane Katrina.

The judge was particularly dismissive of Gore's citing of a scientific study to support his claim that the melting of Arctic ice was causing polar bears to drown. 'The only scientific study either side before me can find is one which indicates that four polar bears have recently been found drowned because of a storm.'[55] Finally he rejected Gore's claim that global warming was responsible for destroying the world's coral reefs, when the science indicated that many other factors were involved, such as over-fishing and pollution.

Gore's film could only be shown in schools, the judge ruled, on condition that additional guidance was sent out by education authorities to ensure that on all these points pupils were given a balancing point of view.[56]

Burton's unprecedented judgment was hardly likely to change history, let alone have any influence on the overall debate on climate change. But at least it was modest judicial recognition of the fact that many of the claims made by Gore in his film went recklessly further than even the 'consensus' promoted by the IPCC.

This curious case also marked a rare exception to the extent to which children in schools all over the Western world were now being routinely subjected to an alarmist view of 'climate change' that was almost wholly one-sided. So all-pervasive had become the psychological power of the 'consensus' over the threat posed by global warming that it seemed entirely reasonable to frighten children with these apocalyptic predictions of their future.

The old rule formerly taught in schools that proper science requires any hypothesis to be rigorously tested by looking at all the evidence against it had in this context, it seemed, been conveniently forgotten.

THE ROAD TO BALI – AND COPENHAGEN

With the IPCC's massive Fourth Assessment Report at last launched on the world, attention now turned to the next great landmark in the 'consensus' calendar, the conference scheduled for Copenhagen in 2009 to agree a successor to Kyoto.

As in 1997 this would be staged under the auspices of the UN Framework Convention on Climate Change. Although 12 previous international meetings had already been held as part of the ongoing 'Kyoto process', the 10-day UNFCCC gathering staged on the island of Bali in December 2007 to plan for Copenhagen was easily the largest since Kyoto itself.

Ten thousand delegates and hangers-on, including thousands of the usual officially-sponsored representatives of environmental NGOs – with 5,000 more representing the media – duly assembled in one of the world's most popular tropical holiday resorts, having arrived from all over the world in hundreds of the gas-guzzling, carbon-emitting jet airliners they affected to despise.

Another conspicuous presence were the commercial concerns now looking to wax rich on the multi-billion dollar international market now being created by all the schemes designed to 'mitigate global warming'. These ranged from lobbyists for the renewable energy industry to world-famous firms such as Lehman Brothers, hoping to make fortunes out of 'carbon-trading' and the sale of 'carbon offsets'.[57]

Much in evidence as the conference began was the UN's Secretary-General Ban Ki-moon, presiding over the vast array of politicians, officials and environmental activists alongside Yvo de Boer, a former senior official of the Dutch housing ministry who had been made head of the UNFCCC in 2006 and who had recently described global warming sceptics as 'criminally irresponsible'.

The first purpose of the delegates, it seemed, was to direct incessant attacks, frequently greeted with applause, at President Bush and the US for having still failed to ratify Kyoto. The initial line argued by the US delegation was the same as it had been since 1997. America was not prepared to agree to curbing its emissions unless similar concessions were made by the fast-growing developing nations led by India and China (shortly about to surpass the US as the world's largest CO_2 emitter).

China and India were equally adamant, as they always had been, that if man-made global warming was a problem, then the blame lay with those already developed countries which had caused it in the first place. The developed world had no right to stop them increasing their emissions until they had caught up.

The EU delegation, headed by Humberto Rosa, insisted that the rest of the world must follow its shining example by signing up to drastic mandatory targets for emission cuts. The US delegation drew boos from delegates before it said it was prepared to compromise by agreeing to cuts. But these should not be mandatory.

After nearly 10 days getting nowhere, the mood of the conference had become increasingly heated and strained. Chairman de Boer at one point had to leave the platform in tears after a tangle over a point of procedure, Ban Ki-moon, having left Bali, rushed back in the small hours of the final day to plead with delegates that they must reach an agreement.[58]

After the usual marathon session of frenzied negotiations lasting through the final night, the chief delegations managed to cobble together what was hailed as the 'Bali Road Map'. Inevitably it fudged the issues in all directions. To the rage of the EU delegation there were to be no mandatory targets. The Chinese and the Indians would still not agree to reduce their emissions. But at least they were all agreed on one thing: that talking should continue, and that the UNFCCC would meet in Copenhagen two years later to hammer out the historic treaty that was to be the successor to Kyoto.

As it was vividly put by the EU's Rosa, 'It is exactly what we wanted. We are very pleased. We will now have two tremendously demanding years, starting in January. Many meetings, many discussions, many people passing hours doing many things.'[59]

The UN itself, reported by the environmentally-aware *Guardian*, calculated that the '15,000 politicians, activists, MPs, journalists and civil servants from 180 countries who travelled to Bali for the talks emitted between 60,000 and 100,000 tonnes of carbon dioxide', through air travel to and from the conference, car travel and the air-conditioning and other use of electricity needed to keep them in comfort while they were there.[60]

The UN boasted that it had offset its own emissions by paying nearly £50,000 of taxpayers' money into its Clean Development Mechanism, handed over to those enterprises in the developing world which were in a position to sell 'carbon credits'. The Indonesian government said that it had planted '79 million trees' to offset the conference's emissions, insisting that these would not be cut down until they had removed the requisite amount of CO_2 from the atmosphere.

The road to Copenhagen was now open – with those two 'tremendously demanding years' of 'many meetings, many discussions and many people passing many hours doing things' to look forward to.

THE BILL MOUNTS UP

Back in the real world the costs of all this talk were beginning to add up. In June 2007 Ekkehard Schulz, chief executive of Germany's largest steel firm ThyssenKrupps, had warned that his government's environmental policies, such as meeting the EU's target of a 20 per cent cut in carbon emissions by 2020, were likely to cost Germany 500,000 jobs, as energy-intensive industries relocated outside the EU to escape its requirements. Such a target was anyway 'illusory', Schulz told *Suddeutsche Zeitung*.[61]

In July, the Federation of Tour Operators, representing some of Britain's leading travel firms, failed to get a High Court judge to agree that Gordon Brown had acted illegally in imposing a 'climate change' tax worth £2 billion a year on everyone buying airline tickets in Britain, at a cost up to £80 per journey.[62]

A survey by the Taxpayers' Alliance found that Britain's council taxpayers were now having to pay £102 million a year for local councils to employ a new army of 'climate change managers', 'carbon reduction advisers' and other climate change-related officials. These included 58 in Tower Hamlets alone, the poorest borough in London.[63] Another of the think-tank's surveys in September estimated that 'green taxes' were now costing the British people £21.9 billion a year, nearly £1,000 for every household in the country.

In Brussels, the EU's anti-fraud commissioner Siim Kallas disclosed in December that, as one of Europe's most lavishly funded environmental pressure groups, Friends of the Earth Europe was now receiving half its yearly income from the EU's taxpayers, including

£425,000 a year from the European Commission itself. Inevitably top of the FoE agenda, as its website proclaimed, was 'Climate change – the biggest threat our planet is facing'.[64]

Meanwhile, back in the not-so-real world, just as the UNFCCC's climate change conference was ending in Bali, Britain's energy minister John Hutton announced that, to meet the EU's 20 per cent renewable energy target by 2020, the UK intended within 13 years to build 7,000 giant offshore wind turbines. Their 33GW of capacity, Hutton claimed, would be enough 'to power every home in the country'.

The minister did not, of course, mention what the cost of this gargantuan enterprise might be. But with the current cost of offshore turbines averaging, according to the Carbon Trust, £2 billion for each gigawatt of capacity, the capital cost alone of installing these 7,000 towers, one for every half a mile of Britain's coastline, would be some £66 billion, quite apart from the billions more that it would cost to connect them all up to the land-based National Grid.[65]

One question which immediately arose from Hutton's prouncement was whether he understood that, thanks to the intermittency of the wind, the 7,000 turbines he was dreaming of would generate on average not 33GW but barely a third of that amount (the average output of offshore turbines was just over 30 per cent of their capacity).

The actual output of his turbines would thus average only 11GW, well under half what would be needed to power every home in the country, and which could be much more reliably produced by six new nuclear power stations at only a quarter of the cost. Indeed the country would need to build several new power stations simply to provide back-up for the times when fluctuations in wind speed created swings in the amount of power produced by Hutton's turbines, which could potentially range, if the wind dropped sharply enough, up to their full 33GW.

Still more fanciful was the idea that such a vast engineering project, bigger than anything Britain had ever undertaken, was even remotely feasible. To meet Hutton's target, Britain would have to install two of these 2,000 ton monsters, many as tall as 850 feet, every day for the next 12 years. Yet Denmark, the country which had more offshore wind resource than any other in the world, had never managed to build more than two in a week. And such were weather and sea conditions round Britain's coasts that the work needed to erect these huge structures could only be safely carried out during four months of the year.

There was thus no conceivable way Hutton's dream could be realised. Yet such was the state of unreality into which politicians had been carried away by the psychological pressure put on them to believe in the threat of global warming – let alone in the ever more fantastical measures now being urged on them to meet it.

400 SCIENTISTS REJECT
THE 'CONSENSUS'

Just before the end of 2007, a minority report from the Environment Committee of the US Senate listed and quoted more than 400 academic scientists from all over the world, many of them current or former participants in the IPCC, who were now prepared to express their dissent, sometimes in the strongest terms, from the IPCC 'consensus' view of global warming.[66]

They included Nobel Prizewinners and many professors, in disciplines ranging from climatology, oceanography, geology and physics to biology, chemistry, mathematics and glaciology. They came from a score of countries and from some of the world's leading universities, including Harvard, MIT, Princeton, Columbia and London. They even included members of the US National Academy of Sciences and employees of NASA, the US National Oceanic and Atmospheric Administration, the US National Center for Atmospheric Research and the Environmental Protection Agency.

Several admitted they had previously been supporters of the man-made global warming orthodoxy but had now changed their minds. Many testified to the pressure they and like-minded colleagues were under not to make their dissenting views known. Dr Nathan Paldor, Professor of Dynamical Meteorology and Physical Oceanography at the Hebrew University of Jerusalem wrote 'many of my colleagues with whom I spoke share these views and report on their inability to publish their scepticism in the scientific or public media'.

One name on the list was Dr Syun-ichi Akasofu, a Japanese American who had been founding director of the International Arctic Research Center at the University of Alaska and was one of the world's leading authorities on the history of the climate of the Arctic.

In July Professor Akasofu had published a note 'to point out that the method of study adopted by the International Panel on Climate Change (IPCC) is fundamentally flawed, resulting in a baseless conclusion'.[67]

In a thoughtful meditation on why, in his opinion, the IPCC had got the story so wrong, he distinguished between 'climatologists' and 'meteorologists'. A great many of the IPCC's scientific contributors were what he called 'meteorologists', concerned with what they saw as the immediate physical factors influencing changes in the world's weather, of which greenhouse gases were seen as the most significant. Another 'large group of scientists in the IPCC study group' consisted of those whose 'primary expertise is in computer modelling', and to them the 'meteorologists' fed the data which enabled them to come up with their projections.

But genuine climatologists, of whom Akasofu argued there were not many in the world, were as much 'archaeologists' as anything. They were aware that there were important natural factors influencing climate in past ages of which we have very little understanding. We did not know why the world's climate went through the extreme fluctuations it experienced during the successive Ice Ages. We did not understand the reasons for the sizeable rises and falls in temperature of the last 10,000 years. We did not know why temperatures fell during the centuries of the Little Ice Age, or why they began to rise again with the beginning of the Modern Warming in the years after 1800. So this had continued up to recent times.

One of the more obvious examples of where the 'meteorologists' and the computer modellers showed how little they understood these natural factors influencing climate, Akasofu argued, was their complete inability to explain the sudden pronounced warming in the 1920s and 1930s. So preoccupied were they with those immediate physical factors which they could programme into their models that they did not begin to recognise how much was getting left out of the picture.

For instance, as an expert on the Arctic, Akasofu emphasised that the recent receding of the Arctic ice was a phenomenon which had begun around 1800. On and off, it had therefore been going on throughout the period of the Modern Warming, up to the present day. The most obvious feature of the climate changes of the past 200 years was that they were all part of that same continuous trend.

Yet the computer modellers of the IPCC had fastened all their attention on just one short segment of that continuing pattern at the end of the twentieth century, extrapolating it into the future, when their theory could not explain anything that had happened before it, for natural reasons such as fluctuations in solar radiation. This had then required the rewriting of what was known about those previous ages, as in the 'hockey stick', simply to make their theory seem plausible.

Such was one distinguished scientist's view of why the IPCC's studies were 'fundamentally flawed', leading to conclusions which were 'baseless'. Meanwhile, as 2007 came to an end, the year had seen a fall in average global temperature of 0.7°C, larger than its entire net rise through the whole of the twentieth century. It may still have been too early to know whether or not this indicated any longer term trend. But at least one thing was certain: that such a drop had not been predicted by any of those computer models on which the IPCC's 'consensus' so heavily relied.

Notes

1. 'Key climate report sparks global call to action', *New Scientist*, 2 February 2007.
2. *Ibid*.
3. Climate Change 2007: IPCC Synthesis Report. Summary for Policy-makers, p. 2.
4. 'Ten years to save the planet', *The Sun*, 30 January 2007.
5. The full Synthesis Report was officially published in Valencia, Spain, on 12 November 2007, according to the IPCC website, although copies were available for a month or two before this.
6. 'Every British teen to see *An Inconvenient Truth*', NSAC Noticeboard and Message Forum.
7. As early as 1962, a landmark paper by Minze Stuiver, a University of Washington biophysicist, correlating tree-ring records with solar activity over the past 1000 years, showed that whenever the sun was active, creating more solar wind to deflect cosmic rays, less carbon-14 was available to be absorbed by the trees.
8. Much of the story below has been based on *The Chilling Stars: A New Theory of Climate Change*, by Henrik Svensmark and Nigel Calder (Icon Books, 2007).
9. E. Friis-Christensen and K. Lassen (1991), 'Length of the solar cycle: an indicator of solar activity closely associated with climate', *Science*, 254, 698–700.
10. H. Svensmark and E. Friis-Christensen (1997), 'Variation of comis ray flux and global cloud coverage – a missing link in soclar-climate relationships', *Journal of Atmosphere and Solar-Terrestrial Physics*, 58, 1225–1232.
11. Svensmark and Calder, *op. cit.*
12. G. Bond, *et al.* (2001), 'Persistent solar influence on North Atlantic climate during the Holocene', *Science,* 294: 2130–2136.

13. Perry and Hsu (2000), 'Geophysical, archaeological and historical evidence support a solar-output model for climate change', *Proceedings of the National Academy of Sciences*, 97.

14. N. Shaviv and J. Veizer (2003), 'Celestial driver of phanerozoic climate?', *Geological Society of America*, 13.'

15. 'NASA study finds increasing solar trend that can change climate', Goddard Space Flight Center press release, 20 March 2003.

16. The SKY experiment is described in full in Svensmark and Calder, *op. cit.*

17. Svensmark and Calder, *op. cit.*

18. The origins of *The Great Global Warming Swindle* lay in a meeting of the World Congress of Science Producers in Tokyo in 2006. Martin Durkin asked why the world's major television networks were paying so little attention to the serious doubts now being expressed by reputable scientists about the basis for global warming 'consensus'. His point was scornfully rejected by Michael Mosley, a senior BBC science producer, arguing that no reputable scientists challenged the 'consensus'. It was suggested that Durkin and Mosley should debate the issue in front of their colleagues at a subsequent meeting of the congress in New York. So forcefully did Durkin argue his case in the debate that many producers were surprised to find themselves agreeing that he had a point. Following this episode Channel 4 commissioned Durkin to make *The Great Global Warming Swindle* (private information from Durkin).

19. See, for instance, H. Fischer, *et al.* (1999),'Ice core record of athmospheric CO_2 around the last three glacial terminations', *Science*, 283, 1712–1714; and N. Caillon, *et al.* (2003),'Timing of atmospheric CO_2 and Antarctic temperature changes across Termination III', *Science*, 299, 1728–1731.

20. Svensmark and Calder, *The Chilling Effect, op. cit.*

21. This was a point which had been powerfully argued by the Danish political scientist Bjorn Lomborg, not least in his book *The Skeptical Environmentalist: Measuring the Real State of the World*, originally published in Danish in 1998. Although he accepted a measure of man-made contribution to global warming, he regarded the measures proposed to tackle it as being both unrealistic and likely to inflict disproportionate damage on the undeveloped world. In 2004 he convened a meeting of eight leading international economists, who agreed what was known as the 'Copenhagen Consensus'. This listed what they believed should be the top 20 economic priorities confronting mankind. Top of the list was HIV/AIDS. This was followed by the need to tackle malnourishment in the Third World, barriers to trade and malaria. Bottom of their list were measures to halt global warming, such as the Kyoto Protocol.

22. George Monbiot, 'Don't let truth stand in the way of red-hot debunking of climate change', *The Guardian*, 13 March 2007.

23. 'Climate scientist "duped to deny global warming"', *The Observer*, 11 March 2007.

24. '"No Sun link" to climate change', BBC website, 11 July 2007. 'No solar hiding place for greenhouse sceptics', *Nature*, 11 July 2007. 'Sun's activity not to blame for climate change', *The Register*, 11 July 2007, and many more.

25. Lockwood, M., and Frölich, C., 'Recently opposite directed trends in climate forcings and the global mean surface air temperature', *Proceedings of the Royal Society A*, published online 13 July 2007.

26. *Nature, op. cit.*

27. *The Register, op. cit.*

28. For a discussion of this point see K. Gregory, 'A critique on the Lockwood/ Frölich paper', *mitosyfraudes.org* website. Svensmark and Friis-Christiansen's own response was given in 'Reply to Lockwood and Frölich – the persistent role of the sun in climate forcing', Danish National Space Centre, September 2007.

29. *http://vortex.nsstc.uah.edu/public/msu/t2lt/tltglhmam_5.2*

30. MIT News Office, 24 June 1998.

31. 'Global warming on Pluto puzzles scientists', *www.space.com*, 9 October 2002.

32. ABC News, 26 July 2006.

33. NASA's Jet Propulsion Laboratory, Pasadena, *mars.jpl.nasa.gov/odyssey/newsroom*, 8 December 2003.

34. *National Geographic News*, 27 February 2007.

35. *USA Today*, 4 May 2006.

36. See Appendix 1, 'A tightly knit group …'.

37. Our summary here is based on papers reconstructing this story by two diligent researchers, David Holland's 'Bias and Concealment in the IPCC Process: the "Hockey Stick" Affair', *op. cit.*; and 'Caspar and the Jesus Paper', published on the Bishop Hill blog, 11 August 2008. For details, see Appendix 1, 'A tightly knit group …'.

38. 'Hot summer on the way, predicts Met', *The Observer*, 8 April 2007.

39. 'Johannesburg gets four inches of snow', Bloomberg, 27 June 2007.

40. 'Buenos Aires gets rare snowfall', BBC website, 10 July 2007.

41. In the US the NBC network was even more generous, giving Gore's concerts a total of 75 hours of coverage in various channels.

42. 'Turbines sacrifice beauty to futility', *Sunday Telegraph*, 16 February 2007. In 2006, at a public inquiry in Somerset, the same inspector had already used the same argument to justify overruling the unanimous rejection by the local council of a single giant turbine overlooking an Area of Outstanding Natural Beauty on the unique Mendip plateau. He con-

ceded that the scheme did not meet the normal statutory protection given to such landscapes, and ignored objections raised against it on the absurdly exaggerated claims made by the developers for the turbine's potential output (e.g. that it would generate at 38 per cent of its 2MW capacity). Yet earlier this inspector had turned down similar schemes for precisely these reasons, i.e. that they would damage valuable landscapes and that their benefits had been greatly exaggerated.

43. *Sunday Telegraph*, 22 July 2007.
44. 'HadCRU3 versus GISS', Climate Audit, 17 February 2007; 'GISS divergence with satellite temperatures since the start of 2003', WUWT, 8 January 2009.
45. McIntyre also discovered that, although GISS had made 'adjustments' to the temperature data from 3,464 surface weather stations to allow for the distortions of the 'urban heat island effect', these were very heavily concentrated in the US and Europe. Markedly fewer adjustments had been made to data from the rest of the world, even though many of their weather stations were sited in places which had been subject to extensive recent development. This would have further reinforced the impression of recent warming (see 'Hansen and the Great White North', Climate Audit, 23 August 2007, and related posts).
46. '1998 no longer the hottest year on record in USA', Watts Up With That, 9 August 2007. See also posts by McIntyre on Climate Audit, such as 'Quantifying the Hansen Y2K errror', 6 August 2007; 'New leader board at the US Open', 8 August 2007.
47. Post by McIntyre on Watts Up With That, 11 August 2007.
48. *Ibid.* Hansen's retraction on this point was only partial, in the sense that he now showed 1934 ahead of 1998 by just 0.2 degrees rather than the 0.6 he had shown eight years earlier.
49. *Ibid.*
50. Hansen, J. E., and Lebedeff, S., 1987, 'Global trends of measured surface air temperature', *J. Geophys. Res.*, 92, 13345–13372.
51. See the Cryosphere Today website, published by the University of Illinois.
52. *http://www.businessandmedia.org/articles/2007/20071220101840.aspx*
53. 'Gore slams global warming critics', *http://archive.newsmax.com/archives/ic/2006/6/20/134405.shtml?s=ic%20*
54. William Nordhaus (2007), *The Challenge of Global Warming: economic models and environmental policy* (Yale University Press).
55. Monnett, *et al., op. cit.* See also 'Where are all those drowning polar bears?', by I. Goldman on the website *theycantsolveit.org*.
56. The authorities did send out the required 'balancing' material, but since this ran to 77 pages the gesture was largely meaningless.
57. One world figure who had been expected to endorse the importance of the Bali conference was Pope Benedict XVI, who earlier in the year had

staged a conference on global warming at the Vatican (which now liked to describe itself as 'the world's first fully carbon-neutral state', after announcing that it was 'offsetting its carbon footprint' by planting a forest in Hungary and installing solar panels on the roof of St Peter's). But 'senior cardinals', it was reported, had since urged the Pope to be wary of the 'over-hyping' of the threat of global warming. His message issued to coincide with Bali disappointed delegates by taking a much more cautious line than anticipated, warning that advocates of global warming should not exaggerate their case and that measures taken in response should not damage the welfare of the poorer peoples of the world (see 'Pope to make climate action a moral obligation', *The Independent*, 22 September 2007, and then 'The Pope condemns climate change prophets of doom', *Daily Mail*, 13 December, 2007).

58. 'Bali conference adopts climate plan after rough night of talks', Associated Press, 15 December 2007.

59. 'Guardians of the planet fly home on a lot of hot air', *Sunday Telegraph*, 16 December 2008.

60. 'The summit's carbon footprint', *The Guardian*, 15 December 2007.

61. 'German government's environmental plans may cost 500,000 jobs', AFX News, *http://www.forbes.com/feeds/afx/2007/06/29/afx3870286.html*

62. 'Judge urged to scrap the £2 billion air tax', *Daily Mail*, 16 July 2007.

63. *Sunday Telegraph*, 22 July 2007, and *www.taxpayersalliance.com/waste/publication/page/2/-*

64. *Sunday Telegraph*, 22 July 2007.

65. See 'Britain has never concocted a crazier plan', *Sunday Telegraph*, 16 December 2007.

66. See US Senate Minority Report, 'Over 400 prominent scientists disputed man-made global warming claims in 2007', website of US Senate Committee on Environment and Public Works, 20 December 2007.

67. Syun-ichi Akasofu, 'On the fundamental defect in the IPCC's approach to global warming research', published on Climate Science website, Roger Pielke Sr News, 15 June 2007.

8

A tale of two planets
Fiction versus truth: 2008

'Global warming has become a symbol and example of the clash between truth and propaganda. The one politically correct truth has already been established, and opposing it is not easy. Yet a large number of people, including top scientists, see the issue of climate change, its causes and its proposed consequences quite differently. They are alarmed by the arrogance of those who advocate the global warming hypothesis and the complementary hypothesis that links the problem of global warming with some particular human activities. They fear the proposed and already implemented measures will radically affect the lives of each one of them – and rightly so. I too share their concerns and anxieties.'

President Vaclav Klaus, *Blue Planet in Green Shackles*, 2008[1]

'It is regrettable that the public debate over climate change, fuelled by the errors and exaggerations contained in the reports of the IPCC, has strayed so far from scientific truth. It is an embarrassment to science that hype has replaced reason in the global debate over so important an issue.'

Nature, Not Human Activity Rules The Climate.
Summary for Policymakers, Non-Governmental
International Panel on Climate Change, 2008

At the start of 2008, as it had in January 2007, the UK Met Office issued its now customary prediction of how the world's climate would perform during the next 12 months. It was based on the computer model jointly run by the Met Office's Hadley Centre and the Climate Research Unit at the University of East Anglia, run by Professor Phil Jones, an honorary member of the 'Hockey Team'. This was the most important of the four official sources on which the IPCC relied for its global temperature projections.

A year earlier the Met Office had predicted that 2007 would probably be 'the warmest year ever', even hotter than 1998. In fact world temperatures during those 12 months had fallen by as much as the entire net temperature increase for the twentieth century.

Somewhat chastened, the Hadley Centre/East Anglia team now predicted that 2008 would be 'cooler globally than recent years', but hastened to add that it would 'still be one of the top ten warmest years' ever recorded. Temperatures would be limited, it explained, by a La Niña event. But once this declined we could look forward to 'sharply renewed warming'.[2]

The real point the Met Office wanted to put across was that such 'cyclical influences can mask underlying warming trends'. 'The fact that 2008 is forecast to be cooler than any of the last seven years', Professor Jones emphasised, 'does not mean that global warming has gone away'. What mattered was 'the underlying rate of warming', and the fact that twenty-first century temperatures had on average been 0.44 degrees higher than the average between 1961 and 1990.

What was to happen next no one had predicted, least of all Professor Jones's very expensive computer.

'THE WINTER FROM HELL'

Over the first three months of 2008, as global temperatures continued to fall, the world endured one of its coldest winters for decades. In January, the northern hemisphere recorded its most extensive snow cover for the month since 1966 (just before those predictions that the world might be entering a 'new ice age'). Not only were there record snow falls across North America, but countries such as Saudi Arabia, Iraq and several regions of China experienced more snow than they had seen for 50 or even 100 years.[3] NOAA and the US National Climate Data Center reported that on land it had been only the 63rd warmest January globally in 114 years.[4]

In February the chill continued. Snow was recorded in the deserts of southern Iran where no one could remember it ever falling before. Jerusalem had its second snowfall in a month. Astonished Athenians gazed up at a snow-draped Acropolis, while more than 200 villages in Greece and Crete were cut off by blizzards. In Turkey the number of villages cut off was estimated at 1,000.[5] Further heavy snows across southern China added to a disaster which had already damaged 10 per cent of the country's forests and devastated thousands of square miles of farmland.

As the four official sources of temperature data agreed that global temperatures had fallen below their twentieth-century average,[6] even

Hansen's GISS figures showed the steepest January-to-January global temperature drop (0.75 degrees) since surface records began in 1880.

In the US in early March there were blizzards as far south as Texas and Arkansas. In the northern US states and Canada what was being called 'the winter from hell' continued to break records for cold and snow going back in some cases as far as 1873. In Afghanistan it was reported that the abnormal snow and freezing weather had killed 1,500 people and 200,000 animals. In Tibet six months of snow and record low temperatures had killed 500,000 animals, leaving a further three million at risk of starvation.

Meanwhile, in Antarctica sea-ice cover was at its highest March level since satellite records began in 1979, nearly a third above its 30-year average. In the Arctic, where sea-ice the previous September had dropped to 3 million square kilometres, its lowest level ever recorded, prompting frenzied media predictions that it would soon be gone altogether, the winter freeze had now returned the ice to 13 million square kilometres, the same level it had been at a year earlier. In western Greenland, the Danish Meteorological Institute recorded temperatures 30°C below zero, while more ice was clogging the strait between Greenland and Canada than at any time for 15 years.[7]

No one had done more to exploit the potential vanishing of the Arctic ice than Al Gore. In particular, there was one image more than any he liked to flash up to illustrate the lectures for which the Nobel prizewinner was now paid $100,000 or more a time all over the world. This was the widely-publicised photograph showing two polar bears standing apparently forlornly on what looked like the fast melting remains of an iceberg,

Gore's message was that this was emblematic of the plight of the bears who were now having to swim so far in their desperate efforts to reach the next fragment of disappearing ice that some had already been found floating dead in the sea. 'Their habitat is melting', he declared when he first used the image at a conference in Toronto in March 2007, 'beautiful animals, literally being forced off the planet'.

Now, however, a Canadian journalist revealed the story behind this picture. It had been taken in August 2004 just off the Alaskan coast by Amanda Byrd, a graduate student in marine biology. As Ms Byrd was happy to explain, the bears were in no danger so near the land. She had pointed her camera at them, not because of global warming or even the bears themselves, but simply because the 'wind-sculpted ice' had made such a memorable image.

Spotted on the ship's intranet by a colleague, her picture was passed to the Canada Ice Service, from where it sent to Environment Canada. On 2 February 2007 one of its employees had sent it to seven press agencies, timed to coincide with the launch in Paris of the IPCC's Summary for Policymakers. From the resulting publicity, the picture was adopted by Gore and others in the global warming propaganda machine as an iconic image which soon came to rank second only in popularity to the 'hockey stick'.[8]

Only a year later had the truth about the picture emerged.

'THE EU LEADS THE WAY' – WITH 'A CRIME AGAINST HUMANITY'

The one part of the world largely spared the record snowfalls and low temperatures affecting the rest of the northern hemisphere in the early months of 2008 was western Europe. This perhaps helped to explain why all these dramatic weather events elsewhere were scarcely noticed by the British or European media.[9]

In Brussels on 23 January an array of EU Commisioners came before the world's media to present their long-awaited 'climate action and renewables package'. This put forward the Commission's proposals as to how those far-reaching decisions taken by the EU's political leaders in March 2007 were to be put into practice. Their intentions had already been flagged up in a document entitled *Combating Climate Change: the EU leads the way*:

> 'The international consensus is growing that the planet is facing irreversible climate change unless action is taken quickly. The EU has already formulated a clear response in the shape of an integrated energy and climate change policy, a commitment to cut emissions of 'greenhouse' gases by at least 20 per cent by 2020 … this will help to prevent the world's temperatures rising by more than 2°C, the level which is increasingly thought by scientists to be the point of no return.'[10]

Now, in two main respects, the Commission was spelling out the details. First, 'central to the strategy', was its plan for a 'strengthening and expansion of the EU's Emissions Trading System'. Phase One of the ETS between 2006 and 2007 had not been an unqualified success. While it had forced up energy prices to EU consumers by up to 13 per cent, the EU's 'carbon emissions', far from falling, had also risen, by 1.9 per cent.[11]

Nevertheless, declaring that the ETS was 'an important building block for the development of a global network of emission trading systems', the Commission now proposed that under Phase Two a single EU-wide cap would be imposed on carbon emissions, to cut them by 21 per cent by 2020. Free allocations of 'carbon allowances' were to be progressively replaced by allowing national governments to auction them off, to create in effect a highly lucrative new stream of tax revenue. The costs, to be passed on to EU consumers, would thus rise to the point where, by 2020, the Commission estimated, that they would reach £38 billion a year (the UK's share £6.5 billion).

Even the Commission conceded that energy-intensive industries such as steel, aluminium, chemicals and cement would have to raise their prices by up to 48 per cent. But when it was pointed out that this would put the EU's industries at a serious competitive disadvantage, forcing some to relocate elsewhere in the world, the Commission's only response was to suggest that tariffs might have to be imposed on imports from countries such as the US and China which had not agreed to comply with Kyoto.[12]

The Commission's other main proposal was for a directive on 'the promotion of energy from renewable sources'.[13] This set out the specific targets allocated to each member state which would enable the EU by 2020 to derive 20 per cent of all its energy from wind, solar, hydro and 'biomass', and 10 per cent of all the power for its transport from 'biofuels'.

Predictably, the plan was warmly welcomed by the array of front organisations set up by the EU to lobby for those industries which stood to benefit from this new renewable energy bonanza. A chorus of statements applauding the Commission's proposals thus emerged from the European Renewable Energy Council, the European Wind Energy Association, the European Solar Thermal Energy Federation, the European Biodiesel Board and the European Bioethanol Fuel Association (all based in 'Renewable Energy House' in Brussels).[14]

Equally, no one was more enthusiastic about the Commission's proposals than Prince Charles, who in February was invited to Brussels to address the European Parliament on a cause now at the top of his personal agenda. Although he was known in the past to have been privately critical of the EU, all this was now thrown aside as the Prince declared 'surely this is just the moment in history for which the European Union was created'. To the evident delight of the Foreign Office officials who accompanied him, he heaped lavish praise on the Commission and its President Jose-Manuel Barroso for all they were doing to 'fight global warming'. The MEPs gave him a standing ovation.[15]

In startling contrast, however, one Commission proposal met with a storm of protest. This was its requirement that by 2020 10 per cent of the EU's transport should be powered by biofuels. Over the previous two years a sea-change had been taking place in attitudes towards biofuels, not least among many of the organisations normally looked on as the EU's closest environmental allies.

As early as 2006 various international organisations, including the IMF, the OECD and the UN's Food and Agriculture Organisation (FAO), had already blamed rapidly rising world food prices on the ever-increasing areas of land across the world being switched from food production to growing crops for biofuels.[16] The FAO published a report suggesting that, for the EU to meet its 10 per cent target from home-grown biofuels, would require a staggering 70 per cent of the EU's cereal land, necessitating a huge increase in EU food imports.[17]

By the end of 2006, the Commission itself was equally aware that the world was about to face a food shortage, which over the next few months would spark food riots in several countries, ranging from west Africa and Egypt to West Bengal. Yet, in their attempts to show that a sufficient acreage of farm land would be available to meet its planned new biofuels target, the Brussels officials resorted to a curious method which involved including the same areas of land more than once.[18]

First the Commission counted in all the 'set aside' land taken out of food production to avoid building up grain mountains and other food surpluses. But much of this land was now being used to grow 'industrial' crops needed for other purposes. It then conceded, without being too specific, that in addition large areas of land would have to be switched from growing food to crops for biofuels. Finally, however, to meet the world food shortage, it then suggested that this same land could also be used to grow more food crops. This bureaucratic sleight of hand came to be compared to 'Enron accounting'.

Thanks to these efforts to make its policy seem plausible, the EU's political leaders in March 2007 nodded through the Commission's 10 per cent biofuels target apparently without questioning whether the sums added up.

It was around this time, however, that, with startling speed, the backlash against biofuels suddenly erupted on all sides. Even before the EU had adopted its new target, fierce criticism of biofuels was coming from those same environmental groups, Greenpeace and Friends of the Earth, which had once been their most fervent advocates. Their particular focus was the damage being done in the developing world, not least by the clearing for biofuels of millions of acres of rainforest in Brazil, Malaysia and Indonesia. It had become distressingly obvious that this was inflicting very serious damage both on locally indigenous peoples and on wildlife, not least by its threat to the survival of Borneo's fast-vanishig orang-outans.

Next to weigh in had been Jean Ziegler, the UN's 'special rapporteur on the right to food', who in October 2007 made headlines across the world by claiming in New York that it was 'a crime against humanity to divert arable land to the production of crops which are then burned for fuel'. Since the 'dash for biofuels', he said, could only bring 'more hunger to the poor people of the world', he called for a five-year moratorium on their use.[19] A report to be published the following year by the World Bank's chief economist, Donald Mitchell, would claim that switching food-growing land to biofuels had been responsible for three quarters of the 140 per cent rise in world food prices which took place between 2002 and 2008.[20]

Most alarming of all, however, was a succession of scientific studies showing that, far from helping to cut global CO_2 emissions, biofuel production could often give off much more CO_2 than it saved – not least by disturbing huge quantities of CO_2 locked in the soil which, according to the University of Minnesota, could release '17 to 420 times more CO_2' than would be saved by the biofuels.[21] A study by Cornell University showed that, thanks to the high-energy inputs needed to make biofuels from farm crops – in everything from machinery and fertilisers to the intensive use of irrigation – they took 29 per cent more energy to produce than was generated by the biofuel itself.[22]

In the week before the Commission published its proposals they were dealt a further devastating blow by its own in-house scientists. Its Joint Research Centre came out with a report dismissing almost every positive claim which had been made for biofuels.[23] The Commission's proposals, it concluded, would not achieve any overall savings in CO_2 emissions. Their energy efficiency was much less than half that of fuel from oil refineries. They would not on balance create any new jobs. And their costs would far outweigh any bene-fits, amounting by 2020 to a net deficit ranging between €33 and €65 billion.

Environmentalist groups, led by Greenpeace, queued up to implore the Commission to abandon its 10 per cent target. A Friends of the Earth spokesman said: 'I just can't see how the Commission can go ahead with its biofuels policy now … it has nothing going for it.' But in no way was Brussels to be deterred from pressing ahead with its policy. Biofuels, it insisted, had not been responsible for the rise in world food prices, which were due to rising world demand, bad weather and international speculation. 'If you don't have targets you don't make progress', said a Commission spokesman, adamant that the 10 per cent biofuels target could not be altered.[24]

In the US, where the powerful farmers' lobby was insistent that nothing should be done to change a subsidy system which, according to the FAO, could soon see nearly a third of US farmland diverted to biofuels, it seemed the 'crime against humanity' was equally set to continue.

'ENVIRONMENTALISTS' VERSUS 'REALISTS' – THE UK FACES A BLACK HOLE

The one country most obviously put on the spot by the Commission's proposals was Britain. This was for two reasons. One was that she derived only 1.3 per cent of her electricity from renewable sources, easily the lowest percentage of any nation in Europe apart from tiny Malta and Luxembourg.[25] This meant that to meet the EU's target would require her to make a far more costly effort to expand renew-able generation than any other country.

Worse still was the fact that, when the small print of the Com-mission's proposals was examined, the proportion of her electricity which Britain was now required to derive from renewable sources by 2020 was not 20 per cent but 38 per cent. This was because the over-all target included other forms of energy which could not be derived from renewables. In other words, the UK would have to increase its output from renewables by a staggering 3,000 per cent, which in practical terms was again not conceivably possible (after fraught discussions with the Commission this would be lowered a few months later to 32 per cent, which was still not remotely achievable).

What made this even more alarming was that the penny had at last begun to drop with at least some of Britain's ministers that within a few years, with the loss of 40 per cent of her generating capacity, the UK would be facing a quite unprecedented energy crisis.

Behind the scenes a serious rift had opened up between the officials of the two ministries whose responsibilities covered energy issues. On one hand were the 'environmentalists' who until now had dominated Britain's policy, as the 2003 energy white paper had showed. These were centred in the Department of Environment, Food and Rural Affairs (Defra), responsible for climate change, and their position was unequivocal. Appointed in 2007 as the department's Chief Scientific Adviser had been Dr Bob Watson, former head of the IPCC. So committed was he to the cause that when in July 2007 Watson stepped down as environmental adviser to the World Bank, Al Gore had sent a personal tribute to be read out at his leaving party hailing him as 'the hero of the planet'.[26]

To the practical problem of Britain's fast-approaching energy gap, Watson and his fellow 'environmentalists' seemed quite oblivious. Obsessed with climate change and wind turbines, they viewed both nuclear power and 'carbon intensive' coal as the work of the Devil. How Britain was to keep its lights on and its computer-based economy running did not concern them.

In BERR, however, the ministry directly responsible for energy policy, there were still a number of senior officials who, in terms of Britain's energy needs, could be described as 'realists'. They had by now been able to impress on their minister John Hutton that unless the government made a very drastic switch of policy Britain would soon be facing major power shortages. As was reflected in that briefing paper leaked the previous August, the 'realists' were acutely aware there was no way the country's energy demands could be met by any number of windmills or solar panels.

Thus in January 2008 Hutton startled MPs by announcing that the government would now support the building of a new generation of nuclear reactors. This, he said, would be a 'safe and affordable' way of securing the UK's future energy supplies while 'fighting climate change', hoping that the first would be completed 'well before 2020'.[27]

Hutton was quick to warn, however, that no government money would be available to subsidise these nuclear power stations. Although he didn't admit it, this would not be permitted under EU state aid rules, which allowed subsidies to 'renewables', such as windfarms, but not to nuclear energy. And if his new strategy was to be realised, it was fraught with practical difficulties. Thanks to Britain having turned its back on nuclear power for nearly three decades, the country no longer had a nuclear industry worthy of the name. Astonishingly, as late as October 2006, Blair and Brown had sanctioned the selling off to Toshiba of Britain's only remaining world-class nuclear construction company, Westinghouse, at the giveaway price of £2.8 billion.

This meant that Britain would be wholly reliant on foreign-owned companies to build the new power stations (before the day was out the French company EDF and the German-owned E-On had both expressed interest). But because many other countries were also now jumping on the nuclear bandwagon, Britain would have to take its place in a fast-lengthening queue (the now Japanese-owned Westinghouse already had orders for 19 new nuclear reactors on its books). Furthermore, as environmentalist groups led by Greenpeace vowed to oppose the new policy all the way, it seemed that legal and planning obstacles might delay the completion of any new reactors until long after most of Britain's existing nuclear power stations had been forced to close.

At least Hutton's approval in principle of nuclear power marked a belated recognition of the grim reality of Britain's plight. He had said nothing yet, however, of what might be done to replace the obsolescent coal-fired power stations which still provided a third of the country's electricity, six of which were soon due to close under the EU's Large Combustion Plants directive. Just as alarming was the fast-dawning realisation of the price Britain would soon be paying for that decision in 1992 to close down most of her remaining coal mines in order to generate up to 40 per cent of her electricity from North Sea gas.

The thinking behind the 'dash for gas' was that it was abundant, cheap, and compared with coal would save on CO_2 emissions. But 16 years later it had become horribly clear that those once abundant reserves of gas below the North Sea were fast running out. A report commissioned for BERR now revealed that, as late as 2005, Britain had still been a net exporter of oil and gas. However, they were now disappearing so rapidly that by 2013 the imports required to meet the country's needs – at a time when gas prices were already rapidly rising – would be running up an annual deficit of 80 million tons, equivalent at then-current prices to £40 billion a year.[28]

Whichever way it was looked at, Britain's energy policy seemed to be on a collision course with disaster. Meanwhile she was still locked into a legal obligation under her EU's renewables target which was not remotely achievable.

One illustration of the absurdities to which this was already leading was the fate of a long-discussed £500 million project to build the 'largest onshore windfarm in Europe'. This was to consist of 176 600-foot turbines planned for the island of Lewis in the Hebrides. The politicians of the Scottish Assembly liked to boast how this would make a major contribution to Britain's EU renewables target. Their claims were dutifully echoed by the media, quite oblivious of the fact that the 200 megawatts of power the turbines might on average generate would be equivalent to only a quarter of the output of a single medium-sized gas-fired power station.

When decision time came, however, in April 2008, the Assembly was bluntly informed by the European Commission that the scheme was illegal and could not be allowed. The environmental damage the monster turbines and the 100 miles of road needed to service them would inflict on a vast area of peat bog, home to Scotland's largest population of golden eagles and other prized birds, would be in breach of the EU's Habitats directive.

Thus, on one hand, the EU was ordering Britain to build thousands of wind turbines, as the only way to meet her environmental obligations on renewable energy. On the other, when a scheme was put forward to do just that, a different department of the Brussels bureaucracy ruled that this would be so environmentally destructive that if the UK allowed it to go ahead she would face a colossal fine in the European Court of Justice.[29]

So desperate were the 'environmentalists' becoming in casting round for ways to meet that wholly unrealisable 38 per cent target that in March ministers had even proposed resurrecting the long-standing dream of building the world's largest tidal barrage across the Severn Estuary, a vast 10-mile long concrete wall between Somerset and Wales containing 300 turbines powered by the second highest tide in the world. This £20 billion scheme, as the media dutifully reported, would create 'generating capacity' capable of meeting '5 per cent of Britain's electricity needs'.

What both politicians and the media failed to grasp was that the power of twice-daily tides, like that of the wind, is intermittent. As had already been recognised even by the Sustainable Development

Commission, the Severn Barrage would on average generate only 22 per cent of its capacity, or 1.9 gigawatts, at a cost of more than £10 million per MW. Yet almost the same amount of power could be generated by a single modern nuclear power station, at barely an eighth of the cost.[30]

Furthermore, by damming the water, the scheme would devastate the feeding ground for millions of birds on the Bristol Channel's tidal mudflats. As in Lewis, this would be illegal under the EU's Habitats directive. Once again, the more extravagant the wishful thinking of the environmentalists became, the more it threw up contradictions which collided with one another.[31]

A further tiny example of the peculiar state of mind into which all this was leading the politicians had been a vote taken in February by members of the European Parliament. One British MEP had noted an angry outburst from Friends of the Earth against the patio heaters which thousands of British and Irish pubs had installed to allow their customers to smoke outside following the ban on smoking in public places. These were emittting so much CO_2, complained Friends of the Earth, that they should also be banned.

So fired up were the MEPs by this opportunity to help save the planet that they voted to outlaw patio heaters by 526 votes to 26. One Conservative MEP, Richard Ashworth, then wrote to the *Daily Telegraph* to point out that the MEPs themselves were guilty of emitting almost the same amount of CO_2 simply by engaging in the farce whereby once a month the entire European Parliament decamped from Brussels to Strasbourg and back, complete with a vast convoy of trucks carrying all their papers.

Such a delightful point doubtless earned Mr Ashworth brownie points with many readers of the *Telegraph*. They might, however, have raised their eyebrows had they known that among the names of the 526 MEPs who voted for the ban was that of Mr Ashworth.[32]

TWO PLANETS – AND THE RISE OF THE 'COUNTER CONSENSUS'

The story thus enfolding in 2008 was of how the two sides to the global warming debate seemed more than ever before to be speaking from two different planets.

On one side, still dominating the field with its extraordinary prestige and influence, was the IPCC. Its claims to represent the 'consensus' view of 'the world's leading climate scientists' were supported by three main groups, each with enormous influence of its own: the politicians (at least in the Western world); the environmental lobby groups; and virtually the entire mainstream media.

On the other side, as the story unfolded, the position of each of these groups was now being undermined and chipped away at. Although the standing of the IPCC might have seemed undiminished, the fact that the shifting pattern of temperatures had not been predicted by those models on which its case ultimately rested was beginning to trouble its scientific allies. This was already prompting attempts to explain what was happening in ways which might keep the basic theory intact, much along the lines of the UK Met Office's insistence at the start of the year that the recent cooling was merely 'masking the underlying warming trend' and that warming would eventually return more strongly than ever.

In May, for instance, considerable media coverage was given to a new study published in *Nature* which conceded that global temperatures might not rise over the next decade, 'as natural climate cycles enter a cooling phase'. But after 2015, *Nature's* readers would be reassured to know, global warming would again pick up, causing temperatures to rise even higher than those of 1998. This was based on the projections of a computer model run by a British scientist, Noel Keenlyside, at the Liebniz Institute of Marine Sciences at Kiel in Germany, which based its results on predicting changes in the Gulf Stream, the 'meridional overturning circulation' (MOC) which brings warmer water across the Atlantic to Europe.

Keenlyside accepted that the IPCC's forecast of a 0.3 degrees temperature rise during the current decade had not been borne out. But this was only, he suggested, because its models were not programmed to take proper account of ocean currents such as the Gulf Stream. His own model, he insisted, confirmed that by 2015 the warming caused by CO_2 would re-assert itself, carrying temperatures up to record levels.[33]

This might have given some cheer to the warmists, but it was hardly a ringing endorsement for the efficiency of the IPCC's models. Indeed, curiously enough, another significant ocean current event overlooked by the IPCC's models was reported by NASA on 21 April. This was the shifting of the Pacific Decadal Oscillation (PDO) 'from a warm to a cool phase'.[34] As was pointed out by Anthony Watts, the alternations of the PDO between its warm and cool phases had coincided with each of the main temperature shifts of the twentieth century: warming after 1905, cooling after 1946, warming after 1977. Now it was again shifting into a cool phase. Was it not odd that the IPCC's models had not been programmed to take account of this?

The politicians, of course, were quite oblivious to such arcane scientific deliberations. As we have seen, they had troubles enough of their own, finding that the more they tried to put into practice all those grandiose schemes designed to combat the IPCC's projected warming, the more fraught with contradictions these seemed to become. The biofuels dream was turning out to be both a farce and a disaster. The EU's emissions trading scheme was not just proving to be colossally expensive but had so far seen emissions rising rather than falling. Despite the billions of pounds, dollars and euros being spent on renewables, notably on building tens of thousands of wind turbines, the amount of electricity they produced was derisory.

As for the environmentalist lobby groups and the media, all that was left to them as indications piled up that the promised global warming disaster was not proceeding quite according to plan, was to keep on recycling the same familiar scare stories – more droughts, more hurricanes, rising sea levels, vanishing Arctic ice and polar bears – while firmly shutting their eyes to any evidence which contradicted their chosen 'narrative'.

A tiny instance of this in the late spring of 2008 was the almost complete lack of coverage given by the British media to what was happening on top of Snowdon, the highest mountain in southern Britain. For several weeks in April, work on building a new EU-funded café on the mountain's summit was halted by heavy blizzards.

This might not have seemed particularly odd except that every spring for five years had seen regular media reports that Snowdon's snow-cover was vanishing due to global warming. In 2003 scientists from the University of Bangor had made headlines by predicting that by 2020 Snowdon might have lost its snowcap forever. In 2007 a local MP, Lembit Opik, was again quoted as saying 'it is shocking to think that in just 14 years snow on this mountain could be just a distant memory'. In November 2007 pictures of a snowless Snowdon shown at a Cardiff exhibition prompted Wales's Environment minister Jane Davidson to pronounce that 'we must act now to reduce the greenhouse gases which cause climate change'. But just five months later, when Snowdon was buried in its heaviest and most prolonged snow for years, the media showed not the slightest interest.[35]

Another curious little episode at this time had shown just how intense was the pressure from 'climate change activists' to keep their media spokesmen on message. On 4 April the BBC's chief climate change reporter, Roger Harrabin, normally a tireless promoter of warmist orthodoxy, reported on his blog that global temperatures had not risen for 10 years and were likely in 2008 to fall below their average of the past two decades. This, he went on, had prompted 'some to question climate change theory'.

This straightforward reporting was based on a statement from the World Meteorological Organisation. But it so infuriated one 'activist', Jo Abbess, of the Campaign Against Climate Change (its honorary president was *Guardian* columnist George Monbiot) that she emailed Harrabin angrily demanding that he 'correct' his item. Harrabin replied that what he had said was perfectly true. There were indeed eminent climate scientists 'who question whether warming will continue as predicted'.

This only angered Ms Abbess further, It was 'highly irresponsible', she said, 'to play into the hands of the sceptics', or even to 'hint that the world is cooling down again'. Harrabin stood firm, responding that even in the 'general media' there were 'sceptics' highlighting the failure of temperatures to rise since 1998 and that to ignore this might give the impression that 'debate is being censored'. His item had after all added that 'we are still in a long-term warming trend'.

This was too much for Ms Abbess. This was not 'a matter of debate', she said. He should not be quoting the sceptics 'whose voice is heard everywhere, on every channel, deliberately obstructing the emergence of the truth'. Unless he changed his item, she said, 'I would have to conclude that you are insufficiently educated to be able to know when you have been psychologically manipulated'. She threatened to expose him by releasing his replies across the internet.

At this point the BBC's man caved in. Within minutes a new version of his blog appeared, given the same time and date as the original. Out went any mention of 'sceptics'. After a guarded reference to this year's 'slightly cooler temperatures', a new paragraph said that they would 'still be above the average' and that 'we will soon exceed the record year of 1998 because of the global warming induced by greenhouse gases'.

As it happened, shortly afterwards the US National Climate Data Center, run by NOAA, issued a statement that January snow cover on the Eurasian land mass had been the highest ever recorded, and that in the US March had been only the 63rd warmest since records began in 1895. Naturally none of this was reported by the BBC, any more than it had covered the other record-breaking events of the 2008 winter. To do so, as Ms Abbess might have put it, would have been 'highly irresponsible'.

As for those eminent climate scientists who, according to Harrabin's original blog, had dared 'to question climate change theory', almost daily now did they seem to be growing in number. In New York in March some 500 climatologists, astrophysicists, meteorologists, geologists, economists and policy-makers (including Vaclav Klaus, President of the Czech Republic) had gathered under the auspices of a free-market think tank, the Heartland Institute, for a three-day 'International Conference on Climate Change'.

There might have seemed nothing particularly odd about this, except that these 500, some of them leading experts in their field, had not gathered together to promote the views of the IPCC. What united them was their unanimous disagreement with the IPCC's claimed 'consensus'.

Published to coincide with the conference by the doyen of US 'climate sceptics', Dr Fred Singer, was a 'Summary for Policymakers for the Non-Governmental International Panel on Climate Change' entitled *Nature, Not Human Activity Rules the Climate*. Signed by 30 authors from 15 countries, citing some 200 scientific papers and with a foreword by Professor Frederick Seitz, past president of the US National Academy of Sciences, it summarised the main scientific grounds for doubting the orthodoxy on global warming in a way most participants in the conference would have been happy to endorse.[36]

The report began by repeating at rather greater length a key point previously made on *The Great Global Warming Swindle*. Since its 1996 report, the IPCC itself had argued that, according to its models, man-made greenhouse gas warming should show a distinctive 'fingerprint'. This was that temperature levels would most obviously increase, not at the earth's surface but in the upper levels of the tropical troposphere. Yet measurements by balloons and satellites had consistently shown the opposite. Recent warming had been greater at the surface and decreased with altitude. This finding had been accepted by a National Academy of Sciences study in 2000 and confirmed by the US Climate Change Science Program in April 2006. Yet the IPCC had wholly ignored its own evidence.

In particular, so skewed were the IPCC's models by their built-in assumption that the main driver of warming was greenhouse gases, that they failed to take proper account of the major natural influences on climate, notably the fluctuations in ocean currents and the variability of the sun. Two charts based on a recent stalagmite study demonstrated the remarkable correlation between solar activity and temperatures over several thousand years.

The report was particularly withering about the inadequacy of the computer models on which the IPCC relied for its projections of future climate. They could not accurately model the role of clouds or water vapour, easily the most significant greenhouse gas of all. They had been shown not to predict the behaviour of ocean currents or to explain the history of polar temperatures or the cooling of the Antarctic. They were not programmed to take account of the climatic impact of solar radiation. 'The climate models used by the IPCC', the report concluded, 'cannot make reliable predictions and should not be used in formulating government policy.'

The report went on to criticise the unreliability of the IPCC's estimates of sea-level rise, pointing out that each successive IPCC report had lowered its predictions of future rises, while scientific mavericks such as Dr Hansen had wildly exaggerated their own model projections without any supporting evidence. It demonstrated how much scientific uncertainty there still was about the mechanisms which caused the oceans to absorb or emit CO_2. Again it showed how the IPCC's persistent claims that warming was leading to more hurricanes and extreme weather events were simply not borne out by the evidence. And it cited a sheaf of scientific papers to show why increases in CO_2 levels and a moderate warming would be beneficial to plant-growth and agriculture, and to human health and prosperity in general.

The report's overall conclusions were that the extent of modern warming was 'less than is claimed by the IPCC and the popular media'; that the 'human greenhouse gas contribution to current warming is insignificant'; and that the best 'empirical evidence suggests very strongly that the main cause of warming and cooling on a decadal scale derives from solar activity via its modulation of cosmic rays that in turn effect atmospheric cloudiness'.

At the end of the conference, those present agreed to a 'Manhattan Declaration on Climate Change', which began by stating 'global warming is not a global crisis'. It went on to assert that the oft-claimed 'consensus' on the causes of climate change did not exist; that there was 'no convincing evidence that CO_2 emissions from modern industrial activity' would 'cause catastrophic climate change'; that CO_2 was 'not a pollutant but rather a necessity for all life' and that 'attempts by governments' to introduce costly regulations designed to reduce CO_2 emissions will 'pointlessly curtail the prosperity of the West and progress of developing nations without affecting climate'.

The Declaration ended by calling on world leaders to reject the views on climate change expressed by the IPCC and to ensure that 'all taxes, regulations and other interventions' designed to 'reduce emissions of CO_2 be abandoned forthwith'.

If a similar conference featuring contributors of similar eminence had been staged to promote the views of the IPCC it would undoubtedly have been given prominent coverage by the BBC and the rest of the media. As it was, although in the US it attracted a little notice, in Britain (with one exception) it was not reported at all.[37]

Had the media been aware of it, however, the significance of this unprecedented gathering in New York was considerable. After years when the 'consensus' on global warming had carried all before it, there were at last clear signs that a 'counter consensus' was emerging – reflecting the growing concern of all those expert scientists whose views had for so long been derided and ignored.

The tide of opinion, like the climate, was changing. It was noticeable that of all the books on global warming published in the previous year, the ones which stayed in the best seller lists were not those rehearsing all the wearisomely familiar arguments in favour of the 'consensus', such as *The Hot Topic* by the British government's former Chief Scientific Adviser Sir David King. What it seemed the book-buying public was now looking for were those which put the other side of the argument, such as *An Appeal To Reason: a cool look at global warming* by the former British Chancellor Nigel Lawson (originally turned down by a succession of publishers, this remained a best-seller for months).[38] Equally noticeable was the growing popularity and soaring hit-rates of such expert sceptical blogs as Watts Up With That and Climate Audit (which had been voted on the internet 'Best Science Blog' of 2007).

The 'counter-consensus' on global warming was finally finding its voice.

FURTHER STILL INTO CARBON
CLOUD-CUCKOO LAND

Through the summer of 2008, the surreal pattern established in the earlier months of the year continued – only becoming yet more surreal.

On 7 June the International Energy Agency, holding a conference in Japan, announced that if the human race was to halve its emissions of CO_2 by 2050, it would need to spend $45 trillion, equivalent to two-thirds of the world's entire current annual economic output. This was by far the largest figure any official body had yet put on the cost of saving the planet from global warming.[39]

Dr Roy Spencer of UAH at the same time reported his NASA satellite measurements as showing that global temperatures in May had fallen by a further 0.2 degrees. This brought the total drop since January 2007 to 7.7 degrees, a full tenth of a degree more than the entire net warming of the twentieth century.

On 4 June Mark Gregory, a business correspondent for the BBC World Service clearly not wholly 'on message', produced a startling report on the workings of the UN's Clean Development Mechanism. This bizarre scheme, introduced under the Kyoto Protocol, administered by Yvo de Boer's UNFCCC and paid for by enterprises in the developed world (to allow them to exceed their official emissions allowance), handed out 'carbon credits' to companies in still-developing countries which could show they were reducing their greenhouse-gas emissions.

Among three beneficiaries of the scheme Gregory tracked down in India was a small chemical company in rural Rajasthan. RFS was annually receiving 3.8 million carbon credits, worth $50 million a year for 10 years, for installing a cheap incinerator to burn off the CFCs from its process. A spokesman for the firm said it was pleased to be receiving a windfall of $500 million dollars for doing something 'we would have done anyway'.[40] Defending his scheme, the UN's de Boer merely said 'I'm happy that a very potent greenhouse gas is being removed'.

The other two projects were not dissimilar. One involved the grant of carbon credits worth several hundred thousand dollars a year to a rice exporting firm for installing a new generator burning rice husks, which again the firm said it would have bought even without the money from the CDM,

On 27 June the only story on the front page of the *Independent* carried a huge headline reading 'Scientists warn that this summer there may be no ice at the North Pole'. What the story didn't say was that, after its record melt in the summer of 2007, the ice in the Arctic had recovered during the winter at record speed. Even though it was now again melting, its extent by midsummer 2009 was now 700,000 square kilometres greater than it had been at the same date in 2007.

On 26 June, to a great fanfare of publicity, Gordon Brown launched in London what he called 'the greatest revolution in our energy policy since the advent of nuclear power. His '£100 billion green energy package' centred on building 7,000 wind turbines, 3,000 on-shore and 4,000 offshore, which he claimed would be enough to meet Britain's EU renewables target.

Thanks to frenzied number-crunching by BERR's energy officials, they had now somehow worked out that, to meet her target. Britain would only need to derive 15 per cent of her electricity from renewables, of which Mr Brown's 7,000 new turbines would be the centrepiece (the rest, he rather vaguely suggested, would come from biomass, tidal, wave and solar power).

Even if BERR's wholly fanciful figures were taken at face value, the numbers still did not begin to add up. On the most generous estimate, 7,000 turbines would only generate on average some 5GW, less than 10 per cent of peak demand, At least five gas-fired power stations would need to be built simply to provide instant back-up for when the wind suddenly ceased to blow at the right speed. And even though Brown was also proposing yet more changes to the planning system, to allow more onshore turbines to be forced through against the wishes of local communities, any idea that those 4,000 giant off-shore turbines could be built at a rate of nearly two every day between 2008 and 2020 amounted to self-deception on a scale verging on lunacy.[41]

Two weeks later Brown joined his fellow G8 leaders on a cloud-wreathed Japanese mountain top, where they solemnly agreed that, to halt global warming, their countries would all halve their emissions of CO_2 by 2050. None of them had any more practical idea than Brown of how such a thing could be done.[42]

A rather longer-time player in the drama also now showing signs of having even further parted company with reality was Dr James Hansen. Speaking at the National Press Club in Washington, the public official in charge of one of the four official sources of world temperatures called for the CEOs of major fossil-fuel companies who 'spread disinformation about global warming' to 'be put on trial', for 'high crimes against humanity and nature'.[43]

On 13 July Gordon Brown was at it again, boasting to an EU 'Mediterranean summit' in Paris that Britain would not only be the first country in Europe to phase out 'energy-inefficient light bulbs' by 2011, but would soon 'become the global centre for offshore wind', making the North Sea 'the Gulf of the future'.[44] The representatives of the Gulf states in his audience (from whom Brown was seeking finance for his offshore wind project) might have been bemused to hear him comparing his 4,000 planned North Sea turbines to the largest oilfields in the world, when their total average output would be less than that of a single large coal-fired power station.

At the end of July, the *Sunday Times* carried a large advertisement from the German-owned company npower, one of Britain's leading electricity suppliers, inviting children to 'save the planet this summer' by becoming 'climate cops'. A picture showed a sleeping father with a notice on his head warning in a childish scrawl that he has been found guilty of a 'climate crime' by 'falling asleep with the TV still on'.[45]

For 'more interactive games and fun downloads', it was suggested that readers should contact npower's 'Climate Cops' website, which explained how children could spy on their parents, relatives and neighbours to catch them out in seven 'climate crimes', such as leaving the TV on standby, putting hot food in a fridge or freezer (as hygiene experts recommend) or failing to use low-energy light bulbs. Children could then record these offences in a 'climate crime case file', while teachers were offered a full 'learning resource pack' for use in schools, including a PowerPoint presentation and posters for classroom walls.

As it happened, npower's own Aberthaw power station in south Wales emitted more CO_2 every two months than was notionally saved by all Britain's 2,000 wind turbines in a year. If merely falling asleep in front of a TV was a 'climate crime', why hadn't the directors of npower put themselves behind bars long ago?

And what newspapers like to call the 'silly season' was only just beginning.

OFCOM: THE IPCC SPINS DEFEAT INTO 'VICTORY'

On 21 July, after 16 months ploughing through a mountain of documents, the broadcasting regulatory body Ofcom at last came up with its rulings on the 265 complaints made the previous year against Channel 4's documentary, *The Great Global Warming Swindle*. These were particularly remarkable for two reasons: firstly, how they were reported by the media, and, secondly, the extraordinary response of the IPCC.

A measure of how seriously the pro-warming establishment had taken this programme was that it had provoked such an unprecedented avalanche of heavyweight complaints, from dozens of establishment luminaries, including Bob Ward's '37 professors' (among them Phil Jones of the 'Hockey Team'), another group including Bert Bolin (who had died of cancer the previous December), Sir David King, Professor Wunsch and, of course, from the IPCC itself.

On the face of how it was presented by their supporters in the media, the IPCC and its allies had won a great victory – 'Channel 4's Great Global Warming Swindle "misrepresented" scientists', was the *Daily Telegraph's* headline. The BBC headlined one of two reports on its website 'Climate documentary "broke rules", quoting Pachauri saying 'this is a vindication of the credibility and standing of the IPCC'.[46]

The BBC's other much longer piece was a highly sympathetic interview with Dave Rado, who had co-ordinated the assembling of the second major complaint, that supported by Bolin and several other leading figures in the IPCC, past and present. Rado described how, on watching the programme, he had been 'flabbergasted both by its brazenness and its unprecedented number of deceptions', and how it was 'a systematic attempt to deceive the public, an out and out propaganda piece masquerading as a science documentary'.

Rado recalled how next morning he had appealed for scientific support in making a complaint on a website run by William Connolley, who 'agreed to peer-review' his complaint. Connolley, a tireless 'green activist', who had once worked for the British Antarctic Survey, was already well known in climate change circles as the chief moderator on global warming issues for Wikipedia, the very widely-read internet encyclopaedia. He had used this position to great effect for the cause, by ensuring that Wikipedia's innumerable entries on the subject, supposedly open to all to contribute, were kept very firmly 'on message'. Contributions arguing a sceptical view were rapidly 'moderated out'; and entries for 'climate deniers', such as Dr Fred Singer, were given short shrift, usually by claiming that their views had been discredited or that they were tainted by links to energy interests or the tobacco industry.[47]

When Ofcom's various rulings were examined, however, the truth of what they contained turned out to be startlingly different from how they had been reported. Although, according to the BBC, Ofcom found that 'Channel 4 did not fulfil obligations to be impartial and to reflect a range of views on controversial issues', with one very minor exception, Ofcom found nothing of the kind.[48]

Of scores of specific complaints that 'errors' in the programme had broken the rules by 'misrepresentation' of the truth, Ofcom did not uphold a single one. Similarly, on the scientific issues, Ofcom did not uphold a single complaint against the programme's lack of 'impartiality'.[49]

The one minor count on which Ofcom ruled that the programme had breached its obligation to be impartial was nothing to do with the science, but was on a political point. It was concerned by the programme's failure to include 'an appropriately wide range of significant views' as to whether the UN's climate change policies were damaging to Africa and the poorer peoples of the world.

Ofcom also – perhaps with tongue in cheek – upheld two personal complaints. One was from Sir David King, who protested that he had been misrepresented as saying that Antarctica would by the end of the century be the only habitable continent on earth. The other was from Professor Wunsch, who complained that he had not been told what was the programme's purpose.[50]

Of all Ofcom's rulings, however, none were more carefully crafted than its responses to the official protest from the IPCC itself. Of six specific complaints, only two were concerned with the content of the programme. The IPCC rather oddly denied that it had claimed that global warming would lead to a disaster, or that it would lead to a spread of tropical diseases. Both these complaints Ofcom rejected.

By way of modest consolation, Ofcom did uphold four procedural complaints, in ruling that the IPCC had not been given enough time to comment on points made by the programme before it was broadcast. Channel 4 had emailed the IPCC asking for comments on 27 February 2007, then again on 1 March, each time receiving no reply.

But since the emails had not mentioned the fact that the programme was due to be broadcast on 8 March, Ofcom ruled that the IPCC had not been given sufficient time to comment. Had Channel 4's emails been sent a week earlier, these complaints would not have been upheld.

This was all the Ofcom ruling amounted to. Every one of the scores of specific complaints relating to the contents of the programme, including those from Ward's '37 professors' and the 175 pages submitted by Rado (endorsed by various luminaries from the IPCC), had been rejected. The seven complaints upheld were little more than minor technicalities relating to procedure.

Then, however, came the most startling feature of the entire affair. No sooner was the Ofcom report released than statements were released to the media by all the leading IPCC figures involved.

Pachauri's began

> *'we are pleased to note that Ofcom has vindicated the IPCC's claim against Channel 4 and upheld most of the formal complaints made by those who respect the IPCC process. It is heartening to see that the review process of the IPCC, and the credibility of the publications of the IPCC were upheld.'*

This was truly bizarre; Ofcom had made no comment on the 'review process of the IPCC' or the 'credibility' of its publications. Pachauri's statement was an absurd misrepresentation of what Ofcom had said.

Even dottier was the statement issued by Sir John Houghton (who of course no longer had any formal connection with the IPCC):

> *'The ruling today from Ofcom regarding* The Great Global Warming Swindle *programme has exposed the misleading and false information regarding the IPCC that was contained in that programme, and that has been wilfully disseminated by the climate-denying community. The integrity of the IPCC's reports has therefore been confirmed, as has their value as a source of accurate and reliable information about climate change.'*

A statement from Dr Bob Watson, who also no longer had any formal link to the IPCC, was more succinct:

> *'I am pleased that Ofcom recognised the serious inaccuracies in* The Great Global Warming Swindle *and has helped set the record straight.'*

Again, Ofcom had done nothing of the kind. It had not 'recognised' a single 'inaccuracy', having been careful to avoid any discussion of the science whatever.

So wildly misleading were all these statements that it might be charitable to imagine that none of their supposed authors had actually read the report before the press releases went out. Whoever drafted them had perhaps counted on the likelihood that few of the journalists who received them would bother to read the report either. If their purpose was no more than spin, then it was rewarded by the unquestioningly one-sided way in which these comments were reported.[51]

NOT '2,500 CLIMATE SCIENTISTS' – JUST 53

If one thing had done more than any other to establish the IPCC's authority in the popular mind it was that oft-repeated claim that its reports represented a 'consensus' of the views of '2,500 of the world's top climate scientists'. Now for the first time a detailed study had been carried out which examined the reality behind that claim.

An Australian IT analyst, John McLean, who had for some time specialised in issues related to climate change, produced a paper looking at the IPCC's 2007 report.[52] He began with a graph of global temperatures from 2002 to 2008, based on the four main official records, showing how they all now agreed that the trend for six years had been downward. He noted that this had not been predicted by the IPCC's computer models and that the AR4 made no reference to it.

He quoted the IPCC's rules of procedure, laying down that its reports should be compiled by a wide range and geographical balance of contributors, and should take account of 'a range of views'. He then focused his attention on what was essentially the key section of the whole report, Chapter 9, entitled '*Understanding and Attributing Climate Change*', since it was really on this that everything else in the report depended. This was the chapter which assessed the reasons for and the scale of climate change, and the other working groups were supposed to base their conclusions on its findings.

Chapter 9 concluded that the evidence for human-induced warming was detectable in every continent except Antarctica, and that this was leading to all the commonly cited consequences, from melting glaciers and sea ice to changing rainfall patterns and more intense cyclone activity,

Who was responsible for putting this crucial chapter together? McLean's analysis showed that, of the chapter's 53 authors, 44 or 83 per cent came from just four English-speaking nations: 20 (38 per cent) from the US, 16 (20 per cent) from the UK, while China, Japan, Germany and four others had just one each. Only 12 of almost 200 countries signatory to the IPCC were represented.

The organisations from which these authors were drawn numbered only 31. No fewer than 10 contributors came from the Hadley Centre or the University of East Anglia, nearly a fifth of the total, and four each from Oxford University, NCAR and the University of Michigan. Where McLean's study became particularly interesting, however, was when he looked at how closely all these contributors were professionally linked to each other. This turned out to be a larger version of the 'social network' analysis contained in the Wegman report of 2006, which showed how intimately interwoven were all the authors of papers defending Mann's 'hockey stick'.

Of the 534 scientific papers cited in support of the views expressed in Chapter 9, 213 or 40 per cent had appeared under the name of at least one chapter author. Forty-two of these papers were written by Peter Stott of the Hadley Centre, a lead author; 36 by Myles Allen of Oxford University, a contributing author (and a complainant against the *The Great Global Warming Swindle*); and 23 by Ben Santer, who played such a key part in rewriting the IPCC's 1996 report. Allen had co-authored papers with 20 other authors of Chapter 9, Stott with 18, and Santer with 15. Of the 53 authors, 70 per cent, including both the 'co-ordinating lead authors', had co-authored papers with other contributors. Only seven authors could be described as truly independent, in that they had no apparent professional connections with other Chapter 9 authors.

It thus turned out that the IPCC's orthodoxy was based not so much on the 'consensus' of '2,500 climate scientists' as on the views of just 53 of them, most of whom were very closely linked. 'The relationships between most of the authors of Chapter 9', wrote McLean, 'demonstrate a disturbingly tight network of scientists with common research interests and opinions'. This perhaps helped explain why 'neither the papers nor the opinions of the growing band of serious climatologists who doubt that humankind has an actually or potentially harmful influence on the earth's climate are adequately represented'.

Having then gone on to draw similar conclusions about the selection of the review editors, who, under the IPCC rules, were supposed to provide an independent critique of the work of the contributing authors, McLean then noted the very high proportion of contributors, such as those from the Hadley Centre, whose work was based on computer models. The words 'model' or 'models', he found, appeared 'a total of 628 times in the 70 pages of chapter 9, demonstrating how heavily the IPCC relies on modelling for its findings'. The very heavy bias towards modellers among the authorship of Chapter 9', McLean observed, 'must have largely prevented any serious questions about the competence of climate models ... to truly represent the future evolution of a complex, non-linear, chaotic object such as the climate'.

He gave several examples of the 'questionable devices' used to make the findings of models seem plausible; or to provide findings which accorded with the *a priori* assumptions of the modellers, as when it had been necessary to 're-tune' models to get them to replicate phenomena such as the cooling between 1940 and 1975 which they had originally failed to reproduce.

Chapter 9, he said, had set great store by examples of where models had come up with similar findings, as if this showed a 'consensus', when the models had clearly been programmed on similar assumptions even before they began processing the data. Since it was 'the *inputs* to the models that determined the extent of the imagined human influence on climate ... analysing the *outputs* to determine the extent to which they demonstrate anthropogenic influences is meaningless and futile'.

The clear biases evident throughout the text, McLean observed, showed that Chapter 9 was 'not science but politics elaborately dressed up' to masquerade as science. The IPCC's exclusion of

> '*scientists who had sufficient knowledge, impartiality and integrity to prevent the numerous fundamental errors of science in Chapter 9 had led to a statistically valueless attribution of the 1976–1998 "global warming" to humankind when, on the evidence, it was merely the continuation of a warming trend which had set in 300 years previously, as solar activity recovered at the end of the Maunder Minimum.*'

There was now evidence, he suggested, that this late-twentieth century warming might have ceased, after a 70-year period when the sun had been more active than at any time in the past 11,400 years. As scientists all over the world were observing, the next cycle of sunspot activity, Cycle 24, was abnormally slow in appearing, indicating the possibility of a prolonged new phase of cooling. Yet the

IPCC's report was so fixated on the 'human-induced climate change' theory written into its charter that it had conspicuously ignored such considerations.

The evidence thus showed that the IPCC's choice of authors, many of whom were selected by each other because of their shared assumptions, had been almost entirely dictated by the extent to which they supported the IPCC's own preconceived position. 'Governments', McLean concluded, 'have naively and unwisely accepted the claims of a human influence on global temperatures made by a close-knit clique of a few dozen scientists, many of them climate modellers, as if they were representative of the opinion of the wider scientific community'.

Many observers had argued this point before, including scientists such as Lindzen who had experienced the IPCC's methods at first hand. But no one had previously done the homework necessary to pin down the charge in detail. The evidence was now incontrovertible.

AMERICA 'COMES IN FROM THE COLD'

Such was the view of the debate as seen from one of the two planets. On the other, few things going on in the world that August were more significant than what was happening in the US, where the 2008 presidential election campaign was now in full swing.

On 'climate change', although it was promoted as one of the central issues of the contest, it was hard to discern any difference between the two candidates, Barack Obama and John McCain. After the years under George W. Bush, when America had been vilified as the 'bad boy' of the planet, the two potential presidents now vied with each other to proclaim how they were going to bring the US in from the cold, by signing up to the full 'green agenda'.

Both candidates supported the Warner-Lieberman 'cap and trade' Bill which had been fought over in the Senate through the summer. This proposed to cut US carbon emissions to 63 per cent below their 2005 levels. The cost of the scheme, it was estimated, would have risen by 2030 to more than $600 billion a year. This represented a cumulative loss to the US economy over 22 years of $4.8 trillion.

Both candidates supported a landmark judgment by the Supreme Court in May 2007, in a case brought by the state of Massachusetts against the Environmental Protection Agency. The court had ruled, by just one vote, that CO_2 was a 'pollutant' – a toxic gas – which the EPA had a legal duty to regulate under the Clean Air Act. The EPA had thus been mandated to set drastic limits on emissions of CO_2 and other gases from almost any source, not just industry and transport but schools, hospitals, even lawn mowers, The potential damage this would inflict on the US economy was so immense that US government departments, from Commerce and Energy to Agriculture, had lined up to protest that it should be considered unthinkable. The Bush White House had accordingly left the judgment in limbo. Now both candidates wished to see it enforced.

Both Obama and McCain were shown in campaign commercials standing in front of the same giant wind farm, to proclaim their support for a massive switch of energy policy from fossil fuels to 'renewables'. So powerful had the influence of 'environmentalists' become that almost any proposal for a new coal-fired power station now faced fierce opposition either from state governments or in the courts, even though the US was still dependent on coal for half its electricity.

As for the suggestion that this could be replaced by electricity form the wind, the candidates' grasp of the technicalities of energy production was so nebulous that neither seemed to have any inkling of just how inefficient were wind turbines in comparison with more conventional power sources. Put all the 10,000 wind turbines already built in the US together and their combined output averaged only 3.9 gigawatts. This represented well under 1 per cent of the country's needs, and was less than the output of a single large coal-fired power station.

The candidates talked blithely about wanting to see vast arrays of solar panels to harness the 'free' energy provided by the sun, when a recent study had shown that the cost of a kilowatt-hour of solar-generated electricity was between 25 and 30 cents, more than four times that of power generated from coal (6 cents).

Rarely in history can the political leaders of any country ever have become so detached from economic reality. But why should they be concerned with such mundane considerations when the future of the planet was at stake?

From the speeches given by the two candidates that August, no one could have guessed that, only weeks away, the US banking system would be in meltdown, as the world's economy plunged into its fiercest recession for more than 70 years.

THE DREAM BEFORE THE STORM

As September 2008 approached, the eyes of environmentalists were fixed firmly on one region of the earth. September always marked the lowest extent of Arctic polar ice, before it began its winter re-freeze. A year earlier the summer melt had reduced the extent of the polar ice to its lowest level since satellite records began in 1979, 3 million square kilometres.

All summer 'green' press releases and the media had been eagerly anticipating the possibility that in 2008 the ice might shrink even further, and that very soon that around the North Pole might actually vanish altogether. WWF had put out its first release suggesting this in April. In June the BBC's environment correspondent Richard Black suggested that the ice was now so thin and melting so fast that the 2008 melt would certainly be as great as in 2007, and that the Arctic might 'be ice-free in summer within five to ten years'.[53]

In July the *Independent* had cleared its front-page to predict that the ice was now vanishing so fast that the North Pole might even be ice-free within a couple of months. At the same time the media reported with great excitement on a forthcoming bid by an Englishman, Gordon Lewis Pugh, to kayak single-handed towards the Pole to wake up world leaders to the disaster unfolding there. The previous autumn in the City of London he had addressed a conference of property men alongside Al Gore, and on 16 July, after posing for the media with his kayak on the Thames, he told the *Times* 'I'm going to try and get all the way to the North Pole to show the world what is happening'.

His 'Polar Defence Project' website proclaimed 'The North Pole is melting'. On 30 August, accompanied by a fossil-fuel powered support ship, Pugh set off in his canoe from Spitzbergen. After only a few days, he found the ice so thick that he could paddle no longer, having reached 80.52 degrees N. He planted on the ice the flags of 192 nations and returned to his mother ship, where he received a congratulatory call from prime minister Gordon Brown and claimed that he had at least 'kayaked further north than anyone has ever kayaked before'.

It did not take long before readers of Watts Up With That came up with a report from a Norwegian consul in August 1922 that Eskimos had just paddled to a point 81 degrees, 29 minutes north. This was followed by a passage from a book by Fridtjof Nansen recording in

1895 how he had paddled above 82 degrees north, 100 miles nearer the Pole than Pugh. A satellite record from 1979 showed that it would have been possible that year to kayak 300 miles nearer the Pole.[54]

It seemed Pugh had been rather too quick to believe what he was told by Gore about what was happening in the Arctic. Had he followed the daily satellite updates on the Cryosphere Today website, provided by the US National Snow and Ice Data Center, he might have seen that the 2008 Arctic ice-melt had stopped some 700,000 square kilometres short of its lowest point in September 2007.

Similarly surreal events were taking place elsewhere on the battlefield. Dr Pachauri, described by the BBC as 'the world's top climate scientist', won widespread media attention when he told a conference organised by Compassion in World farming that everyone should give up eating meat. This was on the grounds that the digestive methane given off by cattle contributed more to greenhouse gases than all the world's transport. As a vegetarian Hindu, Pachauri said nothing about the contribution to global warming made by India's 400 million sacred cows.[55]

In America, Dr Mann made yet another attempt to salvage his 'hockey stick' by publishing a widely-publicised new paper which claimed to have vindicated the original version with 1,200 new proxies 'without using tree rings'.[56] Also published online by the National Academy of Sciences, Mann's new study confirmed, he said, that the previous decade had been the warmest in 1,700 years.

Immediately Steve McIntyre got to work on Climate Audit, entertaining his readers on an almost daily basis as he dug ever deeper into how Mann had come up with his new findings.[57] First, with the aid of expert Finnish readers, he discovered that some of Mann's new proxies, based on the sediments in Finnish lakes, were highly unreliable because settlements had recently grown up on their shores. Then he found that, as 10 years earlier, Mann hid discarded proxies which failed to show the correct 'hockey stick' shape. Then, among many other fundamental flaws, he found that, to get the right curve, Mann had needed to resort to his famous bristlecone pine tree rings after all.

Finally, McIntyre discovered that Mann had smuggled in a version of his original algorithm, giving disproportionate weight to those proxies which confirmed that the present day was much warmer than any time in the previous 1,700 years (although Mann did now concede there was slightly more evidence for a limited Mediaeval Warm

Period than was shown by his previous studies). McIntyre dubbed this idiosyncratic method of dealing with statistical data 'Mannomatics'. But this still didn't prevent Mann's new paper being hailed across the warmist blogosphere as a triumph, not least, of course, by the 'Hockey Team's' own in-house blog, RealClimate.

Then it was again James Hansen's turn to hit the headlines. In the first week of September, six Greenpeace activists appeared at Maidstone Crown Court on charges of having caused 'criminal damage' to the Kingsnorth coal-fired power station on the Kent coast. They had been protesting against E.On's plans to build a more modern coal-fired plant, capable of generating 1.6GW, more than twice as much as the average output of all the 2,000 wind turbines so far built in Britain put together.

Having broken into the plant, the activists had attempted to paint the words' 'Gordon bin it' on a chimney, but after they had written the prime minister's Christian name, the police had intervened. It had then cost E.On £35,000 to repair the damage. All this might have remained no more than a little local incident had not Hansen, who was by now campaigning for all coal-fired power stations to be scrapped, agreed to fly the Atlantic to appear as an 'expert witness' for the accused.

After a private session with the British Foreign Secretary David Miliband, Hansen travelled down to Maidstone to testify that the damage done to the environment by the new power station's CO_2 emissions would be so great that the new plant would contribute to the vanishing from the planet of 'a million species'. The Kingsnorth plant alone would be responsible for the extinction of '400 species'. His evidence was supported by that of Zac Goldsmith, a leading environmental adviser to David Cameron, leader of the Conservative Party. Greenpeace's lawyers argued that the protestors had a 'lawful excuse' to wreak damage on the plant, since this would be far outweighed by the damage done to the world's climate if the power station were built.

So swayed by this evidence were the judge and jury that on 10 September the six activists were acquitted. In reporting this remarkable verdict, the BBC, the *Guardian* and the *Independent* could scarcely conceal their glee. No one seemed to question that a US government official, apparently with the sympathy of the British Foreign Secretary, should have given evidence for six people charged by the British government with having committed criminal offences. Equally odd was why the judge should have ignored the *obiter dicta* of Mr Justice Cresswell in 1993 that an 'expert witness' should only give 'objective evidence' and must not be an 'advocate' for one side or the other on any issue on which experts were divided.[58]

Finally it was the BBC's turn to make waves. Having made no secret at meetings of the World Congress of Science Producers of their rage at Channel 4's documentary *The Great Global Warming Swindle*, the BBC's own environmental team had long been planning a counter-attack. On three Sundays in September, it showed a series, *Climate Wars*, presented by a geologist Dr Iain Stewart, who purported to be acting as an impartial scientist, objectively reviewing the case for and against global warming.

No expense was spared in flying Stewart to locations across the world, from Greenland to California, as in the first programme he laid out the 'consensus' case for man-made global warming. But in the second instalment the BBC revealed its true purpose when it turned to examine three of the main points made by Durkin's film. In each case the programme used the same technique. It caricatured the views of sceptics such as Fred Singer or Roy Spencer by showing soundbite clips of them making seemingly provocative remarks at the Heartland Conference, and then cut them short before they could develop their justification for the point. Stewart was then able simply to assert in each case that their views had been discredited.

Back in the 1990s, for instance, a fault had been discovered in the satellite method of measuring temperatures. This was because satellites slipped in their orbit as they 'decayed', skewing their data. Spencer, as designer of the system for NASA, was shown admitting that a flaw had been identified in the system. But the programme then omitted the rest of the interview, in which Spencer had gone on to explain how, as soon as this and other flaws in the satellite system had been identified, great care had been taken to correct them. He was left only apparently admitting that his satellite data were flawed, thus giving the impression the programme wished to make that satellite data were unreliable.[59]

Stewart accused Durkin's programme of having cut off a graph showing the correlation between temperatures and solar radiation at a point where the data failed to support the thesis (this was the one which Channel 4 had corrected). But Climate Wars itself then did exactly the same, by not extending its own version of the graph to 2008, which would have confirmed Channel 4's point.

Most surreal of all, however, was a long sequence in which Stewart defended the 'hockey stick'. Reverentially fondling the trunks of Mann's famous bristlecone pine trees on a Californian mountainside, he baldly asserted that Mann's graph had withstood all the criticisms the 'sceptics' had thrown at it, without once mentioning McIntyre or the flaws he had identified in it. The BBC then 'proved its point' at great expense by showing a huge blow-up of the 'hockey stick' being triumphantly wheeled round the tourists spots of London on the back of a lorry. As Londoners saw it trundling past them, from Buckingham Palace to the Tower, from Big Ben to Piccadilly Circus, they can only have wondered what was the purpose of this weird publicity stunt.

Scarcely a frame of this unashamed propaganda exercise did not obscure, distort or omit some important point. If all those who complained about Channel 4's film had shown similar devotion to truth and fairness in this case, Ofcom might have been submerged in work for several years.

But the BBC had already made clear that, although its Charter and editorial guidelines committed it to reporting impartially, it did not consider that this applied to coverage of global warming. In a statement repeated to members of the public who complained, it somewhat disingenuously explained

> 'BBC News currently takes the view that their reporting needs to be calibrated to take into account the scientific consensus that global warming is man-made. The BBC's Editorial Guidelines, issued to all editorial staff, state that "we must ensure we avoid bias or an imbalance of views on controversial subjects" and, given the weight of scientific opinion, the challenge for us is to strike the right balance between mainstream science and sceptics since to give them equal weight would imply that the argument is evenly balanced.' [60]

In other words, in the name of reporting impartially, it saw no need to report impartially. To rub this in, the BBC announced that copies of *Climate Wars* would be distributed for showing in Britain's schools – to ensure that its 'impartial' version of the 'truth' prevailed.[61]

THE STORM BREAKS

By the second week of September 2008 the news was dominated by only one story: the domino collapse of many of the largest financial institutions in the western world. As bank after bank teetered on the edge of insolvency, nothing more brought home the shock of what was happening than the announcement on 15 September that Lehman's, one of the world's four richest investment banks, had filed for bankruptcy. So inconceivable in scale was the collapse of the financial system that on all sides there was talk of the world sliding into its worst Depression since the 1930s.

There were at least three ways in which this had relevance to the fight to save the planet from global warming. The immediate cause of the financial crash was that too many institutions had risked too much money on loans and investments which turned out to be secured on assets which had been hopelessly overvalued. And a hugely influential hidden factor in this flight from reality was that so much faith had been placed by the financial markets in the projections of computer models.

When Forbes predicted in April 2008 that shares in Freddie Mac, one of the two monster concerns which dominated the US mortgage market, looked 'cheap at $29', the reason for this was that this assessment had resulted from very expensive computer modelling which completely lost touch with the realities of the company's plight. Five months later the shares stood at just 25 cents, a drop of 99 per cent.

If computer models powered by wishful thinking had proved so disastrously incapable of mirroring all the variables involved in the affairs of a mortgage company, how much could they be relied on to replicate the infinitely more complex variables involved in predicting the future of the earth's climate? [62]

A more specific link between the financial crash and 'climate change' was the plight of Lehman Brothers itself. The bank had lately been investing billions of dollars in a bid to become the global leader in the international market in 'carbon credits', through the EU's Emissions Trading Scheme, the UN's Clean Development Mechanism and the 'cap and trade' system proposed for the US by both McCain and Obama. As Lehman set out in two hefty reports on *The Business of Climate Change* it had hoped to become 'the prime brokerage for emissions permits', in a market predicted soon to be worth trillions of pounds. Lehman was advised by Jim Hansen and Al Gore, a close friend of the bank's erstwhile managing director Theodore Roosevelt IV; and although there were more significant factors in its collapse, the very expensive gamble it had taken on becoming the leading player in what was now the fastest-growing financial market in the world had hardly helped its balance sheet.

The third link between the financial meltdown and global warming promised potentially to become the most far-reaching of all. It was all very well for the politicians to talk about spending trillions of dollars to change the climate when their economies were booming and the western world was floating on a sea of credit. But now, as credit dried up and their economies looked to be on the edge of a fathomless abyss, how long would it be before at least some of those politicians began to say that they could no longer afford such sacrifices, and that other priorities had now intervened, such as the need to fight for their countries' economic survival?

Sure enough, within weeks, spokesmen for the Polish and Italian governments were in Brussels at the front of the queue, putting to Europe's government that this was not the time to be piling onto its economies costs amounting to trillions of euros. Gordon Brown, standing alongside Commission President Barroso, was at the forefront of those insisting that the EU must stick to its guns.[63] As the recession worsened, it seemed unlikely this was the last time that such pleas would be heard.

'NO COAL, NO NUCLEAR, NO FUTURE'

One country where the politicians were not saying anything of the sort was Britain. But in recent months it had become apparent that a major rift was opening up between the country's energy minister John Hutton and some of his Cabinet colleagues.

Hutton had fully taken on board that unless very dramatic steps were taken to close Britain's approaching energy gap, within a few years she would face a massive crisis. Building windmills was not going to have any effect. The only way to close the gap would be to build new nuclear and coal-fired power stations as fast as it could be done (which was why Hutton was now urging Brown to approve the proposed new plant at Kingsnorth).

'Of course we've got to tackle climate change', said Hutton in an interview at the end of August. But

> *'we've also got to be absolutely clear that our energy policy has got to be figured first and foremost with a view to supplying Britain with the affordable and secure enery it needs for the futire. That is why we cannot turn our back on any proven form of technology. We cannot afford to say no to new coal, new gas or new nuclear.'*[64]

A few weeks later, at the Labour Party conference, he spelled out his message even more bluntly. Guaranteeing Britain's future energy supplies had become a 'defining' issue for the country, he said. As North Sea gas ran out, it was no good the UK hoping to rely on importing 80 per cent of its gas from overseas, 'much of it from potentially "unstable" regions'. The only practical hope lay in coal and nuclear: 'no coal and no nuclear means no power, no future.' [65]

Such frank realism did not go down well with Hutton's colleagues. Two weeks later it was announced that he had been relieved of his post and moved to the Ministry of Defence. Gordon Brown had set up a new ministry, the Department of Energy and Climate Change, under Ed Miliband, as fervently committed as his Foreign Secretary brother David to the full global warming orthodoxy.

Thus the 'realists' of BERR, concerned for Britain's parlous energy future, were to be united in the new ministry with the climate change fanatics of DEFRA, presumably with the intention that they should thrash out their differences behind the scenes. As for which way the argument was likely to go, a clue was that the new ministry's chief scientific adviser was to be Dr Bob Watson, formerly chairman of the IPCC and Gore's 'hero of the planet'.

It seemed highly unlikely that Miliband would follow Hutton's lead in declaring that Britain's energy security should take priority over everything else, even if this meant disregarding EU directives. Like his brother, the new Climate Change Secretary was as firm a believer in Britain's governance by the EU as he was in man-made climate change. Furthermore, there was not the slightest public or private indication that he knew anything about the practicalities of Britain's energy needs.

Miliband's first priority was to push through its final stages the most bizarre and expensive piece of legislation ever put before the British Parliament (the episode with which the narrative of this book began). This was the government's Climate Change Bill, imposing a legal obligation on every government for the next 42 years to ensure than by 2050 Britain's carbon dioxide emissions were only 40 per cent of what they had been in 1990. Except that Miliband now wished to amend this to the even more drastic figure of only 20 per cent of their level in 1990.

Short of some technological revolution as yet undreamed of, there was no way this absurdly fanciful target could be achieved without shutting down virtually every aspect of Britain's economy.

On 29 October MPs returned to the Bill, which they had already approved in principle, to spend six more hours debating it again on its Third Reading. This was necessary because of Miliband's new amendment changing the original 60 per cent target by 2050 to 80 per cent, a figure far higher than was as yet being aimed at by any other country in the world.

Only two MPs questioned the need for the Bill, and only one raised the question of what it was all going to cost. This was a former Conservative Cabinet minister, Peter Lilley. The government's own estimate for the cost of the unamended Bill, when the target figure was still at 60 rather than 80 per cent, was £205 billion. But its benefits were estimated at only £110 billion. In other words, what MPs were being asked to vote for was a Bill the cost of which had been estimated to be twice the value of any benefits it would bring (Miliband promised new estimates in light of his raising of the target figure).

It should hardly have seemed an irresistible bargain. But so far had the MPs been swept up into unthinking acceptance of the fashionable mindset that, without having the slightest idea what they were voting for, they trooped through the lobbies to approve the Bill and Miliband's amendment by 463 votes to 3.

Just before the vote was taken, as was recalled at the start of the book, Mr Lilley drew the Speaker's attention to the fact that, outside the centrally-heated building in which they were sitting, London was experiencing its first October snowfall in 74 years. On one planet, where global temperatures had been dropping for 10 years, Britain was just entering its coldest winter for decades. On the other the MPs, somehow convinced that planetary temperatures were soaring, were voting for what – if implemented – would amount to no less than an act of collective economic suicide.

PRESIDENT OBAMA FOLLOWS SUIT

If the winter had started cold in Britain, this was nothing to what was happening elsewhere in the world. Abnormal snowfalls had been reported in October from Canada to China, from the Alps to New Zealand. China's official news agency reported that Tibet had suffered its 'worst snowstorm ever'.[66]

So much snow fell in the US that NOAA reported 63 places having experienced record snowfalls for the month and that 115 had recorded their lowest-ever October temperatures. NOAA ranked it as only the 70th warmest October in 114 years.[67]

So rapid was the refreezing of ice in the Arctic Circle that by late October Cryosphere Today was showing the extent of ice-cover as

30 per cent greater than it had been at the same point in 2007. When WWF attempted in a press release to keep up the alarm over that 'vanishing' Arctic ice, its graph tellingly showed the area of the ice in September 2007 rather than that for 2008.

There was therefore considerable astonishment when, on 10 November, Hansen's GISS announced that the previous month had been globally 'the warmest October ever recorded'. Within hours, after checking through the GISS data, Climate Audit, accompanied by Watts Up With That, had tracked down just why Hansen's October figures were so dramatically anomalous. GISS had simply carried over its Russian temperature data from September, unchanged.[68]

Less than a day after this embarrassing blunder was reported to GISS, new figures were posted to correct most of the anomaly (although GISS did claim to have discovered a new 'hotspot' in the Arctic, which was also surprising, since satellites had simultaneously been showing Arctic ice recovering at remarkable speed). Gavin Schmidt, Hansen's colleague, explained that it had been supplied with the Russian figures by a public body, the Global Historical Climate Network, and that GISS did not have adequate resources to exercise proper quality control over data it received from elsewhere.

This was a startling confession. GISS was one of the four sources of temperature data officially recognised by the IPCC and others all over the world. Yet it was now admitting that it did not have sufficient resources to maintain adequate checks on the reliability of its data.

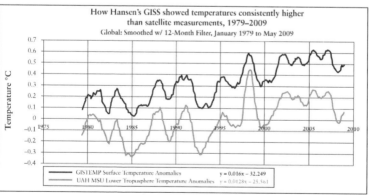

Figure 4: Comparison of temperature data as shown by GISS and by satellite measurements. The upper line shows temperatures as reported by James Hansen's GISS, based on data from surface weather stations, which was increasingly coming under question for its reliability. The lower line shows satellite temperatures from UAH. Hansen's graph consistently shows temperatures up to 4°C higher.

It was perhaps not surprising that Dr Pachauri should shortly afterwards have surprised a university audience in Australia, where he was being given an honorary science doctorate, by claiming that global warming was now taking place 'much faster' than ever, and that '11 of the last 12 years rank among the 12 warmest years' since temperature records began. To illustrate his point he showed Hansen's surface temperature graph cut off in 2000, so that the declining trend since 2002 had been omitted.[69] That evening on television, he dismissed those who disagreed with his views on global warming as 'flat earthers' who 'deny the overwhelming weight of scientific evidence'.

Certainly none of these finer points impinged on the thinking of the new US President Barack Obama, who at the end of November (as was recalled in the Prologue to Part One) recorded on video his second major post-election policy statement. This was intended to be seen not only in the US but by the delegates to a vast UNFCCC gathering in Poland, summoned to discuss the agenda for next year's conference in Copenhagen to agree a successor to the Kyoto treaty.

It was in this statement that Mr Obama wished everyone to know that, under his presidency, the US now intended to 'lead the world' in the fight against global warming. 'The science', he went on to say, 'is beyond dispute'. 'Sea levels are rising, coastlines are shrinking, we've seen record drought, spreading famine, and storms that are growing stronger with each hurricane season.'

On every one of these familiar points, as we have seen, the science was very far from being settled in the way Obama imagined. If sea levels were modestly rising, they were doing so no faster than they had been doing for 200 years. Coastlines were not shrinking, except where land was subsiding. Major droughts were becoming fewer, rather than more frequent. Hurricane activity was lower than it had been in the 1950s, and in recent years had been declining.

Obama then turned to all the practical measures by which his presidency would be leading the fight against climate change. He wanted to see a 'federal cap and trade system', a tax on 'carbon', designed to follow Britain's example by cutting America's CO_2 emissions within 42 years to a level 80 per cent below where they had been in 1990. This would in fact take them back to where they had been in 1867.

He announced his intention to spend $15 billion a year to encourage 'clean energy' sources, such as building tens of thousands more wind turbines. He said that the construction of new coal-fired power plants would be allowed only if these were fitted with 'carbon capture': burying the CO_2 in holes in the ground (even though the technology to do this hadn't yet been developed). And all this, he promised without being specific, would somehow generate 'five million new green jobs'.

The timing of Obama's message, as the American economy continued to disintegrate, was impeccable. As his country entered its coldest winter for decades, much of the US, as far south as New Orleans, had just been hit by heavy snowfalls (even the BBC deigned to notice the first snow in Las Vegas for 30 years, because it was Vegas, but not the rest of it).

The new president's words were received with rapturous applause in the Polish city of Posnan, where at the start of December 10,000 delegates from all over the world gathered in near-zero temperatures to plan the successor to Kyoto. Nevertheless, China and India were still adamant that they would not cut their emissions unless the developed world paid them to do so. The Italians and the Poles were now threatening to veto the Copenhagen proposals on the grounds that the economic crisis made them unaffordable. Poland could not accept the phasing out of coal, the fuel which supplied 95 per cent of her electricity (and was keeping all those 10,000 delegates warm in their hotels and conference halls). In Brussels 11,000 steelworkers demonstrated in protest against the EU's climate change proposals on the grounds that, if they were enforced, much of Europe's steel industry would simply relocate outside the EU.

The sense that the debate over global warming was now being conducted from two totally separate planets, neither remotely able to understand or communicate with the other, could scarcely have been more complete.

'A BLIZZARD OF MAD PROPOSALS'

The strange *danse macabre* whereby countries were now vying with each other to see who could come up with the most drastic commitment to cut carbon emissions was turning into a poker game, played for scarcely imaginable stakes. Obama having now matched Britain's offer of '80 per cent by 2050', it was again Britain's turn to raise the bid. Sure enough, to coincide with the Posnan conference in the first days of December, the offer came in the shape of a set of recommendations from something called the 'Committee on Climate Change', chaired by a member of the government's Great and Good, Lord Turner of Ecchinswell.

Few people outside the 'climate change industry' would have heard of this body, although its chairman was better known as Adair Turner, with his day job as chairman of the Financial Services Authority, charged with sorting out the havoc in Britain's financial sector which the FSA had done nothing to foresee or prevent.

When Turner had the previous March been appointed Britain's first 'climate czar', the main reason why this hit the headlines was his suggestion that, as a first step towards saving the planet, men should stop wearing ties and suits to the office, and women should give up wearing skirts. This, he said, would lessen the need for air-conditioning and encourage them to cycle or walk to work.[70]

His committee was made up of various 'professors of climate change' and other unworldly academics, all hard-line believers in man-made global warming, only one of whom had the slightest experience of the business world. Their task was to work out practical ways in which Britain could lead the world in what was now its statutory obligation to cut emissions of CO_2 to just 20 per cent of where they were in 1990. After eight months hard at work, they had come up with their recommendations.

The timing, as so often that winter, was immaculate. As Turner's committee issued its first report on how Britain was to meet the terrifying threat of runaway global warming, blizzards had closed roads and schools across northern England and Scotland. Large parts of the country were carpeted with snow for the third time that winter.

One of their proposals was that the British should switch from eating beef and lamb to 'less carbon-intensive types of meat'. Another was that within 11 years they wanted to see 40 per cent of all the cars on Britain's roads powered by electricity. This was in the same week when it was being reported that sales of all-electric cars had in 2008 halved from 374 to 156 (one of only two companies making them had just gone bankrupt).

Nor, of course, did Turner's wise men and women explain where all the electricity to power these vehicles might come from. They seemed blissfully oblivious, for instance, to the fact that, within a few years, Britain would face a shortfall of 40 per cent in the supply of electricity she needed to meet her current demand. They insisted that no more coal-fired power plants should be built unless they could be fitted with 'carbon capture', seemingly unaware that, even if this were technically possible, it would double the cost of electricity and make Britain even more dependent on the Russian and other imported coal which already supplied 70 per cent of her needs.

So what did they suggest would provide the power for those millions of imaginary electric cars, let alone keep Britain's lights on? Inevitably they wanted to see the building of thousands more windmills. But nothing better illustrated the Neverland in which these academics lived than a graph in their report showing how, by 2020, Britain would have enough of them to meet her EU target of deriving a third of her electricity from 'renewables'.

These, they claimed, would provide 28GW of 'capacity', exactly half the 56GW which Britain needed to meet peak demand. Yet, of course, thanks to the intermittency of the wind, those thousands of turbines would only generate on average some 7.5GW. This would represent a mere 13 per cent of current peak demand, leaving Britain woefully short of her agreed EU target while doing little or nothing to plug that fast-looming 40 per cent gap in her supplies.

In other words, a more vacuously dotty ragbag of proposals it would have been hard to conceive of. The only possible competitor was the plan to save the planet put forward the same week by George Monbiot of the *Guardian*. The 'Great Moonbat', as the revered environmental campaigner was affectionately known, wanted to see air travel reduced by 95 per cent. 'Key roads' should be barred to private cars. And a total ban should be imposed on grouse-shooting, because burning the heather on grouse-moors created, according to Moonbat, 'a staggering proportion of UK emissions'.[71]

Monbiot was far from alone in the UK media. Just as the politicians competed with each other in their pledges to cut carbon emissions, so did the environmental journalists of the BBC, the *Independent*, the *Daily Telegraph* and others now vie with each other to produce the scare story of the day, usually based on the avalanche of press releases now being put out by the army of pressure groups and government bodies keenly aware that Copenhagen was now only a year away.

What was strange was the readiness of these journalists to publish whatever claims were fed to them, without pausing to check out whether there might be some other side to the story. When Butterfly Conservation Europe, for instance, put out one of its regular releases claiming that global warming could cause the disappearance of many butterfly species, such as the Mountain Ringlet and others indigenous to the uplands of northern Britain, the journalists reporting it never seemed to ask any of the more obvious questions, such as how did such species manage to survive those times in the past when the climate was warmer than the present.[72]

When the *Daily Telegraph* published two pictures showing the alarming retreat of the Rongbuk glacier below Everest between 1968 and 2007, it had no doubt as to what was the cause. It had been unequivocally attributed by a group of Indian meteorologists to the effects of global warming, which they predicted could cause all the Himalayan glaciers to vanish by 2035.[73] Yet only two days earlier, unmentioned by the *Telegraph's* article, the UN Environment Program had claimed that the melting of the glaciers was due, not to global warming, but to a vast 'atmospheric brown cloud' hanging over the region, made up of soot particles from southern Asia's sharply increased burning of fossil fuels and the vast areas of forest being torched in Indonesia and Malaysia (not least for biofuels).[74]

Again, two years earlier, a British study, published by the American Meteorological Society, had shown that glaciers were only shrinking in the eastern Himalaya. Further to the west, in the Hindu Kush and the Karakoram, glaciers were 'thickening and expanding'.[75] But even this, they claimed, was due to the different effects in different places of 'global warming'.

ITN News was at the same running a week-long series on the vanishing of the Arctic ice and those 'doomed' polar bears. Naturally it never bothered to tell its viewers that Arctic ice cover was now above its 30-year November average and that polar bear numbers were at record levels.[76]

With the countdown to Copenhagen having begun, the only thing which mattered was to keep climate change hysteria at fever pitch, regardless of the evidence. Truly did it seem that the two sides to this battle now inhabited totally different planets. But which planet was who trying to save?

Notes

1. Vaclav Klaus, *Blue Planet In Green Shackles* (Competitive Enterprise Institute, Washinghton, 2008).
2. Met Office press release, 'Global temperature 2008: Another top-ten year', 3 January 2008.

3. 'Jan 08 snow Northern Hemisphere snow cover: largest anomaly since 1966', Watts Up With That, 9 February 2008.
4. 'NOAA/NCDC: Jan08 colder than 20th century average', WUWT, 7 February 2008; 'Climate of 2008: January in historical perspective', NCDC, 14 February 2008.
5. 'Weather wreaks havoc in Greece and Turkey', *New York Herald Tribune*, 18 February 2008.
6. 'January 2008: 4 sources say "globally cooler" in the past 12 months', Watts Up With That, 2 February 2008; 'A look at temperature anomalies for all 4 global metrics', WUWT, 28 February 2008; 'Even the warmists can feel the chill', *Sunday Telegraph*, 24 February 2008.
7. 'Ice between Canada and SW Greenland: highest level in 15 years', WUWT, 16 February 2008.
8. Carole Williams, 'How the environmental extremists manipulate the masses', NewsWithViews website, 26 January 2008.
9. 'Even the warmists can feel this chill', *Sunday Telegraph*, 24 February 2009; 'Climate dissent grows hotter as chill deepens', *Sunday Telegraph*, 9 March 2009.
10. *http://ec.europa.eu/publications/booklets/move/70/index_en.htm*. So fixated now was the EU on global warming that a reference to it was among various additions to the EU Constitution, now in 2008 resurrected as the Lisbon Treaty. Under Article 191, requiring the 'Union' to contribute to international measures on 'environmental problems', the phrase was now added 'and in particular combating climate change'. This was the first time that any country in the world had included a reference to global warming in its constitution.
11. European Union Emission Trading Scheme wikipedia.
12. 'EU plans to see our economy blown away', *Sunday Telegraph*, 27 January 2008.
13. 'Proposal for a directive of the European Parliament and the Council on the promotion of energy from renewable sources', COM(2008) Final.
14. 'Commission scientists blast EU biofuels policy', EurActiv, 18 January 2008.
15. *Sunday Telegraph*, 17 February 2008.
16. 'US biofuel subsidies under attack at food summit', *Guardian*, 3 June 2006.
17. 'Food Outlook No,1', FAO briefing, 1 June 2006.
18. Sec(2006) 1721, Commission Staff Working Document, Accompanying document to the Communication from the Commission to the Council and the European Parliament, Biofuels Progress Report, Report on the progress made on the use of biofuels and other renewable fuels, 10 January 2007: *http://ec.europa.eu/energy/energy_policy/doc/08_biofuels_progress_report_annex_en.pdf*

19. BBC website, 27 October 2007.

20. 'A Note on Rising Food Prices', Donald Mitchell, World Bank Policy Research Working paper 4682, World Bank Development Prospects Group, July 2008.

21. University of Minnesota Biofuels Database.

22. *http://cip.cornell.edu/biofuels/* Biofuels: Environmental Consequences and Interactions with Changing Land Use.

23. 'Biofuels in the European Context: facts and uncertainities', European Commission Joint Research Centre, Institute for Energy, with input from the JRC Institute for Environment and Sustainability, January 2008.

24. For further background see 'The Great Biofuels Con', *Daily Telegraph*, 13 July 2008. In April 2008, under previous EU legislation, it became mandatory for 2.75 per cent of all fuel served on Britain's forecorts to come from biofuels, wiith the intention that by 2020 this should rise by stages to 10 per cent.

25. 'States handed ambitious renewable energy targets', EurActiv website, 24 January 2008.

26. The letter from Gore hailing Watson as 'hero of the planet' was read out by Jack Gibbons, Watson's former boss in the Clinton-Gore White House, and recorded on a World Bank video, 13 July 2007, *http://info. world bank.org/etools/BSPAN/PresentationView.asp?PID=2129&EID=963*

27. 'New nuclear plants get go-ahead', BBC News website, 10 January 2008.

28. Mike Earp, UK Continental Shelf: Oil and Gas Production and the UK Economy, BERR, 2008 (graph on p. 57). Although we reported on this in the *Sunday Telegraph* on 8 July 2008, it appears that this report has since been removed from the ministry's website.

29. 'Brussels steps in to stop a windfarm', *Sunday Telegraph*, 3 February 2008; 'Save the planet from environmental pargets', *Sunday Telegraph*, 27 April 2008.

30. The cost of the new nuclear power plant then under constriction at Olkiluoto in Finland was £2.7 billion, to generate 1,600MW of electricity and 4,300MW of thermal energy.

31. 'The Severn Barrage is a washout', *Sunday Telegraph*, 30 March 2008.

32. 'Tory MP is hoist with his own canard', *Sunday Telegraph*, 3 February 2008.

33. N. Keenlyside, *et al.* (2008), 'Advancing decadal-scale climate predictions in the North Atlantic sector', *Nature*, 453, 84–88 (1 May 2008). See also 'Global warming may "stop", scientists predict', *Daily Telegraph*, 30 April 2008; 'Next decade "may see no warming"', BBC News website, 1 May 2008.

34. 'Larger Pacific climate event helps La Nina linger', NASA website. 21 April 2008. See also 'NASA: PDO flip to cool phase confirmed – cooler times ahead for West Coast?', Watts Up With That blog, 29 April 2008.

35. This was noted in 'Anti-warming evidence piles up on Snowdon', *Sunday Telegraph*, 4 May 2008.
36. *Nature, Not Human Activity Rules The Climate*, Summary for Policy-makers, Non-Governmental Panel on Climate Change, edited by Dr Fred Singer (Science and Environmental Policy Project, March 2008).
37. 'Climate dissent grows hotter as chill deepens', *Sunday Telegraph*, 9 March 2008.
38. David King, Gabrielle Walker, *The Hot Topic: How To Tackle Global warming And Still Keep The Lights On* (Bloomsbury Publishing, 2008). Nigel Lawson, *An Appeal to Reason: a cool look at global warming* (Duckworth, 2008).
39. 'International energy agency says world faces $45 trillion push to halve carbon output', *The Times*, 7 June 2008.
40. Mark Gregory, 'The great carbon bazaar', BBC News Channel website, 4 June 2008.
41. 'Gordon Brown vows to drive out fossil fuels', *Daily Telegraph*, 26 June 2008. 'UK plans big wind power expansion', BBC News website, 26 June 2008.
42. 'Our leaders are in carbon-cloud cuckoo land', *Daily Telegraph*, 10 July 2009.
43. 'NASA scientist: put CEOs on trial for global warming lies', Fox News website, 24 June 2009.
44. For full speech see 'The post-oil economies of the future', Oil Drum Europe website, 15 July 2008.
45. 'Energy firm recruits children as "climate cops"', *Sunday Telegraph*, 3 August 2008.
46. 'Climate documentary "broke rules"', BBC News website, 21 July 2008. See also, for instance, 'Channel 4's Great Global Warming Swindle "misrepresented" scientists, says Ofcom', *Daily Telegraph*, 21 July 2008.
47. See 'The Opinionator: at Wikipedia one man engineers the debate on global warming and shapes it to his views', Lawrence Solomon, *Financial Post*, 3 May 2008. Solomon pointed out that Connolley gave himself an absurdly long entry on Wikipedia, emphasising his passionate support for the global warming orthodoxy. The article argued that, because Wikipedia had become 'the single biggest reference source in the world', its ruthlessly one-sided coverage of global warming-related issues, and its personal 'smearing' of anyone who dissented from the orthodoxy was not only a matter of serious public concern but also broke Wikipedia's own proclaimed editorial rules.
48. See Ofcom website for rulings, 21 July 2008.
49. A more detailed account of the Ofcom rulings can be found in Appendix 2.

50. For details, see Appendix 2.

51. For a full discussion of the points raised by this episode see the lengthy posts by Steve McIntyre on Climate Audit: 'Ofcom decision: a humiliating defeat for Bob Ward and the Myles Allen 37', 21 July 2008; David King, 'hot girls and cold continents', 22 July 2008; 'Ofcom: the IPCC complaint', 23 July 2008. In light of his experiences with the IPCC over its 2007 report, McIntyre was particularly struck by the IPCC's protestations in its evidence to Ofcom as to the 'openness and transparency' of its review process.

52. John McLean, *Prejudiced authors, prejudiced findings* (Science and Public Policy Instutute, 2008).

53. 'Arctic ice melt "even faster"', BBC New Channel website, 15 June 2008.

54. See reports on Watts Up With That website, such as 'Polar Defense Project deletes the tough questions', 9 September 2008, in which Watts related how his attempt to make these points on Pugh's website were denied entry.

55. *Sunday Telegraph*, 14 September 2008.

56. M. Mann, *et al.*, 'Proxy-based reconstructions of hemispeheric and global surface temperature variations over the past two millennia', PNAS, 9 September 2008, 195, 36.

57. See the series of commentaries on Climate Audit, beginning with 'Mann *et al.* 2009', 2 September 2008, including 'Non-MWP proxies', 'Mann 2008: the bristlecone addiction', and several more.

58. *Sunday Telegraph*, 14 September 2008.

59. The advocates of the orthodoxy were particularly anxious to discredit the reliability of satellite temperature data, because of the criticisms which had been levelled at the reliability of surface measurements. The satellite data tended to show significantly less global warming than weather stations. For a discussion of flaws found in the satellite method see 'Spence UK' on the comment thread of 'BBC Climate Wars', Climate Audit, 16 September 2008.

60. Copies of letters sent to the author. The BBC's deliberate bias in favour of the 'consensus' on global warming was later confirmed by one of its senior newsreaders, Peter Sissons, who wrote in 2009 that he was one of only 'a tiny minority of BBC interviewers who have so much as raised the possibility that there is another side to the debate on climate change'. The BBC's 'most famous interrogators', he wrote, 'invariably begin by accepting that "the science is settled" when there are countless reputable scientists and climatologists producing work that says it isn't'. 'But it is effectively BBC policy', he continued, 'enthusiastically carried out by the BBC's environment correspondents, that those views should not be heard'. Sissons described an episode when, following a 'climate change

rally' in London in December 2008, he had been asked to interview the leader of the Green Party, Caroline Lucas. When he pointed out to her that Britain was going through a severe winter, after 10 years which had seen no rise in world temperatures while CO_2 emissions continued to increase, Lucas was 'outraged'. She told him angrily it was 'disgraceful that the BBC should be giving any kind of publicity to those sort of views' (Peter Sissons, *The Mail on Sunday*, 12 July 2009).

61. 'BBC stitches up sceptics in counter-attack over climate change', *Sunday Telegraph*, 21 September 2008.
62. See Michael R. Smith, 'Common sense and the perils of predictions', Watts Up With That blog, 12 June 2009.
63. *Sunday Telegraph*, 19 October 2009.
64. 'No more cheap energy, warns Cabinet minister John Hutton', *Daily Telegraph*, 27 August 2008.
65. 'Energy security "vital" – Hutton', *Daily Telegraph*, 22 September 2008.
66. 'Tibet's 'worst snowstorm ever', WUWT, 31 October 2008.
67. 'The world has never seen such freezing heat', *Sunday Telegraph*, 16 November 2008.
68. 'Did Napoleon use Hansen's temperature data?', Climate Audit, 10 November 2008; 'GISS releases (suspect) October data', Watts Up With That, 11 October 2008; 'Corrected Gistemp data as been posted', WUWT, 12 October 2008. See also *Sunday Telegraph*, above.
69. For discussion, including screen grab of graph used in Pachauri's University of New South Wales lecture, see the Australian Climate Madness science blog, 8 and 9 November 2008.
70. 'Blizzard of mad proposals descends on the UK', *Sunday Telegraph*, 7 December 2008.
71. Monbiot, 'Whistling in the wind', *Guardian* website, 2 December 2008.
72. 'Butterfly species may be lost to Britain through climate change', *Daily Telegraph*, 10 December 2008.
73. 'Himalayan glaciers could disappear completely by 2035', *Daily Telegraph*, 14 November 2008.
74. 'Widespread and complex climate changes outlined in new UNEP atmospheric brown cloud report', UNEP News Centre website, 13 November 2008.
75. B. J. Fowler and D. R. Archer, 'Conflicting signals of climate change in the Upper Indus basin', *Journal of Climate* 19, Issue 17, pp. 4276–4293.
76. 'Stubborn glaciers fail to retreat, awkward polar bears continue to multiply', *Sunday Telegraph*, 23 November 2008.

9

Countdown to Copenhagen
Colliding with reality: 2009

'Barack Obama has only four years to save the world. That is the stark assessment of NASA scientist and leading climate expert Jim Hansen who last week warned only urgent action by the new president could halt the devastating climate change that now threatens Earth.'
                                   The Guardian, 18 January 2009

'The US President has just four years to save the planet'
                                   Professor James McCarthy, president of the
                                   American Association for the Advancement
                                   of Science, February 2009[1]

'The best scientific projections indicate that we have very little time left – indeed less than 100 months – in which to alter our behaviour drastically.'
                                   HRH the Prince of Wales, 26 May 2009[2]

At the start of 2009, the UK Met Office and its Hadley Centre proudly announced that they had bought from Japan a new £33 million super-computer. Capable of 125 trillion calculations a second, it would help them, they said, to produce even more accurate predictions of future climate change (and also improve their 'short-term forecasting of Britain's weather'). Even if it used so much power that it emitted 10,000 tons of CO_2 a year, this was nothing, the Met Office claimed, compared to what it would eventually save the world by bringing 'an acceleration in action on climate change' through more accurate prediction of its risks.[3]

As was now customary, the Met Office also marked the start of 2009 with a forecast for the year ahead, based on the calculations of its existing super-computer. A year earlier this had predicted that 2008 would be one of the 'top ten warmest years' ever, just as global temperatures were plunging way below their 30-year average. Now they upped the ante by forecasting that 2009 would be one of the 'five warmest years on record'.

By far the most dominant theme of the year was to be the run-in to the mammoth conference scheduled for December in Copenhagen, where it was hoped the nations of the world would be able to agree on a very much tougher successor to the Kyoto treaty. Through the next 11 months, this was to preoccupy the attention of the world's 'climate change community' in two separate ways.

The first of these would be a concerted campaign by the IPCC's myriad supporters to soften up world opinion by raising the stakes over the threat of global warming even higher. Scarcely a day was to go by without some alarming new study or press release being published somewhere, all with a common theme. Whether they were talking about vanishing polar ice or the disappearance of the Amazon rainforest, rising sea levels or the increased risk of hurricanes, the message was to be invariably the same: the plight of the planet was 'much worse than had been predicted'.

The other thread through the year, attracting considerably less attention from the media, was the continuing impasse, evident in one round of talks after another, over what might actually be achieved at Copenhagen. The fundamental division, as it had been ever since Kyoto, was between the richer nations of the developed world and those poorer but fast-growing countries which were still developing.

On one side, most developed countries, already pledged to drastic curbs on their own use of fossil fuels, were calling on the developing world to do likewise. On the other, led by China and India, the still-developing countries insisted that the problem had largely been created by those who had industrialised before them. Poorer countries could not be expected to cut down their own emissions unless the richer nations paid them astronomic sums of money in compensation.

This seemingly intractable equation was now being further complicated by the fact that the developed countries were themselves now on the rack of the sharpest recession for decades. This naturally made the more realistic of them increasingly reluctant to agree to further economic sacrifices they could less than ever afford.

Another new element in the equation, however, was the arrival of new governments in the two industrialised countries which had hitherto failed to ratify Kyoto, but were now anxious to make amends: the US and Australia. Politically the big event at the start of 2009 was the arrival in the White House of President Obama, promising that the US would now 'lead the world' in the fight against global warming.

Even before he took office, Obama had signalled his intentions by the appointments he had made to all the senior posts in his administration responsible for energy and environment policy. Acclaimed as 'the green dream team', every one of them was committed to the belief that man-made climate change was the most serious challenge facing mankind.

Obama's new Secretary of State for Energy was a somewhat unworldly Nobel Prize-winning physicist, Professor Stephen Chu, who had already gone on record as saying that he wanted to see taxes raised on fossil fuels, to make the US's cheap gasoline as expensive as it was in Europe.

Appointed as chief scientific adviser to the White House was Professor John Holdren, whose record as a prophet of planetary doom went back to the 1970s, when he had famously co-authored a paper with the most apocalyptic doom-sayer of them all, Paul Ehrlich of *The Population Bomb*. As an adviser to Gore on *An Inconvenient Truth* and director of the Wood Hole Research Institute, a think-tank dedicated to climate alarmism, Holdren was a much more obviously hard-line advocate for drastic action on warming than Chu. Like Maurice Strong before him, he believed in 'moving towards some kind of world government', to ensure that rich countries reduced their selfishly high standard of living in order to redistribute wealth to poorer countries.

Other Obama nominees who wanted to put climate change at the top of their agenda included Liza Jackson, the first African-American head of the Environmental Protection Agency and Jane Luchenco, the new director of the National Oceanic and Atmospheric Administration.

Just before Obama's inauguration another federal employee Dr Hansen again hit the headlines by warning that the new president had 'only four years to save the world'. On 21 January, more than a million people gathered in a chilly Washington to hear the most eagerly-awaited inaugural address since John F. Kennedy's in 1961.

In a speech full of indications as to how he wished to see America reborn to itself after wasted years of betrayal under Bush, Obama made only two surprisingly brief references to energy and climate. In one he promised 'we will harness the sun and the winds and the soil to fuel our cars and run our factories'. In a quite different part of the speech he promised 'we will work tirelessly to lessen the nuclear threat and roll back the spectre of a warming planet'.

That was it. Not a huge amount to go on. But no one greeted his speech more rapturously than the BBC, which sent 400 people to Washington to give it many more hours of coverage than any inauguration had ever received before. None of this was more reverential than that from its leading current affairs programme *Newsnight*. Craftily editing Obama's two sentences together to make them sound much stronger than they did at the time, the programme used this as the text for its science editor, Susan Watts, to deliver a paean of gratitude that the world at last had a US President prepared to listen to 'the science', after the dark days of 'religious' obscurantism personified by President Bush.

After years when they could not speak openly on this subject, said Ms Watts, 'scientists calculate that President Obama has just four years to save the world'. She did not explain that the only scientist who had said anything so silly was Hansen, and that it was also he who liked to claim that the Bush administration had tried to 'muzzle' him on global warming, a claim which surprised all those under the impression that he scarcely ever stopped talking about it.

Only that same week Hansen's former supervisor Dr John Theon, formerly in charge of all NASA's work on climate and meteorology, had been provoked at last to protest publicly that Hansen had never been 'muzzled'. This was despite the fact, said Theon, that his more extreme statements on global warming over the years had 'embarassed' NASA, and were quite contrary to its own official views. Now retired, Theon further said that in his opinion climate models were 'useless', because they could not hope to replicate all the factors which influenced climate. On man-made global warming, he declared, he himself was a 'sceptic'.[4]

None of this, of course, was reported by the BBC, although it gave ample coverage to a global warming publicity stunt involving a giant plastic replica of a polar bear on an iceberg being moored in the Thames next to the Palace of Westminster. This gave the BBC a cue to wheel on its favourite naturalist, Sir David Attenborough, to claim, somewhat implausibly, that he had once been a 'sceptic' on man-made global warming. But, naturally, he now found the 'science' entirely convincing.*

---

* 'BBC abandons impartiality on warming', *Sunday Telegraph*, 1 February 2009. The only other candidate for the title of 'the BBC's favourite naturalist' would formerly have been the bearded conservationist Professor David Bellamy, who featured in more than 400 BBC programmes from

WHEN GILL MET HARRY: FIASCO
IN THE ANTARCTIC

The BBC was again among those who fell for a farcical attempt to remedy what had long been for the global warming lobby one of the more embarrassing contradictions in their argument: the failure to warm up of Antarctica. Containing 90 per cent of all the ice on the planet, the prospect of a melting Antarctic ice sheet was crucial to their more apocalyptic visions of sea-level rise. But for several decades, while temperatures everywhere else were rising, those in Antarctica had cussedly failed to follow. All evidence showed that the coldest continent had in fact in recent decades got slightly cooler.

The warming propagandists had tried to obscure this by concentrating attention on the Antarctic Peninsula, the one small part of that huge continent which had anomalously been warming because of a local rise in the temperature of the surrounding ocean. Few images of nature had been more regularly exploited in their cause than those showing immense chunks of ice sliding off into the sea: the Larsen A ice shelf in 1995, the Wilkins ice shelf in 1998, the Larsen B, the size of Connecticut, in 2002. All these had been repeatedly used as photographic evidence for global warming in action. But they had all taken place on and around the Antarctic Peninsula. Meanwhile the land-ice over the vast interior of the continent had been thickening. The extent of sea-ice around its shores had risen 30 per cent above its average since satellite data began in 1979.

Then, out of the blue, Nature came up with a startling cover story, eagerly promoted by the BBC and others. Antarctica was not cooling after all. A new study, turning all the received scientific wisdom upside down, had established that for 50 years the continent had been warming up by as much as 0.6°C. Western Antarctica had even been warming faster than the rest of the world. The only possible cause of this, the BBC wanted to emphasise, was 'rising greenhouse gas levels in the atmosphere'.[5]

It just happened that the study's lead author, oceanographer Professor Eric Steig, was a board member of RealClimate and a member of the 'Hockey Team'. One of his co-authors, advising on

---

the 1970s onwards. In the late 1990s, however, he was dropped when he, first, began to protest at the futility of windfarms and then said that, as a scientist, he could not accept that global warming was man-made ('BBC shunned me for denying climate change', *Daily Express*, 5 November 2008).

the computer model on which the study was based, was Michael Mann.

Unsurprisingly, a number of experts at once examined their study (published as a 'letter' to *Nature* rather than as a formal paper), to see how the Steig team had managed to come up with results so markedly different from anything scientists had observed before.[6] They found the team's findings had emerged from a computer model based on combining satellite data with that from surface weather stations. But because Antarctica contained so few weather stations, the computer model had been programmed to fill in all the gaps by guessing what surface measurements might have been if they could have been recorded – what the paper called 'sparse data infilling'.

This methodology was so curious that it provoked scepticism even from Dr Kevin Trenberth, a senior member of the IPCC establishment. 'It is hard to make data', he dismissively observed, 'where none exists'. Ross Hayes, an atmospheric scientist who had visited Antarctica for NASA, wrote Steig a caustic email ending 'with statistics you can make numbers go to any conclusion you want. It saddens me to see members of the scientific community doing this for media coverage'.

Even more surprising, however, was what emerged when the study was subjected to analysis by Climate Audit and Watts Up With That (which had been just voted 'Best Science Blog' for 2008, following Climate Audit's victory the previous year). McIntyre was, of course, an expert on computer models, Watts on weather stations. What they and their readers teased out was that the evidence which enabled Steig *et al.* to reach their remarkable conclusion was largely based on splicing together the data from just two weather stations, 'Harry' and 'Gill', hundreds of miles apart.

The difference between these two records had provided the apparent 'jump' in temperatures. But, thanks to the algorithm used to enable that 'sparse data infilling', this discrepancy had then been projected by the computer model across other parts of the continent where no weather stations existed, Furthermore, photographic evidence showed that 'Harry', the station which recorded the higher temperatures, had been buried in snow. This would have insulated its thermometer enough to produce the readings accounting for a 'rise' in temperatures which turned out to be just an illusion.[7] This embarrassing discovery was not, of course, reported by *Nature* or the BBC.

'MUCH WORSE THAN PREDICTED'

By now, with Copenhagen fast approaching, similar bids to raise the temperature over global warming began to come thick and fast. Their most conspicuous feature, so consistent that it was clearly an agreed party line, was to claim that things were much worse than previously predicted.

On the morning of Sunday, 15 February, for instance, the BBC led its news programmes with a report that 'the severity of global warming over the next century will be much worse than previously believed', according to 'a leading climate scientist'. The world's future climate, Professor Chris Field had told a Chicago conference of the American Association for the Advancement of Science, 'will be beyond anything predicted'.[8]

The mystery as to why the BBC should have made this the main news of the day only deepened when it emerged that Field was not a climate scientist at all, but a professor of biology in an ecology department. To promote its cause, the BBC website even posted a video explaining how global warming would be made much worse than forecast by 'negative feedback'. 'Negative feedback', of course, reduces temperatures rather than raising them. This elementary howler inspired such a gale of derision from Watts Up With That that the BBC had hurriedly to pull the video off its website.[9]

In an interview that same morning in the *Observer*, Dr Hansen launched his most vitriolic call yet for the closing down of all the coal-fired power stations which were the world's chief electricity source, describing them as 'the single greatest threat to civilisation and to all life on our planet'. 'Coal fired power plants are factories of death', he told the *Observer*: 'the trains carrying coal to power plants are death trains'. This deliberate use of the phrase used to describe trains carrying Jews and others to Nazi extermination camps recalled the likening of 'climate sceptics' to 'Holocaust deniers'.[10]

Hansen was also calling on university students across America to join him in Washington on 2 March to shut down the ancient coal-fired power plant which had formerly supplied the Capitol with a third of its electricity (it was now used for heating and air-conditioning). Although billed in advance as 'the largest ever act of civil disobedience over climate change', with a prediction that 'hundreds of thousands of demonstrators' would turn out, when the day came Washington was blanketed in nearly a foot of snow. The few hundred eco-zealots who joined Hansen outside the plant had to huddle next to its coal-powered pipework to keep warm.

The blizzards which had swept down the east coast of America were not by now unfamiliar. The winter had again been unusually cold across the northern hemisphere, with many places in the US and Canada for the second year running registering unprecedented snowfalls and record low temperatures. In Britain, following the Met Office's prediction that 2009 would be 'one of the five warmest years on record' and that Britain's winter would be 'milder than average', more snow had fallen than for years. In February, even the Met Office was forced grudgingly to admit that it had been 'the coldest winter for 13 years'.*

Also hampered at the end of February by 'an unusually heavy snowfall' was the departure from Britain of another ambitious and expensive bid to 'heighten awareness of global warming'. This was the Catlin Arctic Survey, an expedition to the North Pole led by a British adventurer, Pen Hadow. With two companions, his plan was to trek to the Pole across the ice, taking measurements all the way to show how dangerously it was thinning. These were to be fed into a computer model in California run by Professor Wieslaw Maslowski, whose team according to the BBC was 'well known for producing results that show much faster ice-loss than other modelling teams'.[11]

Although the expedition had an array of corporate sponsors, including Nokia and Panasonic, its main backers, after whom it was named, were a City insurance group which had invested heavily in the fast-growing market for insurance against the damage caused by climate change. The expedition was also billed to receive regular coverage on the BBC and Google Earth. Its website carried glowing

---

* One place in the world more worried by heat than cold at this time was the Australian state of Victoria, where in February bushfires caused by the highest temperatures since 1908 had destroyed 1,800 homes and left more than 200 dead. Inevitably this was blamed by 'green' activists and others on global warming (Allianz insurance group website). They did not explain why temperatures had been as high 100 years earlier, or why the 2009 bushfires had caused such unprecedented damage. The chief culprits, it emerged, were the 'greens' themselves, who had successfully lobbied for strict laws to prohibit clearing of brushwood and trees to create fire-breaks round settlements and homes. Liam Sheahan of Reedy Creek had in 2004 been fined $50,000 for felling 247 trees to protect his property. In 2009, when fire swept through Reedy Creek, his was the only house left standing ('Fine for illegal clearing, family now feel vindicated', *The Age*, 12 February 2009).

endorsements from the WWF (who said 'it could make a lasting difference to policy-related science'); and Prince Charles ('for the sake of our children and grandchildren, I pray that we will heed the results of the Catlin Arctic Survey, and I can only commend this remarkably important project').

Scarcely had the intrepid trio been landed on the ice by a twin-engined Otter to embark on their 1,000 kilometre journey than they were reporting back via the BBC that the Arctic was a very much colder place than they expected, with temperatures as low as 40 degrees below zero. They were being 'battered by wind, bitten by frost and bruised by falls on the ice'. Thanks to the constant shifting of the ice, it was 'disheartening', said Hadow, to find that 'when you've slogged for a day', you could wake up in the morning to discover that 'you have drifted back to where you started' the day before.

As for the much-advertised scientific value of their expedition, it seemed that, thanks to the intense cold, the electronic equipment with which they hoped to measure the thinning of the ice had broken, leaving them to acquire their data with the aid of an old tape measure (calibrated, as Watts Up With That gleefully noted, in feet and inches). Meanwhile, as WUWT also noted, the Arctic ice was also being already rather more reliably monitored by a network of US Army buoys. Their current finding was that, since March 2008, the ice had on average thickened by 'at least half a metre'.[12]

Meanwhile, as Hadow and his companions battled on, in Copenhagen 2,500 government and UN-funded delegates from 80 countries gathered in rather greater comfort for a three-day 'Congress on Climate Change'. Planned as a warm-up to the Copenhagen main event later in the year, the proclaimed purpose of this vast conference, addressed among others by Pachauri, Stern and Hansen, was to hear more than 1,400 'scientific presentations' updating on all the new evidence on climate change which had emerged since the IPCC's 2007 report.[13]

From the extensive media coverage given to its proceedings, however, it was only too clear that the conference's real purpose was not scientific but political. The one consistent message speakers were instructed to put across to the world was that the future for the planet now looked much blacker than even the IPCC had predicted. Sea level rise by 2100, said one report, could be 'much greater than the 59cm predicted by the last IPCC report'. Global warming, said another, could kill off 85 per cent of the Amazon rainforest, 'much more than previously predicted'. The ice caps in Greenland and Antarctica were melting 'much faster than predicted'. The number of people dying from heat could be 'twice as many as previously predicted'.[14]

As was reflected in the conference's official report, every possible stop was pulled out:

> *'Recent observations show that greenhouse gas emissions and many aspects of the climate are changing near the upper boundary of the IPCC range of projections. Many key climate indicators are already moving beyond the patterns of natural variability within which contemporary society and economy have developed and thrived. These indicators include global mean surface temperature, sea level rise, global ocean temperature, Arctic sea ice extent, ocean acidification, and extreme climatic events. With unabated emissions, many trends in climate will likely accelerate, leading to an increasing risk of abrupt or irreversible climatic shifts.'*[15]

At least two other conferences relating to climate change were taking part that same weekend. At one, organised by the Centre for Psycho-Social Studies at the University of the West of England in Bristol, 130 therapists, 'climate activists' and 'eco-psychologists', accompanied by several professors, met to discuss whether 'denial of climate change' could be properly classified as a form of 'mental disorder'.[16]

At the other, attracting infinitely less media attention than Copenhagen, 800 climatologists, geologists, meteorologists, statisticians, economists, politicians and business leaders assembled in New York for the second conference on climate change organised by the Heartland Institute. Its title was 'Global warming: was it really a crisis?'

This gathering, on a rather grander scale than its predecessor the previous year, was addressed by dozens of expert scientists, several of world rank, such as Richard Lindzen, Syun-ichi Akasofu, Willie Soon, Nir Shaviv and Paul Reiter, who for professional standing put those speaking at Copenhagen in the shade.

The proceedings began with a powerful address by President Vaclav Klaus, the solitary 'climate sceptic' among the world's leading politicians. Since the Czech Republic was now holding the EU's six-monthly rotating presidency, as Czech head of state he was also now the acting-president of the EU.

Klaus recounted how had recently attended the World Economic Forum in Davos, along with President Obama, Gordon Brown and an array of other world leaders. He had been forcibly struck by how rigidly closed their minds were to anything but the 'consensus' view on global warming. Yet none of them seemed to know anything about the science behind it or were even willing to discuss it. Such reliance on dogma uncomfortably reminded him, he said, of the Communist system under which he had lived for much of his life.

The Czech president was followed by Professor Lindzen, who spoke of how profoundly the scientific community had become intellectually corrupted by the way federal and corporate funding had become conditional on acceptance of the 'consensus' view. Not afraid to name names, he singled out as one example his MIT colleague and near-neighbour Carl Wunsch, who 'professionally calls into question virtually all alarmist claims concerning sea level, ocean temperatures and ocean modelling, but assiduously avoids association with sceptics', because 'if nothing else, he has several major oceanographic programs to worry about'.

Lindzen also described the backstairs methods used by the global warming lobby to ensure that their allies were picked to head such leading professional bodies as the National Academy of Sciences (of which he was a member) or the American Association for the Advancement of Science (of which Obama's chief scientific adviser John Holdren had recently been president).[17]

Most of the 70-odd speakers over the next two days spoke with authority just on their specialist concerns. Akasofu talked about how the recent warming of the Arctic was only a continuation of a 200-year old trend. Soon talked about the latest evidence linking temperatures to solar radiation, Reiter spoke with dry humour about the IPCC's failure to grasp that global warming was irrelevant to the spread of tropical diseases. McIntyre also spoke with humour about the latest developments in the 'hockey stick' saga. Anthony Watts revealed that of the 919 US surface weather stations his investigations had now covered (75 per cent of the total), only 11 per cent met the official siting criteria. This meant that 89 per cent of the stations on which the US temperature record relied (and therefore much of the global record relied on by the IPCC) had 'estimated measurement contamination errors' of between 1 and 5°C.[18]

As the conference unfolded, however, it became clear that it represented a 'counter consensus' on global warming to which almost everyone participating could have subscribed. The major influences shaping climate change, all agreed, were not related to CO_2 but natural, notably solar radiation and ocean currents. Computer models, they were equally agreed, had been proved wholly incapable of replicating all the climate's complex workings. The IPCC's 'consensus', based on erroneous *a priori* assumptions, was therefore dangerously misconceived. The political measures adopted on the basis of its findings could thus have little or no effect on influencing the earth's future climate. So economically crippling would they be, however, that the only real 'global warming crisis' facing mankind was that which those measures themselves were bringing about.[19]

Such was the essence of the scientific 'counter-consensus' which had been emerging in the previous few years, and which by now would have been subscribed to, privately if not publicly, by a significant proportion of thinking scientists in the many relevant disciplines across the world.

In terms of influencing policy, however, the views of these scientists were wholly irrelevant. So far as the politicians were concerned, as had again been confirmed to Klaus by his experience at Davos, all they knew was what the official 'consensus' told them to think. That 'consensus' was now telling them that the terrifying threat of runaway global warming was even worse than anything previously predicted. The practical implications of this were now terrifying in a way very few politicians had yet begun to grasp.

THE ABYSS OF UNREALITY

Just how far the politicians had now become detached from reality by the scare over climate change might have been brought home by a succession of events in that same month of March.

The first of these was the publication of two sets of new figures by the British government. The previous October the House of Commons had almost unanimously approved the Climate Change Act, committing Britain to reducing its 'carbon emissions' by more than 80 per cent in four decades. At the time the only official estimate of what this might cost had been based on the original target figure of a 60 per cent cut. The MPs had thus voted for a measure which the government told them would produce benefits worth £110 billion at a cost of nearly twice that figure, £205 billion.

Now the new Department for Energy and Climate Change slipped out on its website, without telling Parliament, a new set of estimates based on the 80 per cent target. These now showed that the costs of the Act would be nearly double the original figure, £404 billion. As the government's website admitted, this would cost the British people, through their electricity bills and in many other ways, no less than an additional £18 billion a year every year until 2050. This averaged out at £720 a year for every household in the country. But the benefits of the Act, the government conveniently calculated, now showed a staggering 1,000 per cent increase to £1,024 billion, or £4,000 a year for every household.

In themselves, these figures, arrived at by a computer model, bore not the faintest relation to any reality. They might just as well have been plucked from the air by a man sitting in the corner of a pub with a large drink. But even if taken at face value, they were so mind-bogglingly huge that their only significance lay in the complete lack of interest shown in them by the ranks of Britain's politicians. The solitary exception was Peter Lilley, the only MP who back in October had asked the minister Ed Milband what it had been estimated the Act might cost.

Then another ministry, BERR, published a second set of figures. One of the claims politicians had increasingly been using to justify all their climate change measures was that these would create huge numbers of 'green jobs'. Obama in the US had talked about creating 'five million green jobs'. In Britain Gordon Brown had talked about '400,000 new green jobs'. But no one had specified where or how these imaginary jobs might be created, until BERR published an analysis for which it had paid one of the many firms of consultants now springing up to cash in on the 'low carbon economy' bonanza.[20]

Under what BERR called 'the Green New Deal', the report used a computer model to estimate the likely increased number of jobs in three 'low carbon and environmental' sectors of the economy by 2015, just six years away. In renewable energy, the model predicted, the wind industry would create 69,300 new jobs, biomass would create 22,900, the 'geothermal' energy sector 39,300 (yet since this virtually non-existent sector was already stated to employ '75,000' people, this alone should immediately have flagged up that the model's figures were wholly fictitious).

The various planet-saving activities listed under 'environmental', covering anything from air pollution to waste management, would, according to the model create 43,000 new jobs (ever since 1991 the

EU had regarded recycling as one of its climate change policies).*
Under 'emerging low carbon', the model estimated that 114,500
new jobs would be created in producing biofuels, 47,500 in 'green'
building technologies, 13,500 in 'carbon finance' and 1,400 in 'carbon capture and storage'. All this added up to 393,000 additional
jobs, according to the computer model. As for the cost of it all, BERR
itself estimated that the 25,000 new jobs to be created in waste management alone would cost up to £30 billion, or £1.2 million per job.

In reality, of course, all this was as meaningless as the estimates
given by that other computer model of the costs and benefits of the
Climate Change Act. Yet it was on such wholly illusory figures that
ministers relied to make their case.

A very different view of such dreams was presented in a report
just published in Spain, the first attempt at a detailed study of just
what the creation of subsidised 'green jobs' could mean for a country's economy.[21]

The report began by describing a visit made by president-elect
Obama in January 2009 to an Ohio factory making components for
wind turbines. Renewable energy, he said, could ' create millions of
additional jobs and entire new industries'. 'Think of what's happening', he went on, 'in countries like Spain, Germany and Japan,
where they're making real investments in renewable energy. They're
surging ahead of us.'

Using official figures, the report then analysed what this had meant
for one of the economies Obama had held out as a shining example.
Between 2000 and 2008, to comply with EU targets, Spain had subsidised its renewables industry to the tune of $36 billion, giving it the
third highest number of wind turbines in the world. This policy had
created 50,000 'green' jobs, at an average cost of €571,138 each
(new jobs in the wind industry had cost more than €1 million). But
two thirds of these were involved in construction and manufacture,
a quarter in administration and marketing and only one in ten in
maintaining and operating the installations thus created. All this
was to provide Spain with well under 10 per cent of its electricity,
unreliably, inefficiently and very expensively, at a subsidy cost alone
equivalent to 5.6 per cent of Spain's corporate taxes.

---

* Among the provisions of the new Climate Change Act, it empowered
  ministers to tax or ban the use of plastic bags and to introduce penalties for
  putting excess rubbish into wheelie bins.

The report went on to estimate, however, what effect this huge diversion of public and private resources had meant for the rest of Spain's economy. For a start it had pushed up electricity prices so high that this had inflicted serious damage on Spanish industry, causing many firms to reduce production and lay off workers, or even to relocate to countries such as Poland where energy prices were lower. In addition, the same level of investment could have created much more productive jobs in more efficient sectors of the economy.

On this admittedly speculative basis, the study concluded that the number of jobs lost to the Spanish economy, as the price of creating 50,000 new 'green jobs', was 110,000, or 2.2 jobs lost for each one created. Extrapolating to the US, this would mean that if Obama was to create his 5 million new 'green jobs', the US economy could look to lose 11 million jobs, at astronomic financial cost.*

In fact a US study had already indicated that replacing two-thirds of its coal-based energy with higher-priced renewables could alone cost more than 4 million US jobs.[22] A study from John Hopkins University had shown that such an increase in the price of electricity, hitting the poor hardest, could also lead to 150,000 extra premature deaths a year.[23]

Whether such calculations were any more than academic guesswork, they were certainly no more unrealistic than the kind of mad figures now being banded about by the politicians on the other side. Nor could such considerations have been further from the minds of the thousands of delegates from 175 countries who, at the end of March, descended on the headquarters of the UNFCCC in Bonn for 10 days of negotiations on the forthcoming Copenhagen treaty. This was intended to be the first of three mammoth sessions designed to hammer out the broad outlines of the treaty, before the delegates convened in December to agree the final text.

Before they arrived in Bonn, a 16-page document was circulated by the UNFCC setting out its own proposals for what should be

---

* In fact an academic study into where Obama's '5 million green jobs' were to come from had already been published by a team at Duke University, financed by a leading environmental lobby group, the Environmental Defense Fund, and four trade unions, The first five sources of new jobs identified by the study would be in 'LED lighting', 'high-performance windows', 'auxiliary power units for long-haul trucks', 'solar power' and 'super soil systems, or new technology for treating hog wastes' (see 'Manufacturing climate solutions', Center for Globalisation, Governance and Competitiveness, on Duke University website).

the agenda. According to one account, based on a copy leaked in advance, it envisioned 'a huge re-ordering of the world economy, likely involving trillions of dollars in wealth transfer, millions of job losses and gains, new taxes, industrial relocatopns, new tariffs and subsidies and complicated payments for greenhouse gas abatement schemes and carbon taxes – all under the supervision of the world body'.[24]

Virtually no reference was made In the UN document to the cost of its proposals. These envisaged extensions of the kind of 'cap and trade' scheme now endorsed by the Obama administration; 'carbon taxes' on aviation and energy-intensive industries; and higher subsidies for renewables, biofuels and other commodities considered to be 'environmentally sound'. Governments might also be asked to reconsider plans for new road, rail and airport projects.

The UN conceded that cap and trade schemes might induce some industries to relocate to 'less regulated host countries', which would 'involve negative consequences for the implementing country which loses employment and investment'. But some of this might be compensated for by 'border carbon adjustment', which would allow those countries affected to impose tariffs on goods imported from nations which operated more relaxed 'carbon policies', or to demand that such countries paid for 'carbon credits' before their goods could be imported. Goods would have to be labelled to reflect the amount of carbon emitted in their manufacture, and the 'economic and social consequences' of all these regulations might 'for some countries and sectors be significant'.

No mention was made, of course, of the actual money all this might cost. The delegates were also provided with a new paper by Lord Stern which called for 'most of the world's electricity production' to have been 'decarbonised' by 2050.[25] In the US and Britain, to name but two of many, this would mean eliminating nearly 80 per cent of their existing generating capacity.

When the officials got down to some hard negotiating, the head of the Chinese delegation immediately repeated his country's demands that the developed (Annex 1) countries must not only cut their own carbon emissions to 40 per cent of their 1990 levels by 2020, but must give much more financial and other assistance to developing countries such as his own. Yet China, now the world's largest carbon emitter, was still building two new coal-fired power stations every week.[26]

One hundred and thirty developing countries, led by India and Brazil, joined forces to make similar demands. No figures were yet formally on the table, but informally it was indicated that they would not be prepared to agree to a deal unless the developed countries not only cut their own emissions by more than 40 per cent within a decade but also paid the poorer countries hundreds of billions of dollars a year.[27]

Not surprisingly, the Bonn talks ended on 8 April in impasse. But there were still eight months of talking to go, before the climate change circus finally arrived in Copenhagen.

BRITAIN'S POLITICIANS FLOAT EVEN FURTHER INTO FANTASY-LAND

In April, as yet more snow blanketed Britain, it was back to surreal play-acting. Three weeks before his Chancellor announced his annual Budget, Gordon Brown broke Parliamentary rules by leaking to the media that a highlight of the budget speech, as a 'major part' of his government's plan to revive Britain's fast-shrinking economy, would be the creation of those famous '400,000 green jobs'.

Brown also enthused about how the British would soon be switching *en masse* to driving electric cars, praising in particular an Indian-made model known as a G-wiz. Costing up to £15,795, these could only travel rather slowly for 75 miles before their batteries needed several hours of recharging. As usual when 'eco-friendly' electric cars were being touted, Brown seemed oblivious to where this electricity was to come from. Professor Stanley Feldman reminded him in a letter to the *Daily Telegraph* that this would be the National Grid, 75 per cent powered by fossil fuels. Taking account of transmission losses, by the time the power reached the charging points its CO_2 emissions would be nearly twice those given off by the equivalent amount of diesel.[28]

If this showed breathtaking naivete on the part of Britain's prime minister, it was only paralleled by that of the man who hoped to replace him, David Cameron. As evidence of their commitment to the environmentalist agenda, senior Conservatives liked to boast that they used only 'green' electricity. Cameron had even, a while earlier, summoned the media to watch his shadow cabinet all sitting in front of laptops, with Zac Goldsmith, editor of *The Ecologist*, signing up to supply companies which offered 'green' tariffs, supposedly providing power from 'renewable' sources.[29]

The Tories might have liked everyone to imagine that their electricity would thus all come from windmills and solar panels. In fact, of course, it all came from the grid, where the tiny amount of power from wind just got mixed in willy-nilly with all the 'dirty' electricity from proper power stations. Cameron himself signed up with a company called 'npower juice', which claimed to derive most of its power from a large wind farm off the North Wales coast; a deal which was fine for npower, which made £9 million a year from subsidies to its wind farm, plus another £9 million from the electricity itself. But the power coming into Cameron's home from the grid was no more 'renewable' than anyone else's. Official figures showed that 'npower juice' derived 46 per cent of the electricity it supplied from gas, 38 per cent from coal and only 3 per cent from 'renewables'.[30]

Equally carried away by the excitement of fighting climate change had become the 'Sustainable Development Unit' of the NHS. This august body had issued a report, Saving Carbon – Improving Health', recommending that whenever possible Britain's NHS hospitals should no longer serve their patients with meat or dairy products but instead should be given 'nutritious fruit, veg and pulses'.[31]

This was because the production of meat and milk was deemed to involve the emission of an excessive amount of greenhouse gases. The report also recommended that health workers, patients and their visitors should whenever possible walk or cycle to and from their hospitals rather than taking cars. All these suggestions were necessary, said the report, because 'unless we take effective action now, millions of people round the world will suffer hunger, water shortages and coastal flooding as the climate changes'.

A rather more practical reason why the NHS had been recruited to the ranks of climate alarmists was that it was the biggest single CO_2 emitter in the public sector, responsible for no less than 3 per cent of all Britain's emissions. Under the EU's Emissions Trading Scheme this meant that the NHS had to pay out ever more millions of pounds a year for the right to continue 'polluting' the planet (in the scheme's first two years of operation, four Glasgow hospitals alone had to pay £500,000 from the budget which was meant to help them look after patients). Therefore the patients would have to eat 'nutritious pulses' rather than planet-destroying meat.

The moralistic pronouncements of environmental campaigners were becoming ever more extreme. Caroline Lucas, leader of Britain's Green Party, made headlines by arguing on television that flying to

Spain was morally equivalent to knifing someone in the street, because air travel was causing people to die 'from climate change'. The director of the Scottish branch of WWF said that failing to ensure one's home was 'energy efficient' was a 'moral crime' as 'anti-social as drink driving', and that 'we should be having a discussion as to whether it should become an actual crime'.[32] This recalled a recent comment by the Climate Change Secretary Ed Miliband that opposing windfarms should become as 'socially unacceptable' as driving without a seat-belt.[33]

Lord Stern, now treated with reverence across the world as one of the high priests of the 'climate change community', heralded the approach of Copenhagen by publishing a new book entitled *Blueprint for a Safer Planet: How to Manage Climate Change and Create a New Era of Progress and Prosperity*. In an interview to publicise his work, he said 'those who deny the science look more and more like those who denied the association between HIV and Aids or smoking and cancer'.[34]

Stern was quoted as warning that, unless something was done to curb CO_2 emissions, temperatures could rise 'by up to 6°C, with catastrophic consequences – Florida and Bangladesh could disappear, alligators could live at the North Pole and millions of people would have to emigrate' (on the same page, Oxfam was reported as predicting that disasters caused by climate change 'will affect 400 million people within six years').

Not that Stern needed the royalties from his book to make a handsome living. He had now been appointed head of the Grantham Research Institute for Climate Change and the Environment, set up at the LSE with an endowment of £12 million from a billionaire fund manager. The Institute's aim was to promote research into climate change-related issues and to earn money advising companies on how they could benefit from investing in renewable energy technology, carbon trading, carbon-capture and all the other ingredients in what was now one of the world's fastest-growing industries.

Meanwhile, as MPs were being daily pilloried in the media over revelations of how they had been abusing their allowances system, claiming taxpayers' money for everything from non-existent mortgages to watching pornographic films, Climate Change Secretary Miliband announced to a virtually empty House of Commons on 23 April that no new coal-fired power stations would be permitted unless they used at least a partial system of 'carbon capture'.[35] To this end, as had been announced in the previous day's budget, the government proposed to fund four pilot schemes, at a cost estimated to be around £750 million each.[36]

Miliband conceded that the technology needed to carry away millions of tons of CO_2 in huge pipes, to bury it in holes under the sea, hadn't even been developed yet, and that there was no guarantee that it would be so even by 2020. But he believed it was worth spending more than £3 billion on having a try.

Instead of laying into the crazy unreality of such a proposal – even in 2009 £3 billion was still an astronomic sum of money – the only response from the Conservative opposition was to demand that no new coal-fired plants should be allowed unless they were fitted with this technology immediately, even though it didn't yet exist.

At least Britain's ministers now had some glimmering of the gravity of the crisis now fast approaching the UK, when it lost two-fifths of its generating capacity. But so lost were Cameron and his Conservative colleagues in their 'green bubble', they seemed quite oblivious to the probability that within two or three years after they succeeded to power (as now seemed likely), Britain's lights would go out. And they wouldn't have the slightest clue why, let alone what to do about it.

'BILLIONS WILL DIE'

May 2009 brought an end to the farce of the Catlin expedition's forlorn bid to prove that the Arctic ice was about to vanish. After two months of frozen misery, having managed well under half their planned trek to the North Pole, the hapless trio were finally lifted off the melting ice to safety, having discovered nothing of any scientific value.

At least they had managed to reassure Prince Charles by satellite telephone that the ice was 'thinner than expected'. But even the BBC, flying in a camera team to film the moment of their rescue, carefully avoided the subject of whether the expedition had achieved anything useful.

Shortly before being forced to abandon their potentially suicidal publicity stunt, the 'Catlin three' heard the sound of a passing aircraft. They little realised that this was a DC-3 containing a team of German and Canadian scientists from the Alfred Wegener Institute in Bremerhaven, using the latest electro-magnetic induction equipment to carry out a systematic survey of the ice's thickness all the way to the Pole. The finding of these millions of measurements was that the ice 'was somewhat thicker than during the last years in the same regions'.[37]

None of this prevented UN Secretary General Ban Ki-moon from announcing the same week that the polar ice caps were 'melting far faster than was expected two years ago'. His claim was apparently based on 'recent studies', such as that of Steig *et al.*, which seemingly confirmed the alarmist view. Yet the latest data from the US National Snow and Ice Data Center showed that, after the third slowest April melt of Arctic ice in 30 years, the extent of polar sea ice was now in fact above its average level for early May since satellite records began in 1979.[*]

With the Copenhagen conference now barely six months away, the campaign to whip up alarm over the world's climate was becoming obvious in all directions. Kofi Annan, Ban Ki-moon's predecessor as head of the UN, launched a 103-page report produced up by a firm of consultants for something called the Global Humanitarian Forum, claiming, without any evidence, that global warming was already 'killing 300,000 people a year'. Even Annan conceded that this was not 'a scientific study' but merely 'the most plausible account of the current impact of climate change'.[38]

A team from the Massachusetts Institute of Technology pitched in with a truly bizarre study reported as claiming that, 'on the basis of evidence which had come to light since 2003', world temperatures could rise by 2100 by 7°C, 'killing billions of people worldwide and leaving the world on the edge of total collapse'.

In London, Prince Charles convened a three-day gathering of '20 Nobel Laureates' at St James's Palace (including two African winners of the prizes for literature and peace), to warn that the world was

---

[*] 'Unprecedented incoherence in the ice message', WUWT, 5 May 2009. This led to an entertaining little episode when I reported these figures in the *Sunday Telegraph*. The *Guardian's* revered environmental columnist George Monbiot was prompted to a triumphant riposte on his blog headed 'How to disprove Christopher Booker in 26 seconds'. This was how long he said it had taken him on the internet to find that the data I had quoted were wrong. After several readers had piled in to congratulate him, calling for me to be sacked, a sharper-eyed reader politely pointed out that Monbiot had been looking at the wrong figures. He graciously posted a disclaimer headed 'Whoops – looks like I've boobed. Sorry folks'. Not often was the 'climate change' debate conducted so politely.

now in 'the last chance saloon' to stop climate change. After hearing speeches from the Prince, Lord Stern, Professor Chu and others, they issued a declaration comparing the threat of global warming to that of all-out nuclear war. Chu, Obama's energy secretary, solemnly assured his distinguished audience that, if all the world's buildings and pavements were painted white to reflect the sun's rays back into space, this would be equivalent to taking all the world's automobiles off the road for 11 years.[39]

At the end of June came a curious little episode which showed how determined the professional promoters of the 'consensus' were becoming to keep the pre-Copenhagen scare machine roaring ahead without any risk of a dissenting voice. A meeting had been convened in Copenhagen of the Polar Bear Specialist Group, part of the International Union for the Conservation of Nature/Species Survival Commission. In light of the way the 'threatened polar bears' had become a central icon of warmist propaganda, it was vital that the group should come up with a suitably alarming message to be used in the months before December.

One of the world's leading experts on polar bears was Dr Mitchell Taylor who, although recently retired, had been studying the status and management of polar bears for 30 years, as both an academic and an employee of the Nunavut provincial government in northern Canada. He had first joined the Polar Bear Specialist Group in 1981, but he held two opinions which were not shared by the rest of the group.

The first, based on his detailed studies of polar bear groups all round the Arctic Circle, was that the bears were not in danger. Of 19 main polar bear populations, only two had for local reasons shown a modest decline in numbers. The rest were either at their optimum size for their food supply or had been markedly growing, so that total numbers were several times larger than they had been in the 1960s.

Taylor's other difference of opinion with the rest of the group, many of whom based their work on computer models rather than direct observation, was that, although he had observed that the Arctic in the past decade was warming, he did not attribute this to man-made global climate change. The chief causes, he believed, were an increase in warm water entering the Arctic from the Pacific, and winds blowing in from the Bering Sea.

Although Taylor was no longer formally a member of the PBSG, which had not met sine 2005, another member asked that he should be invited to attend. He had already been promised Canadian funding. Shortly before the meeting, however, he received a series of startling emails from the group's chairman, Dr Andrew Derocher.

Taylor was told that his presence in Copenhagen was not wanted. This, he was assured, was not because of his undoubted expertise on polar bears: 'it was the position you've taken on global warming that brought opposition', Derocher told Taylor, and that his views 'running counter to human-induced climate change' were 'extremely unhelpful'. Taylor's greatest mistake, it seemed, had been to sign the Manhattan Declaration, in which 500 scientists stated that the causes of climate change were not CO_2 but natural, such as changes in the radiation of the sun and the changing patterns of ocean currents. This, said Derocher, was considered 'inconsistent with the position taken by the PBSG'.[40]

And so, armed with a suitably scary prediction about the threat posed by global warming to the bears' survival, the Copenhagen bandwagon rolled on. As for the endless fraught negotiations over the planned treaty, the economic implications of these were becoming almost more alarming than the over-heated predictions of the officially-approved scientists.

The demands now being made of the world's developed countries by 130-odd developing countries as their price for co-operation at Copenhagen were rising ever higher. China and India were insisting on a sum equivalent to 1 per cent of the developed countries' GDP. This equated to $300 billion every year. African countries were putting in for a further $267 billion a year. South American countries were asking for hundreds of billions of dollars more. Meanwhile the latest costing of the 'cap and trade' scheme now before the US Congress, supported by President Obama, was $1.9 trillion. This would represent a yearly average cost to each American family of $4,500.[41]

Hardly surprisingly, the impasse over the treaty continued. At the end of May, after yet another international meeting in Paris, Germany's environment minister Sigmar Gabriel warned that Copenhagen was 'heading for disaster'. 'There have been no real advances between emerging economies and industrial nations', he said, 'neither in regard to the question of how to reduce greenhouse gas emissions nor in how we are to finance adaptations or technology transfer.'[42]

In early June, it was reported in Brussels that the 27 EU nations were so deadlocked over how much financial assistance they were prepared to pay to the developing world that they could not even agree on a communique. Poland opposed any new obligations whatever.[43]

While another mammoth 11-day UNFCCC conference was under way in Bonn, the Chinese government accused rich countries of 'constantly seeking to shirk their responsibilities to fight climate change', and warned that negotiations on any climate pact faced 'deep disputes'.[44] It was reported that, when EU heads of government met at the end of June, any decision on how to provide financial assistance to developing countries was likely to be postponed.[45]

The Japanese prime minister horrified environmentalists (and the BBC) by announcing at a nationally televised press conference that, as one of the world's leading CO_2 emitters, Japan would agree only to a target barely below what it had signed up for at Kyoto.[46] 'Prime minister Aso's plan is appalling', said the WWF, quoted by the BBC's Richard Black in the opening line of his report.[47]

Russia's President Dmitri Medmedev announced that his country planned to increase its greenhouse gas emissions by 20 per cent by 2020. 'We will not cut off our development potential', he said.[48] In Bonn, as the UNFCCC talks drew to a close, India, China, Brazil and all the major developing countries proposed that the developed countries should agree to cutting their emissions to 40 per cent below 1990 levels by 2020.[49]

With the Bonn talks ending in acrimonious deadlock, *China Daily* asked 'which war are we fighting? The war against climate change or the war over climate change?' If things carried on as they were 'we (by that I mean all the people in the world) will most likely have a war of the second sort'.[50]

In Europe, Poland's leading trade union, Solidarnosc, warned that, following the latest EU climate change legislation, 800,000 jobs would be lost in countries heavily dependent on coal such as his own. A spokesman poured scorn on the idea that job losses would be offset by the creation of new 'green jobs'. A senior spokesman for one of Europe's leading steel companies, ArcelorMittal, warned that, for the same reason, firms like his were now looking to relocate outside the EU.[51]

Meanwhile it was reported that, thanks not least to the abnormally cold weather in many parts of the world in the first half of 2009, there was a possibility of a renewed global food shortage. After a fearsomely cold winter in north America, there had been further heavy snowfalls as late as June across large parts of western Canada and the farm states of the US midwest, seriously delaying the summer planting of corn and soybeans. Stocks were predicted to be 15 per cent down on the previous year.

Elsewhere in the world there had been abnormal snowfalls not just in Australia and New Zealand where it was winter, but in Norway, Scotland and even Saudi Arabia at midsummer. Other freak weather conditions, ranging from devastating hail storms in China to prolonged droughts in Brazil and Argentina, led to forecasts that crop yields would be seriously down in many countries (a veteran US grain expert said that 'in 43 years I've never seen anything like the decline we're looking at in South America').[52]

Both UAH and RSS reported that global temperatures in June had again fallen, after a rise from their 2008 low, to exactly their average level over the 30 years since satellite data began.[53] From the Arctic it was reported in late June that average temperatures across the Arctic Circle had still not risen above 0°C. This was the latest date known for such a prolonged freeze in 50 years of record-keeping.[54]

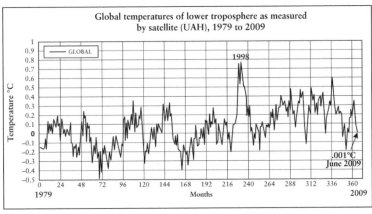

Figure 5: Global temperatures as recorded by satellites (UAH) between 1979, when satellite data began, and June 2009. The graph shows the El Niño 'spikes' in 1998 and 2006, the sharp fall in 2007–2008, and temperatures in June 2009 reaching their average level for the previous 30 years.

Across north America many places had also recorded abnormally low temperatures for the month. In New York City, where it had been the eighth coolest June on record, temperatures failed to top 85°F for the first time since 1916.[55]

KYOTO'S PRODIGALS JOIN THE FOLD

The closing days of June had seen very significant internal political battles in the two countries which had most conspicuously failed to ratify the Kyoto Protocol, America and Australia.

In the US, debate had been raging for weeks over the so-called Waxman-Markey bill, which was intended, with Obama's endorsement, to give America its own 'cap and trade' scheme. Very much following the EU's examples, the Clean Energy and Security bill proposed that within 11 years the US should cut its greenhouse gas emissions by 17 per cent below those of 2005. It should generate 15 per cent of its power from tens of thousands more wind turbines and other 'renewables'.

At the rate the US population was growing, it was calculated that this would mean a cutting down by 28 per cent on the use of fossil fuels, requiring – as even supporters of the bill acknowledged – a significant curtailment of America's addiction to such creature comforts as central heating, air-conditioning and hot water.

To avert the closure of most of the nation's conventional power plants, 50 per cent of them coal-fired, the bill also allowed fossil fuel users to offset their emissions by buying 'carbon permits' from elsewhere. Many of these would have to be purchased from developing countries overseas, under the UN's Clean Development Mechanism.

Fifty per cent of all 'certified emission reduction' credits under the CDM were now being bought from China which, despite being the world's largest CO_2 emitter, was also able to claim billions of dollars worth of credits, not least thanks to its massive programme of hydro-electric projects, such as the Three Gorges scheme on the Yangtse. An Asia Development Bank report had estimated that the world's leading CO_2 emitter could expect an annual income of up to $2.25 billion a year, representing its claimed annual 'savings' of 225 million tons of carbon dioxide equivalent'.[56]

The most obvious beneficiaries of the bill, however, would be firms involved in 'renewable' energy, such as the developers and makers of wind turbines; and the traders who stood to make fortunes from the vast new market opening up to buy and sell 'carbon credits'. As had already become clear, no one would be responsible for policing whether these 'credits' were justified or not. Those generated from, say, a newly-planted Brazilian forest might be sold more than once to several customers. There was also nothing to prevent the owners then cutting down the trees, to claim again for planting the new 'carbon sink' which replaced them.

As an academic observer, Professor James H. Rust, wryly put it, such a scheme 'should make investors with similar dispositions to Bernard Madoff weep for joy'.[57] One politician-turned-businessman who certainly stood to benefit from the new legislation was Al Gore, now chairman of a new 'Alliance for Climate Protection' which had recently launched a $300 million advertising campaign to promote the bill's aims and the virtues of a 'low-carbon' economy. But Gore could also look forward to the business the bill would bring to GIM, the private firm of which he was also chairman, which invested in renewable energy, 'low-carbon technology' and trading in 'carbon offsets'.[58] As one commentator put it, Gore thus used 'one of his multi-million dollar organisations ... to put pressure on government to promote the low-carbon lifestyle that will furnish one of his other multi-million dollar organisations ... with booming business'.[59]

Initial estimates of the annual costs the bill would impose on the US economy, to be paid indirectly by every American family, had ranged up to $4,500 per household, in addition to the damage it threatened to inflict on energy-intensive industries. As the bill worked its way through the House, however, concessions and inducements were showered out to win the support of those wavering Congressmen, particularly Democrats. whose states would be hardest hit.

At 3.09 am on the day before the House of Representatives voted on 28 June, the bill's proposers, aided by the House's fanatically committed Speaker Nancy Pelosi, tabled a further 300 pages of amendments. By the time the vote was taken, it was thus inconceivable that most Congressmen could have read all of what they were voting for. After much last-minute arm-twisting, the bill narrowly scraped through by just seven votes, 219 in favour, 212 against.

So riddled was the final draft with compromises that no one attacked it more vociferously than James Hansen. In its final version, he exploded on the pro-warmist Huffington Post blog, the bill was 'a monstrous absurdity, hatched in Washington after energetic insemination by special interests'.[60] 'The climate course set by the bill', raged Hansen, 'is a disaster ... it's less than worthless.'

The bill now, however, passed to the Senate, where the outcome looked even harder to predict. At a hearing of the Senate's Environment and Public Works committee, Energy Secretary Chu clashed with Liza Jackson, the new head of the EPA, when she confirmed an EPA analysis showing that if the US acted unilaterally on curbing emissions, this would have no effect on the world's climate. Chu said he did not agree with the EPA's analysis.[61]

The EPA was also now at the centre of a rather more significant row. This was over an internal report concerning the key role the agency would soon have to play in regulating US carbon emissions, under the Supreme Court ruling in 2007 that CO_2 was a 'pollutant' which had to be controlled under the Clean Air Act.

Back in March, a senior EPA analyst, Alan Carlin, had been asked to produce an internal report on the scientific justification for such a policy. His resulting 90-page paper was not at all what the agency expected. Having examined the evidence, he recommended that the EPA should commission a properly independent review of the science of its own. This was because, in his view, the CO_2 theory put forward by the IPCC was now looking indefensible.

Carlin argued that, on the latest evidence, the most significant influences shaping climate appeared not to be CO_2 but fluctuations in the radiation of the sun and ocean currents. These seemed to fit the observed data much better. In other words, Carlin found the 'counter-consensus' view convincing. His EPA superiors read his report with dismay. The document was stopped dead in its tracks by the 'Director of the National Center for Environmental Economics (NCEE)' on the grounds that it was much too late to raise objections to what was now the EPA's official policy. Carlin was immediately taken off any work concerning climate change.[62]

All this had happened behind the scenes. Now, however, three months later, a leaked draft of Carlin's report had appeared on the internet, along with internal EPA emails explaining why it had been suppressed. This provoked a considerable media furore, in which Carlin gave dignified but quietly angry interviews on major TV news programmes.

Across the world, meanwhile, another remarkable drama had been unfolding in Australia, where the new Labour government under Kevin Rudd had belatedly joined the 'consensus' by introducing a Bill to give Australia a 'cap and trade' scheme of its own. This triggered off a fierce political debate, with the opposition Liberal Party claiming that such a scheme would devastate Australia's economy, 80 per cent dependent on coal.

Although the bill passed the lower house, where Rudd and his Climate Change Minister Penny Wong could rely on a majority, it still had to pass the 76-member Senate. Here its supporters and opponents were so equally divided that it looked as though, when decision day came in August, the casting vote would be given by an independent Senator, Stephen Fielding.

Fielding let it be known that, before deciding which way to vote, he was going to talk to expert scientists on both sides of the argument. He even travelled to Washington at his own expense, to meet Obama's advisers in the White House and also to attend a third Heartland conference, including leading spokesmen for the 'counter consensus' such as Professor Lindzen.

So crucial had Fielding's Senate vote now become that Wong agreed to see him with four of his expert advisers, all leading Australian scientists. These included Professor Bob Carter, long an outspoken critic of the IPCC orthodoxy; Bill Kinninmonth, a former head of Australia's National Climate Office; and Dr David Evans, formerly the government's top climate modeller on greenhouse gases.

The significance of this interview was that it was the first occasion on which any Western government had allowed itself to be drawn into directly debating the science behind the case for man-made global warming with senior scientists representing the 'counter consensus'.

Fielding and his advisers met the minister on 15 June, flanked by two professors of her own, and put to them some very basic questions, under three headings. First, was it the case that CO_2 levels had increased since 1998 by 5 per cent, while temperatures had cooled? If so, how could human CO^2 emissions be blamed for causing dangerous warming?

Secondly, did the minister agree that the rate and magnitude of warming between 1979 and 1998 was not unusual in the light of previous warmings in the world's history? If so, why was CO_2 perceived to have been the cause of just this latest warming, and why was warming seen to be such a problem if the planet had survived similar episodes in the past?

Thirdly, was it the case that IPCC's computer models had predicted continuous warming between 1990 and 2008, whereas in reality temperatures had shown eight years of warming followed by nine of cooling? If so, was it suitable that long-term climate projections by the same models should be used as the basis for public policy-making?

It was clear from the written answers subsequently produced by the minister's advisers that they found it difficult to provide plausible responses to these questions. All too often they had wandered off into irrelevances, or simply relied on rehashing statements from the IPCC as if they carried an authority which could not be questioned.

So woolly were the replies, even containing elementary errors, that Fielding's team responded by publishing a 50-page commentary of their own.[63] Their paper, headed 'Due Diligence', tore the minister's experts apart. Senator Fielding announced that, in light of the inadequacy of the government's reply, he would be voting in August to reject the bill.

On 12 August the Senate rejected the bill by 42 votes to 30. What swung it so decisively was that five Green MPs joined Fielding in voting against it because in their view it should have been much more draconian. A new vote was expected in the autumn.[64]

'WORLD GOVERNMENT' REACHES DEADLOCK

By the end of June 2009, the political divide threatening to stifle any hope of a meaningful treaty in Copenhagen was deepening still further.

On 30 June, India's environment minister, Jairam Ramesh, emphatically stated that there was no way his country could agree to any limitation on its greenhouse gas emissions. This was because it would undermine the energy consumption India needed for economic growth, its transport system and its ability to feed its people. 'India', he said, 'will not accept any emission reduction, period. This is a non-negotiable stand'.[65]

The following day China said that it was 'firmly' opposed to provisions in the Waxman-Markey climate bill which would allow the US to impose penal tariffs on imports from countries which had not agreed to emissions reductions, and that this would be illegal under World Trade Organisation rules.[66] However, the WTO itself rushed out a joint-statement with the UN Environment Program to say that such tariffs would not be illegal.[67]

On 2 July, Brazil joined India, China and South Africa in insisting that the only acceptable basis for imposing emissions reductions in the treaty would be on the basis of each country's past record in creating the problem. If anyone was to reduce carbon emissions, it must be the developed nations, while countries like themselves must be left free to catch up.[68]

The same day, at a World Conference of Scientists in London, David King conceded that hopes of agreeing a treaty at Copenhagen were 'faltering'. He hinted that ways were being explored to 'find a legal formula' which would allow the conference 'to be concluded with a general statement and a commitment that a protocol would follow in 2010'.[69]

Four days later, on 6 July, King was at it again, having organised in Oxford a 'World Forum on Enterprise and the Environment', sponsored by *The Times*, at which the star speaker was Al Gore. Gore was reported by *The Times* itself as comparing 'the battle against climate change with the struggle against the Nazis'.[70] Since the article went on to quote him more accurately as saying only that 'Winston Churchill aroused this nation in heroic fashion to save civilisation in World War II', the original provocative headline was hurriedly changed to 'Al Gore invokes spirit of Churchill in fight against climate change'.[71]

The reason for the timing of these conferences was that two days later a quite unprecedented gathering was due to take place in Italy, at which all the world's top political leaders were expected to hammer out a common position on the Copenhagen treaty.

On 8 July, hosted by Italy's prime minister Silvio Berlusconi, scores of politicians and thousands of officials assembled in the central Italian mountain town of L'Aquila, which earlier in the year had been devastated by an earthquake. Headed by President Obama, they not only represented the G8 nations, the world's richest economies. At the same time they were due to join with the leaders of the next 11 richest nations, plus the European Union, to take part in a meeting of the 'G20'. Together they described themselves, under Obama's chairmanship, as the 'Major Economies Forum', or MEF.

Apart from the UN itself, this was the nearest thing the world had yet seen to a meeting of a world government; and top of its agenda was the need to reach agreement at Copenhagen.

First it was the turn of the G8, which it was hoped might agree on specific commitments to cut their emissions. Despite tireless negotiations behind the scenes, all they could come up with was an agreement in principle to 'halve their pollution' by 2050 in order to hold down the rise in global temperatures by a maximum of 2°C. But they carefully omitted to name any baseline-year from which this reduction could be calculated.

It was also agreed in principle that developed countries should lead the way by making an 80 per cent cut in their own CO_2 emissions. But immediately afterwards Arkady Dvorkovich, the top economic adviser to Russia's President Medvedev, made clear that this was 'unacceptable and likely unattainable'. He told journalists 'we won't sacrifice economic growth for the sake of emissions reductions. Everyone spoke about this'.[72]

The G8's failure to come up with anything more specific drew a tirade of criticism from India, Brazil and other developing countries. The UN's Ban Ki-moon angrily rebuked the G8's leaders, saying 'the policies that they have stated so far are not enough'. 'This is the science', he said, 'we must stick with the science.'[73] Dr Pachauri for the IPCC was even more outspoken. 'It's pretty ridiculous', if you ask me', he said; 'I mean, I'm surprised I didn't see the fallacy that they were introducing this pledge by not defining the baseline at least'.[74]

Now it was the turn of the 'G20', including the developing countries themselves. The only version they and the 'MEF' could come up with was even more lukewarm than that of the G8. They merely committed themselves to recognising 'the scientific view that the increase in global average temperature above pre-industrial levels ought not to exceed 2 degrees centigrade'. They thus pledged themselves to 'substantially reducing global emissions by 2050', an expression of intent so vague that it meant nothing at all.

With just five months to go to Copenhagen, it was clear that the prospects of getting everyone to agree to a treaty which pinned them to firm commitments were zero. The best hope, as was now being widely hinted, was that they should agree in December simply to keep talking, with another conference to be held at a later date.

Not everyone, however, had given up the cause. In faraway Peru, the BBC reported, almost 250 children below the age of five had died in 'a wave of intensely cold weather'. Freezing temperatures had arrived in March, three months earlier than normal. 'Experts', claimed the BBC, blamed Peru's freak winter on 'climate change'.[75]

Over at Real Climate, the 'Hockey Team' hadn't given up either. It was true, they conceded, that global temperatures were falling. They might even continue to fall for many years yet. But, never fear, that warming trend that had got everyone so excited in the years leading up to 1998 was still there. It was simply being masked by a couple of decades of cooling. But eventually it would return. And when it did it would be worse than ever. 'We hypothesize', said one of their contributors,

> 'that the established pre-1998 trend is the true forced warming signal, and that the climate system effectively overshot this signal in response to the 1997/98 El Niño. This overshoot is in the process of radiatively dissipating, and the climate will return to its earlier defined, greenhouse gas-forced warming signal. If this hypothesis is correct, the era of consistent record-breaking global mean temperatures will not resume until roughly 2020.' [76]

Then there was cheer too from Hansen and Schmidt at GISS. Despite the satellite data from UAH and RSS showing that global temperatures in June had again dropped, by 0.075°C, GISS reported that, on the contrary, June temperatures had risen by a staggering 0.63 degrees. This was the largest 'June anomaly' since the El Niño spike of 1998. Way out on their own, it seemed that Hansen and his colleagues were claiming that temperatures had risen in a single month by an amount more than the entire net warming of the twentieth century.[77]

Twenty-one years after Hansen had first set the great global warming scare in train with his testimony to Congress in July 1988, it looked like a last gallant bid to keep the flag of the scare flying – as the evidence piled up relentlessly in the opposite direction.

A FRANKENSTEIN'S MONSTER

After all those wearying years of conferences, millions of hours of talking and those desperate attempts to pretend that everything was 'worse than has been predicted', it seemed the politicians' efforts to reach the historic new planet-saving agreement so eagerly anticipated ever since the aftermath of Kyoto in 1997 were about to hit a dead end.

There were three main reasons for this. The first and most obvious was that unbridgeable gulf between the handful of rich Western nations and the mass of developing countries, who could see no reason to accept any limits on their right to catch up economically with those who had been able to enjoy the fruits of industrialisation before them.

The second, as the Copenhagen moment of truth approached, was that a growing number of politicians across the globe could now see just what an abyss would loom up ahead of them if they committed their countries to those massive cuts in 'emissions' that were being so airily proposed. At present, despite talk of nuclear fusion and moving forward to a 'hydrogen economy', no practical technology had yet been devised which could enable any country to cut its 'carbon' emissions by such huge percentages without having to shut down much of its economic activity. Not all the biofuels and wind-mills and solar panels in the world could make up the gap, enough to keep their transport and industries running, their homes lit and their people adequately fed.

The third reason for the faltering in momentum was simply that the scientific theory which had for 20 years been driving the global warming scare forwards no longer inspired the old confidence, that it was unquestionably right. Of course few politicians would yet dare admit it. But the fact remained that, had global temperatures gone on rising as they had done before 1998, it would have been very much easier to maintain that sense of urgency that something was happening so terrible that only the most drastic action could hope to save the planet from catastrophe.

However, it had not been like that. The temperatures had not gone on rising. The Arctic ice had not melted away. The polar bears had failed to drown. Those hurricanes had failed to happen. The planet might environmentally be in a terrible mess, thanks to the insatiable appetites of mankind, with vanishing forests and shrinking Himalayan glaciers and species being driven to the edge of extinction. But, despite the efforts of the 'environmentalists' to enlist them under the one all-embracing cause, none of these things were obviously the result of 'human-induced climate change'. They all had much more local and specific causes, which may not have said much for the ability of the human race to live 'sustainably' on the earth, but which had little or nothing to do with that runaway warming which somehow no longer seemed to be materialising.

To this sense of a mighty onward charge that was losing its way, there were two glaring exceptions. China, India, Russia, Japan and many other countries might all be pulling back from the brink, con-vinced that they should not plunge their economies into sharp decline by agreeing to those devastating cuts in their CO_2 emissions the Western world was proposing. But in the Western world itself, two governments were already committed to make even greater cuts, seemingly regardless of the immense economic price that would inevitably have to be paid for them.

One of these countries was Obama's US, still the richest economy in the world, despite the damage done by its banking crash and deepening recession. The Clean Air and Energy Security bill might still be having to win approval from the Senate. But Obama himself, and the team of environmental zealots surrounding him, were now fervently committed to reducing America's carbon emissions within four decades to a level only 20 per cent of where they had been in 1990. This was an amount so small that it was way below anything the US had known in the twentieth century, a level so low indeed that it had last been registered by the US economy as long ago as 1867.

Quite apart from the Waxman-Markey bill itself, the tide of 'environmentalism' had been running so strongly in the US that she would still be having to fight hard to replace the ageing power stations she needed to keep her electricity flowing. There were huge question marks over the extent to which she would be permitted to exploit her still enormous reserves of gas, oil and oil shale. Her industries, hospitals, schools and even her private householders still had to face the threat of draconian new restrictions on their use of 'carbon' when the EPA moved in to regulate any use of CO_2 as a 'pollutant'.

Just two decades after the panic over global warming had first exploded into American consciousness, a mighty shadow was rising over the future of the world's most successful economy in a way which back in the 1980s would have been quite unimaginable. And, ironically, one of the few Americans who stood to become extremely rich out of that shadow was the man who more than anyone else had helped to conjure it into being, Al Gore.

Apart from Australia, the other government which was as committed as the US to making potentially crippling reductions in its 'carbon emissions' was, of course, that strange entity the European Union. By the peculiar way in which it was constructed, not all the 'member states' making it up were likely to be equally damaged by the array of laws which the EU had now issued in the hope of cutting back their 'carbon emissions' by more than 60 per cent by 2050.

France, generating 80 per cent of her electricity from nuclear reactors, was better placed than any. Other countries, when it came to ensuring their own economic survival, were likely to ignore the EU's policies when it suited them, such as Germany, already building 26 new coal-fired power stations; or Italy, largely dependent on imported energy; or Poland, which could not possibly afford to close down the coal-fired power stations which provided 95 per cent of its electricity.

The one country uniquely vulnerable to all the policies inspired by the fear of global warming was Britain, This was because its politicians, more than any others in the EU, were so completely under the spell of the 'climate change' ideology that Britain was the only country in the world already legally committed by Act of Parliament to reducing its 'carbon emissions' to a fifth of their 1990 level by 2050.

What made Britain still more vulnerable, however, was the devastatingly distorting influence already exercised on her energy policy for nearly 20 years by the 'environmentalists'. It was this which had persuaded Britain in the 1980s to abandon the building of any new nuclear power stations; and in the 1990s to close her coal mines in order to become overly-dependent on electricity derived from that 'low carbon' North Sea gas which was now fast running out.

It was this blinkered vision which since 2000 had lulled her politicians of all parties into their infatuation with wind turbines, of which they didn't have the slightest practical understanding. And it was this in turn which had for so long diverted their attention from the need to plug that fast-approaching 'energy gap' which within a few years would leave Britain without 40 per cent of the generating capacity she needed to keep her lights on and her economy functioning in any recognisable form.

So carried away into this fantasy world was Gordon Brown's government that, only a week after the fiasco of the G8 summit in July 2009, his ministers were announcing their intention to increase yet further the number of wind turbines planned to meet the EU target which required Britain to generate 32 per cent of all her electricity from 'renewables' by 2020.[78]

For this, still at a claimed cost of £100 billion, Brown's ministers now hoped to double to 6,000 the number of new turbines to be built across Britain's countryside, at a rate of 10 a week. They still hoped to build 4,000 even larger turbines around Britain's coasts, at a rate of one a day, when nothing remotely like this had proved achievable anywhere else in the world.

Not only was it inconceivable that Britain could build more than a fraction of the number these ministers were talking about (even though they were now bending the planning laws still further in a desperate effort to do so). Even if in practical terms it were possible, the maximum amount of electricity these windmills could hope intermittently to produce would average out at 5 gigawatts, well under 10 per cent of Britain's total energy needs and well below a third of the 32 per cent Brown's ministers were claiming. Yet opposition politicians were as much lost in this fog of ignorance and self-deception as the ministers themselves. The only response from the Conservative Party was that the government was 'stealing' its own policies.[79]

It was hard to recall any issue on which British politicians *en masse* had ever become so detached from reality. Yet, with one or two exceptions, these Quixotic proposals were solemnly reported by the unquestioning media, without any hint that they were pure wishful thinking.

As usual, however, more serious still was the way all this phantasmagoria was diverting attention from the need to meet the real crisis bearing down on Britain, when 40 per cent of her conventional power stations would have to shut down, leaving a gaping shortfall which no amount of wind machines could hope to remedy.

Any objective assessment of what lay ahead for both America and Britain, if they persisted in the policies they had now adopted in the name of the 'fight against climate change', could only reach one conclusion. The two countries which more than any had created the modern world by pioneering and developing the industrial revolution based on fossil fuels seemed now to be heading for a self-inflicted catastrophe on a scale for which history could offer no precedent.

But, of course, the US and Britain would not be entirely alone. So powerful and all-pervasive had the militant ideology of 'climate change' become that, even if the Copenhagen conference resulted in only a meaningless fudge, with promise of yet more negotiations continuing into the future, there were few countries in the world whose economies would not in some way be seriously affected as they were drawn into following milder versions of the same path.

The inescapable fact was that there was not yet any significant replacement for the fossil fuels on which every country in the world to a greater or lesser degree relied keep its economy functioning and its people fed – and from which the emission of CO_2 was inseparable.

Yet the pressure to reduce 'carbon emissions' was now so intense, reinforced by every kind of global body, from the UN to the World Bank to the WTO, that few countries would be able completely to resist or ignore it. Even enforced cuts as small as 10 or 20 per cent – let alone the 40, 50, 60 or 80 per cent targets so blithely bandied about by the politicians – would inevitably create economic havoc.

Undoubtedly the countries likely to sustain the most serious damage would be those Western nations, led by the EU and the US, whose governments were most obviously in thrall to the belief that carbon dioxide, the gas on which all life on earth depends, had become a 'pollutant', to be ruthlessly taxed, regulated and suppressed in the name of 'saving the planet'.

It was equally likely that the countries most likely only to pay lip service to this ideology would be those whose economies were now growing fastest, such as China and India, and whose 'carbon footprints' would similarly continue to grow at such a rate as to cancel out any supposed 'gains' achieved by reducing emissions in the West.

In other words, while the obsessive self-regulation of the West undermined still further its ability to compete economically with the rest of the world, this would only speed up the process whereby the more efficient of the developing countries, led by China and India, took on the world's economic leadership.

For 20 years the Western world, at least on a political and media level, had been talking itself up into an obsessive belief that global warming was the most terrifying threat the world had ever faced. For a long time this had given rise to little more than an infinite amount of wearisomely repetitive talk. But it was now becoming clear was that what this obsession had conjured into being was a Frankenstein's monster: a mighty political engine which threatened to inflict damage on the economic and social life of humanity of a type and on a scale for which there had never been any parallel.

Having been summoned into existence, the monster was about to wreak havoc that was unimaginable. Yet it was at just this same time that scientific evidence was piling up in all directions to suggest that the simple theory which brought all this about might have been hopelessly, tragically wrong.*

How on earth could such a thing have come about?

---

* The summer of 2009 saw significant revolts by members of two of the leading US scientific bodies against their associations' dogmatic support for the 'consensus'. Fifty-four physicists belonging to the American Physical Society, led by one of the most respected physicists in the country, Professor Will Happer of Princeton, wrote an open letter to the Society strongly protesting against its 'policy statement on climate change' issued in November 2007. Asking the Society to respect proper science, Happer and his colleagues wrote that current global temperatures were no higher than had been experienced many times in the past, that 'natural processes, including ocean cyclesand solar variability' were sufficient to 'account for variations in the Earth's climate' and that 'current computer models' appeared to be 'insufficiently reliable properly to account for natural and anthropogenic

Notes

1. 'Obama "must act now" on climate', BBC News website, 12 February 2009.
2. Foreword to special supplement, 'The Climate Challenge: the fierce urgency of now', to mark the St James's Palace Nobel Laureate Symposium, *The Times*, 26 May 2009.
3. 'Met Office forecasts a super-computer embarrassment', *The Times*, 17 January 2009.
4. 'James Hansen's former NASA supervisor declares himself a skeptic', including the full text of Theon's letter, Watts Up With That, 27 January 2009.
5. Richard Black, 'New evidence on Antarctic warming', BBC News website, 21 January 2009.
6. Steig, E. J., Schneider, D. P., Rutherford, S. D., Mann, M. E., Comiso, J. C., and Shindell, D. T., 2009, 'Warming of the Antarctic ice-sheet surface since the 1957 International Geophysical Year', *Nature*, 457, 459–462.
7. See sequence of posts on ClimateAudit archived as 'Steig *et al.* 2009'; and similarly posts on Watts Up With That, e.g. 'Snow job in Antarctica: digging out the data source' (with pictures of Harry being dug from the snow), 4 February 2009.
8. 'Global warming "underestimated"', BBC News website, 15 February 2009.
9. 'Climate change rhetoric spins out of control', *Sunday Telegraph*, 22 February 2009.
10. 'Coal fired power plants are death factories. Close them', Interview with James Hansen, 'one of the world's foremost climate experts', *The Observer*, 15 February 2009.
11. 'The "Global Warming Three" are on thin ice', *Sunday Telegraph*, 22 March 2009.
12. 'Arctic ice measured from buoys', WUWT, 18 March 2009.
13. Synthesis Report from Climate Change, Risks, Challenges and Decisions'. Copenhagen, 2009, 10–12 March, published by the University of Copenhagen.

---

contributions to past climate change, much less project future climate'. In July dozens of members of the American Chemical Society ('the world's largest scientific society') similarly wrote in to protest at an editorial in the society's bulletin stating that 'the science of anthropogenic climate change is becoming increasingly well-established' and blaming 'deniers' for trying to derail meaningful efforts to respond'. Typical of the vitriolic response was the letter from one scientist who told the editor 'your editorial was a disgrace. It was filled with misinformation, half-truths and *ad hominem* attacks on those who disagree with you' ('American Chemical Society members revolting against their editor for pro-AGW views', WUWT, 30 July 2009).

14. 'Nobody listens to the real climate change experts', *Sunday Telegraph*, 15 March 2009.
15. Summary of Synthesis Report, *op. cit.*
16. This description, reported in the *Sunday Telegraph* on 8 March 2000, was taken from the website of the University of the West of England at the time, but appears later to have been edited.
17. On 16 February 2009 the American Association for the Advancement of Science gave its Award for Scientific Freedom and Responsibility to James Hansen and its International Scientific Co-Operation Award to Robert Watson.
18. For full text of speeches, see Heartland Institute website.
19. Most of the speeches are available on the website of the Heartland Institute. For a summary from one of the main speakers, the Australian palaeoclimatologist Bob Carter, see the Quadrant website.
20. 'Low carbon and environmental goods and service: an industry analysis', report by Innovas on BERR website. For analysis see also 'What would you pay for 400,000 new green jobs' by Ben Pile, on Theregister website.
21. 'Study of the effects on employment of public aid to renewable energy sources', edited by Gabriel Calzada Alvarez, published March 2009 by the King Juan Carlos University, Madrid.
22. A. Z. Rose and D. Wei (2006), 'The economic impact of coal utilisation and displacement in the continental United States, 2015', Pennsylvania State University.
23. Harvey Brenner, 'Health benefits of low cost energy, an economic case study', *Environmental Manager*, November 2005.
24. 'UN "Climate Change" plan would likely shift trillions to form new world economy', Fox News website, 27 March 2009. This gives a link to the UNFCCC document, entitled 'Ad Hoc Working Group on Further Commitments for Annex 1 Parties under the Kyoto Protocol'.
25. Lord Stern, 'Key elements in a global deal on climate change'.
26. 'China warns Obama: no climate deal without wealth transfer', Xinhua News, 31 March 2009. See also Norm Kalmanovitch, CCNet, 7 April 2009.
27. 'Developing nations join forces against Western climate policy', Reuters, 1 April 2009.
28. Letter from Professor Feldman to *Daily Telegraph*, 10 April 2009.
29. 'Camron goes green in his lunch hour', *Daily Telegraph*, 18 January 2006.
30. 'The Tories must prepare now for lack of power', *Sunday Telegraph*, 8 March 2009. Figures taken from *www.electricityinfo.org.* website.
31. 'Saving Carbon – Improving Health', NHS Carbon Strategy for England, published January 2009.

304 The Real Global Warming Disaster

32. 'Save the planet rhetoric reaches crazy heights', *Sunday Telegraph*, 19 April 2009.

33. ' "Opposing windfarms should be socially taboo", says Ed Miliband', *Guardian*, 24 March 2009.

34. 'Climate sceptics "like those who deny Aids link" ', *Daily Telegraph*, April 2009.

35. Commons *Hansard*, 23 April 2009, Col. 382 *et seq*.

36. A recent McKinsey report had estimated that to set up between 10 and 12 'carbon capture' pilot plants would require subsidies of £7.9 billion.

37. 'Catlin Arctic Ice Survey: an Annie Hall moment', WUWT, 17 May 2009.

38. 'Global warming of 7 degrees C "could kill billions this century" ', *Daily Telegraph*, 20 May 2009.

39. 'Prince Charles says world in "last chance saloon" to stop climate change', *Daily Telegraph*, 28 May 2009; 'Global warming must stay below 2 degrees C or world faces ruin, scientists declare', *The Times* on-line, 28 May 2009; 'Meanwhile, back in the real world', *Sunday Telegraph*, 7 June 2009.

40. 'Polar bear expert barred by warmists', *Sunday Telegraph*, 29 June 2009. This article was based on sight of the email exchanges between Dr Taylor and Dr Derocher and private information.

41. Figures taken from a paper presented by Professor Bob Carter to the energy and environment committee of the New Zealand parliament, May 2009 (supplied by the author, but figures were supported from various other sources).

42. 'Copenhagen climate summit heading for disaster', Deutsche Presse Agentur, 26 May 2009.

43. *Suddeutsche Zeitung*, 6 June 2009.

44. 'China fires warning shot at green zealots', Reuters, Beijing, 5 June 2009.

45. 'EU leaders hold off climate funding decision', EurActiv, 9 June 2009.

46. 'Japan's mid-term CO_2 target just 2% below Kyoto', *New York Times*, 19 June 2009.

47. BBC News, 10 June 2009.

48. Reuters, 19 June 2009.

49. 'Developing nations join forces, harden stance', *Indian Express*, 22 June 2009.

50. Yuo Nuo, *China Daily*, 15 June 2009.

51. EurActiv, 25 June 2009.

52. 'Crops under stress as temperatures fall', *Sunday Telegraph*, 14 June 2009.

53. WUWT, 10 July 2009.

54. 'Arctic temperatures still not above 0 degrees C', WUWT, 25 June 2009 (data from Danish Meteorological Institute).

55. 'NYC fails to reach 85° F in June – first time since 1916', WUWT, 13 July 2009.

56. 'People's Republic of China: establishment of the Clean Development Mechanism fund', Asian Development Bank, technical assistance report, June 2006.

57. 'Some effects of the American Clean Energy and Security Act', message sent to Dr Benny Peiser and circulated on the academic Cambridge Conference Network (ccnet), 5 July 2009.

58. GIM was a privately-owned investment company, co-founded by Gore in 2004, based in London and New York. Its purpose was to invest in all forms of 'sustainable development', which as stated on its website 'will be a primary driver of industrial and economic change over the next 25 years'. Gore's partner David Blood was a council member of the Copenhagen Climate Council, the international collaboration of business and scientific organisations dedicated to profiting from all the new investment opportunities created by the fight against 'climate change'. Brendan O'Neill, 'Green-industrial complex gets rich from carbon laws', *The Australian*, 3 July 2009.

59. Brendan O'Neill, 'Green-industrial complex gets rich from carbon laws', *The Australian*, 3 July 2009.

60. 'NASA warming scientist Hansen blasts Obama's "counterfeit" climate bill – calls it "a monstrous absurdity … less than worthless!" ', Climate Depot website, 9 July 2009.

61. 'EPA's Jackson and Energy Sec. Chu on Senate hot seat', WUWT, 7 July 2009.

62. For the text of the Carlin report see the website of the Competitive Enterprise Institute, *cei.org/...\cei-releases-global-warming-study-censored-epa*. See also 'Released – the censored EPA CO2 endangerment document', WUWT, 27 June 2009.

63. 'Minister Wong's Reply to Senator Fielding's Three Questions on Climate Change – Due Diligence', June 2009.

64. 'Australian Senate rejects Rudd's cap and trade emissions plan', Bloomberg, 12 August 2009.

65. *Times of India* and other sources, 1 July 2009.

66. 'China blasts US climate bill carbon tariffs', Agence France Presse, 2 July 2009.

67. 'WTO and UNEP joing forces: western carbon tariffs on poor nations are legal', EurActiv, 1 July 2009.

68. 'Brazil joins China, India in opposing Western climate demands', Reuters, 2 July 2009.

69. 'Hopes of climate treat fading', COP15 website; Daniel Nelson, OneWorld, 2 July 2009.

70. 'Al Gore likens fight against climate change to battle with Nazis', *The Times* first edition, 7 July 2009.
71. 'Gore and Nazis', WUWT, 7 July 2009.
72. 'G8 emissions pledge unravels as Russia objects', AFP, 8 July 2009. 'Russia rejects G8 emissions cut target', RIA Novosti, 8 July 2009.
73. 'UN chief rebukes G8 over climate failures', Associated Press, 9 July 2009.
74. ABC News, 9 July 2009.
75. 'Children die in harsh Peru winter', BBC News, 12 July 2009.
76. 'Warming interrupted: much ado about natural variability', RealClimate, 12 July 2009; 'RealClimate gives reason to cheer', WUWT, 14 July 2009.
77. The GISS version was also supported by NOAA and the NCDC, from which GISS acquired much of its data. They both now claimed that the previous month had been the second warmest June on record (see 'GISS for June – way out there', WUWT, 15 July, and 'NOAA/NCDC: June 2009 – second warmest on record globally', WUWT, 16 July 2009).
78. 'Britain must accept "invasion of wind farms"', *Daily Telegraph*, 16 July 2009; Gordon Brown, Britain's green revolution will power economic recovery', *The Observer*, 12 July 2009.
79. 'Labour "stole our green energy ideas"', *Daily Telegraph*, 16 July 2009.

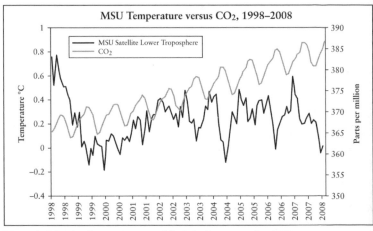

Figure 6: CO_2 rises but temperatures fall: their divergence after 1998.

STOP PRESS: Just as this book was going to press in August 2009 it was announced by the German renewable energy institute IWR that global CO_2 emissions had risen for the tenth year running, by a further 1.9 per cent, and were now 40 per cent above their level in 1990, the base-year for the Kyoto treaty (Reuters, 11 August 2009).

Epilogue
Saving the planet from whom?

'Future generations will wonder in bemused amazement that the early twenty-first century's developed world went into hysterical panic over a globally averaged temperature increase of a few tenths of a degree and, on the basis of gross exaggerations of highly uncertain computer projections combined into implausible chains of inference, proceeded to contemplate a roll-back of the industrial age.'
Richard Lindzen, 2007[1]

By any measure, the story told in this book represents one of the most extraordinary episodes in human history. It has certainly been one of the most extraordinary episodes in the history of science. It has equally been one of the strangest chapters in the history of politics. It even provides one of the more fascinating case studies in the history of collective human psychology.

This curious saga could only have unfolded as it did through a combination of factors which happened to come together at a particular moment in the closing years of the twentieth century. To see this fateful coincidence in its widest context, we may first, by way of a prelude, draw a perspective on how the human race came to arrive at this unique moment in its time on earth.

A HISTORICAL PRELUDE

Way back in the succession of ice ages known to geologists as the Pleistocene, one form of life, alone among all the billions of species on earth, had begun to emerge from a state of nature. Breaking out of that wholly instinctive frame of existence in which all other animals live their lives, this evolving new species gradually found ways to exploit the materials and resources of the natural world around it to makes its own life easier, as by discovering fire and learning to use stone and wood for weapons and tools.

After the earth had emerged from its last major glaciation around 12,000 years ago, a new prolonged warming phase, the Holocene Optimum, in due course created the conditions in which this new species, *homo sapiens*, could begin moving towards a more pronounced extension of his ability to reshape nature to his own ends. He learned how to herd animals and plant crops, how to construct dwellings to protect himself from the extremes of weather and eventually how to work metal and build the first cities. All the time he was separating himself ever further from that instinctive state of nature from which he long since begun to emerge.

As the warmth associated with Bronze Age gave way to the Iron Age, the world was again slightly cooling. But this gave way in turn to those 600 years which were to become known as the Roman Warming, associated with the rise of the most advanced form of human society the world had yet known. After four more centuries of a markedly colder climate associated with the Dark Ages, the renewed warming of the early Middle Ages, both in Europe and China, saw a new flowering of technical skills and the attributes of highly developed civilisations.

By the time this gave way to the four centuries of the Little Ice Age, mankind was launched on that new stage of intellectual evolution which was to give rise to a wholly new understanding of the world based on science. And by the time temperatures again began to rise at the start of the Modern Warming, around the end of the eighteenth century, this coincided with the beginnings of that industrial revolution which was to transform man's relationship with the rest of nature on a scale dwarfing anything which had gone before.

The first phase of this transformation, lasting through most of the nineteenth century, was based on coal, the fossil fuel which powered the new factories and railways. A second phase began towards the end of that century, now based additionally on electricity and the internal combustion engine, powered by another fossil fuel, oil. These gave rise to electric light, motorised transport, aeroplanes, refrigeration, wireless, the cinema and much of what symbolised twentieth-century civilisation.

In 1945, at the end of the second of two catastrophic world wars, a third phase began. The harnessing of nuclear fission marked an entirely new stage in man's relationship with nature. For the first time he now had the power to destroy all life on the planet. With the world now ideologically divided between two mighty armed camps, mankind lived under the shadow of the unimaginably threatening power which was now at its command. But during those years after the Second World War, man's fast-developing technological skills again transformed his world as never before.

The advent of the age of electronics brought television and the computer, which in turn made possible the rise of the space age, culminating in the landing of the first men on the Moon in 1969. New chemicals, transforming food production, together with advances in medical knowledge, helped to create that explosion in the earth's human population – more than doubling in 40 years – which put more demands than ever on the earth's natural resources.

Then, in the 1960s, this vast new extension of man's technological powers led quite suddenly to a disturbing new awareness of what he was doing to the natural world around him. Rachel Carson's book *Silent Spring* (1962), with its apocalyptic picture of the damage being done to nature by the reckless use of pesticidal chemicals, was one of the first signs of that profound shift in consciousness which over the next few years was to bring into being the ideology known as 'environmentalism'.

The significance of this was huge. For the first time since man emerged from a state of nature, he was sensing alarm and even despair at what all his new technological power was doing to the natural world itself. Those affected by this new concern for the 'environment' were coming to see mankind as a greedy and reckless cuckoo in the nest of creation, capable not just of wreaking immeasurable damage on all other forms of life but of destroying it altogether.

Nothing better symbolised this new awareness than 'Earthrise', the unforgettable picture taken in 1968 by the Apollo 9 astronauts of a softly blue planet Earth rising in space above the lifeless surface of the Moon. This image struck an instant chord with the awakening mood of the time because it so vividly embodied the fragile beauty of the only place in the universe which human beings could call home, yet which now seemed under threat as never before.

As some 'environmentalists' began banding together to protest at what was happening, the essence of what drove them was a combination of fear and anger: fear of what men were now capable of doing to the complex eco-systems that sustained life on the planet, and anger towards those they saw as primarily responsible, from corporate industry and governments to the 'morally irresponsible' scientists seen as having made it possible. If mankind in general now came to be viewed as the enemy of life, then certain groups in particular were identified by the 'environmentalist narrative' as its chief villains. Mixed in with fear and anger, as in any form of moralistic puritanism, was a great deal of self-righteousness.

The year of 'Earthrise' also saw the publication of Paul Ehrlich's *The Population Bomb*, his doomsday vision of a species on the way to destroying itself through technology, poisonous chemicals, over-population and over-exploitation of the earth's resources. The next year or two saw the founding of Greenpeace and Friends of the Earth, originally set up to protest at how man was threatening both his own survival and that of all life on earth through his splitting of the nucleus of the atom.

It was around this same time that the attention of a handful of scientists – notably including geologists – was drawn to the fact that for several decades the earth's climate had been cooling, leading them to speculate as to whether this might herald the approach of a new ice age. Initally they viewed such a potentially devastating climate shift as likely to be just a natural phenomenon, a continuation of those fluctuations in temperature which had intermittently given rise to severe glaciations for well over a million years.

Other scientists, however, influenced by the new 'environmentalism', began to surmise that if the climate was changing then the blame might lie with man himself. Such was the significance of that Schneider and Rasool study in 1971 speculating that the earth's cooling might have been caused by aerosols from the burning of fossil fuels. Equally significant was the fact, thanks to recent advances in computing power, that their study was based on their colleague James Hansen's use of an early computer model to replicate the workings of the climate.

This idea that man's activity might be capable of having an effect on something so vast and complex as the earth's climate, although it had been foreshadowed by Arrhenius and Callender, was now taking on a wholly new force. It was aptly in Arrhenius's Sweden that, at the same time and also assisted by computer models, the meteorologist Bert Bolin had begun to theorise that increased human emissions of CO_2 might eventually lead to a planetary warming – even though, when he first began suggesting such a possibility in the 1950s, the world was still cooling.

Among those to whom Bolin communicated his ideas was the man who in 1972, reflecting the powerful rise of the new 'environmentalist' movement, organised in Bolin's Stockholm the 'UN Conference on the Human Environment'.

Maurice Strong's primary interest was not in the 'environment' as such. The real driving force of his life (apart from making money) was his 30-year-old dream that the UN might be a stepping stone to full world government. And now, through his association with the apocalyptically minded Club of Rome, he had come to see 'environmentalism', transcending national boundaries, as the most powerful instrument whereby his own great ambition might be brought about. His setting up in 1972 of the UN Environment Program, with its own international commissariat, able to command funding from national governments, was a step towards realising his dream.

In 1979 Strong's UNEP was a co-sponsor of the first 'World Climate Conference', at which Bolin was a prime mover in urging the world 'to prevent potential man-made changes in climate that might be adverse to the well-being of humanity'. By this time, of course, global temperatures had just begun to reverse their 35-year downward trend and were again rising upwards. The fact that this was what Bolin had predicted lent him a new authority, which was again to the fore at the UNEP/WMO conference in Villach in 1985, calling on the UN to set up an 'intergovernmental panel' to advise the world on the dangers of global warming.

Equally significant in the same year was the international alarm over the discovery of the hole in the ozone layer over the Antarctic. Here, it seemed, was a potentially devastating climatic phenomenon which could be blamed directly on human agency. It led with dramatic speed in 1987 (again thanks not least to the influence of Strong) to the signing of the Montreal Protocol, phasing out the use of CFCs. This treaty set a precedent for the nations of the world, under the auspices of the UN, agreeing to take drastic collective action to halt a major threat to the global environment.

In that same year, 1987 (again through the influence of Strong and Bolin), the UN's Brundtland Report on 'sustainable development' called for the UN to set up both a panel of experts to advise on the threat of global warming and a world 'summit conference', building on the precedent of Montreal, to agree measures to be taken to respond to it.

Before 1987 was ended, Strong's UNEP and the WMO had agreed that the following year the new 'Intergovernmental Panel on Climate Change' would come into being, under Bolin's chairmanship. The stage was beginning to be set. But before the cause of global warming could really take off, several other factors would be needed to reinforce Bolin's initiative. In 1988 they would all finally come together.

PROFESSOR BOLIN'S GAMBLE

Looking back on 1988, we can see that Bolin, by that time a highly politicised scientist, was talking the world into an unprecedented gamble. On the basis of barely 10 years of a renewed upward rise in global temperatures, he predicted that this would continue until it had reached catastrophic proportions.

For years Bolin had personally been convinced that human emissions of greenhouse gases would eventually lead to a potentially dangerous warming of the atmosphere. But he had initially conceived his theory at a time when, despite CO_2 levels rising, global temperature had for years been falling.

Naturally he had been excited when, towards the end of the 1970s, temperatures turned upwards again. It looked as though his theory might be confirmed sooner than he expected. But by 1988, when he had convinced others to allow him to run his new IPCC, the world had only been warming again for little over a decade. Yet it was on this basis that he persuaded so many others that humanity might soon be facing an unimaginable crisis.

This should have raised some rather large questions. Temperatures had risen just as fast and far back in the 1920s and 1930s, long before there was any measurable rise in CO_2. If CO_2 was not the cause of warming at that time, what had caused that pre-war temperature rise? What indeed had caused their generally upward trend through the nineteenth century, as the world emerged from the Little Ice Age? And why, when CO_2 levels noticeably began to rise in the 1950s, had temperatures not risen with them, but remained so cool that more than a decade later some were predicting a new ice age?

As we saw back in Chapter One, by no means all those scientists concerned with such matters yet believed that the relatively modest warming which had taken place since the late 1970s was caused by rising CO_2. But by now Bolin was far from alone in expressing alarm over the rise in temperatures. And of those who had come to accept his thesis none was more important than a highly influential figure

who was not a scientist, and whose interest in global warming originally stemmed from quite different motives.

The man who more than any, apart from Bolin himself, had
pushed for the setting up of the IPCC was Strong, who had also now
got his way by winning the UN's support for his plan to stage a
global conference to discuss what should be done to combat global
warming. He would need the IPCC to provide scientific input for
his 'world summit'. But its purpose would then be to lay the ground-
work for a historic international treaty, modelled on the Montreal
Protocol, committing the world's governments to the measures his
conference agreed. It would be the most far-reaching step towards
turning the UN into a 'world government' since Strong first conceived his ambition that it should become so during World War Two.

None of these moves might have earned the political and media
profile they needed for success had it not been for the extraordinary
publicity given in July 1988 to James Hansen, for the testimony he
gave at his carefully staged appearance before that US Senate committee. It was Hansen's sensational claim, in the middle of a heat
wave, that, thanks to man's activity, the 1980s had been the warmest
decade ever recorded and that 1988 promised to be the hottest year
ever, which finally raised the threat of global warming to the top of
the US media's 'scare agenda'.

The media, not just in America, were peculiarly attuned to promoting 'scare stories' at this time – food scares, lead in petrol, dioxins,
white asbestos and many others.[2] But the nightmare vision conjured
up by global warming was clearly bigger than all the rest put
together. It offered the media the chance to conjure up a real life
'disaster movie' scenario which even Hollywood might have envied,
with nothing less than the entire future of the planet at risk, threatened by intolerable heat, melting icecaps and whole cities sinking
below the rising waves.

The coverage given to Hansen's claims certainly helped the politicians to wake up to the fact that something big was afoot, an issue
to which they needed to pay attention. But it also struck a powerful
chord with the leading 'environmentalist' groups, such as Greenpeace
and Friends of the Earth, which for nearly 20 years had focused their
campaigning on the nuclear threat to the planet posed by the Cold
War and by the building of nuclear reactors.

At this very time, however, the crumbling of the Soviet empire
meant that the nuclear shadow of the Cold War was at least tem-

porarily lifting. In the aftermath of Chernobyl nuclear power had also dropped off the agenda. And for the environmental activists this meant that they stood to lose the cause which more than any other had been central to all their campaigning and fund-raising.

Now, at just the opportune moment, along had come a new cause which even better fitted that apocalyptic narrative which had sustained them for two decades. With remarkable speed, saving the planet from global warming replaced the nuclear threat at the top of the enviromentalists' agenda. No cause could be more cosmic in its implications or have more emotional appeal. And they could now castigate the human greed and arrogance which they saw person-ified in multi-national corporations such as those running 'Big Oil' and the energy industry as the supreme enemies of mankind.

As significant as any of these factors, however, was the way in which they created a new pressure for governments to pour immense sums of public money into funding research into any branch of science which could be related to global warming. In 1989 even President George Bush's sceptical White House advisers authorised a stag-gering increase in the federal funding allotted to 'climate-related' researches, which in just the four years of the Bush presidency was to rise from $134 million in 1989 to a total by the end of 1992 of $2.8 billion.[3]

In Britain, influenced by advisers who had also been swayed by Hansen's evidence, Mrs Thatcher promised lavish funding to John Houghton, now Bolin's most senior colleague in the new IPCC, to set up his Hadley Centre, part of the Met Office, as a 'world-class centre of research into climate change'.

Not the least reason why the researchers wanted so much money was that a large part of it was needed to pay for those huge super-computers with which they would attempt to predict the complex workings of the world's climate as far as 100 years and more ahead. But invariably these models would be programmed to assume that the most important 'forcing' factor in dictating the future of the world's climate and temperatures was the rising levels of CO_2 and other greenhouse gases.

Along with IPCC itself, those computer models would in important respects turn out to be the central player in the entire story.

'2,500 CLIMATE SCIENTISTS CAN'T BE WRONG'

Rarely can any public body have been so misrepresented or misunderstood as the IPCC. The oddest thing about the IPCC, when it first convened in November 1988, was how totally different was the picture of it generally presented to the world from the reality of what it was about.

From the moment the IPCC published its first report in 1990, it came to be treated by the media and the politicians of the Western world as a uniquely reliable authority on the science of climate change. It was routinely portrayed as being made up of '1,500' or '2,500' of 'the world's top climate scientists' from many different countries, who had been brought together to provide an objective assessment of all the relevant evidence on global warming.

In fact, as we have seen, the IPCC was never anything of the kind, nor was ever intended to be. The two men initially responsible for setting it up, Bolin and Houghton, were both wholly committed believers in what they called 'human-induced climate change'. Far from representing a cross-section of scientific opinion from across the world, most of the IPCC's key contributors on the science of 'climate change' were drawn from a surprisingly small network of not more than a few dozen predominantly American and British academics and government employees, who were already as firmly committed as Bolin and Houghton to the belief that global warming was serious and caused by man-made greenhouse gases. A surprising number were to come from Houghton's own Hadley Centre, which would also play a key part in selecting many of the authors.

The prime purpose of the IPCC's reports was thus not to provide a balanced assessment of all the evidence. It was to put together as strong a case as their editors dared for their own already firmly held view: that potentially dangerous global warming was a reality, caused primarily by humanity's use of fossil fuels.

It was true that a minority of the scientists nominated by governments to contribute to the IPCC's reports over the years were by no means wholehearted subscribers to its orthodoxy. Right from the start, however, when the IPCC's first report emerged in 1990, it was clear that the caveats and expressions of dissent by such contributors had been buried away in the hundreds of pages of the full technical report. By the time the all-important Summary for Policymakers came to be written, initially drafted by Houghton with political input from governments, any expressions of disagreement or uncertainty were either toned down or disappeared altogether – a process which in subsequent reports was to become even more obvious.

The most glaring instance of this was to be the IPCC's second report, that which in 1996 aroused such ire from Professor Seitz. Not only did the Summary read by politicians and journalists present a highly tendentious version of what was actually contained in the full technical report. Even parts of the technical report itself, to the dismay of some of its contributors, had been rewritten after they had already agreed it. In particular a whole series of comments expressing doubt about the 'consensus' view were simply removed, again after contributors had approved what they were told was the final text.

Apart from the way they were compiled and edited, nothing did more to skew the IPCC's reports than their dependence on those computer models which had been programmed to predict future temperatures on the assumption that the main driver in determining them would be CO_2. As Lindzen and many others were to point out over the years, they thus failed to take proper account of all the other important factors potentially shaping the earth's climate, from the negative feedback of clouds and water vapour to the changing radiation of the sun and shifts in major ocean currents.

The opinions of the scientific community from which the IPCC drew its contributors were finally distorted still further by the immense pressure now being applied on both sides of the Atlantic for researchers only to come up with findings which agreed with the 'consensus'. This pressure was powerfully reinforced by the way the vast majority of funding was allocated only to scientists willing to meet these requirements. As was to happen again and again, any projects liable to reach conclusions unacceptable to the 'consensus' would fail to win approval for grants.

So obvious did this use of funding to produce desired results become that it recalled a telling passage from the final State of the Union address delivered by President Eisenhower just before he left the White House back in 1960. The most often-quoted line from that speech was his warning about the dangers of allowing 'the military-industrial complex' to win a stranglehold over public policy and funding.

What had generally been forgotten was that Eisenhower immediately went on to deliver a second, equally minatory warning. Referring to the ever rising cost of the research involved in the technological revolution of the post-war years, he pointed out how 'a steadily increasing share' of it was 'conducted for, by or at the direction of, the Federal government'. The prospect of the 'domination of the nation's scholars by Federal employment, project allocations, and the power of money', he warned, 'is ever present and is gravely to be regarded'.[4]

Little could Eisenhower have imagined how, 30 years later, the power of the federal government's money would be used to persuade thousands of his country's academics that their prime duty should not be to establish scientific truth (however much many would believe that this was what they were doing) but essentially to come up with findings which supported one particular, officially prescribed theory.

All these devastating criticisms of the IPCC would not infrequently be made public over the next 20 years, either by expert observers who had examined its methods from the outside, such as Professor Seitz, or, still more tellingly, by those shocked scientists who had directly observed its workings from the inside, such as Professors Lindzen and Reiter. As far as most of the media and the politicians were concerned, however, such comments could be brushed aside as irrelevant. As the accepted narrative had it, the IPCC consisted of '2,500 of the world's top climate scientists' who had all agreed by 'consensus' that global warming was happening and getting worse; and that the only causes of it which mattered were those man-made emissions of greenhouse gases.

The IPCC was never in any meaningful sense a scientific body, nor was it intended to be. It was essentially a political organisation, using the prestige of science to promote the purposes of those who ran it. And they had only one very simple political message to put across.

THE ABDICATION OF THE POLITICIANS

Just as odd as the role of the IPCC in this story was the curious role in it to be played by the politicians.

In allowing the UN to set up the IPCC as the unquestioned arbiter of whether or not the earth faced an unprecedented threat from global warming, the governments of the world had already made a remarkable concession of authority to an international body driven by an agenda which it was itself allowed to dictate. There was no hint of questioning from any major government as to whether the IPCC was really fulfilling the objective scientific role entrusted to it.

This abdication of responsibility became even more obvious four years later when Strong staged his extraordinary 'world summit' in Rio de Janeiro, to approve the UN Framework Convention on Climate Change.

More than half the prime ministers and presidents of the world turned up to participate in this bizarre event, the tone of which was set by the vast crowd of 20,000 'environmental activists', led by Greenpeace, Friends of the Earth and other adherents of the 'Climate Action Network', whose attendance on such a scale had only been made possible by the millions of tax dollars Strong had been able to distribute to ensure that they would be there to support him.

Dutifully, to the applause of the activists, the politicians lined up to sign the Rio 'convention', the contents of which had essentially been drafted by the officials working for Strong's own commissariat. Despite the private reservations of many governments, not least that of the US, so heady was the collective enthusiasm generated around the conference that none of the politicians present dared question what was happening. Swept along by the pressure of the general euphoria, they thus committed their countries to a set of general principles dictated by Strong's officials, and to turning up at the next conference – to take place in Kyoto five years later – at which they would agree to specific targets, requiring their nations and peoples to make very drastic cuts in their CO_2 emissions.

One major government in the world, that of what was about to become the European Union, had already for its own reasons laid out the template for all the new laws and regulations it proposed to introduce, to comply with the recommendations of the IPCC's first report. These had been drawn up by the officials of the European Commission in Brussels, after discussions with officials from the governments of the member states. The elected politicians of those countries had nodded all this through, on the instructions of the unelected officials who advised them that this was what the IPCC had recommended.

The next five years were to see an endless succession of meetings, as part of what was now the 'UNFCCC process', to negotiate the contents of what was to become the Kyoto treaty. These were almost entirely conducted between officials of all the countries signed up to the Rio treaty, with elected politicians playing only a peripheral role. A rare exception was the appearance at one of these meetings in 1996 of Tim Wirth, a senior member of the Clinton-Gore administration, with the purpose of explaining that the latest IPCC report, which he had done his best to push in the right direction, would prove helpful in persuading the US to participate fully in Kyoto and whatever was agreed there.

The other politician who was much more prominently an exception to all this was Vice-President Gore. But his role at this stage was not so much that of a spokesman for the US administration as to act as a cheerleader and campaigner in his own right. This was why he was invited to give the keynote speech at Kyoto and even proceeded to sign the treaty, although his President and the Senate had both already made clear that the US would not ratify it.

As the world's politicians left the conference, their duty was to go home to persuade their governments to ratify a treaty which, even if implemented to the full, its supporters could only claim was likely to hold back the process of global warming for at best six years.

For Strong, however, this was the crowning moment of his lifelong dream that the UN might eventually be transformed into a fully-fledged world government. He was never to play such a leading role on the world stage again, not least because of a curious episode which had occurred five months before the Kyoto conference took place.

In July 1997, as was eventually to emerge, Tariq Aziz, the foreign minister of Iraq, had handed nearly $1 million in cash to a Korean contact of Strong's, on the understanding that the money would be used to persuade the UN to allow Saddam Hussein's government more favourable arrangements under its 'oil for food' programme. This was a project devised to allow certain exemptions from the UN's ban on Iraqi oil exports, on condition that the proceeds were used to feed the impoverished Iraqi population.

Although it was only to come to light eight years later, Saddam's money was passed to Strong in the form of a cheque, which he personally endorsed to be paid into the account of one of his family's companies. In 2005, after a rather wider web of corruption surrounding the 'oil for food' programme had come to light, an independent inquiry conducted by Paul Volcker unearthed the story of the money paid to Strong, who consequently stepped down from the post he had been given as a UN Under-Secretary by Kofi Annan.

Since Kyoto, Strong had been acting as a personal intermediary for Annan on various UN missions, not least in maintaining contact with the hardline Communist regime in North Korea, for which

Strong also acted as the country's UN envoy. After the exposure of his part in the 'oil for food' scandal, he retired to Beijing, which he had visited many times as a longtime friend of the Chinese Communist government. He liked to boast that he had been close to those at the top of that totalitarian government for 40 years, going back to the time of the Cultural Revolution under Mao-tse-Tong. After his disgrace, he lived quietly in the Chinese capital in a penthouse flat, at the top of a building occupied by various UN agencies.[5]

With Rio and Kyoto, however, Strong's chief ambition had been achieved. He had used the issue of global warming to persuade the politicians and governments of the world to accept the supranational authority of the UN on a scale it had never enjoyed before, handing it powers considerably more far-reaching than anything in the minds of those who drew up its original Charter. It was the biggest single step towards turning the UN into an unelected world government since its foundation half a century before.[6]

Then came what, in retrospect, we can see in some ways to have been the central defining episode of the whole story.

THE 'HOCKEY STICK' AND 'PEER REVIEW'

In the aftermath of Kyoto, the IPCC's case that the world was being threatened by an unprecedented warming seemed more convincing than ever. If temperatures had risen in the 1980s and in the 1990s higher still, in 1998, the year after Kyoto, all four official data sources agreed that they had soared to their highest level yet.

There were still, however, those last niggling doubts as to whether these dizzyingly high temperatures were actually without precedent in human history. There was still that long-accepted evidence that, 1,000 years earlier, at the start of the Mediaeval Warm Period, the world had entered on a time when it was even hotter than it was in the present, long before this could have been blamed on human activity. And if that mediaeval warming, like the Roman Warming before it, had come about entirely through natural causes, why might not similarly natural causes lie behind the warming of the late twentieth century?

We may never know the exact circumstances behind the emergence of the 'hockey stick' graph, which was to transform the debate over global warming like nothing else before or since. What cannot be questioned, however, is that what came out of the computer model run by a group of hitherto comparatively unknown government-funded scientists was the one piece of evidence which the IPCC and its allies would have wanted more than anything else; something they could present as final proof that the world's current warming was quite without precedent. Such an abnormal rise in temperatures could only be unnatural, and could therefore be ascribed beyond doubt to a human cause.

All this was reflected, of course, in the extraordinary speed with which the IPCC and its supporters at once rushed to promote the 'hockey stick' as the supreme icon of their cause, and for several years it seemed to carry all before it (as in how it was given pole position at the start of the British government's 2003 energy White Paper).

It was not until that same year, 2003, that the 'hockey stick' first came seriously to be questioned, initially by Soon and Baliunas, in their paper showing how many academic studies over the years had come up with a vast range of evidence contradicting the 'hockey stick' version of climate history; and then in the devastating exposure by McIntyre and McKitrick of the statistical techniques used to create the graph in the first place.

To begin with, it was easy for the 'hockey stick's' supporters to brush such criticisms aside. Who were McIntyre and McKitrick anyway? Their paper hadn't been 'peer-reviewed' and they weren't even qualified scientists, let alone 'climate scientists'. McKitrick might have been an academic but only a professor of economics, which scarcely qualified him to pronounce on matters of science. McIntyre wasn't even an academic, just someone from the business world who earned his living from analysing statistics generated by computers.

But this, of course, was precisely the point: that McIntyre and McKitrick were expert statisticians, who had long been professionally familiar with all the tricks that can be played with computer models. The key to unravelling all that was wrong with the 'hockey stick' did not require any knowledge of climate science. The 'hockey stick' was a statistical artefact. The only technical expertise relevant to uncovering its fatal flaws was precisely that which the obsessively meticulous McIntyre in particular possessed to an unusual degree.

All this would in due course be confirmed by the two inquiries set up by the US Congress, particularly that chaired by Edward Wegman as one of the most respected statisticians in America. By the time those expert inquiries had reported, the 'hockey stick' was so comprehensively discredited that, as we saw, its academic defenders and the IPCC had to resort to the most bizarre devices to keep it in play at all.

The most significant point, however, was that made by McKitrick to the Lords committee in 2005: how was it that the 'hockey stick', with all its glaring statistical flaws, had come so readily to be accepted, first by *Nature* and then by the IPCC, without either of them having subjected it to any of those basic validation tests which any scientific paper should be expected to pass before it is accepted for publication? If two outsiders could identify the basic methodological errors behind the graph after it had been given such remarkable prominence, why hadn't these been spotted before it was published by those under a strict professional obligation to do so?

A claim which from now on was to be heard ever more often from supporters of the 'consensus' was that some paper which aroused their hostility had 'not been peer-reviewed'. This came to be used like a mantra, the simplest way they knew to dismiss any paper which challenged their beliefs; in contrast to the sources they themselves relied on, which they liked to insist could be trusted because they had passed the test of 'peer review'.

In its theoretical intention, the time-honoured practice of 'peer review', whereby a new scientific paper is sent out to other experts in the field to assess whether it merits publication, is of course entirely commendable. But one obvious way in which this system is open to abuse is when those chosen to decide on the merits of a scientific study do not represent a sufficiently balanced range of expertise to prevent bias creeping in.

Such distortions of the process of peer-review had long been familiar in the scientific world. But never had they become so blatant as in the highly politicised debate over global warming, where, as Wegman and others were to demonstrate, the comparatively small number of those prominently involved in 'climate studies' on the 'consensus' side of the debate made up such a tight 'social network' that many of them would not only co-author papers with each other but would also be chosen as reviewers to approve each other's work for publication.

A particular example of this incestuous tendency to promote bias was the way it was used to promote the 'hockey stick'. Not only was there the IPCC's initial failure to subject the graph to those basic tests which would have exposed its fundamental flaws before it was published. This was later compounded by the sleight of hand used to protect the 'hockey stick's' reputation after it had been torn apart by some of the most expert statisticians in north America.

Some day in the future students may be asked to review the saga of the 'hockey stick' as a salutary case study in how far, when politics and science become too closely intertwined, the proper disciplines of the scientific process can fall apart. But through most of the time this curious story was unfolding, other than on the internet it attracted virtually no detailed public attention whatever.

WHAT IS A 'SCIENTIST'?

A related issue was the notably loose way in which the debate over climate change prompted many people to use the term 'scientist'.

So wide-ranging were the factors governing the earth's climate, past, present and future, that there was, of course, no single scientific discipline which exclusively qualified someone to pronounce on it. Those whose expertise might have some bearing on understanding such an immensely complex field of study included atmospheric physicists, astronomers, oceanographers, geologists, meteorologists, chemists, experts in sea levels and carbon dating, students of ice cores, boreholes, tree rings, tropical diseases and heaven knows what besides (not of course forgetting statisticians, when it came to assessing the methodology used to programme those all-important computer models).

So powerful had become the psychological pressure to go along with the orthodoxy, however, that the general term 'scientist' often came to be allowable only when it was applied to someone who supported the 'consensus'. Anyone who in some way dissented from it could be attacked as not being a proper 'scientist'.

A famous example of this was the savage campaign waged between 2001 and 2003 against the Danish political scientist and statistician Bjorn Lomborg for his best-selling book *The Skeptical Environment-alist*. Ironically, although Lomborg was critical of some of the wilder claims made by the proponents of global warming, he did not dispute that human activity was contributing to climate change. In this sense he was far from being a full-blown 'sceptic'. He was, however, more concerned to argue that the vast sums of money now being dedicated to 'halting climate change' would be better spent on directly helping the poorer peoples of the world to adapt to its consequences, and on providing them with more immediately tangible benefits, such as clean water and proper medical aid.

When Lomborg's book appeared, to widespread acclaim, it was subjected to a vitriolic assault from the leading scientific journals, including *Nature* and *Scientific American*.[7] Among those who sought to discredit both Lomborg and his book were Stephen Schneider and John Holdren, and these attacks were then made the basis for a complaint to the Danish Committees on Scientific Dishonesty. Relying on the basis of these venomous personal criticisms rather than on examining Lomborg's expertly-referenced arguments, the DCSD ruled that his book had been 'clearly contrary to the standards of good scientific practice', and that 'objectively speaking', it was therefore found to have fallen 'within the concept of scientific dishonesty'.

When this very odd ruling provoked considerable uproar, the Danish Ministry of Science, Technology and Innovation eventually overruled it, and the committee was forced to reverse its verdict. But this was not before headlines had gone round the world, to the effect that Lomborg was not a proper scientist and had been found guilty of breaching 'good scientific practice'.[8]

The contrary tendency was to use the terms 'scientist' or 'climate scientist' to build up the authority of anyone speaking in favour of the 'consensus', however irrelevant their scientific qualifications might be (or even, in some instances, where they had none at all).* A conspicuous example was the respect accorded by politicians and the media to the utterances of Professor Sir David King, the Blair government's 'Chief Scientific Adviser', when he began to play an active part in the public debate in 2004.

---

* In an article in August 2009 headed 'Who's a climate scientist – depends which side you're on', Myron Ebell cited the recent instance of an Australian professor Andrew Macintosh, described in a newspaper article as a 'prominent Australian scientist', who had 'spent months modeling 45 different climate change scenarios', concluding that the emissions reduction targets agreed by the G8 would not limit global temperature increase to 2°C. Ebell checked out Macintosh's credentials, to find that he was not a scientist at all but a lawyer, helping to run a 'Centre for Climate Law and Policy'. Ebell then, however, tracked down an ABC radio broadcast in which Professor Bob Carter was interviewed as a 'climate sceptic' who had just given evidence to a parliamentary commission. The programme immediately wheeled on a 'climate scientist' to point out that Carter was 'not a reputable climate scientist'. It went straight on, however, to quote 'Professor Andrew Macintosh' claiming that proposed emissions cuts were not enough, without questioning his 'scientific' credentials at all (Competitive Enterprise Institute's *globalwarming.org* website, 3 August 2009).

It soon became apparent that, as a specialist in 'surface chemistry', King was far from being at home with all the quite different disciplines involved in discussing global warming. This showed, for instance, when he launched forth on his theory that a rise in atmospheric CO_2 to 1,000 ppm had been responsible for the mass-extinction of species which took place at the end of the Mesozoic. Quite apart from the fact that this was in itself a startlingly novel hypothesis, he on different occasions described this event as having happened '55 million years ago', and '60 million years ago'. Yet to anyone versed in basic geology, the more usual date given for the end of the Cretaceous is 65 million years ago.

It showed again when, to the Lords committee in 2005, King joined Houghton in dismissing Linden's views on the feedback effect of water vapour, on grounds so facile that Lindzen himself said he could only regard them with 'astonishment'.

Just how out of his depth King was with all the multi-disciplinary science of climate change was embarrassingly brought home when he made his ill-fated visit to Moscow in July 2004. Why this episode merited so much space in Chapter Five was that it highlighted the way in which the supporters of the 'consensus' had come to live in such a self-contained 'bubble' that, when confronted with genuinely expert scientists who happened to disagree with them, they hardly knew how to respond, except with bluster and ill-tempered impatience.

So used were they to talking only to their fellow-believers that King and his scientific team had never before encountered a whole roomfull of expert authorities who didn't agree with the 'consensus'. As Ilarionov made clear at his press conference after King and his team walked out, the leading Russian scientists were not convinced by the CO_2 theory. They believed that the prime causes of climate change lay much more plausibly in fluctuations in the radiation of the sun and ocean currents. Yet when they had tried to engage the IPCC in serious dialogue on their concerns, by submitting a series of questions, they received no answer.

When King arrived in Moscow, seeking Blair's support for his demand that the conference agenda should be rewritten and two-thirds of the invited speakers thrown off the list, he was behaving not as a scientist but as a politician. However knowledgeable he might have been about his own discipline of 'surface chemistry', when he was challenged on a fairly simple point relating to the science of climate change the impression he gave his audience was that he was floored for an answer. But because he had been vested by journalists and politicians in the mystical aura of a 'scientist', they treated his views on global warming with reverential deference, even though in reality he spoke with little more specialist authority on the subject than a man holding forth in the pub.[9]

Later this kind of credulity was to find even more reckless expression, when the title of 'the world's top climate scientist' would be variously accorded by the BBC and other journalists to Dr Pachauri (with his academic qualifications in railway engineering); to Dr Hansen (the one-time astronomer turned 'climate activist'); and even, by one particularly wide-eyed US Congressman, to the economist and former Treasury official Lord Stern.

THE FIRST 'GREAT DIVIDE'

Unquestionably the moment when hysteria over global warming reached its height was in the summer of 2006, when Gore's *An Inconvenient Truth* began hitting cinema screens across the world. Scarcely a single passage in the film was not either exaggerated or demonstrably wrong. Yet millions of those who saw it found it terrifyingly plausible, not least because the media had for so long been carried away by the scare themselves that their coverage of the global warming issue had not provided enough balanced information for most members of the public to recognise just how far the film was no more than an ingenious exercise in propaganda.

Another symptom of the hysteria prevailing at this time was the change which came over the style of language being used by supporters of the 'consensus' to express their scorn for those who did not agree with them. It had formerly been customary to discredit the views of scientists critical of the 'consensus' by claiming that they were funded by 'Big Oil' or the energy industry. But now most of the major oil companies were investing heavily in the boom in 'renewables', such as wind farms, and were devoting huge sums to proclaiming their 'green' credentials (in 2004 British Petroleum had begun to advertise that 'BP' now stood for 'Beyond Petroleum').

It was in 2006 that it became customary for the cheerleaders of the 'consensus' to use rather more extreme language to dismiss those dissented from their orthodoxy, by equating them with 'Holocaust deniers', 'members of the Flat Earth Society', or with those cranks who liked to believe that the first moon landing in 1969 had been 'staged on a movie lot in Arizona'.*

This was only a more public expression of the similar collective pressure which had long been evident in the academic community, applied to any scientist who dared express even the mildest scepticism towards the 'consensus'. This had led frequently to verbal insults or abusive emails, in some cases to dissenters being downgraded or pointedly moved to less salubrious working accommodation, even on occasion to their being dismissed from their posts altogether.

At this stage, by the end of 2006, it still seemed plausible to maintain the thesis that the earth might be in the grip of runaway global warming, not least because during that year global temperatures had shown another upward El Niño spike. Although they had never risen again to the height they reached in the earlier El Niño year of 1998, their average level since 2001 was still higher than it had been in the 1990s.

But at this point the story began to move into a wholly new stage. We can see in retrospect how it was beginning to split apart into two quite different and barely connected 'narratives'. A gulf was opening up between those still caught up in the bubble of the 'consensus' and the reality of what was happening in the world outside it.

For a start, global temperatures in 2007 began that sharp drop which for the first time revealed a distinct gap between the predictions of the computer models that they would continue to rise by 0.3°C per decade, and what was happening in the real world. For more than 20 years nothing had more obviously made the CO_2 thesis seem plausible than the fact that temperatures had continued to rise. Such was the chief support of the gamble which Bolin, Hansen and others had persuaded the world to take back in the late 1980s. But now, for the first time, as the overall trend in temperatures since 2001 was downwards, it began to look as though the gamble might not be coming off after all.

At the same time the scientific 'counter-consensus', for so long muted or silenced, was at last beginning to find its voice. In media

---

* In 2009 two of the US astronauts who had walked on the moon, Dr Buzz Aldrin and Dr Harrison 'Jack' Schmitt (who later became a US Senator), both also qualified scientists, publicly expressed their rejection of the consensus' view of global warming. In April 2009 Gore nonetheless repeated his comparison of 'climate deniers' to those believing that the Apollo 11 moon landing was 'staged on a movie lot in Arizona' (testimony to the US Congress, 24 April 2009).

terms, the most conspicuous instance of this, provoking outrage from the IPCC and supporters of the 'consensus', was Channel Four's *The Great Global Warming Swindle*, allowing an array of sceptical scientists to put arguments which had never been given such a prominent public airing before.

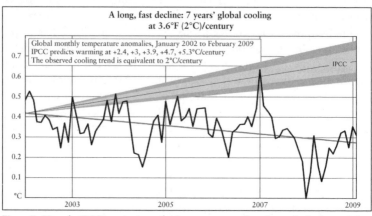

Figure 7: How the IPCC's projections of rising temperatures have increasingly diverged since 2001 from the trend in actual temperatures. Source: Science and Public Policy Institute.

In his *National Post* column in Canada, under the title of 'The Deniers', the veteran environmentalist Lawrence Solomon was running a series of interviews with many of the world's most distinguished academic global warming-sceptics, several of whom had never publicly admitted their scepticism before.[10] Books began appearing by scientists arguing the 'counter-consensus' case, such as Fred Singer's *Unstoppable Global Warming, Every 1,500 Years*, *Climate Confusion* by Dr Roy Spencer, in charge of the UAH official temperature record[11]; and Henrik Svensmark's *The Chilling Stars*. The hit-rates of the leading sceptical scientific blogs, such as McIntyre's Climate Audit and Watts's WUWT, were rising by the month.

Meanwhile, inside the 'consensus bubble', wholly unconcerned by any of this, the governments of the Western world were at the same time, after years of talk and grand policy declarations, moving towards concrete commitments which, if carried through, could only have an increasingly devastating impact on their economies and way of life.

The leaders of the EU in 2007 were formally committing their countries to reducing CO_2 emissions by 60 per cent; to a massive increase in wind turbines and other forms of 'renewable' energy; and to such an increase in the compulsory use of biofuels that this might within 13 years require as much as 70 per cent of their farmland to be taken out of food production. In the US, where the drive for subsidised biofuels was similarly threatening to usurp a third of all the land used for food crops, the Supreme Court ruled that carbon dioxide, the gas on which all life on earth depends, was should now be officially classified as a 'pollutant'.

Few issues more neatly illustrated the extent to which the politicians had lost contact with practical reality than their continuing infatuation with wind-turbines. Taken in by the self-promoting claims of the wind industry, they consistently exaggerated the potential of windpower by some 300 per cent, through confusing the 'capacity' of windfarms with their actual output. The politicians seemed unable to grasp that windmills were a remarkably expensive, unreliable and inefficient way to generate only derisory amounts of electricity (in Britain, for instance, which contributed barely 2 per cent of all the world's CO_2 emissions, while China was increasing its emissions by more than that every year, building 10,000 wind turbines would make no difference to the global CO_2 total whatever).

Even more revealingly naive was the politicians' obsession with the idea that coal-fired power stations should only be allowed to continue operating if they were fitted with 'carbon capture', piping off their CO_2 emissions to be buried in underground caverns or the remains of exhausted oil and gas fields beneath the sea. Not only had the technology to do this not yet been properly developed, but even if they could be made to work, such schemes would involve doubling the amount of coal required by the generating plants, thus doubling the cost of their electricity.

So fanciful was the idea of burying carbon dioxide in holes in the ground to save the planet that it recalled Lemuel Gulliver's visit to the inventor in the Academy of Lagado who was working on a project to extract the energy of sunbeams from cucumbers. When the 'projector' had explained to Gulliver that his process was well on the way to being proven, he held out his hand for a fat subsidy to enable his scheme to be brought to completion. Naturàlly Swift's hero moved on. But the rather less worldly politicians of the twenty-first century were only too happy to pledge billions to the developing of an idea scarcely less fanciful, with the astronomic bill to be picked up in due course by all users of electricity.

Just as odd as the dream world of the politicians, however, was that inhabited by most of the media. In the early years it might have been understandable that the media should be seduced by scientists' predictions of runaway global warming, because it provided such an entertaining scare story, set in the comparatively distant future. But as the story had continued to unfold, most journalists remained so locked into the narrative that, with honourable exceptions, they abandoned any attempt to exercise their supposedly ingrained professional scepticism, continuing to accept the claims of the 'environmentalist' lobby at their face value, however absurd.

On wind power, for instance, they proved just as gullible as the politicians, when only a little rudimentary homework could have shown them that the claims made for the value of wind energy were being ludicrously overstated. They were equally credulous towards the IPCC, as was reflected in that routine claim that it represented the views of 'the world's 1,500 (or 2,500) top climate scientists'. Had they bothered to spend any time investigating its workings, the journalists might have found a story rather more interesting to their readers than just the rehashing of IPCC press releases.

Just as significant as what did get reported about the 'climate change story' was how much the media chose to overlook, particularly when evidence began to mount in contradiction of the 'consensus' view. It was remarkable how few journalists deigned to notice the decline in global temperatures after 2006 or the abnormally cold winters being experienced in so many parts of the world, let alone the increasingly pointed arguments now being put forward by the more eminent of the scientists representing the 'counter-consensus'.

In Britain the most conspicuous failure of the media to give balanced coverage to all the various aspects of the climate change story was that of the BBC, which actually took pride in abandoning any pretence of the impartiality required by its Charter, and gloried in the way its reporting had become no more than highly specious pleading for one side of the story.

This was never better exemplified than in the BBC's 2008 television series *Climate Wars*, designed as a response to *The Great Global Warming Swindle*. From caricaturing the opinions of those whom it clearly saw as 'enemies' to its dishonest editing of interviews, the programme scarcely missed a trick in its efforts to discredit the views of the 'sceptics' representing the 'counter-consensus'. Rarely can even the BBC have plumbed such tendentious depths as in the sequence where it showed a giant mock-up of the 'hockey stick' being driven round

London, in an attempt to convince viewers that this celebrated rewriting of climate history had triumphantly survived all the 'sceptics'' attempts to undermine it, and that temperatures were still continuing to hurtle upwards exactly as Mann's graph had suggested they would.

In fact one of the biggest stories of 2008 was the continuing rise of that massive array of vested interests now benefiting financially from the alarm over global warming. There were the billions going into every kind of academic research, making it the fastest-growing sector in the academic world.[12] Tens of billons more were going into every sector of the 'renewables' industry. Further vast sums were going to 'expert consultants' advising governments and industry on how to move towards a 'low carbon economy'.

The greatest bonanza of all, however, scarcely yet recognised by the public at large, was the exploding global trade in 'carbon credits', officially estimated in 2008 at $126 billion. Buying and selling the right to emit CO_2 was now growing so fast that it was estimated that it could eventually be costing the world anything up to $10 trillion a year, which would make 'carbon' the most valuable traded commodity in the world.*

So astronomic were the profits already on offer in the 'climate industry' that it was fast becoming a significant player in the global economy. So rich and powerful were the interests involved that they would certainly from now on be at the forefront of opposing any attempt to urge that the dangers of global warming might have been overstated. Those driving the 'consensus' bubble forward had won some very substantial allies.

As 2009 approached, the divide between those inside the 'bubble' and the world outside it only widened further. As the northern hemisphere entered a winter even colder and snowier than the year before, the trend in global temperatures since 2001 was now conspicuously downwards. The predictions of the IPCC's computer models, like the theory on which they were programmed, looked more obviously than ever at odds with reality.

---

* Nova, *op. cit.* Among those who now stood to make fortunes from 'carbon trading' was Maurice Strong, who had been on the board of the Chicago Climate Exchange, one of the world's foremost centres for broking 'carbon' deals. He was now reported as being involved in setting up the Tianjin Climate Exchange, the first in China, the world's biggest seller of 'certified emission reduction' credits under the UN's Clean Development Mechanism (Claudia Rivett, WSJ, 11 October 2008, *op. cit.*

At just this time, however, Britain's MPs led the world in committing their country to reducing its 'carbon' emissions more drastically than was yet being contemplated anywhere, promising to take them back by 2050 to a level not known since shortly after the start of the industrial revolution. Not one of those politicians could have provided a remotely coherent explanation for how this could be achieved, other than by closing down much of Britain's economy.

In America, as the US entered its fiercest recession since the 1930s, Barack Obama was elected President on a strikingly similar programme. Like Britain, he was prepared to commit his country to a 'carbon' reduction so great that it would take the US back to levels not known since the mid-nineteenth century. Like Brown, he promised thousands more wind turbines, when those already built contributed barely 1 per cent of his country's electricity needs. He talked blithely of creating 'five million green jobs' when no one could begin to explain how in practice this could be brought about. On top of all this he supported both a 'cap and trade' scheme which would add thousands of dollars a year to his countrymen's electricity bills, and regulation of CO_2 by the EPA as a 'pollutant', for reasons which even one of the EPA's own senior experts could not begin to justify.

Yet again, so locked into their dream world were those inside the 'bubble' that the practicality of all these Quixotic declarations of intent were scarcely questioned.

In Britain, as 2009 began, the media again remained strikingly oblivious to the abnormally cold weather affecting large parts of the world, even though, between October and April, Britain itself was experiencing its most frequent snowfalls for years. As the UK Met Office's computer model again predicted one of the 'warmest years ever' and that Britain would enjoy a 'barbecue summer', just before the rains came down and summer temperatures remained stubbornly low, newspapers were still almost daily peddling little stories about how the south of England would soon be growing tropical crops and how all kinds of wildlife, from migrating birds to dragonflies, would find it impossible to survive those soaring temperatures.

The great divide between those in the bubble and the world outside it was all but complete. But now, as the deadline of the Copenhagen conference approached, the world was faced with a second 'great divide' which threatened to change its future just as dramatically as the first.

THE SECOND 'GREAT DIVIDE: THE WEST VERSUS THE REST

For 12 years, the conference due in December 2009 had been billed to become even more of a landmark in the history of the world than Kyoto. But the fatal obstacle to it becoming so was precisely the one which had caused such grief in 1997, and which now looked like becoming even more insurmountable.

On the one hand were the industrialised Western countries, led by the EU and now joined by the US and Australia, which had signed up to commitments adding up to what looked, on all the evidence available at the time, to be the most weirdest economic suicide note in history. If all those commitments were honoured, this could lead only to the self-induced decline and even collapse of their economies, on a scale without any historical precedent.

On the other hand were the still developing countries, led by India, China, Russia and Brazil, which were not prepared to have any of it. None of them really believed in man-made climate change, a theory which had been largely developed by American and British scientists. None of them were prepared to reduce their use of fossil fuels in such a way that would hold back their attempts to catch up economically with the West.

The only way such countries might be prepared to make even the slightest moves in that direction was if the Western nations paid them scarcely imaginable sums of money to make what would be little more than token gestures. Some of them indeed, such as India and Russia, had already indicated that they were not prepared even to do that, declaring that nothing whatever would persuade them to hold back on the economic growth which it was their first duty to their peoples to keep in being.*

---

* An article published in July 2009 by Fiona Kobusingye, chairman of the human rights and economic development group, CORE Uganda, described how, 'day after day, Africans are told that the biggest threat we face is – global warming. Conferences, news stories, television programs, class lectures and one-sided "dialogues" repeat the claim endlessly. We are told using oil and petrol, even burning wood and charcoal, will dangerously overheat our planet, melt ice caps, flood coastal cities, and cause storms, droughts, disease and extinctions.' Yet the real problem for Africans was that 'fake science, hysterical claims and worthless computer models', were being used 'to justify telling Africans that ... we shouldn't develop, or have electricity or cars', because Western countries were

Not only did the possibility of any meaningful agreement at Copenhagen in 2009 thus look extremely remote. It seemed as though the Western countries were now locked into policies which – unless they eventually made a very dramatic change of course – could only ensure their own relative economic decline, while the rest of the world was determined to remain forging ahead.

The net result of all this would be a mighty shift in the world's economic balance of power, to accelerate a tendency which had already been in evidence for more than a decade, Europe had already been sliding down the comparative league table since the 1990s; and America, under President Obama, now seemed doomed to follow. This would leave the world to be dominated by the two giant economies of Asia, with between them nearly 40 per cent of the world's population, while Russia exercised an ever greater stranglehold over the industrialised economies of the EU, ironically because of her vast resources of fossil fuels.

This had the potential to create such dislocation across the entire global economy that it might lead to social and political breakdown on a scale that was hard to imagine or predict. Yet it had all come about because, for 20 years at the end of the twentieth century, global temperatures had risen by a few tenths of a degree, as had happened countless times before in the earth's history. On this occasion, however, thanks to a peculiar combination of historical circumstances, such a natural event had prompted a handful of scientists to predict that the end of the world must consequently be nigh – and the politicians had believed them.

This left above all two questions to be answered. How might the human race escape from this unique mess it had got itself into? And what were the deeper reasons why such a wholesale flight from reality should have come about in the first place?

'worried about global warming'. But 'not having electricity' meant that 'millions of Africans don't have refrigerators to preserve food and medicines', people didn't have 'lights, computers, modern hospitals and schools ... or offices, factories and shops to make things and create good jobs'. Because Africans were told that they could not have electricity and economic development', except for what could be 'produced with some wind turbines or little solar panels', this in reality consigned many of them to 'disease and death'. This, wrote Miss Kobusingye, was 'immoral, a crime against humanity' ('Africa's Real Climate Crisis', Chronwatch website, 30 July 2009).

WHAT HAPPENS NEXT?

There wasn't one person in the world in 2009 who could say with absolute certainty what was likely to happen to the earth's temperatures in the decades ahead, There were many people who believed that they would rise. There were others who believed they might fall. But that was all it amounted to: a matter of belief.

The only thing which could be said with certainty was that all those predictions made on the basis of computer models that temperatures would continue to rise in line with the rise in greenhouse gases had been proved wrong. In the early years of the twenty-first century, the models had turned out to be such unreliable prophets of the future that even some of those who continued to believe in the basic theory on which they had been programmed were having to come up with new theories to explain why their prophecies hadn't worked out. They put their faith instead in predicting that in due course, after a temporary lull, the climate would resume its warming just as before. But this, like their earlier belief, was still no more than a matter of faith.

Ultimately there were two things which should long have aroused much more widespread suspicion of the 'consensus' than they did.

The first had been the readiness of its supporters to manipulate the evidence. They had been prepared to endorse the rewriting of climate history by methods which eventually turned out to be more than questionable. They had been prepared to doctor the agreed text of IPCC reports to come up with the findings they wanted. In the name of 'scientific accuracy' they had 'adjusted' the official global temperature record. If the theory behind their belief in 'human-induced climate change' had genuinely rested on sound science, why had it so often been necessary for the evidence supporting it to be rigged?

Equally revealing had been the peculiar form of intolerance shown by supporters of the 'consensus' towards anyone who didn't share their beliefs. Nothing had become more familiar in discussions of 'man-made climate change' than how often it prompted its 'true believers' to resort to *ad hominem* abuse, suggesting that those who disagreed with them could only be doing so from corrupt and venal motives. Rather than being willing to engage in debate, they were more likely to respond with insults.

On so many occasions that it had become a consistent pattern, attempts were made to prevent those dissenting from the orthodoxy from putting their case in public. Papers and articles putting a 'sceptical' point of view had been refused publication times without number. Similarly familiar, as was famously seen in Moscow, were the attempts to prevent dissenters from the 'consensus' putting their case on public platforms.* The hostility and resentment displayed towards those who could be dismissed as 'deniers' or 'contrarians' scarcely belonged to the measured discourse of science but recalled the impatience of religious zealots, enraged by anyone daring to challenge their 'revealed truth'.

By 2009, however, this psychological bulldozing had created such a mighty edifice of legislation, financial interests and dogmatic assumptions not to be questioned that it was hard to imagine how it could easily be dismantled. If the 'sceptics' were right and global temperatures failed to rise, how many years would it take before the remorseless momentum built up over two decades could be reversed?

A serious problem was that so many people and organisations now had such a strong political, financial or intellectual interest in perpetuating that edifice. Above all there were the governments which had imposed such an avalanche of measures in the name of 'halting climate change', spewing out new regulations, new taxes and controls in all directions. How could all those politicians who had been blindly swept along by the 'consensus', without ever properly understanding it in the first place, bring themselves to admit that they might have been wrong?

Then there were whole new industries called into being by the fear of global warming: those who had invested billions in developing

---

* Two more examples came to light as this book was going to press. When in they summer of 2009 one of Australia's leading geologists, Professor Ian Plimer, was touring universities in Australia and New Zealand to talk by invitation about his scientifically erudite and best-selling book *Heaven and Earth: global warming, the missing science* (Quartet, 2009), several times vice-chancellors intervened at the last minute either to cancel his meetings, or to insist that they must be given no publicity. In London, Avril Terri Jackson, founder and first chair of the Energy Group at the Institute of Physics, had been invited to write an article on climate change for the autumn 2009 newsletter of the Institute's London branch. When her paper turned out to be highly critical of the man-made global warming thesis, she was told that it wouldn't appear. In 2008 Lord Lawson had similarly been invited by the Energy Group to discuss his book *An Appeal to Reason*. When the Institute learned of this, his invitation was cancelled (personal information).

wind turbines and biofuels; the armies of 'carbon traders' and 'carbon brokers', the sellers of 'carbon offsets' and insurers against 'the risks of climate change'. Although some might privately have had their doubts about the realities of global warming, they had seen a huge new business opportunity in the making and they would resist to the last any attempt to reverse the accepted view of that which was making them rich.

How could all those academics benefiting from the billions being poured into 'climate change' research justify changing their minds about a scientific theory which had become the basis of their livelihood? How could all those journalists who had built their careers on writing up the latest scare story about vanishing polar bears or killer heat waves or drowning Pacific islands suddenly change their tune and report that these things weren't happening after all? How could all those teachers who for years had been earnestly indoctrinating their pupils with the officially-approved line that the future of Planet Earth was menaced by this vast shadowy threat suddenly turn round to tell their classes that the whole thing had been a misunderstanding?*

In other words, the Frankenstein's monster had been called into being and wasn't going to be easily stuffed back into its grave. Even if the trend in global temperatures continued to drop, it would inevitably be years before the juggernaut could be reversed. Meanwhile 'green' taxes would continue to rise; electricty bills would continue to soar; controls on every kind of 'carbon intensive' activity, from driving cars to flying on holiday to using the 'wrong' type of light bulb, would become ever more restrictive; industries would slip away to parts of the world where the madness had not taken hold; and ever more of the landscape would become dominated by useless windmills, making their owners rich and the 'environment' poorer.

As odd as anything was that, as this new world had been brought about, the two professions best positioned publicly to question it had been so conspicuously reluctant to do so. Remarkably few politicians or journalists had ever dared to challenge the array of assumptions on which it was based, or to ask what all these measures were really

---

* So far had the 'consensus' view pervaded public education in Britain that it had even been built into the school examination system. As a columnist in 2009 I was sent by readers various GCSE and other exam papers, not just in science subjects but even in English, on which students could not have scored high marks unless their answers echoed the official line on global warming.

going to achieve. It had thus been allowed to creep up on the peoples of the West like a dank, silent fog, seeping into every corner of their lives. Without knowing it, they had been led into sleepwalking towards a disaster. And at the end of it, all they could now see, if their eyes were sufficiently open and their brains sufficiently engaged, was a slow but steady erosion of that relatively comfortable, relatively free way of life which they had for a few brief decades come to take for granted.

So why, when much of the rest of the world had remained immune to this strange card house of delusions, had the nations and governments of the affluent West become so compulsively possessed by it?

A 'STORY' FOR OUR TIME

As we have seen, there were essentially four reasons why, as the twentieth century approached its end, the fear that mankind might be heating up the earth to the point of destruction had mushroomed into the greatest and potentially most expensive scare the world has ever known.

The first of these, preparing the ground for all that followed, was that profound shift in consciousness which took place in the 1960s, giving rise to what came to be known as 'environmentalism'. For all those caught up in it, this gave them a new way of looking at man's place in the world as 'the cuckoo in the nest', thoughtlessly wreaking untold havoc on the natural world around him and seemingly bent on destroying all life on earth.

We all of us, much more than we are consciously aware, see the world in terms of stories, 'narratives' which help shape the way in which we try to understand the world around us: explaining how it works, where we have come from and where we may be heading for. All ideologies in this way have their own narrative, and 'environmentalism' was no exception.

The central problem of the world, as the 'environmentalist' narrative had it, was the uncontrolled selfishness with which human beings had come to exploit its resources at the expense of the rest of nature. Unless they made very drastic moves to change their ways and to develop a completely new set of values, both they and the planet were doomed.

Certainly it was remarkable how many people spontaneously experienced that change of perception in the 1960s and how quickly it pervaded Western culture, finding expression in everything from pop songs of the time to the rise of those environmentalist campaigning groups at the end of the decade. But initially this was focused on a wide range of environmental threats, of which global warming was not one.

A second crucial factor was the way Maurice Strong used his influence to harness this new 'environmentalist' mood of the time to his lifelong dream that the United Nations should move forward towards becoming a 'world government'. The answer to all these threats crowding in on the planet, he argued, lay in the creation of new UN structures to tackle them. His purpose in setting up the UN's first 'World Environment Conference' in 1972, followed by his launch of of the UN Environment Program, was not just to enhance the UN's global role by identifying it with humanity's response to environmental challenges, but also to further his socialist ideals by redistributing wealth from the rich nations of the West to the under-developed world.

Without Strong's tireless lobbying behind the scenes, the UN would never have come to play such a central shaping role in the drama that followed. And the key to the power it came to exercise lay in that third crucial factor which entered the story when Bert Bolin provided Strong's campaign with its ideal focus: an environmental cause which could not have been more cosmic in its implications. Thus, thanks to Strong's lobbying, did the UN's IPCC take its central place on the stage, followed by his 'world summit' in Rio, leading in turn to Kyoto.

Even all this could not have come about as it did, however, without that fourth factor which had entered the equation with the collapse around the same time of Soviet Communism. The lifting of the nuclear threat of the Cold War and the crumbling away of the ideology of Marxism left a psychological vacuum in Western society, which the new ideology of 'environmentalism' was ideally placed to fill.

The environmentalist narrative had much in common with the Marxist version it for so many people replaced. It divided the world into the exploiters and the exploited. It identified many of the same 'enemies', the power of America and of multi-national corporations, particularly those involved in oil and energy. It saw the rich nations of the world, led by the US, living at the expense of the poor. And above all it provided for its adherents the heady sense of being caught up in a great idealistic cause, aimed no longer just at freeing the world from the evils of capitalism but at something more cosmic altogether, saving nothing less than the entire planet from the greed and selfishness of humanity.

It had often been observed that Marxism had many parallels with the more extreme forms of organised religion. It similarly had its revered prophets and 'sacred texts'; its dogmatic explanations for everything; its intensely moralistic view of the world; and above all its capacity to inspire its followers to a kind of righteous fanaticism, convinced that it was their destiny to save mankind from those 'heretics' and 'unbelievers' who did not share their world-saving creed.

One of the first people to note that the belief in saving the planet from global warming had also come to display many of the characteristics of a secular religion was the novelist Michael Crichton in 2004, but by 2009 such an observation had become commonplace. The true believers in global warming similarly exhibited a moralistic fanaticism, justified by the transcendent importance of their cause. The basic narrative by which they lived was one familiar from the history of religious sects down the ages, the conviction that the end of the world was nigh, thanks to the wickedness of mankind, and could only be saved if humanity acknowledged its sins and went through a profound change of behaviour.

The vision of the coming apocalypse conjured up by their prophets, such as Al Gore and James Hansen, and confirmed by those 'sacred texts' handed down by the IPCC, had much in common with ancient myths and Biblical tales of the world being visited with 'extreme weather events', plagues, fires, mighty winds and above all floods so immense that whole cities would vanish below their waves.

But all this, of course, was dressed up in new and very different language, deriving its authority not from invocations of the wrath of the Almighty but from that ultimate source of authority in the modern age, the pronouncements from on high of 'science' and 'scientists'.

The only problem was that even the scientists had to rest their prophecies of the future not on absolute and provable scientific certainty, such as governs the workings of the law of gravity, but on belief. And here the scientists themselves had to look to a higher authority on which to base their certainties: namely the predictions made by those terrifyingly powerful computer models which they themselves had programmed.

No theme has run more consistently through the story told in this book than that quasi-religious faith shown in the power of computer models to replicate the complex workings of the earth's climate and to predict what it might be doing in 10, 20, 50, 100 years time. The whole of the global warming scare has ultimately centred on this reverence for the computer model. It stands at the heart of the story like some mysterious fetish at the centre of a jungle clearing, attended by those modern versions of witch doctors who are the consecrated interpreters of its oracular powers.

The trouble is that those oracular projections rely only on what has been fed into the model by the same witch doctors in the first place. They see in the smoke which emerges from their Delphic caverns only those teasing images which arise from the oils and incense and herbs they themselves have placed on the fire. And ultimately they cannot resolve those teasing images into certainty, because predicting the climate 100 years ahead is such a complex task that they cannot know what magical ingredients they may inadvertently have left out of the mixture.

I began this book with one of my favourite quotations from Shakespeare, which gives such a profound clue to so much of the way we human beings perceive and try to make sense of the world, and also to why we so often fall prey to self-deceiving illusions. As Theseus puts it in *A Midsummer Night's Dream*:

'In the night, imagining some fear.
How easy is a bush supposed a bear.'

What Shakespeare is identifying, with his usual unerring insight, is the way, when we are not presented with enough information for our minds to resolve something into certainty, they may be teased into exaggerating it into something quite different from what it really is. We see at night a mysterious vague shape moving near us. Because we cannot see it clearly, our minds cannot resolve the image. We imagine that it is a burglar, a wild animal, a ghost, something that momentarily inspires terror in us.

It is the trick of human perception which I have long since termed a 'nyktomorph', from the Greek words for 'night shape': that which provokes the mind into wild imaginings because it hasn't been given enough data to identify the source of our panic correctly. Then a light comes on, or we see the object more clearly, and we see that what we had imagined to be a terrifying bear is only a bush blowing harmlessly in the wind.

We cannot yet be absolutely certain of it, any more than those scientists gazing into the entrails of their computers can be absolutely certain of what they see there. But it begins to look very possible that the nightmare vision of our planet being doomed by runaway global warming may be just a nyktomorph, an imaginary bear that is gradually resolving into a familiar bush.

If this turns out to be the case, then it will turn out to be one of the most expensive, destructive and foolish mistakes the human race has ever made. The next few years are going to be increasingly uncomfortable but very interesting. At the moment, it begins to look in many ways as though the lunatics have taken over the asylum. One of the greatest challenges confronting us in the years ahead may be to find ways of pulling them and ourselves back from that headlong rush towards chaos and self-destruction which is now hanging over our blindly comfortable Western world very much more than most of us yet realise.

Notes

1. Jacket copy for Christopher Horner's *The Politically Incorrect Guide to Global Warming* (Regnery Publishing, 2007).
2. See Booker and North (2007), *Scared To Death: From BSE to Global Warming – How Scares Are Costing Us The Earth*, *op. cit.*
3. Based on official US government figures, published in *The Climate Industry: $79 billion so far – trillions to come*, by Joanne Nova, Science and Public Policy Institute website,
4. President Eisenhower's 'Second Warning', State of the Union Address, 17 January 1961.
5. 'Maurice Strong named in UN oil-for-food report', CTV News website, 8 September 2005; Claudia Rosett, 'The UN's man of mystery', *Wall Street Journal*, 11 October 2008.
6. More than was generally appreciated, the UN had already moved to play the role of a 'world government' in at least two other areas. One covered food safety and veterinary standards, drawn up by a body known as the Codex Alimentarius Commission. This was subordinate to the World Health Organisation and the Food and Agriculture Organisation, each of which in turn were subordinate to the UN. These rules bound national governments throughout the world and were implemented in Europe, for instance, through legislation drafted by the European Commission. Another was the drawing up of standards governing the safety of road transport. These were passed on to Europe through a body known as UNECE (the UN Economic Commission for

Europe), and again implemented by Brussels, issuing directives and regulations which its member governments had no power to question and with which they were legally obliged to *comply*.

7. 'No need to worry about the future', *Nature*, 414, 8 November 2001; 'Misleading math about the earth: science defends itself against *The Skeptical Environmentalist*', *Scientific American*, January 2002.

8. For an account of this episode see Christopher Horner's *Red Hot Lies: how global warming alarmists use threats, fraud and deception to keep you misinformed* (Regnery Publishing, 2008), pp. 119–125.

9. Christopher Booker, 'Beware the politician posing as a scientist', *The Spectator*, 8 March 2009.

10. This was later (2008) turned into a book under the same title, *The Deniers: the world-renowned scientists who stood up against global warming, hysteria, political persecution and fraud*, *op. cit.*

11. Roy W. Spencer, *Climate Confusion: how global warming hysteria leads to bad science, pandering politicians and misguided policies that hurt the poor* (Encounter Books, 2008).

12. By 2009, according to government figures, US federal spending alone on 'climate-related' research had totalled $32.6 billion since 1989, with another $36.1 billion having gone into climate-related technologies (figures, with sources, taken from Nova, 2009, 'The Climate Industry', *op. cit.*).

Appendix 1
'A tightly knit group ...'
When temperature data became a 'state secret' – with further details on how the IPCC 'saved' the hockey stick

One of the more arcane sub-plots of the global warming drama was the concerted effort made between 2003 and 2006 to defend the 'hockey stick' graph against the attacks levelled against it by McIntyre and McKitrick.

This story had wider significance because it showed how closely linked was the small but strategically placed group of scientists who master-minded the defence of the graph, with the intention that it could be rehabilitated for use again in the IPCC's 2007 report. They included not only the co-authors of Mann's original studies, including his supervisor, Raymond Bradley, and Malcolm Hughes, but also Professor Phil Jones, director of the Climate Research Unit at East Anglia, in charge of HadCrut, one of the IPCC's four official sources of global temperature data. Jones was also a key player at the top of the IPCC. His junior CRU colleague Keith Briffa was chosen to be a 'lead author' for Chapter 6 on 'Palaeoclimate' in the IPCC's 2007 report, on which the attempt to resurrect the 'hockey stick' was to be centred.

Between 2003 and 2005 Mann and Jones co-authored no fewer than four papers defending the 'hockey stick'. Two were written by them alone, while on the others their co-authors included Bradley, Hughes, Briffa and Caspar Ammann.[1] Ammann and his UCAR colleague Eugene Wahl were the authors of the two key papers which in 2005 were chosen as the spearhead of the campaign to rehabilitate the 'hockey stick' by discrediting the analysis of it by McIntyre and McKitrick.

The complex story of how this was carried out was reconstructed in separate papers by two British researchers, David Holland and Bishop Hill.[2] Although Chapter 7 included an outline of the story based on their accounts, some details are so arcane that they have been reserved for this appendix.

As Chapter 7 explained, the papers by Ammann and Wahl were submitted to two separate scientific journals, *Geophysical Research Letters* and *Climatic Change*. When the paper submitted to GRL, supposedly in response to an earlier paper by McIntyre, was rejected, this left only the second, longer paper which had been submitted to Climatic Change.

This purported to have replicated the methodology which created Mann's 'hockey stick' and found it technically valid. At the time of the original UCAR press release in 2005, Ammann and Wahl had published the computer code they had used for this study, so that when McIntyre was sent their paper for 'peer review', he already knew how they had arrived at their findings. One of the more suspicious weaknesses in Mann's original study had been his persistent refusal to publish his 'r2 validation statistics'. These are an essential tool for demonstrating the technical validity of a complex statistical model, because they can be used to demonstrate whether or not it has been soundly constructed. McIntyre was now aware that if he could persuade Ammann and Wahl to divulge their own validation statistics, these would reveal that their attempt to replicate Mann's work suffered from the same flaws as Mann's original. The 'r2' number would be so low that it would show their 'hockey stick' to be of no more scientific value than Mann's version. Far from confirming the integrity of the 'hockey stick', their study had in fact vindicated his exposure of its flaws.

McIntyre therefore asked to see their validation statistics. Just as Mann had done earlier (and in contravention of the journal's rules) they refused. Ammann and Wahl tried to justify this by claiming that their rebuttal of McIntyre's work had been confirmed in the paper submitted to *Geophysical Research Letters*. But this, McIntyre knew, had already been rejected.

However, the editor-in-chief of *Geophysical Research Letters* then intervened by taking over personal responsibility for responses to McIntyre's earlier paper. Shortly afterwards, Mann was able to announce on RealClimate that both the Ammann and Wahl papers would shortly be accepted. The significance of this, as explained in Chapter 7, was that, if the two papers were to be cited in the IPCC's 2007 report, they had to be 'accepted for publication' by a 16 December 2005 deadline, now only two months away.

The new version of the *Climatic Change* paper was 'provisionally accepted' on December 12. It attempted to get round the problem of the missing validation statistics by cross-referring to their other paper, that which they hoped was about to be published by *GRL*. But in March 2006 GRL confirmed its earlier view that the paper was not fit for publication. Ammann and Wahl were thus left with a single fundamentally flawed paper, for which there were no validation statistics. Over a year went by, without the crucial paper appearing in *Climatic Change*. From the IPCC's point of view, however, it was irrelevant that the paper hadn't actually been published. All that mattered was that, by breaking the rules (the date on the 'accepted' paper was in fact February 2006, two months after the deadline), the paper was 'in press'. It could therefore be cited in the IPCC's 2007 report as the authority proving that McIntyre and McKitrick's criticisms of the 'hockey stick' were 'unfounded'.

The rest of this story, describing how the IPCC used the controversial paper to discredit McIntyre and McKitrick in Chapter 6 of its report, with the aid of Jones's colleague Briffa as a lead author, was outlined in Chapter 7.

This was not, however, to be the last tussle between Jones and McIntyre. In 2007 McIntyre became interested in the extent to which the two official temperature records based on surface weather stations had become distorted by the 'urban heat island' effect and other factors. On his Climate Audit blog he identified serious inconsistencies in the data used by one of the two records, Hansen's GIStemp. But he wondered whether there might be also be problems with the data supplied to compile the other surface record, Jones's HadCrut.

When McIntyre put in a Freedom of Information request for data on the weather stations used by HadCrut, this was refused. But by now the attention of another researcher, a British mathematician Dr Doug Keenan, had been drawn to the 84 Chinese weather stations whose data were supplied to the CRU as part of their HadCrut record.

In 1990 two papers had appeared on these stations, one in *Nature* by a team led by Professor Jones, the other by a US scientist Professor Wei-chyung Wang, who also contributed to Jones's paper.[3] The Jones paper stated that HadCrut had chosen stations 'with few, if any, changes in instrumentation, location or observation times'. This was confirmed in almost identical words by the Wang paper. Both papers referred to a report produced jointly by the US Department of Energy and the Chinese Academy of Sciences, making a similar claim.

When Keenan examined this report he found that it contained information on only 35 of the 84 stations. But the locations of at least half of these had been moved during the period 1954–1983, in one case five times, by as much as 41 kilometres. This not only cast serious doubts on the reliability of their data but belied the claims made by Jones and Wang in their papers.

When Keenan approached them for an explanation, Jones stated that the weather stations had been selected by Wang. Wang eventually replied that he had checked with a Ms Zeng in China, who confirmed that the chosen stations had experienced 'relatively few, if any, changes in instrumentation, location or observation times'. It turned out that Zeng had been a part-author of the joint report, which itself contained evidence showing this not to be true.

Considering how important it was that data used to compile one of the four internationally-recognised global temperature records was reliable, Keenan in 2007 submitted a report to Wang's university at Albany, New York, alleging that the professor was guilty of 'fraud'. After carrying out an internal inquiry, without interviewing Keenan, the university ruled, without giving reasons, that the charges were baseless.[4]

In 2009, McIntyre again put in a Freedom of Information request to the UK Met Office and Jones's CRU for sight of the data used to compile the HadCrut temperature record. He was told that this information was confidential, and that to release it would damage 'international relations' between the UK and those countries which supplied the data.[5] In other words, the data used to compile one of the four official temperature records were a state secret.[6]

Furthermore, the Met Office said that to reveal the data supplied to Jones could 'damage the trust that scientists have in those scientists who happen to be employed in the public sector'. It was ironic that this claim was made in the same week that the Met Office was under fire in the media for having had to withdraw its claim that Britain in 2009 would enjoy 'a barbecue summer', when July and August were again turning out to be abnormally wet. Their forecasts, which had now proved disastrously wrong three years running, were made with the aid of the same HadCrut computer model used by Jones and his colleagues to provide the IPCC with its climate projections for 100 years ahead.

McIntyre then discovered that some of the station data he had asked for was still publicly accessible to those who knew where to look on the CRU website, When the two organisations' refusal to disclose data provoked consternation, including a report in the *Sunday Telegraph*, Jones's CRU team promptly removed from their website many files of data which had been publicly available for years.

Worse was to come. In August the CRU announced on its website that, thanks to moving its office in the 1980s, it could no longer find much of its 'original raw data' from earlier years, only that which it had subsequently processed.

In other words, not only was one of the four official sources of global temperature data on which the IPCC and everyone else relied now trying to explain that it could not reveal its original data because these were a state secret, but CRU was now confessing that much of the data had been lost anyway.[7]

Notes

1. Mann, M., Ammann, C., Bradley, R., Briffa, K., Jones, P., Osborn, T., Crowley, T., Hughes, M., Oppenheimer, M. and others, 2003, 'On past temperatures and anomalous late-20th century warmth', EOS 84, 256–257. Mann, M., and Jones, P. D. (2003). 'Global Surface Temperatures over the past two millennia', *Geophysical Research Letters* 30, (15). Jones, P. D., and Mann, M. E. (2004), 'Climate over past millennia', *Reviews of. Geophysics.*, 42, RG2002. Rutherford, S., Mann, M. E., Osborn, T. J., Bradley, R. S., Briffa, K. R., Hughes, M. K. and Jones, P. D. (2005), 'Proxy-based Northern Hemisphere Surface Temperature Reconstructions: Sensitivity to Method, Predictor Network, Target Season, and Target Domain', *Journal of Climate*, 18, 2308–2329, American Meteorological Society.
2. D. Holland, 'Bias and Concealment in the IPCC Process: the "Hockey Stick" Affair', *op. cit.*; 'Caspar and the Jesus Paper' published on the 'Bishop Hill' blog, 11 August 2008.
3. Jones, P. D., Groisman, P. Y., Coughlan, M., Plummer, N., Wang, W.-C., Karl, T. R. (1990), 'Assessment of urbanization effects in time series of surface air temperature over land', *Nature*, 347, 169–172. Wang, W.-C., Zeng, Z., Karl, T. R. (1990), 'Urban heat islands in China', *Geophysical Research Letters*, 17, 2377–2380.
4. For a full account of this episode, see 'Climate science fraud at Albany University', WUWT, 5 March 2009.
5. See various posts on Climate Audit website, beginning with 'UK Met Office refuses to disclose station data once again', 23 July 2009, and 'CRU refuses data once again', 24 July 2009.
6. 'Weather records are a state secret', *Sunday Telegraph*, 2 August 2009.
7. 'CRU responds', Steve McIntyre on ClimateAudit, 11 August 2009.

Appendix 2
The IPCC spins 'victory' out of defeat
Further details on Ofcom's response to complaints against Channel 4's The Great Global Warming Swindle, *21 July 2008*

What was remarkable about the general response to the rulings by Ofcom on the 265 formal complaints made by the IPCC and others against Channel 4's *The Great Global Warming Swindle* was the glaring discrepancy between media reports of the rulings and what Ofcom actually said.

The rulings were widely presented by the BBC and others as somehow a victory for the complainants, supported in particular by the statements issued by various luminaries of the IPCC. When the rulings were examined, however, the truth turned out to be very different.

Of the mass of complaints that the programme had 'misrepresented' the science, Ofcom did not uphold one. This was because it was careful not to get involved in arguments about the science. But it was prepared to rule that the programme 'did not materially mislead the audience so as to cause harm or offence'. In particular Ofcom noted that, when an error had been pointed out in one of the programme's graphs, the mistake was promptly corrected before its second showing.

Similarly, on scientific issues, Ofcom did not uphold a single complaint against the programme's lack of 'impartiality'. Under the broadcasting code, producers were only under an obligation to present an issue impartially when it was considered to be still subject to debate. Since the complainants had repeatedly insisted that the science on global warming was no longer a matter of debate, Ofcom turned this back on them by ruling that they could hardly now argue that the matter was still controversial.

The only count on which Ofcom did rule that the programme breached its obligation to be impartial related to the sequence near the end, where it was argued that the policies of UN and western governments were causing the world's poorer countries to suffer by hold-ing back their economic development in the name of controlling climate change. Ofcom ruled that, since this was 'a major matter relating to current public policy', the programme should have included 'an appropriately wide range of significant views'.*

Ofcom also upheld the two personal complaints by Sir David King and Professor Wunsch. King claimed that he had been misrepre-sented in the closing sequence of the programme where Dr Fred Singer was filmed saying:

> 'there will still be people who believe that this is the end of the world –
> particularly when you have, for example, the chief scientist of the UK
> telling people that by the end of the century the only habitable place on
> the earth will be the Antarctic. And humanity may survive thanks to some
> breeding couples who moved to the Antarctic. I mean this is hilarious. It
> would be hilarious actually, if it weren't so sad.'

King protested that, as the 'chief scientist' referred to, he had never said in 2004 that the Antarctic would be 'the only habitable place' on earth. What he had said to a House of Commons committee was that 55 million years ago the Antarctic was the 'most hospitable place for mammals, and the rest of the earth was rather uninhabit-able because the earth was so hot'. He also said that, unless global warming was stopped, similar conditions would prevail on earth by the end of the twenty-first century. These remarks had later been quoted by the *Independent* under the headline as 'Antarctica is likely to be the world's only habitable continent by the end of the century'. King had not on that occasion asked for a correction, but now that a similar interpretation of his views had been echoed by Channel 4, King demanded redress.

Ofcom went into this issue at great length (seven pages), ruling that 'Professor Singer's comment amounted to a significant allegation which called into question Sir David's scientific views and his cred-ibility as a scientist'. This, it said, was in breach of the rules, and Channel 4 would have to broadcast a correction.

Ofcom also upheld Professor Wunsch's complaint that he would never have agreed to take part in the programme if he had known its true nature. This was despite Channel 4's evidence to Ofcom that its programme makers had explained this to him at length, both in writ-ing and in conversations at the time of the filming (all except the programme's title, which was only chosen at the last minute). At the time he had raised no objection, and had, off-camera, been critical of the media's tendency to over-sensationalise the dangers of climate change.[1]

Of the six specific complaints against the programme from the IPCC, only two were concerned with the content of the programme. The IPCC claimed it had been misrepresented as arguing that global warming would lead to the northerly spread of malaria (the point Professor Reiter had been contesting with the IPCC for years). It also denied that its 1990 report had predicted 'climatic disaster as a result of global warming'. Ofcom refused to uphold either of these complaints (observers were amused to note that the IPCC now seemed to be denying that warming would lead either to a spread of tropical diseases or to a 'climatic disaster').

The four IPCC complaints Ofcom upheld related only to the charge that Channel 4 had not given it enough time to comment on points made by the programme before it was broadcast. These were its references to the criticisms by Reiter of the IPCC's findings on malaria and of the way the IPCC selected its authors; Professor Seitz's comments on the 1996 report; and Professor Stott's observation that the IPCC was 'politically driven'.

Channel 4 first approached the IPCC about the programme in October 2006 and had merely been referred to its website. When the programme was all but complete, it then emailed the IPCC asking for comments on specific points, first on 27 February 2007, then again on 1 March. Each time it had no reply. But since the emails had not mentioned the fact that the programme was due to be broadcast on 8 March, Ofcom ruled that the IPCC had not been given the 'eight working days' notice considered the minimum time it should have been allowed to come up with a response.

This was all the Ofcom ruling amounted to. Every one of the hundreds of complaints relating to the contents of the programme had been rejected, including those from Ward's '37 professors' and the 175 pages submitted by Rado (endorsed by leading figures from the IPCC). The seven complaints upheld were little more than minor technicalities relating to procedure.

It was this which the media, aided by the wildly tendentious statements issued by the IPCC on behalf of Pachauri, Houghton and Watson, somehow conjured up into a victory for the complainants. Pachauri, for instance, claimed that Ofcom had upheld 'most of the formal complaints'. It had in fact upheld only seven out of 265, all very trivial compared with most of those it rejected. The idea that Ofcom had 'vindicated' the 'review process of the IPCC and the credibility of the publications of the IPCC' was laughable.

Equally ridiculous was Houghton's claim that Ofcom had 'exposed the misleading and false information regarding the IPCC' put over by the programme, and had 'confirmed' the value of the IPCC's reports as 'a source of accurate and reliable information about climate change'. Ofcom had deliberately avoided any consideration of such issues.

The same applied to Watson's claim that Ofcom had 'recognised the serious inaccuracies in *The Great Global Warming Swindle*'. Again it had done nothing of the kind. But in the way all this was presented by the BBC and others, it was Channel 4 which had lost the day.

Notes

1. Evidence given to Ofcom by Channel 4 and private information from the programme's director Martin Durkin.

A personal note from the author, with acknowledgements

The story behind this book dates back to a day in 2003, when my attention was caught by a report that Denmark, the country which had more wind turbines per head than any other in the world, was planning a moratorium on building any more. This was because, when the wind blew at the right speed, most of the electricity they generated had to be exported to Norway, and when it was not blowing, Denmark had to import large quantities of power from Germany, helping to make its electricity the most expensive in Europe.

This seemed so remarkable that I thought it worthy of investigation for my column in the *Sunday Telegraph*. My old friend Brigadier Anthony Cowgill, who has extensive contacts in the energy industry as director of the British Management Data Foundation, put me onto Angela Kelly of Country Guardian. She turned out to be a remarkable woman in her 70s who, from a remote cottage in Wales, provided via the internet an invaluable information service on every aspect of wind power to a network of readers all over the world.

Thanks to Angela and one of Country Guardian's technical advisers, Dr John Etherington, a retired university lecturer on environmental issues, I was able to learn enough about the technicalities of wind energy to produce the first of what were to become many articles in my weekly column, on a subject which I soon found had been astonishingly misrepresented, not least by some of my fellow-journalists, and was therefore widely misunderstood.

Having assumed, like most people at that time, that wind turbines were a comparatively cheap and attractive way to produce power, I was startled to discover just how little electricity they, very inefficiently and expensively, manage to generate. Thanks to the hidden subsidy system, however, they generate such handsome rewards for their owners that my first article dubbed it 'the great wind scam'.

I soon learned at first hand just how ruthlessly the government was using its power to force more and more wind turbines through the planning system, when I became chairman of a local action group set up to protest at a proposal to build a single turbine on the Mendip Hills where I live in Somerset. Although the local council voted unamimously to reject the scheme, which flouted all normal planning rules, it was overruled by a government inspector on the grounds that Somerset's need to meet its share of Britain's EU target for 'renewable' energy overrode all other considerations.

Inevitably this introduction to the shabby futility of the 'great wind scam' led me to take rather more interest than I had done previously in the cosmic cause which was being used to justify building all these wind turbines: the fear that the world was facing catastrophe through runaway global warming (one of my neighbours, a university scientist specialising in chemistry, expressed fanatical support for our local turbine, on the grounds that we should do all we could to prevent the 1,000-foot high Mendip hills being submerged by the rising seas).

When I began reading up on the subject, nothing intrigued me more than the number of times it seemed that rather important questions had been raised by the methods scientists and others had used over the years to promote the alarm over global warming. Early on, for instance, I came across an internet article on the famous 'hockey stick' graph, written by John Daly, a impressively knowledgeable amateur scientist who had emigrated from England to Australia, and who died there in 2004. Looking further into the extraordinary story behind the 'hockey stick' and other episodes in the history of concern over global warming, I found that these inevitably prompted reflection as to why, if the science behind the theory of man-made global warming was as soundly based as its supporters insisted, it had so often been necessary to distort and manipulate the scientific evidence used to promote it.

The more I read into the subject, the more instances there seemed where those ringing alarm bells over global warming had made claims which were either wildly exaggerated or which had no factual basis at all. By contrast, the books, papers and articles which dissented from the 'consensus' view often seemed rather more convincing, not least because they included so much evidence which supporters of the 'consensus' tried to ignore.

One of the first books I read, for instance, was *Unstoppable Global Warming* by Dr Fred Singer, one of the scientists who had been questioning the 'consensus' over global warming almost as soon as we were told there was one. I was grateful to him and his co-author Dennis Avery for providing such a well-referenced perspective on climate history and the global warming thesis in general, which also included many important points sidestepped by more conventional accounts of the subject.

I was equally grateful for an essay written back in 1992 by that other distinguished veteran in the debate, Professor Richard Lindzen, magisterially showing even then how false was the idea that there was some kind of 'consensus' among scientists that the world's modest recent warming was primarily due to human activity. Dr Patrick Michaels was another long-time combatant in the debate, whose book *Meltdown: the predictable distortion of global warming by scientists, politicians and the media* (2004) was a useful resumé of some of the more absurd and disprovable claims made by reputable scientists, politicians and journalists who had got caught up in the rush to hype up panic over man's overheating of the planet.

With my colleague Dr Richard North, I was just embarking at this time on a book analysing the 'scare phenomenon'. Our purpose in *Scared To Death* was to examine the readiness of our age to fall for every kind of scare which later turns out to have been unjustified by the evidence, from BSE causing brain disease to the 'millennium bug', which was going to create havoc by closing down the world's computers. And by now I had learned enough about the global warming story to recognise how uncannily in many ways it fitted into the classic pattern of all the other scares we had reported on, indeed so much bigger than all the rest that it merited the longest chapter in the book.

Looking back on those days, in the aftermath of Al Gore's film *An Inconvenient Truth*, we can now see it was around that time that the hysteria over global warming was at its height. In conversation one day with my *Private Eye* colleague Ian Hislop, I remarked casually how flimsy it seemed was much of the evidence behind the global warming scare, only to receive an almighty put down to the effect that George Monbiot of the *Guardian* knew a great deal more about the subject than I did and that I should think twice before daring to challenge such expert authority. When Ian said dismissively that Monbiot had read many more books on global warming than I had, I rather feebly responded that possibly Professor Lindzen, of whom he had never heard, had read even more about it than the great Monbiot.

Even before our own book was published in the autumn of 2007, as it happened, it was becoming increasingly clear that the scientific foundations beneath the great global warming scare were beginning to look very much more shaky than they had done even a year or two earlier.

In 2008, when Richard and I twice visited America to talk about the book, we had a very enjoyable dinner with Fred Singer. We met some of the writers working for 'think tanks', such as Myron Ebell and Chris Horner of the Competitive Enterprise Institute, who had been eloquently putting the 'sceptical' case on global warming in books and articles for some years. And, with the 2008 presidential campaign then in full swing, we were so shocked to learn just how far America's economic future was now being threatened by a tidal wave of scientifically and technically illiterate 'greenery' that we decided that our original chapter on global warming in *Scared To Death* should be expanded and updated into a book in its own right.

Another discovery by this time, without which this book could not have been written, had been the remarkable coverage of the scientific issues involved in the debate given by the two leading 'sceptical' science blogs, Steve McIntyre's Climate Audit based in Toronto and Watts Up With That?, run by the Californian meteorologist Anthony Watts.

Nothing has generally transformed the nature of the debate on climate change more than the remarkable accessibility of technical information provided by the internet, but in particular the contributions made by McIntyre and Watts have been invaluable. It was no accident that in 2007 and 2008 their two blogs were voted in succession 'Best Science blog' of the year, although other blogs and websites have also made a very useful contribution, such as those run from Australia by Jennifer Marohasy and Dr John Ray (Greenie Watch), Dr Craig Idso's CO2 Science and the website of the Science and Public Policy Institute in Washington.

In March 2009 I had the honour of being invited to join the 70 other speakers at the second Heartland Conference in New York, where I had the pleasure of hearing and meeting many people whose work I had been reading and writing about for so long, including Professors Richard Lindzen and Paul Reiter, Dr Singer, Steve Mac-Intyre and Anthony Watts ('my favourite weatherman'). To each of them I owe a great debt for all they have unwittingly contributed to this book.

Later in London I also had the pleasure of meeting two genial Australian professors, Bob Carter, with whom I had long been corresponding, and Ian Plimer, whose admirably comprehensive and weighty book *Heaven and Earth: global warming, the missing science*, with its thousands of scientific references on every aspect of climate change, became both in Australia and Britain one of the more surprising best-sellers of 2009.

I am also grateful to the *Sunday Telegraph* for giving me the space and freedom to give fairly obsessive coverage to the unfolding drama of the climate change debate in my weekly column. I thus became the most conspicuous 'denier' in the British press (both on global warming and windfarms), at a time when most journalists still seemed happy to promote the views of the 'consensus'.

The fact that twice at the end of 2008 my columns became 'the most viewed' item of the year on the entire *Daily* and *Sunday Telegraph* website was an indication of the huge interest this topic was now arousing. The hundreds of comments frequently attracted from readers were again a measure of how much more informed about the issues many members of the general public were becoming. It was very noticeable from the general tone of these contributions, as of those on the comment threads of the main science blogs, how much more restrained and courteous critics of the 'consensus' usually tended to be (although there were exceptions), in contrast to the striking readiness of many of its supporters to post bilious and abusive responses, often bristling with hate.

I must also thank Myron Ebell for putting me down to speak at the Heartland Conference; Chris Horner for his splendidly combative book *Red Hot Lies: How Global Warming Alarmists Use Threats, Fraud and Deception to Keep You Misinformed*; Viscount Monckton of Brenchley for his equally combative part in the ongoing debate and for many useful and enjoyable conversations; Nigel Calder for guidance on Svensmark's solar thesis; Steve McIntyre for his invaluable background guidance when the Press Complaints Commission received a complaint against me from Dr Michael Mann; Martin Durkin, producer of *The Great Global Warming Swindle*, who knows far better than I do how much time can be wasted in dealing with such complaints from the 'warmist' lobby; Marc Morano of Climate Depot for keeping us all somewhat breathlessly briefed with his emails; and my son Nicholas Booker, for his presence in New York and informed encouragement on many occasions.

Special thanks are also due to Dr Benny Peiser for his invaluable daily bulletins on ccnet, appreciated by a wide academic readership, without which Chapter 9 on the 'Countdown to Copenhagen' would in particular have been much more difficult to compile.

I must thank my publisher Robin Baird-Smith, for agreeing to publish this book against a very tight deadline, and Tony Lansbury for his usual meticulous copy-editing under similar pressure.

I owe a particular debt to my colleague Richard North, who was originally to be a co-author of the book until his attention became understandably distracted by the need to complete a book of his own, *Ministry of Defeat*, recounting the disaster of the British occupation of Iraq after 2003. But he has walked with me much of the way, and many passages in the book have benefited from our late-night conversations.

My final debt is due to my wife Valerie, who, not for the first time, has allowed me to spend far too many hours of day and night locked in the obsessive research that writing a book like this requires.

It is inevitable that such a book will contain errors for which I am solely to blame. But I look forward to the zeal with which they will be picked out and fastened on by hostile reviewers and commentators, claiming that, if I have got this or that fact wrong, then this proves that the whole book can be dismissed as worthless. Such techniques are, alas, only too famliar from the 'warmist' side of the argument. But what will really annoy them more than anything is that I have at least got most of the story right.

Index